6000 Years of Mankind Chronology Papers

Official Edition

by

Walter R. Dolen
President of the Becoming-One Church

Trade Cloth Fifth Edition
ISBN: 978-1-61918-0642
Also found on digital versions

March 2026 Printing
with correction for JC's Passover date
30AD v. 31AD
(typo and format corrections)

Note: In this edition there are corrections/additions in text and
renumbering of dates in chapter 5 (CP5) in the Table of the Chronology
Future updates to this book will appear at: https://beone.ws/chronology

BeComing-One Publications
https://becoming-one.org/books.htm

Information on the author:
www.walterdolen.com or www.walterdolen.ws

Acknowledgment

I thank my wife Shirley Clare and others for their help with editing the grammar, spelling and for my wife's patience in the long hours I spent on my projects. I also thank all biblical scholars who wrote helps (concordances, interlinear Bibles, grammars, computer programs, creation v. evolution books, etc.) and critiques of doctrine, for they made my work easier. Lastly, I thank all scholars of serious books (philosophy, science, biology, etc.) for their work, for no one person can think through all opinions pertaining to subjects: we need to compare our knowledge with others in order to ascertain the truth of the matter. Spiritually, I want to thank our creator for the Spirit and knowledge given to me, for without this I would not have recognized the obvious hints throughout the Bible.

Walter R. Dolen
2024

About the Author

Walter Dolen is an author/editor of several books, using the scientific method[1] including: *My God is the BeComingOne: God Papers*; *New Mind Papers*; *6000 Years of Mankind*; *Becoming-One Bible*; *Harmony of the Gospels*; *Harmony of the Good News*; *Male and Female He Created Them*; *Prophecy Papers*; *Einstein Light Time and Relativity*; etc. These books were researched and written between 1969 and 2024. Walter has worked with his hands (carpenter/builder), with his mind (publisher/writer/building designer) and with his soul (President of the Becoming-One Church).

For more information about the author see his web site:
www.walterdolen.com or www.walterdolen.ws

---

[1] (1) Perceive a problem; (2) examine and analyze all the available evidence; (3) examine and imagine different hypotheses in attempt to solve the problem in a logical manner; (4) form a theory that answers the problem; (5) test the theory; (6) always have an open mind for better theories or answers to the problem; (7) change the theory if new evidence is inconsistent to your prior theory.

Contents

Chronology Table, p. 139

CP1: Chronology Introduction

cp1» The study of chronology is very difficult because you must rely on historical sources that are fragmented and ambiguous. Secular or Biblical chronology isn't as exact as some may think. Throughout this work we point out the difficulties. In part two (CP2) and part three (CP3) of this book we point out the major problems with secular chronology, and the many different dating methods used by cities, states and kingdoms over the centuries. In part four (CP4) we show the difficulty in determined the birth and death of Jesus Christ, which our modern reference dating system uses (BC/AD). When historians claim that such and such an event happened, you should take it with a grain of salt. There are many problems. Despite the difficulties, this book is a Biblical chronology based primarily on the Hebrew scripture and secondarily on secular sources. We use the Bible as our main source of study because the Bible contains a chronology of about 4000 years and because the Bible has proven more trustworthy than secular sources. The Bible is full of old customs and an amazing amount of detail. It names cities, places, kings, nations, laws, and even dates, lots of dates. Myths do not contain vast amounts of detail. Many of the Biblical details have been confirmed in the last two centuries by archeology (see example see: *Archaeology and the Old Testament*, by Merrill F. Unger; etc.). In this book we do our best to show that the dates of the Bible are the best source for evidence to help establish the chronology of mankind.

cp2» Our Biblical chronology starts with the creation by God in the first year of man (YM). That is, in the first year that mankind existed we begin the chronology of the history of man. Yes, we understand the bias against a short chronology for mankind, but we also understand the dubiousness of secular chronology and the theory of evolution, which must have a long chronology. Some say the Bible was not meant to be used to ascertain the chronology of mankind. They speak of gaps in the Biblical chronology. But although the Bible's purpose is not primarily for chronology it does have a chronology built into it. There is a fine line of chronology that runs through the Bible. The ambiguity of certain areas will make it difficult, if not impossible, to have an absolutely correct biblical chronology: correct for each year. But we can ascertain a chronology that is relatively correct; much more correct than secular chronology, because the Bible's chronology is the longest and most detailed of all chronologies.

cp3» Contrariwise, we distrust secular sources for chronological evidence mainly because secular sources are dubious and fragmented, and because in the past there was no universal dating system: there was no universal calendar (see CP3). Each country, even each city, had their own calendar. Concerning the ancient Greek cities:

- "The tenth day of the month for the Corinthians is the fifth for the Athenians, and the eighth somewhere else....the beginning and the end of months in various Greek cities did not coincide....The battle of Plataea (479 BC) took place on 27 Panamos according to the Boeotian calendar, but on 4 Boedromion according to the Athenian calendar; at that time the beginning of the Athenian month came seven days later than the Boeotian...It happened, rarely, that two cities agreed to begin the months on the same day...Each *polis* had its own mode of time reckoning as it had its own month names and numerals... (pp. 32-33, *Chronology of the Ancient World*, Bickerman; in chap. 3 of *Greek and Roman Chronology*, Alan Samuel details 96 Greek calendars).

cp4» The lack of a universal calandar makes it extremely difficult to interpret past secular dates. Today we use the universal dating system called the *Christian Era* system (BC-AD). From this system we can actually compare events in different parts of the earth by their chronological order. But this was not the case in the past.

cp5» In this book we have connected Biblical dates with the *Christian Era* system (BC-AD). We use "absolute dates" to do this, that are based on many astronomical phenomena, not just one vague eclipse. Contrary to what many think, there are few *absolute dates* before Christ's time. Chronological schemes based on so-called "absolute dates" using only eclipses are making a major mistake. Herein we identify a few real absolute dates and show the fatal flaw in using just one eclipse to identify ancient dates.

Earth is Old Theory

Two Views: Earth is old; Earth is young

cp6» There are two general views of history that are polarized. One is that the cosmos is old, very old, billions of years old. The other view is that the cosmos is young, very young, only thousands of years old.

cp7» Those who believe that the earth is billions of years old have various theories to "prove" that the earth is billions of years old. They speak of the Uranium to Lead method of dating, or the Thorium to Lead method of dating. They speak of bones that they say are millions of years old. When you are educated in an environment that dogmatically indicates that the earth is billions of years old it is ludicrous to believe that the earth is only thousands of years old. To believe that the earth is thousands of years old is to be uneducated or ignorant, and you are ripe for belittling by the "educated." But every belief system has it foundations. The "earth is old" system of belief is related to the "evolutionary" system of belief. Those who believe in evolution *must* have an old earth. The magic of evolution needs billions of years of "natural selection" in order to work its miracles. But all methods of dating events and materials billions, or even millions of years old, are baseless, illusionary, and arbitrary.

Foundations for the "Earth Is Old System"

Theory of Evolution

cp8» **(1)** The theory of evolution is the first foundation for the "earth is old" theory. Evolution needs an old earth for its development. There are numerous works that examine the theory of evolution (see list in *Beginning Papers*). Because the theory of evolution needs an old earth, it found an old earth through selective perception. Any method that indicates a great age is an acceptable method for evolutionists. Any method that indicates a young earth is a rejectable method for evolutionists. Evolutionists don't even feel a need to examine other points of view. Their minds are made up. They have a mindset. Their selective perception reaffirms to them each day that evolution is correct. Thus, any method that proves an old earth is correct; any method that proves the contrary is foolishness.

Radioactive Dating Methods

cp9» **(2)** The radioactive dating method is the second foundation for the "earth is old" theory. All radioactive dating methods start with a parent element which through radioactive decay turns into a daughter element. The decay rate is measured in half lives. The half life of Uranium 238 is said to be about 4.5 billion years. A unit of Uranium 238 turns into ½ lead and ½ Uranium after about 4.5 billion years. The Uranium 238 is the parent element and Lead 206 is the end or final daughter element. There are other daughter elements between Uranium 238 and Lead 206. For example, Uranium 238 first decays into the daughter element Thorium 234 after about 4.5 billion years, and then after about 25 days turns into Protactinium 234, then after 1 minute turns into Uranium 234, then after 300,000 years turns into Thorium 230, then after 80,000 years turns into Radium 226, then after 1600 years turns into Radon 222, then after 4 days turns into Polonium 218, and continues its decay until it reaches Lead 206 (Krauskopf and Beiser, *Fundamentals of Physical Science*, 5th Ed., p. 252, see p. 562).

cp10» If the rate of decay is constant, then we have a clock in which to tell time, **if, and only if**, we know the ratio of Uranium 238 in the earth compared to Lead when the earth was formed/created, either by God or by the magical evolution. Because the decay rate of Uranium 238 is so slow compared to the decay rates of other elements in the series only the amount of the end daughter, Lead 206, is considered when ascertaining the age of the rock. The earth is believed to be about 5 billion years old according to evolutionists. But, of course, 5 billion years ago there was no man to observe the ratio of Uranium in the rocks compared to Lead. It is nothing but guesswork and nothing else when someone arbitrarily says that at the beginning there was such and such ratio of Uranium as compared to Lead. Guesswork is not scientific work.

Constant Decay Rates?

cp11» Furthermore it was believed at first that these decay rates were constant.

"Radioactivity was discovered by Becquerel in 1896. In 1906, Millikan stated, 'Radioactivity has been found to be independent of all physical as well as chemical conditions. The lowest cold or greatest heat does not appear to affect it in the least. Radioactivity seems to be as unalterable a property of the atoms of radioactive substances, as is weight itself.' This state of mind established the modern view, which is quite generally held today.... The electroscope and spinthrascope were used in early study of radioactive alpha-decay rates. The inherent limitations of these early instruments led to erroneous conclusions:

- That radioactive decay rates are constant.
- That these rates cannot be altered by change of the energy state of the electrons orbiting the nucleus.
- That radioactivity results from processes which involve only the atomic nucleus.

Refinements in electronics resulted in the development of sophisticated counting apparatus. The equipment was used in the demonstration by scvcral investigators (1949-73) of rather easily induced changes in the disintegration rates of 14 radionuclides, including ^{14}C, ^{60}Co, and ^{137}Cs. **The observed variations in the decay rates, (changes in the half life) were produced by changes in pressure, temperature, chemical state, electric potential stress of monomolecular layers, etc. ... The decay 'constant' is now considered to be a variable.**" [H.C. Dudley, "Is There Ether?,"*Industrial Research*, Nov 15, 1974, p. 42; my emphasis]

cp12» Even a small amount of variation in the decay rate can make a big difference in the assumed age of the rock:

> "Measurement of nuclear disintegration parameters has been done for about fifty years. To my knowledge no major research effort has been mounted to determine whether nuclear decay parameters vary at all with time [he is speaking of time not pressure, chemical state, etc]. Once values of the decay index for a particular nuclide are obtained and a particular value is agreed upon, this value is generally accepted. Usually no further measurements are taken....

> If a small amount of exponential variation occurs in the nuclear decay index, then the half lives of the radiometric nuclides are drastically reduced — orders of magnitude. In the case of U 238 the half life is reduced by a factor of 10^5"
> (Theodore W. Rybka, *ICR Impact Series* No. 106)

Decay Rates not Constant

cp13» As we see above temperature, pressure, chemical state, and other factors do change the decay rate of radioactive elements, and this drastically changes the so-called clock of radioactivity. Atomic clocks even seem to change their rates of decay by the direction in which they travel in an airplane. Those going westward gained time; those going eastward lost time (Hafele, Keating, 1972, "Around-the-world atomic clocks," *Science* 177 [4044]).

Radiohalos

cp14» Robert V. Gentry's work on radiohalos has cast a shadow on the premise that the decay rates are constant. "Radiohalos" are microscopic, ring-like discolorations caused by radioactivity in certain minerals. Early work seemed to indicate that the radiohalos exhibited dimensions predictable on the basis of modern decay rates. But Gentry who worked at the Chemistry Division of the Oak Ridge National Laboratory in the 1960's "set out to review previous work on the subject, then began his own painstaking study of thousands of halos in rocks from around the world. Almost immediately he found that all was not in order in this long neglected field. Gentry discovered that, although uranium halos, for example, are readily identifiable by the number and relative rough diameters of their rings, their actual dimensions often vary substantially, even within a single crystal" (Ralph E. Juergens, "Radiohalos and Earth History," *Kronos*, III:1, pp 7 ff; read article, and Gentry's articles noted in footnotes). Gentry has shown that the "halos furnish no proof that [the decay constant] is constant" (Gentry, *Science*, April 5, 1974, pp 62-66; Also see Don B. De Young, "The Precision of Nuclear Decay Rates," CRSQ, Vol. 13, No 1 [1976]; and John Lynde Anderson and George W. Spangler, "Radiometric Dating: Is the 'Decay Constant' Constant?," *Pensee*, Vol 4 No. 4 [1974]; *Scientific Creationism*, 2nd Ed., 1985, Chapter VI; and other works.).

Dubious Premises

cp15» Evolutionists use the elements with the slowest rates of decay to measure the age of the earth, and they use the highest ratio of the parent element to daughter element at the time of formation/creation in order to give a high age. Remember there were no human observations made at formation/creation to help establish the correct ratio. The ratio may have been low. Thus, even if the Uranium-Lead method is correct, the earth is still young since there was a low ratio at first.

cp16» Also there are other elements that decay at much higher rates. At the far extreme from Uranium 238 is Astatine 216 with a half-life less than a second as is Polonium 214. Why didn't they choose a faster decaying element to clock the earth's age? It is because they assumed a great age for the earth, therefore they arbitrarily chose an element with a slow decay rate along with a high parent to daughter radio instead of a low parent to daughter ratio, so as to self-fulfill their view.

Different Methods of Dating Don't Agree

cp17» There is also the problem of variation of the ages arrived at by using various elements and methods to date the earth. One system of dating gives one date, another gives a contradictory date. Or one set of rocks gives one age, while another set of rocks gives a different age for the earth. What does the believer in the "earth is old" theory do? With the Carbon 14 dating method (C14) they merely pick the result they wanted to begin with, "If a C14 date supports our theories, we put it in the main text. If it does not entirely contradict them, we put it in a footnote. And if it is completely 'out of date,' we just drop it" (T. Save-Soderbergh, "Carbon 14 and Egyptian Chronology," *Nobel Symposium 12 Radiocarbon Variations and Absolute Chronology*, Stockholm, Almquist and Wikwell, p. 35; quotes from R.D. Long, CRSQ, Vol 10, No 1, p. 19; *Science, Scripture, and the Yound Earth*, 1989 Edition, pp.42ff). This is the way some quote the Bible. If a verse agrees with a belief it is quoted, if not it is ignored. And this is like the "identification game" used in astronomical retro-calculations (see CP2).

Great Distances in Space

cp18» **(3)** Great distances in space is the third foundation for the "earth is old" theory. The "earth is old" group believes in such things as the "big-bang" theory. (Although lately there have been articles critical of this theory.) All matter came from a big explosion and has been spreading out ever since. Since the earth to them *must* be billions of years old, then the matter in the universe has been traveling after the explosion for billions of years. Matter has spread out great distances since the beginning; the larger the universe, the older the universe. Thus they look for methods that "prove" great distances in space. Of course they have come up with methods for great distance and have rejected any method or theory that may show a small universe or young universe. They use the red-shift method of dating, which is partly based on Einstein's relativity theories. But others have shown the shaky foundation of this red-shift method as well as the unstable foundation of the special theory of relativity and consequently the general theory of relativity (See *Science Papers*; Field, Arp, and Bahcall, *Red-Shift Controversy*,1973; Herbert Dingle, *Science at the Crossroads*, 1972; Walter R. Dolen, Einstein: *Light, Time and Relativity*; etc.).

Foundations for the "Earth is Young System"

(1) No Scientific Evidence For Evolution

cp19» The first foundation for the "earth is young" theory is the lack of real evidence that the earth is old. There is sound evidence against the red-shift method for ascertaining distances in space, against radioactive dating methods, and all other methods of dating the earth as old (see my *Science Papers*; Jeremy Rifkin, *Algeny*, 1983; Field, Arp, and Bahcall, *Red-Shift Controversy*, 1973; John C. Whitcomb and Henry M. Morris, *The Genesis Flood*, 1961; etc.).

(2) Proof that the Earth is Young

cp20» The second foundation for the "earth is young" theory are the *many* methods that prove the earth is young. They are at least 76 methods that prove the earth can not be older than 500 million years and of these 24 indicate that the earth is no older than 20,000 years. These methods include such things as the influx of titanium, or cobalt, or zinc, or mercury, or silver, or copper, or gold, or silicon, or nickel into ocean via rivers. If the earth was billions of years old, the ocean would be a soup of pollution without any life in it. And such methods as the influx of meteoritic dust from space, or development of total human population, or lack of vast amounts of ancient cultural debris, the decay of the earth's magnetic field, the decay of C-14 in pre-Cambrian wood, the growth of active coral reefs, the formation of river deltas, decay of short-period comets, and the instability of rings of Saturn show a young earth. These 76 methods are based on the assumption that there were constant rates, no initial daughter components, and all were in a closed system. These methods lead to an even younger age for the earth if, for example, there were some initial daughter components at the beginning (see *Scientific Creationism*, 2nd Ed., Chapter VI; Harold S. Slusher, *Age of the Cosmos*; Henry M. & John D. Morris, *Science, Scripture, and the Young Earth*, 1989 Edition, Chapter 8; Henry M. Morris, "The Young Earth," *ICR Impact Series*, No. 17).

(3) Biblical Chronology

cp21» The third foundation of the "earth is young" theory is the belief in the Biblical chronology, or in creation without mixing the false theory of evolution into the picture. And this in turn is based on the proof that the Bible is a sound document, more sound than any other ancient document ("Bible Paper" [BP3]). And this in turn is the belief in a powerful God, not a belief in a powerless and mystical God or the false belief in the magical evolution.

Your Mindset Limits You

cp22» What system you believe in depends on your belief, your research on *both* belief systems, your biases, your world view, and your mindset (perceptual set). The more you research different points of view, the more you see that the world sees through filters that color its perception of reality. To the Evolutionist the world is old. To the Creationists the world is young. It is difficult for either group to prove their case to the other group. Since the only witness to the Beginning (Creation) was either the powerful God or the magic of Evolution, it is only through inductive thinking that we can come to a conclusion. We must piece evidence upon evidence. But for most of us our "mindset" or "world view" interferes with our judgment. We see what we want to see and subconsciously disregard what we do not want to see.

Premises for this Chronology

1) There is a God Being, otherwise know as the all powerful, all knowing Being.

2) This very smart Being created the universe and its natural laws. DNA is one piece of evidence of this as well as the complexity of the "simple" cell. Evolution is a myth.

3) The God Being gave us a book that reveals the truth about himself and his creation (Read the *God Papers*).

4) That book is what we call today the Bible, the so-called Old Testament and the New Testament.

5) There is a fine line of chronology in the Bible; it can be relied upon more so than any other document or documents because

6) Two centuries ago there was little evidence (except faith) that the places and people mentioned in the Bible ever existed. But archaeology since have helped to confirm many of the details written about in the Bible. The Bible is real history with abundance of details. Myth does not have details that can be confirmed.

7) There is a *pattern* of seven: six days of work, one of rest (see our *New Mind Papers*: NM15 & NM16 etc.). There is the type and antitype pattern. A day to God is like a thousand years (Psalms 90:4; 2 Peter 3:8). There is the Book of Revelation and its 1000 year period, a Kingdom of God, a rest period from evil. Putting this together we can see the type (the seven day week) and the antitype (the seven millennium week). This pattern is strong and points to 6000 years of man at "work" and the coming 1000 years for rest. We use the scientific method to study the Bible and its chronology. Without a correct chronology we cannot understand history as it really occurred.

CP2: Secular Chronology's Problems

Contradicts Bible
Reconstructed Lists
Astronomical Calculations
All About Eclipses
Identification Game
Secular Dates & Ptolemaic Canon
Juggling Economic Texts
Reading Dates into Texts
77 years of Missing Dates
Other Problems

Secular Chronology Before 626 BC is Dubious

cp23» *Overview of This Section.* There are three points that make today's secular and Biblical chronologies questionable and I believe incorrect in many areas. In ordered to understand history you must have its various events in the correct chronological order. Otherwise, your history will be of little value in understanding what happened in the past.

Contradicts Bible (1)

cp24» The first point (1) that make today's secular and Biblical chronologies questionable is that all secular chronologies that I am aware of contradict the Biblical evidence. This, in itself, means little to someone who thinks the Bible is largely myth. But there is much evidence that contradicts this negative view of the Bible (see "Bible Paper" [BP3]). One should also learn to distinguish between Biblical evidence and Biblical interpretations of evidence. Because I believe in the veracity of Biblical facts, I, of course, give great weight to point (1).

King Lists (2)

cp25» The second point (2) that make today's secular and Biblical chronologies questionable is that most secular and even Biblical chronologies give great weight to such things as king lists. I will show the dubiousness of these lists and that you should give little weight to them for the most part.

Astronomical Calculation (3)

cp26» The third point (3) that make today's secular and Biblical chronologies questionable is that most modern chronologies rely on "astronomical calculation" especially retro-calculations of eclipses. I will show that most astronomical evidence is of questionable value and should be given little weight except for a few cuneiform tablets that also contain times and positions of several planets as well as times of eclipses. After you study this book you will understand how dogmatic and naive the claim is that the Egyptian, or Assyrian, or Grecian chronologies, or areas in them, are "astronomically confirmed."

1: Contradicts the Bible

cp27» Most contemporary-secular chronologies before 626 BC contradicts the chronology of the Bible. This in itself is not evidence to many that the Biblical chronology is correct. It is merely a beginning point in our examination of conventional chronology.

cp28» William F. Albright said, "The Babylonian Chronicle ... and the Assyrian eponym lists, with the aid of the eclipse of the year 763 ... enable us to correct the transmitted chronology of the Bible" (*Recent Discoveries in Bible Lands*, 1936). Notice he says "*to correct*" the chronology of the Bible.

> [An Eponym list is a list of persons officiating as an eponym for a certain year; each year a different person or king or official or governor was designated as that years' eponym: instead of the year being designated by a number, the year was named after the person who was eponym for that year.]

Edwin R. Thiele

cp29» Thiele is an author of a popular rendition of chronology. His chronology is considered a Biblical one. He is widely quoted by secular and Biblical scholars. But Edwin R. Thiele indicates in his writings that Biblical chronology must conform to the Assyrian eponyms along with the apparent 763 BC eclipse of the sun (*A Chronology of the Hebrew Kings*, 1977, pp 28-30, 82-85).

cp30» Even though he is considered a Biblical chronologist, he nevertheless "corrects" the Bible by using the reported eclipse of 763 BC and by using an Assyrian list of eponyms. I disagree here. Thiele does not understand the uncertainty of using an eclipse to date events or the dubiousness of using the Assyrian list of eponyms to "correct" the Bible.

Some of the things mistaken with Thiele's chronology are as follows:

(A) Thiele Foundation was the 763 BC Eclipse

cp31» Thiele in his 1977 paperback book, *A Chronology of the Hebrew Kings*, tries to show that Biblical scripture on the reigns of the kings are hopelessly mixed and contradictory by mentioning some *apparent* contradictions and by quoting some words of noted scholars to the same effect (Chapter 1). But in this book all these apparent contradictions are successfully harmonized following the premises we listed in part one of this book. Thiele is too quick to embrace "evidence" he thinks he found instead of the inspired evidence in the Bible. Thiele at the end of Chapter one says in effect that he has the solutions, but his solutions ignore scripture and he reasons against some scripture ([1977 book], chap. 7, pp. 54ff).

(B) Thiele Tries to fit Biblical Chronology into Assyrian's Chron.

cp32» Thiele *establishes* his chronology based not on the Bible but on secular chronology ([1977] Chapter 3, pp. 28ff). He uses the eclipse that is reported to have occurred on June 15, 763 BC along with the reconstructed Assyrian eponym list(s) ([1977] pp. 28ff). For example he states that:

> "For many years Old Testament scholars have noticed that a total of 128 regnal years for the rulers of Judah from the accession of Athaliah to the end of Azariah ... was about a quarter of a century in excess of the years of contemporary Assyria ..." ([1977] p. 44).

He tries to solve this problem of the missing 25 years by squeezing the Biblical chronology together so that it will agree with the Assyrian chronology by using "dual dating" and "overlapping regnal" patterns ([1977] Chap. 4 to 7). This is not necessarily wrong since there were overlapping regnal years among kings. But this problem has to do with overlooking or miscalculating overlapping years of kings **and** relying too much on a incomplete and contrary Assyrian kings' list(s) and/or by giving too much credit to an apparent eclipse in 763 BC instead of believing in Biblical evidence.

(C) Thiele Changes Scripture to fit his Views

cp33» In chapter 6 of *A Chronology of the Hebrew Kings* [1977], Thiele tries to fit Israel's king Pekah's reign before king Pekahiah in order to squeeze the Biblical chronology into the Assyrian chronology. But the Bible clearly says that before king Pekah became king (he became king by killing Pekahiah) he was the captain of king Pekahiah:

> "But Pekah the son of Remaliah, a captain of his [Pekahiah], conspired against him, and smote him in Samaria, in the palace of the king's house ... and he killed him, and reigned in his room" (2 Ki 15:25).

cp34» This scripture clearly shows Pekah reigning only after he killed Pekahiah, for Pekah was a captain of the king before this event. How can Thiele have Pekah coming to reign before Pekahiah? He does this by changing scripture to suit his own theories and by saying without any proof that the scriptures were "late calculations" of records that were lost (pp. 57-60ff).

cp35» In Thiele' 1983 version of his chronology, *The Mysterious Numbers of the Hebrew Kings*, he is very aware of the problem his chronology causes for the scripture concerning Pekah, for he goes to great lengths to defend his own idea (pp. 120, 129-137, 174).

(D) Thiele Twists Hoshea and Hezekiah reigns

cp36» Thiele's twisting and "reasoning" against scriptures concerning the reigns of Hoshea and Hezekiah is way off the mark (chap 7. [1977 book]). Thiele's main apparent goal is to fit Biblical chronology into the broken Assyrian chronology. But the Assyrian chronology cannot be trusted (see # 2 & 3 below: "2: Reconstructed Eponym List(s) and King List(s)" and "3: Astronomical Calculations").

(E) Bible just misunderstood

cp37» At the end of chapter 1, Thiele tries to indicate that he does not really think the chronology of the Bible is wrong, but only misunderstood:

- "In the pages to follow, the solutions to the various problems involved will be given. It will be shown that once the methods of chronological procedure employed by the early Hebrew recorders are understood, the data of synchronism and lengths of reign can be woven together into a pattern of internal harmony that is in accord with the years of contemporary chronology at every point where a precise contact occurs" ([1977] p. 13).

(F) In Thiele's own words

cp38» In actual fact, Thiele thinks there are several parts of the Biblical chronology that are wrong and that is why he changes the natural flow of certain king's reigns such as Pekah's and Hoshea's ([1977] chap. 6 and 7) and disregards certain scripture as mistaken late calculations by editors of the Bible ([1977] chap 7, p. 54).

cp39» From his book, *The Mysterious Numbers of the Hebrew Kings*, 1983:

- "If Biblical chronology seems to be at variance with Assyrian chronology, it may be because of errors in the Hebrew records" (p. 34).

- And, "Assyrian chronology back to the beginning of the ninth century B.C. rests on a highly dependable basis" (p. 67).

- And, "the chronologies of these two nations [Assyria & Neo-Babylonia], at least for the period with which we are most concerned, have been definitely established" (p. 67).

- "From some period very early in their history — possibly from the very beginning of the kingdom — to the end, the Assyrians followed the practice of each year appointing to the office of eponym, or limmu, some high official for a calendar year, and to that year was given the name of the individual then occupying the position of limmu. Historical events in Assyria were usually dated in terms of these limmus" (p. 68).

- "One item of unusual importance is a notice of an eclipse of the sun that took place in the month Simanu in the eponymy of Bur-Sagale. Astronomical computation has fixed this as 15 June 763. With the year of the eponymy of Bur-Sagale fixed at 763 B.C., the year of every other name of the complete canon can likewise be fixed. The Assyrian lists extant today provide a reliable record of the annual limmu officials from 891 to 648 B.C.; and for this period they provide reliable dates in Assyrian history" (p. 69).

- "Since Ptolemy's canon gives precise and absolutely dependable data concerning the chronology of a period beginning with 747 B.C., and since the Assyrian eponym canon carries us down to 648 B.C., it will be seen that there is a century where these two important chronological guides overlap and where they may be used as a check on each other" (p. 71).

- "When the student has at his disposal chronological materials so dependable as the assyrian eponym list and the ptolemaic canon, he may have complete assurance that he has a solid foundation on which to build" (P. 72).

What Thiele does not understand here is that the king list was *reconstructed* in order to reflect the Ptolemaic Canon (See "Ptolemy and Chronology" below).

cp40» But in contradiction to this last clear statement, Thiele then goes on and argues concerning some contradictions within the eponym lists about the eponymy Balatu, whether he was an "extra eponymy" and if there was an "extra year" ([1983]p. 73). And Thiele goes on to raise further doubt about the Assyrian chronology:

- "A determination of the question of whether there were one or two eponyms during the year 786 and whether the longer or the shorter chronology is correct" ([1983]p. 74).

- "It is extremely rare, however, that an Assyrian inscription provides an account of every year without a gap. The eponym canon deals with every year, and a very few other inscriptions give annual reports; but the usual rule is many omissions in the record. Seldom is there any indication as to just how large or small a gap may be, whether many years or only a few" ([1983]p. 126).

- "The eponym Chronicle has been of invaluable service to scholars in their endeavor to fit properly together facts gleaned from other sources. But in spite of the splendid work that has already been done, it is admitted by careful historians that future study may indicate the necessity of making some modifications in results already achieved" ([1983]p. 143).

2: Reconstructed Eponym List(s) and King List(s)

cp41» **Secular chronology before 626 BC cannot be relied on because** it is based in part on lists of Assyrian eponyms and kings from *different* cuneiform sources which has been **reconstructed** so as to show an almost continuous list of reigns of Assyrian kings starting with Enlil-nasir II (1432-1427 B.C.) down to about 647 B.C, conventional dating (see Grayson, *Assyrian Royal Inscriptions*, Vol. 1 & 2; etc.). Even Egyptian and Sumerian chronologies in part rely on the Assyrian lists (see below). There are at least 66 Assyrian kings listed before Enlil-nasir II, but the King List is too fragmented and incomplete in details prior to his reign so that it is impossible to give dates for these kings with any reliability. I am not saying that the King list after Enlil-nasir II is reliable. An analysis of some of the data concerning the reconstruction can be found in Anstey's *Chronology of the Old Testament* (Kregel edition, 1973, pp. 98ff & 110ff). Also in the *Cambridge Ancient History*, Volume I (1923), it gives information and references on the reconstruction of these eponyms (see, copy of this 1923 volume in archive.org).

(chap. IV, see pp 149ff; also see *The Cambridge Ancient History*, 3rd Ed. Vol. I, Part 4 [1970], pp. 193-200; and see Rogers, Robert William *A History of Babylonia and Assyria*, 2nd Ed., Vol I [1901], [a 1901 copy, 2nd Ed., can be found on archive.org], pp. 323-325, 312-348; Grayson *Assyrian and Babylonian Chronicles, [ABC]* pp. 196, 269; and see E.R. Thiele, *The Mysterious Numbers ...*, 1983, pp. 142-149.)

Some quotes from these latter sources that cast doubt:

Eponym List(s)

cp42» "While the early Mesopotamians and Babylonians named their years after important events, the Assyrians named theirs after *limus*. The *limu* was a title assumed by a different high official each year, the officials following one another according to a definite order. Thus the names of the *limus* were ready-made year names and the Assyrians did not have to compose year names as the early Mesopotamians did. In the same way that the early Mesopotamians compiled lists of the year names as chronological aids, so the Assyrians compiled *limu* or eponym lists" (Grayson, *Assyrian and Babylonian Chronicles*, p. 196).

cp43» "A number of copies of the eponym canons must have existed, for numerous fragments have come down to us. These [*sic*] it has been possible to piece together in the correct order largely *by means of the Canon of Ptolemy*, to be mentioned below" ([1901] Rogers, p. 323, my emphasis).

cp44» Sir Henry Rawlinson found four copies or canons or lists of Eponyms; there were about seven lists or fragments found by 1913 (Anstey, *Chron. of the Old Test.*, 1973 reprint, p. 110).

cp45» "The eponym-lists, except for one small fragment, do not reach back beyond the eleventh century B.C" (*Cambridge Ancient History*, Vol I [1970], p. 195).

cp46» "Babylonian Chronological Materials. The Babylonian priests, historiographers and chronographers have left us an enormous mass of chronological materials, all now in a fragmentary state..." ([1901] Rogers, p. 312).

King List(s)

cp47» "The Assyrian King List is a list of the kings of Assyria beginning with the earliest monarchs and coming down in time as far as the reign of Shalmaneser V (726-722 B.C.). The list is divided into sections by horizontal lines. Each of the first few sections mentions several kings but thereafter each section deals with the reign of only one king. The information given concerning the early kings is sparse owing to lack of sources, as the ancient author admits. The list provides an excellent chronological framework but is not infallible. On occasion kings are omitted, the regnal years are not always accurate, the filiation is sometimes erroneous, and the order of the rulers is not entirely correct. The list seems to have been compiled in the form in which we now know it during the reign of Shamshi-Adad I" (Grayson, *Assyrian Royal Inscriptions*, 1972, Vol. 2, p. 61).

cp48» "These two King Lists have been repeatedly copied, collated, and verified. The chief literature upon them is as follows: (a) *Proceedings of the Society of Biblical Archaeology*, 1884, pp. 193-204 (Pinches). (b) ..." ([1901]Rogers, p. 313, footnote 1 & 2). We must note here that when you "collate" two lists you are taking some from one list and some from the other list: making one list out of two. There are at least four versions of the lists not two.

cp49» "There are four versions (here designated A, B, C, and D) of the Assyrian King List." "There are two fragments.." (Grayson, *Assyrian and Babylonian Chronicles*, 269 & 270).

cp50» "The eponym-list which is behind the Assyrian king-list was damaged, or otherwise deficient, for the interval between Shamshi-Adad I and Adasi. There is also heavy damage to the king-list, in all three copies, for the reigns between Erishum I and

Shamshi-Adad I. Before Erishum I no figures were quoted. This means that the king-list is not a reliable source for the period prior to the beginning of the dynasty of Adasi. For the next few centuries we have no means of verifying its reliability ..." (*Cambridge Ancient History*, Vol. I [1970], p. 195).

cp51» "Although the royal names are rather deformed, it is possible to connect Ptolemy's Canon with the Assyrian lists, and in this manner all the dates can be fixed as far back as the beginning of Adad-nirari's reign" (*Cambridge Ancient History*, Vol I [1923], p. 149).

cp52» As described above there is a difference between the Assyrian Eponym lists and King lists. The Eponym lists are less fragmented than the King lists. But from the fragmented nature of these lists and because they were *reconstructed* by scholars in the last hundred or so years (by scholars who lived thousands of years after the facts), I wouldn't give much credence to "facts" based on the Assyrian kings list or Eponym list. At best these lists are approximate. As previously quoted from Grayson, "the Assyrian royal scribes were prone to hyperbole, hypocrisy, and even falsehood."

Egyptian Chronology and King Lists

cp53» For the most part Egyptian chronologies rely on contradictory copies of the Manetho's king list and on some vague astronomical observations such as the one that was supposed to have occurred in 1536 BC as well as some connection to the Assyrian king lists (see Budge, *The Book of the Kings of Egypt*, Vol. 1, pp xxviii-xxix, xl-xlii; lii-lix"Radical Exodus Redating Fatally Flawed," by Baruch Halpern, *Biblical Archaeology Review*, Nov./Dec., 1987, footnote 1, p. 61).

cp54» "The Egyptian chronology is based on the list of the Pharaohs, made by Manetho under Ptolemy II" (Bickerman, *Chronology of the Ancient World*, p. 82; Budge, *The Book of the Kings of Egypt*, Vol 1, Chap. 2).

cp55» Finegan in his *Archaeological History*, mentions other Egyptian king lists beside the list of Manetho, the list on the Palermo Stone, the Table of Abydos, the table of Saqqara (Sakkara), and the Turin Canon of Kings (p.184).

cp56» W.B. Emery in his *Archaic Egypt*, also mentions different king lists:

"The old Egyptian records consist of five king lists. These are:

1. The 'Tablet of Abydos' inscribed on the walls of a corridor of the temple of Seti at Abydos, listing a series of the *nesu* names of seventy-six kings from Menes to Seti I.

2. The 'Tablet of Karnak,' now in Paris, originally listed the *nesu* names of sixty-two kings from Menes to Thotmose III, but it does not compare with the Abydos list in value, for it was largely based on tradition rather than on formal chronicles.

3. The Tablet of Sakkara, found in the tomb of the Royal Scribe Thunery and now in the Cairo Museum, lists the *nesu* names of forty-seven kings beginning with Merbapen (Enezib) and ending with Rameses II....

4. The Turin Papyrus, written in hieratic, presents a list of kings with the length of each reign in years, months, and days. Unlike the monumental lists of Abydos, Karnak, and Sakkara, it does not stop with unification and the First Dynasty, but goes back beyond mortal kings to the dynasties of the gods....

Valuable as it is, the Turin Papyrus is a tragedy, for more than half its value has been lost by careless treatment. Originally in the possession of the king of Sardinia, it was sent to Turin in a box without packing and it arrived at its destination broken into innumerable fragments. For years, scholars have worked to fit together what remained, but even so, in it restored state, many important gaps occur and the order of some of the kings remains in consequence a matter of debate. Of the seventeen kings of the Archaic Period, only ten are definitely recognizable.

5. Finally we have the so-called Palermo Stone which, like the Turin papyrus, represents another tragedy for archaeological research. Only five small fragments of a great stone slab, originally about 7 ft long and 2 ft high, are in our hands and no record remains which will give a clue to where these pieces were found.... The slab of black basalt was lightly inscribed with the annals of the first five dynasties and also the names of the kings of Upper and Lower Egypt who ruled the two separate kingdoms before the Unification.

Of the Classical sources Herodotus was of limited value, for he trusted too much in the stories related to him by the dragomans who guided him in his travels in Egypt, apparently making no attempt to establish the historical truth of the information thus obtained. But the fragmentary extracts taken from the writings of Manetho by Josephus and by the Christian chronographers Africanus (A.D. 300) and Eusebius (A.D. 340) were of immense importance and formed the framework on which Egyptian history has been built" (pp. 21-23).

Link to web page with links to information on Egyptian king lists and chronology.

https://www.beone.ws/assets/egyptian-chronolog-wikipedia.pdf

cp57» In Budge's *The Kings of Egypt*, he writes:

• "Now if we compare these lists [Tablet of Abydos & Tablet of Sakkarah] with each other, it becomes at once clear that, although they are both supposed to cover the same ground, they differ considerably in many places. Thus the Tablet of Sakkarah opens with the name of Merbapen, which is the sixth in the Tablet of Abydos, and the Tablet of Abydos contains a batch of eighteen names for which there is no equivalent in the Tablet of Sakkarah. We are therefore obliged to conclude that those who drew up these lists have only given us series of selected names. Moreover, monuments bearing numbers of royal names which are not included in either list are well known to Egyptologists. The order of the names is substantially the same in each list, but we may note that in the Tablet of Sakkarah names Nos. 37-46 are written in reverse order. Each list stops at the beginning of the XIX dynasty, and therefore we can obtain no help from either in constructing a list of the remaining kings of that dynasty, or of the following dynasties. For help in this difficulty recourse must be had to the famous List of Kings, which tradition says was drawn up for Ptolemy Philadelphus in the third century before Christ by Manetho of Sebennytus.... His work is lost, but four versions of the King List are extant, and are found in the 'Chronography' of GEORGE THE MONK, the Syncellus of Tarasius, Patriarch of Constantinople, who flourished in the VIIth century of our era. The oldest version of the King List is that of the Chronicle of JULIUS AFRICANUS, a Libyan who flourished early in the IIIrd Century A.D., which is preserved in the Chronicle of EUSEBIUS, Bishop of Caesarea (born A.D. 264, died about 340). Eusebius himself gives a King List, which contains many interpolations. If the versions of the King List of Manetho according to Africanus and Eusebius be compared, it will be seen that they do not agree in the arrangement of the dynasties, or in the lengths of the reigns of the kings, or in the total number of kings assigned to the different dynasties. Thus Africanus makes 561 kings reign in 5524 years, while Eusebius gives the number of kings as 361, and he says their total reigns amount only to 4480, or 4780 years. The version of Africanus agrees better with monuments than that of Eusebius. It is probable that Manetho drew on the writings of the best authorities available in his time, but it is very doubtful if the sources of his information were complete or wholly trustworthy" (Budge, *Kings of Egypt*, p. xl-xli).

cp58» Budge summarizes it:

- "In dealing with Egyptian Chronology it must always be remembered that, comparatively speaking, little is known about it. Many writers on the subject have spent much time and ingenuity in trying to make facts derived from the monuments square with Manetho's King List, and the result of their torturing of the figures and their manipulation of the names has frequently obscured the truth" (Budge, p. xllii).

- "To construct a perfectly complete series of the kings of Egypt, with their dates, we need a complete set of monuments which would tell the order of the succession of the kings, and the length of each king's reign. Such a set of monuments does not exist, and therefore no complete system of Egyptian Chronology can be formulated" (Budge, p. xlii).

Egyptian Kings' Multiple Names

cp59» Manetho used a Greek form for the names of the Egyptian kings. This makes the identification of Manetho kings difficult because of the radically different spelling. Furthermore, as just quoted from Emery's *Archaic Egypt*, some king lists used *nesu* names of the kings. The kings of Egypt had many different names: *Horus* name (Ka or 'double' name); *nesu* name; *nebti* (nebty) name; *insibya* name; *prenomen* name or throne name (Suten Bat); or even the kings personal name, *nomen* (son of Ra name) (Emery, pp. 21-23, 33ff; Finegan, p. 185ff; Budge, pp. xi-xxvii).

Rameses II had at least 72 names (E.A. Budge, *The Book of the Kings of Egypt*, Vol. 1, pp. 165-177).

cp60» "The difficulty does not lie in the order of succession of the kings according to their Horus names.... The difficulty and subject of dispute ... lies in the identification of the Horus names with those submitted by Manetho and those shown on the monumental lists" (Emery, p. 32).

cp61» *Manetho.* There is great "diversity of opinion among Egyptian historians," and this equals "vexed question of chronology" (Emery, p. 28). "There is reason to doubt the strict accuracy of Manetho's figures, for they show every sign of being distorted by the carelessness of his copyists" (Emery, p. 29, he then gives examples between different versions of Manetho's list; Budge, *...Kings* also compares different versions, pp. lxi-lxxiii).

cp62» Breasted in his *A History of Egypt*, also stated that the chronology of Manetho is a late and careless compilation especially of the earlier kings which were "built up on folk-tales and popular tradition of early kings" (pp. 18, 10, Bantam edition). "The dating of the earlier Egyptologists, placing the foundation of united Egypt in the region of 4400

B.C., has long been discarded" (Emery, p. 28). At the time Emery wrote his *Archaic Egypt* (1961) the 4400 BC had been reduced to *3100 BC - 2800 BC* where it now stands (p. 28).

cp63» "By vocation Manetho was an Egyptian priest associated with the city of Serapis. He was not only well versed in the high Greek culture of his day, but he was also thoroughly familiar with Egyptian lore and could read hieroglyphics. He was the first Egyptian to write a history of his country in Greek.

cp64» Manetho was also, like so many of the well-educated Hellenistic Egyptians, anti-Jewish. Indeed, he figured prominently in the Egyptian emergence of anti-Jewish polemical literature in the third century B.C., especially in Alexandria. Ironically, a Jewish historian was responsible for preserving most of the fragments of Manetho's writing. Josephus, the famous Jewish historian of the first century A.D., quotes extensively from Manetho, and it is primarily in this way that Manetho's work has come down to us" ("Jacob in History," Aharon Kempinski, Jan - Feb 1988, *Biblical Archaeology Review.*).

Where are the co-reigns, the co-kings in Egypt?

cp65» As you will see later in this book, there are co-reigns where two kings or princes reign at the same time. One reason is that the first king may become ill or is fighting a war or even wars and he wants to protect his dynasty, so he declares or anoints or crowns one of his sons for co-rulership. We see that in the kings of Judah, Babylonia and other states. But we don't see co-kings on the king or pharaoh lists in Egypt. If the list of kings had groups of two kings reigning at the same time this would cut down the total years for all the kings in Egypt. It would shorten the chronology of Egypt:

> "Any working Egyptologist will agree that discussions of alleged coregencies bulk large in the literature concerned with the history of ancient Egypt. Over the years scholars have accumulated a large body of material that suggests that a number of the pharaohs ruled jointly with their predecessors for at least a part of their reigns" (William J. Murnane, "Ancient Egyptian Coregencies," *Studies in Ancient Oriental Civilization*, No. 40, Th Oriental Institute, Chicago, Ill [1977]).

William J. Murnane then precedes to fill 272 pages with evidence that points to co-regencies in Egypt. It would be very unusual for Egypt to not to have co-reigns. This is another weakness to the list of kings as it pertains to their chronology and the history of Egypt.

Egyptian Dates Astronomically Fixed?

cp66» Many think wrongly that Egyptian chronology is fixed in the heavens, that it is astronomically fixed. Kathleen Kenyon in her *Royal Cities of the Old Testament* makes just such a statement:

- "Dates for Palestine are dependent on the Egyptian calendar, which was based on astronomical observations. These can be astronomically related to the modern calendar. With a varying degree of precision, the recorded regnal years of the Egyptian rulers can be fitted in to the astronomical calendar. There are elements of doubt, and the dates preferred by different scholars vary" (p. x).

cp67» In James Henry Breasted, *A History of Egypt*, in his "Chronological Table of Kings" he indicates many dates in his table are "astronomically fixed." How these dates are "astronomical fixed" he doesn't say. It cannot be based on eclipses since, "from the enormous wealth of written documents from ancient Egypt we have only one doubtful reference to a partial solar eclipse of 610 B.C.... Not a single Egyptian observation is quoted in the Almagest... There exists one Coptic eclipse record of 601 AD..." (O. Neugebauer, *Exact Sciences in Antiquity*, notes for Chap IV). Neugebauer from his book, *Exact Sciences in Antiquity*, sums it up:

- "In summary, from the almost three millennia of Egyptian writing, the only texts which have come down to us and deal with a numerical prediction of astronomical phenomena belong to the Hellenistic or Roman period. None of the earlier astronomical documents contains mathematical elements; they are crude observational schemes, partly religious, partly practical in purpose. Ancient science was the product of a very few men; and these few happened not to be Egyptians" (p. 91).

cp68» "The present writer [Budge] has no wish to belittle in any way the importance of the help which astronomical calculations may afford the Egyptologist in his chronological difficulties, or to deny their general accuracy, but the variations in the results obtained by the different authorities from the same data must tend to make every one hesitate to accept blindly dates which are declared by their advocates to have been ascertained astronomically, and to be 'absolutely certain'" (Budge, p. lvii).

cp69» As we will see in the "Astronomical Calculations" [cp86] section, eclipses and other so-called astronomical evidence are very dubious. The so-called total eclipse of the moon in the time of Takelot II of the so-called XXII Egyptian Dynasty reads:

- "...the heaven could not be distinguished, the moon was eclipsed (literally *was horrible*), for a sign of the events in this land...." (H. Brugsch-Bey, *A History of Egypt*, London, 1894, p. 226)

Please see our "Astronomical Calculation" section to understand that such vague references to 'eclipses' are worthless for date setting.

Egyptian King Lists: Conclusion

cp70» Because of the nature of the king lists of Egypt, with its internal contradiction, because it lists no co-reigns, because the same Egyptian king used many names, because of the different ways cuneiform names can be spelled [cp282-288], because I know of no comprehensive study on how the Hebrews spelled the king's names of Egypt or what names they did use, I cannot harmonize the pharaohs of Egypt with the chronology of the Bible at this time. Those who say that the Egyptian chronology is based on astronomical evidence don't understand how vague and unreliable is the evidence. The so-called astronomical evidence used to prove the Egyptian dates has to do with the fallacious "Sothic period," vague reports of eclipses and new moons, and even through the use of the Assyrian King lists because of certain associations between Egypt and Assyria. See Donovan A. Courville in his *The Exodus Problem and its Ramifications*, Vol 2, Chapter IV for arguments against Sothic dating.

(Budge, ...*Kings*, pp. xlv ff; Baruch Halpern, "Radical Exodus Redating Fatally Flawed," *Biblical Archaeology Review*, Nov.- Dec. 1987, footnote 1, p. 61; Hall, *Cambridge Ancient History*, Vol., p. 170; for critique see Velikovsky, *Peoples of the Sea*, pp. 206ff, 215ff; and see Courville, *The Exodus Problem*, Vol 2 pp. 48ff; and see "Astronomical Calculation," below)

Sumerian Chronology And Hammurabi

cp71» *Were Sumerians, called Sumerians?* The Sumerians are felt to be one of the most ancient nations. (The evidence is too dubious for me to date the so-called Sumerians: too much is made of too little evidence.) "By the end of the fourth millennium B.C. Sumerian civilization was fully developed. This statement involves a question which has often been discussed, 'Who were the Sumerians?'. The adjective 'Sumerian' has been formed by modern scholars from the place-name 'Sumer' which from the late part of the third millennium B.C. was the name regularly used for southern Mesopotamia as opposed to 'Akkad,' the northern part of the river valley; but the inhabitants did not call themselves 'Sumerians,' they were simply 'The people of Sumer'. For the modern historian the invention of the adjective 'Sumerian' was convenient for distinguishing a particular language, a particular people, and a particular civilization" (C.L. Woolley, *Ur of the Chaldees*, [1982], p. 44).

cp72» This is why the Sumerians are not named in the Bible. The Sumerians had another name or names, or where just the people who lived in a region called, "Sumer," but so far no scholar has ascertained it. Not only is the name of this people unknown, but a noted author on the Sumerians, admits that the history of Sumer is dubious:

> "The second chapter deals with the history of Sumer from prehistoric days ... to the early second millennium B.C... Because of the fragmentary, elusive, and at times far from trustworthy character of the sources, not a few of the statements in this chapter are based on conjecture and surmise, and may turn out to be true only in part or even to be entirely false" (*The Sumerians*, Samuel Noah Kramer, 1963, pp. vii-viii).

Hammurabi

cp73» The chronology of Sumer is keyed to the reign of Hammurabi:

> "Let us now turn to the problem of dating in order to see what justifies the statement made in the preceding pages that Sumerian literature represents the oldest written literature of any significant amount ever uncovered. The tablets themselves, to judge from the script as well as from internal evidence, were inscribed in the Early Post-Sumerian period, the period following immediately upon the fall of the Third Dynasty of Ur. Just as a rough point of reference, therefore, the actual writing of the tablets may be dated approximately 1750 B.C.[a]" (pp. 18-19, *Sumerian Mythology*, by Samuel Noah Kramer, Harper Torchbooks:1961)
>
> > "[a] The date 2000 B.C. assigned to the clay tablets on which the Sumerian compositions are inscribed should be reduced by about 250 years as a result of recent studies which point to a date as low as about 1750 B.C. for Hammurabi, a key figure in Mesopotamian chronology" (p. 120, Supplementary Notes, Kramer, 1961).

cp74» At first Hammurabi was believed to have reigned about 450 earlier than 1750 BC:

- L.W. KING in his *The Letters and Inscriptions of Hammurabi*, (1900), dated Hammurabi from about 2200 BC.
- "The chronology of this period is only approximately fixed, and any attempt to definitely settle the various problems it presents and to assign the accession of each king of the First Dynasty to a particular year must be

regarded as purely provisional. If the List of Kings were perfectly preserved this would not be the case; as it is, the principal evidence by which the general date of this dynasty is fixed consists of two passages in cylinders of Nabonidus. From one of these we learn that Burna-Burias lived 700 years after Hammurabi, and from the other that Sagasalti-Burias lived 800 years before Nabonidus. Since Burna-Burias and Sagasalti-Burias are both kings of the Third, or Kassite, Dynasty, these two references enable us to roughly fix the date of Hammurabi at 2200 B.C."

(L.W. King, *The Letters and Inscriptions of Hammurabi*, 1900, pp. LXIX-LXX, AMS Press reprint)

cp75» The revision of the contemporary date of the reign of Hammurabi has to do with his contemporary, the Assyrian king Shamshi-Adad I, who is found in the Assyrian King List (*Assyrian Royal Inscriptions*, Albert Kirk Grayson, Vol. 1, 1972, p. 157, "1813-1741").

cp76» From Jack Finegan's, *Archaeological History of the Ancient Middle East*, we see that in the "tenth year name" of Hammurabi the text:

- "also dates the record of a legal action in Babylon involving a person of probable Assyrian origin, in this the usual oath-formula names both Hammurabi and Shamshi-Adad. Thus, an important synchronism shows that this king of Assyria, Shamshi-Adad I (1813-1781), was still on the throne in the ninth year of Hammurabi (1784)" (p. 61).

cp77» The palace of these rulers at Mari, which was defeated by Hammurabi:

- "preserved royal archives in the form of more than 20,000 cuneiform tablets, almost all in the Babylonian language... These include administrative and economic documents, political and diplomatic communications, and a few literary and religious compositions.

- The diplomatic correspondence touches upon events in the reigns of ... Shamshi-Adad I of Assyria ... and of Hammurabi of Babylon. The correlations thereby provided have much to do with the fixing of the chronology of this period. Similar historical and chronological importance also attaches to cuneiform tablets found at Alalakh (Tell Atchana, on the road from Aleppo to Antioch and the Mediterranean)" (pp. 63-64).

cp78» E.J. Bickerman in his *Chronology of the Ancient World*, writes:

- "Yet, recently discovered documents prove that Hammurabi was contemporary with Shamshi-Adad I of Assyria, who, according to the Assyrian list, reigned in the second half of the eighteenth century. Should we bring Hammurabi down or move Shamshi-Adad up? The rather fluid chronology of the Pharaohs and the Hittites and vague archaeological inferences led recent scholars to suggest 1792-1750 or 1728-1686 as the most probable dates of Hammurabi. Other scholars prefer to place him in 1848 or even *c.* 1900. As a matter of fact, the Assyrian kings themselves disagree with each other and with the information supplied by the royal list when they state the interval between a given king and some predecessor" (pp. 84-85).

cp79» Hammurabi's years were lowered over 400 years mainly because of the Assyrian King List. But Jacobsen doubts this data because he distrusts the older parts of the Assyrian list (*The Sumerian King List*, pp. 191-193ff).

cp80» Jacobsen has reasons to doubt the older parts of the Assyrian king list:

- "The list is divided into sections by horizontal lines.... The information given concerning the early kings is sparse owing to lack of sources, as the ancient author admits. The list provides an excellent chronological framework but is not infallible. On occasion kings are omitted, the regnal years are not always accurate, the filiation is sometimes erroneous, and the order of the rulers is not entirely correct" (Grayson, *Assyrian Royal Inscriptions*, Vol. 2, p. 61).

cp81» Instead of dating Hammurabi by using the Assyrian king list, Jacobsen wants to date Hammurabi with "synchronisms with Egyptian chronology" (p. 193). But the Egyptian chronology is based on even more dubious evidence even though some modern writers think the Egyptian chronology is an accurate one because it is believed to be based on astronomical evidence (see "Egyptian Chronology," and "Astronomical Calculation").

cp82» Therefore the new date for Hammurabi is a reduction of 450 years. Courville in his *The Exodus Problem*, reduces Hammurabi's years even more to about 1411 - 1368 BC (p. 300). There is some evidence that he may be much later than 1750, that is some time after the Exodus. In *The Letters and Inscriptions of Hammurabi*, L.W. King, 1900, Vol III, page 12ff, it shows an order by Hammurabi to Sin-Idinnam ordering him to insert an intercalary month (a second Elul) in the calendar. There is some evidence that the year used to be 360 days before the Exodus and that an astronomical catastrophic event changed the year to the 365 1/4 day year either at the Exodus or much later than the Exodus (See "Catastrophic - Astronomical Events" in CP2 and "Astronomical Chaos" in CP3). The real time when Hammurabi lived I do not know, nor will I guess when Hammurabi lived.

Sumerian King List

cp83» "The first fragment of the Sumerian King List of any importance was published by Hilprecht in 1906... As was natural, considering the fragmentary state of the material and the gradual way in which it accumulated, most of these studies were concerned primarily with the reconstruction of the text, the placing of the known fragments, and the filling up of gaps. The reliability of the information contained in the fragments was rarely seriously questioned. Most scholars inclined to accept it at face value.." (*The Sumerian King List*, Thorkild Jacobsen, 1939, pp. 1-2).

cp84» But by 1923 there grew a wave of "rapidly growing skepticism." Studies showed that "several dynasties listed as consecutive in the King List must in reality have been contemporaneous ... so many kings who were to be expected in the King List are not mentioned there and that so many of the older rulers mentioned appear with unbelievably long reigns, center most of the comments on the King List after 1923" (pp. 2-3).

cp85» "In late years the study of the King List has come almost to a standstill, and its evidence is hardly ever used for purposes of chronology" (p. 4). "But our manuscripts of the King List give opportunity for such study only to a very limited degree. The majority are small fragments. It is therefore relatively seldom that many of them overlap, and passages common to several versions, where we might observe the spread of variants, are few" (p. 14). "The view which we have stated here (...), that our texts are copies, or copies of copies, of a single original document, seems to be generally held by scholars..." (footnote 31, p. 14).

3: Astronomical Calculations

cp86» And point (3), secular chronology before 626 BC cannot be relied on because it is based in part on an *apparent* solar eclipse that has been identified as the eclipse that was supposed to have occurred on June 15, 763 BC according to astronomical calculation, and based on other supposed eclipses.

> (*Handbook of Biblical Chronology* [1964], Finegan, ¶ 159; "Radical Exodus Redating Fatally Flawed," by Baruch Halpern, *Biblical Archaeology Review*, Nov./Dec., 1987, footnote 1, p.61; see (2) above)

cp87» Although the reported 763 BC eclipse deals mostly with Assyrian chronology, this astronomical event is interrelated with other chronologies because of the king lists and the interplay of the Assyrian, Babylonian, Egyptian and other cultures. What applies to this so-called eclipse also applies to others used to prove other secular events and chronologies.

cp88» We need to examine what "astronomical calculation" is all about in order to understand why there is no real proof of secular chronology prior to 626 BC. Because of the finding of some astronomical cuneiform tablets dating after 626 BC, it is possible to verify some conventional dates after 626 BC. But this is not to say that secular chronology after 626 BC is entirely correct or mostly correct. It so happens that two astronomical cuneiform tablets dated after 626 BC (568 and 523 BC) help to prove the Biblical chronology and some of the conventional chronology (see CP3).

cp89» Some set their chronology by the calculation of past solar and/or lunar eclipses:

- "For the year when Bur-Sagale, governor of Guzana, was eponym, the record states that there was a 'revolt in the city of Assur. In the month of Simanu an eclipse of the sun took place.' Astronomical computation has fixed this date as June 15, 763 B.C. This notation is of immeasurable value for Assyrian chronology, for the date of the eponymy of Bur-Sagale being established as 763 B.C., the year of every other name on the complete list can likewise be fixed. It is thus that we have absolutely reliable dates for each year of Assyrian history from 892 to 648 B.C" (Edwin R. Thiele, *A Chronology of the Hebrew Kings*, [1977] p. 29).

cp90» No wonder that those who lack the time to research such statements about the *certainty* of Thiele's chronology are positive that the present conventional chronology is the absolutely correct one because of astronomical calculations it is based on. But the reason Thiele uses eclipses is because he wrongly thinks the Bible is mistaken in its chronology:

- "But as these Biblical numbers are examined, they appear to be in almost constant contradiction with each other, and it seems impossible to work out a harmonious pattern of reigns for either Judah or Israel that is in accord with the numbers in Kings or that *agrees with the established chronology of ancient history*" ([1977] p. 10, my *emphasis*).

cp91» At the end of chapter 1, Thiele tries to indicate that he does not really think the chronology of the Bible is wrong, but only misunderstood:

- "In the pages to follow, the solutions to the various problems involved will be given. It will be shown that once the methods of chronological procedure employed by the early Hebrew recorders are understood, the data of synchronisms and lengths of reign can be woven together into a pattern of internal harmony that is in accord with the years of contemporary chronology at every point where a precise contact occurs" (p. 13).

cp92» In actual fact, Thiele thinks there are several parts of the Biblical chronology that are wrong and that is why he changes the natural flow of certain king's reigns such as Pekah's and Hoshea's (chap. 6 and 7) and disregards certain scripture as mistaken late calculations by editors of the Bible (chap 7).

See "1: Contradicts the Bible" above for more information on Thiele's chronology.

All About Eclipses

cp93» Thiele's chronology and others like his are based in part on the calculation of past eclipses. But these apparent past eclipses and the calculation of them are a *weak* link in this established chronology.

Vagueness of Ecliptical Records

cp94» As just quoted from Thiele's paperback book (p. 29) there was an apparent eclipse when Bur-Sagale was eponym: "In the month of Simanu an eclipse of the sun took place." Or it can be translated as, "the sun was *obscured*" (*Pensee*, Fall 1973, p. 21). If calculations are correct the eclipse was located in northern Assyria, but only a partial (97to99%) in Assyria's capital of Nineveh.
[http://eclipse.gsfc.nasa.gov/SEhistory/SEplot/SE-0762Jun15T.pdf]:

Total Solar Eclipse of -0762 Jun 15

Ecliptic Conjunction = 14:04:43.5 TD (= 08:11:12.9 UT)
Greatest Eclipse = 14:07:32.0 TD (= 08:14:01.4 UT)

Eclipse Magnitude = 1.0596   Gamma = 0.2715

Saros Series = 44   Member = 39 of 72

Sun at Greatest Eclipse
(Geocentric Coordinates)
R.A. = 04h53m47.3s
Dec. = +22°54'17.4"
S.D. = 00°15'43.8"
H.P. = 00°00'08.6"

Moon at Greatest Eclipse
(Geocentric Coordinates)
R.A. = 04h53m46.1s
Dec. = +23°10'35.4"
S.D. = 00°16'24.0"
H.P. = 01°00'11.4"

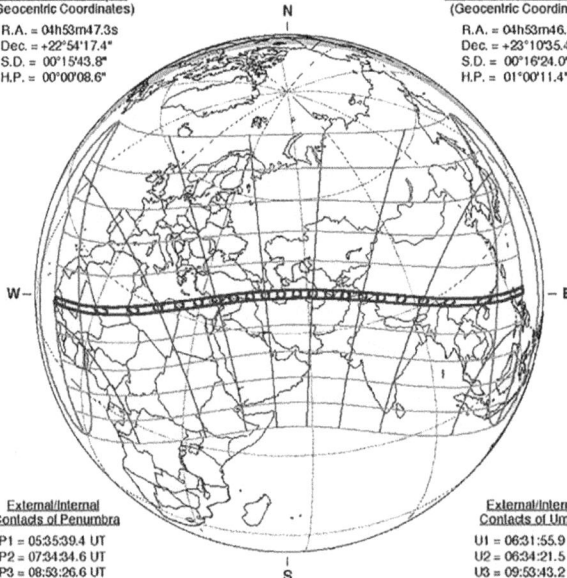

External/Internal
Contacts of Penumbra
P1 = 05:35:39.4 UT
P2 = 07:34:34.6 UT
P3 = 08:53:26.6 UT
P4 = 10:52:27.2 UT

External/Internal
Contacts of Umbra
U1 = 06:31:55.9 UT
U2 = 06:34:21.5 UT
U3 = 09:53:43.2 UT
U4 = 09:56:05.1 UT

Local Circumstances at Greatest Eclipse
Lat. = 38°52.0'N   Sun Alt. = 74.0°
Long. = 054°19.9'E   Sun Azm. = 178.9°
Path Width = 203.8 km   Duration = 05m00.2s

Constants & Ephemeris
ΔT = 21210.6 s
k1 = 0.2724880
k2 = 0.2722810
Δb = 0.0"   Δl = 0.0"
Eph. = VSOP87/ELP2000-82

0   1000   2000   3000   4000   5000
Kilometers

Geocentric Libration
(Optical + Physical)
l = 3.51°
b = -0.29°
c = -8.11°
Brown Lun. No. =-33203

F. Espenak, NASA's GSFC
eclipse.gsfc.nasa.gov/eclipse.html

As we will see below a partial eclipse is hardly even noticeable to most people. If the year of the eclipse is correct we have no proof that the apparent years in eponym list are correct (eponyms may be missing or there were two for one year because one died in the year, etc.). As we will see below solar eclipses repeat themselves in the same areas of the earth even as close as one or two years apart.

cp95» Concerning the so-called eclipse of 763 BC Robert R. Newton writes:

- "With regard to the magnitude, *Fotheringham* [1920] argues: 'As the eclipse is the only eclipse mentioned in this Chronicle, which covers an interval of 155 years, there can be no reasonable doubt that it had been reported as a total eclipse.' This is not a safe conclusion. Even in annals the recording of eclipses is highly variable, as *Dubs* [1938] has shown for Chinese records. Over a span of five centuries, the *Anglo-Saxon Chronicles* recorded six solar eclipses, of which one (809 Jul 16) was probably far from total. (During this time the *Chronicles* missed ten or more eclipses that must have been large if not total.) " [*Ancient Astronomical Observations and the Accelerations of the Earth and Moon,* by Robert R. Newton, 1970, p. 60]

What Newton is saying here is that chronicles that apparently mention eclipses do not necessarily give all of them, or even most of them, or even the larger ones of the chronicle's time period.

cp96» Most ancient so-called eclipses are not identified as total or partial. The following have been interpreted as eclipses:

- "in the seventh year the day was turned to night, and fire in the midst of heaven" (p. 58, Newton)

- "the sun has perished out of heaven" (p. 29, Mitchell's *Eclipses of the Sun*)

- "turned mid-day into night" (p. 29, Mitchell).

cp97» There is a great vagueness in ancient texts as regard to eclipses. If you could be sure that a reported eclipse was total, it would make it easier to find the year of the eclipse, but not easy, for in any century there are hundreds of eclipses.

cp98» Robert R. Newton writes:

"The total eclipse of the sun is a rare and spectacular event....

It is rare, of course, because the zone of totality is narrow, typically of the order of 100 km. The duration of totality at a particular point is of the order of 4^m [minutes]. Thus a simple observation of totality, coupled with an observation of a place where totality occurred, is an astronomical observation of considerable accuracy. The time is needed only to identify the eclipse; an accuracy of a decade in reporting the time is enough in some cases. Unfortunately these simple ingredients of an accurate report are often missing.

Many eclipse reports are found in national annuals or chronicles that reported events of interest anywhere in the country. Sometimes the exact place can be recovered from the annals, often it cannot....

Some reports by an individual do not give the place....

In considering the accuracy of an observation of totality, one should note first that many reports simply state that an eclipse occurred, with no accompanying detail" (Newton, *Ancient Astronomical Observations ...*, 1970, p. 35-36).

cp99» Newton classified ancient observations of eclipses into one appearing in (a) technical reports, (b) annals and chronicles, (c) assimilated eclipses, (d) magical eclipses, and (e) literary eclipses. Newton says the "magical and literary eclipses can be put into a family that can be called myth" (p. 470). While assimilated eclipses are eclipses that were real but were mixed with the wrong time or place or another event. Eclipses found in ancient technical reports and annals may have "typographical errors" and authors of annals or chronicles may have dramatized the reported eclipses.

Frequency of Eclipses

cp100» There is a possibility of as many as seven eclipses in a calendar year:

- "five of the sun and two of the moon, or four of the sun and three of the moon. The smallest number possible is two — both of the sun" (*Astronomy*, by William T. Skilling and Robert S. Richardson, 1949, p. 249).

- "Since eclipses of sun and moon are possible only when the sun is near one of the nodes of the moon's orbit, eclipses, in general, will occur at intervals of about 6 months. Since the lunar eclipse limits are smaller than the solar, it is possible that no eclipses of the moon will occur in any calendar year. Two solar eclipses must occur under these conditions, however. In this century there are 14 years when only two solar and no lunar eclipses take place. Under the most favorable circumstances there may be as many as seven eclipses, two of the moon and five of the sun or three of the moon and four of the sun, in any one year.... From A.D. 1901 to 2000 there will be a total of 375 eclipses, according to Oppolzer's 'Canon der Finsternisse,' 228 of the sun and 147 of the moon; an average of nearly four per year" (*The Elements of Astronomy*, by Edward Arthur Fath, 1944, pp. 166-167; see Theodor von Oppolzer, *Canon of Eclipses*, 1962, Dover reprint, or Oppolzer's 1887 work).

Saros versus Ecliptic Interval

cp101» Lunar and solar Eclipses repeat themselves every 18 years 10 1/3 days (6585.32 days), a period of time mistakenly called a saros.

- "Another document to be considered under category A is the Eighteen-year Interval List. This is a list of eighteen-year intervals beginning with the seventh year of Nabonidus (549 B. C.) and ending with the 21th year of the Seleucid Era (99 B. C.) When first published, the nature of this document was misunderstood and it was incorrectly called the Saros Tablet. The mistaken interpretation of the text and its misnomer arose from a misunderstanding of the term saros. O. Neugebauer [*The Exact Sciences in Antiquity*, 1956] has shown that although Berossus used the term saros (from Sumerian *sar*) as a designation of a period of 3600 years, a later misunderstanding led to the erroneous conclusion that saros was the Babylonian designation for a period of 223 months (= 18 years + 10.8 days [Note: Grayson speaks here of the period of 19 returns of the sun to the same node, not 223 synodic months]). When the present tablet was first discovered and published by Pinches, Oppert immediately connected this list of eighteen-year intervals with the idea that saros was the Babylonian designation for an eighteen-year period.

He claimed that this was a list of such periods and called it the Saros Tablet. Since it is now known that saros is not a term for an eighteen-year period, this text cannot possibly be a Saros Tablet" (Grayson, *Assyrian and Babylonian Chronicles*, p. 195, col 2 to p. 196).

Series of Eclipses

cp102» An eclipse repeats itself every 18 years 10 1/3 days or 6585.32 days (Fath, p. 167). But this is the interval between two eclipses of the same series. Remember there can be as many as seven eclipses within a calendar year. There are series of eclipses:

- "Each individual eclipse, whether of the sun or moon, belongs to a series.... Though an eclipse repeats itself only after eighteen years, there are several eclipses of some kind each year. This is because there are many series going on all the time; there are about 28 series of lunar eclipses, and 42 of solar. Thus there must be a total of about 70 eclipses in every 18 years, or nearly an average of four a year, including eclipses of both sun and moon" (Skilling & Richardson, *Astronomy*, 1949, p.249).

cp103» Because when a certain eclipse in a series repeats itself, it is 1/3 of a day past the position of the last eclipse, then the eclipse will appear on the earth:

- "1/3 of the way around the earth to the west of where it came before. The earth has time to turn 1/3 of the way around (to the east) farther than it did before. But since an eclipse of the moon always covers at least half the earth, and the eclipse path of the sun may extend more than a third of the way around the earth, two successive eclipses will overlap each other. This makes it possible for a person favorably located to see two successive eclipses of the moon, and at least the partial phase of two successive solar eclipses. At each return the eclipse comes on the average about 180 miles north or south of its previous latitude. Half of the series work northward and half southward." [Note: This is because 19 returns of the sun to the same node is .46 of a day more than the moon's synodic period, 6585.78 days versus 6585.32 days (Fath p. 167). This causes the eclipse to fall "a little north or south of where it was before [6585.32 days earlier]. Whether it is farther north or farther south depends on whether the eclipse is at a descending node or at an ascending node" (Skilling, p. 251-252).]

- "At each third repetition of a solar eclipse, that is, once in 54 years, the longitude of the eclipse should be nearly the same that it was before, for the series would have traveled all the way around the earth in 54 years. That often [every 54 years] the partial phase, at least, of a solar eclipse should be seen in the same locality" (Skilling and Richardson, pp. 249-250).

cp104» Thus it is possible for an eclipse of the sun or moon (of specific series) to occur in approximately the same location as often as every 18 years for each series of eclipses, but more likely for the sun every 54 years. From a certain location, the repetition of a *full* solar eclipse will not occur every 18 years, and may not occur every 54 years because of the eclipse's north or southward movement of approximately 180 miles each synodic period.

Types of Eclipses

Annular Eclipses

cp105» If the moon is in its apogee position (furthest distance from the center of the earth) as compared to its perigee position (nearest distance from the center of the earth), the eclipse of the sun will not in any case be a total eclipse, but an *annular eclipse*. In annular eclipses, the moon appears smaller than the sun, thus a ring, or annulus, of the sun's disk remains uncovered. "Annular eclipses are 20 percent more frequent than total eclipses" (Baker & Fredrick, *An Introduction to Astronomy*, 7th Ed., p. 194).

Partial and Total Eclipse

cp106» Of the solar eclipses during the 20th century only 28 percent were total, while 35 were partial and 33 percent annular. About 4 percent were annular-total (*Eclipse*, Bryan Brewer, p. 67).

Penumbral v. Umbral Eclipses

cp107» Furthermore some of the eclipses of the moon cannot be seen at all even in good weather because the eclipse is of the penumbral shadow and not the umbral shadow. The *umbral* shadow is the dense part of an eclipse shadow while the *penumbral* shadow is the less dense part of the shadow. In a recent eclipse of the moon, Oct 7, 1987, the only shadow cast on the moon was the penumbral shadow. Even though this is counted as an eclipse of the moon in such canon of eclipses as Jean Meeus and Hermann Mucke (1979), and even though I knew ahead of time when it was to occur, I could not detect any shadow on the moon by eyesight. About 36 percent of all lunar eclipses from -2002 to +2526 will have been penumbral eclipses, according to calculations (*Canon of Lunar Eclipses, -2002 to +2526*, by Jean Meeus and Hermann Mucke, 1979, p. XIII).

Observable Eclipses

cp108» **Most solar eclipses, except total ones, are not even noticeable to most people.** A total eclipse only lasts about 4 minutes on average, at the very most 8 minutes. A penumbral eclipse of the moon is basically invisible, at most the color of the moon changes. **A partial eclipse of the sun below 99 percent, or an annular eclipse of the sun is also basically invisible**:

- "We find that the overall partial p-type eclipses of Oppolzer were never noticed and even the annular r-type were often missed. Most of the early records relate to eclipses that were total, either at the place of observation or within a few hundred miles of the track of totality.... The total phase seldom lasts more than five and never more than eight minutes.... Long before totality commences, Venus is usually visible, but during totality, planets and a few stars may be seen.... Total eclipses are rare; at any one place the average is three times in a millennium.... The intensity of daylight may not be greatly reduced so that an annular eclipse may not even be noticed... Annular-total eclipses are classified with fully total eclipses as Central [but nevertheless are not easily noticed].... [concerning partial eclipses] Such eclipses are more frequent than is usually supposed, for they occur about once every 2 ½ years at any given location. However, the loss of light is smaller than heavy clouds would produce and partial eclipses usually passed unnoticed by the astronomically-unsophisticated chronicler.... Astronomers, and those who have been forewarned, may notice an eclipse of magnitude 0.70 [percent] (cf. AD 808) if they see it in a reflection, at sunset or through thin cloud or haze, and then the moon shaped black crescent suggests that a large bite is taken out of the Sun. The average person notices a thin solar crescent of a solar eclipse only when the magnitude reaches 0.99 [percent]" (D. Justin Schove, *Chronology of Eclipses and Comets*, [1984], pp. x-xv).

Lunar eclipses are visible whenever the moon is above the horizon to the observer and can be seen over more than half the earth during its duration. Umbral eclipses can last almost 4 hours, counting from when the moon's first contact with the umbra until the moon exits the umbral shadow. While the total shadow over the moon can last over1 hour and 40 minutes. For example, one of the longest total lunar eclipses ever occurred on January 30, 30 BC. It lasted 3 hours and 54 minutes (from first contact of the umbra to the last contact), while the total eclipse lasted about 1 hour and 42 minutes. This eclipse was seen in Jerusalem and in North America.

'Average' Time Between Eclipses

cp109» Remember there are many *series* of eclipses going on in a 54 year period. This means full eclipses of the sun from *different* series of eclipses may be seen from the same position on the earth more often than every 54 years. In certain circumstances an eclipse can be seen within two years of the last eclipse. In the vicinity of the city of Halifax in Nova Scotia people were able to see two total solar eclipses; one in 1970 and one in 1972 (Baker and Fredrick, *An Introduction to Astronomy*, 1967, p.196). See chart called, "Important Solar Eclipses," p 253, *Astronomy*, by Skilling & Richardson, where it shows several solar eclipses visible in certain areas on the earth within different two or three year periods.

cp110» In *Eclipse*, by Bryan Brewer (1978, p. 70) we read:

- "Partial phases of solar eclipses can be seen about every 2 ½ years from the same spot. The best estimate for total eclipses is to say they recur at the same location about every 360 years on the average. This figure is based on the average width of eclipse paths, the total surface area of the Earth, and the overall frequency of total eclipses. But the actual facts vary, sometimes widely, from this estimate. The table below helps illustrate the apparent random nature of the recurrence of eclipses at the same place. The examples were chosen, not to prove any lack of pattern, but to present the flavor of the variation involved."

Consecutive Eclipses

Location	Total Eclipses	Interval
London	Oct.29,878 AD to	
	Apr.22,1715 AD	= 837 years
Jerusalem	Sep.30,1131 BC to	
	July 4,336 BC	= 795 years
	...	
Southern		
New Guinea	June 11,1983 A.D. to	
	Nov.22,1984 A.D.	= 1 ½ years

Identification Game

cp111» All this above, especially since the ancient so-called eclipses are vague as to type or magnitude (partial to total), vague as to exact location, and vague as to time period makes it extremely difficult to identify the year of their occurrence. This enables chronologists (Ptolemy included) to play the "identification game."

cp112» The "identification game" is explained by Robert R. Newton in his *Ancient Astronomical Observations* (pp. 45-47). It is played by chronologists when they think they know the ancient writer or chronologist's approximate location, the approximate date within decades of the occurrence of the eclipse, and when they have a copy of solar charts in such works as *Oppolzer Canon* (1887). When they have this information they merely,

- "identify the eclipse as the one with the greatest calculated magnitude." Then they use,"this possibility alone in using the eclipse to improve the astronomical constants or the accelerations." Thus, "they lead to a successful 'identification' for almost any set of times and places chosen at random. It is only necessary for there to be a modest uncertainty in either the time or place. Further, the calculated path of the 'identified' eclipse, by the rules of the game, passes close to some chosen point. Thus, if the 'eclipse' report is used to improve the constants that went into the eclipse computation, by making the calculated path go through the chosen point, it is almost guaranteed that the changes in the constants will be acceptably small" (R. Newton, p. 46).

cp113» An example of this identification game in process is shown in, *The Story of Eclipses* [1912], by George F. Chambers. **Notice this game was played with the chronologically important 763 BC eclipse:**

"The discovery to which I allude is a contemporary record on an Assyrian tablet of a solar eclipse which was seen at Nineveh about 24 years after the reputed date of Amos's prophecy. This tablet had been described by Dr. Hinckes in the British Museum *Report* for 1854, but its chronological importance had not then been realized. Sir H. Rawlinson speaks of the tablet as a record of or register of the annual archons at Nineveh. He says: — 'In the eighteenth year before the accession of Tiglath-Pileser there is a notice to the following effect — 'In the month Sivan an eclipse of the Sun took place' and to mark the great importance of the event a line is drawn across the tablet, although no interruption takes place in the official order of the Eponyms. Here then we have notice of a solar eclipse which was visible at Nineveh ... and which we may presume to have been total from the prominence given to the record, and these are conditions which during a century before and after the era of Nabonassar are alone fulfilled by the eclipse which took place on June 15, 763.'

This record was submitted to Sir G.B. Airy and Mr J.R. Hind, and the circumstances of the eclipse were computed by the latter, by the aid of Hansen's Lunar Tables and Le Verrier's Solar Tables. The result, when plotted on a map, showed that the shadow line just missed the site of Nineveh, but that a very slight and unimportant deviation from the result of the Tables would bring the shadow over the city of Nineveh, where the eclipse was observed, and over Samaria, where it was predicted. The identification of this eclipse, both as regards it time and place, has also proved a matter of importance in the revision of Scripture chronology, by lowering, to the extent of 25 years, the reigns of the kings of Jewish monarchy" (Chambers, pp. 76-77).

cp114» **Notice that even though the "shadow line" missed the site of Nineveh** in the tables it was close enough for the "identification game" being played here. It is not clear to me what Chambers means by this "shadow line" in the table. By looking at the 1983 *Canon of Solar Eclipse* by Mucke and Meeus, page 685, it shows the shadow line representing the total eclipse missing the area of Nineveh, but at this site, if Mucke and Meeus' work is correct, people at or near Nineveh saw a solar eclipse that was approximately 97-99% total (thus almost invisible [see cp108], if weather permitted the observation, and if the earth and planets were still in the same orbit as now. Remember, the eclipse was retro-calculated. There is evidence of catastrophic-astronomical events in the past. See "Catastrophic - Astronomical Events" in CP2 and "Astronomical Chaos" in CP3.

cp115» Airy was also responsible for the present identification of the eclipse of Thales of Miletus as happening on May 28, 585 B.C.:

- "The exact date of this eclipse was long a matter of discussion, and eclipses which occurred in 610 B.C. and 593 B.C. were each thought at one time or another to have been the one referred to. The question was finally settled by the late Sir G.B. Airy, after an exhaustive inquiry, in favour of the eclipse of 585 B.C. This date has the further advantage of harmonizing certain statements made by Cicero and Pliny as to its having happened in the 4th year of the 48th Olympiad" (Chambers, p. 94).

cp116» Airy method is the identification game method as is shown by how he identified other eclipses:

- "Sir G.B. Airy, having had his attention called to the matter, examined roughly all the eclipses which occurred during a period of 40 years, covering the supposed date implied by Xenophon. Having selected two, he computed them accurately but found them inapplicable. He then tried another (May 19, 557 B.C.) which he had previously passed over because he doubted its totality, and he had the great satisfaction of finding that the eclipse, though giving a small shadow, had been total, and that it had passed so near to Nimrud that there could be no doubt of its being the eclipse sought" (Chambers, p. 97).

- "The tables used by Baily were distinctly inferior to those now in use, and Sir G.B. Airy thought himself justified in saying that to obviate the discordance of 180 miles just referred to 'it is only necessary to suppose an error of 3 minutes in computed distances of the Sun and Moon at conjunction — a very inconsiderable correction for a date anterior to the epoch of the tables by more than twenty-one centuries.' " (Chambers, pp 104-105)

cp117» Airy by just adjusting the computation a little comes up with what he wants. This is another dubious aspect of using eclipses to establish chronology — the present computation of ancient eclipses may or may not be correct. If the present computation of ancient eclipses is wrong a whole new can of worms is opened or a whole new area of dubiousness enters the picture. See F. Richard Stephenson, "Historical Eclipses," *Scientific American*, Oct. 1982, pp. 170ff, especially p. 180 top, for some information about the possibility of the sun shrinking, or earth spin slowing down and their effect on retro-calculation of past eclipses.

1000 Years Difference

cp118» In Robert R. Newton's *Ancient Planetary Observations and the Validity of Ephemeris Time*, he shows us a swing of over 1000 years in the identification of a solar and lunar eclipse and other astronomical phenomena:

> "*Kugler* published and discussed a text that he dates to the months IV through IX of the year 40 of Artaxerxes I (the year SE -113). The text makes statements about the number of days in each month, and about the dates of full moons, of first and last visabilities of the planets and of Sirius, of the summer solstice and the autumnal equinox, and of one lunar and one solar eclipse. It has been claimed that the statement about the lunar eclipse is a highly accurate and reliable observation of the lunar eclipse of -424 October 9, and much weight has been put upon this alleged observation. However, I do not see any reason to assume that the text contains an observation of a lunar eclipse at all.

> I did not originate this conclusion. Kugler reached it in the cited reference sixty years ago, and he emphasized it at least two places that the text contains no observation, but only calculations" (pp 127-128).

> "It is interesting that Kugler used the word 'alleged' in referring to these records, just as I have done, but for a different reason. He referred, in the caption of his relevant section, to alleged records from the middle of the second millennium before Christ'. The text in its present form has no indication of year, and students before Kugler had assigned it to a year near -1500. Kugler assigned the year SE -113 [-424] from an analysis of the astronomical information in the text" (p. 130).

Notice that Kugler assigned the year -424 because of his analysis of the astronomical information in the text, but students before him for the same reasons assigned it to a year around -1500. The "identification game" is very liberal. What is a 1000 years or so?

Calculations versus Observations

cp119» In summarizing this same cuneiform text Robert Newton writes:

- "In summary, if the year is SE -113 [425 BC], it is certain that at least one of the eclipse records in the text is calculated, and there are various reasons to conclude that all records in the text are calculated. If the year is not SE -113, it is mathematically possible that both eclipse records represent observations. In either case, however, there is no basis for the assumption that the text records an observation of the lunar eclipse of -424 [425 BC] October 9. If the year is right, we are dealing with calculations and not observations. If the year is wrong, we are not dealing with the date -424 October 9 at all" (p. 130).

cp120» So Newton is not even sure about the present identification of the text. Newton also brings up that many of the cuneiform text of astronomical events were calculations and not observations. This makes it even more difficult to use astronomical calculations to prove chronology.

Identification Game, More on the

cp121» Lynn E. Rose put the same identification game into the following words:

"Let us now turn to the general context within which the received opinions about such matter as intercalation have developed. Over the years there has been a close cooperation between Assyriologists and astronomers. The interpretation of texts has been carefully guided by astronomical retrocalculation, in accordance with uniformitarian principles. *The Venus Tablets of Ammizaduga* (London, 1928) is a microcosmic replica of the sort of cooperation that has pervaded scholarship generally: Langdon was an Assyriologist, Fotheringham was an astronomer, and Schoch was a mathematician, concentrating here on tables to facilitate astronomical retrocalculation.

... A historian may consult an astronomer regarding an eclipse or other astronomical event. The astronomer will calculate possible dates for the event. The historian will then arrange his chronology so as to fit the astronomer's retrocalculations. Then some time passes, and the chronology becomes orthodox. The grounds for the chronology are forgotten, and it is *assumed* to rest on solid historical evidence. No one remembers or can even find out any more that it rests on astronomical retrocalculations. Then a new generation of astronomers and historians play the game again, this time in reverse direction. The chronology is taken as independently fixed, and the eclipse or other event is taken as datable on purely historical grounds. Then someone retrocalculates in the same manner as before, but not in order to set up the chronology this time — just to check it. And of course all the pieces fit. Different generations have made the same numerical computations and obtained the same results" (*Kronos: A Journal of Interdisciplinary Synthesis*, Vol IV, No. 2, Winter 1978, "Just Plainly Wrong: A Critique of Peter Huber," by Lynn E. Rose, p. 39).

cp122» This quote is from Rose's critique of Peter Huber. It is interesting to quote from Peter Huber concerning the matter of the observation of Venus:

"4.3 The Old Babylonian Venus observations

Apart from minimal changes (to be mentioned below) we followed the text established by E. Reiner and D. Pingree, *The Venus Tablet of Ammisaduqa*...

4.3.1. Data screening

To avoid possible misunderstandings, I must present the analysis of these very poor data in considerable detail. As a rule, apparent gross errors and conjectural emendations were included in the astronomical calculations, but otherwise treated like missing values and excluded from statistical tests. However, I struggled with the Venus Tablet data long enough so that the treatment is not wholly consistent between calculations I did seven years ago (i.e. before RP) or more recently.

The text contains dates of 49 distinct phenomena; if it ever was complete, it covered 52. The data set is the worst I ever have encountered as a statistician. From the number of internal inconsistencies (between dates of disappearance and reappearance and the stated duration of invisibility) and of discrepancies between duplicates, one may guess that at least 20 % to 40 % of the dates must be grossly wrong. This entails that we must perform some data screening to eliminate the clearly wrong values, ...

It should be emphasized that this screening is independent of chronological assumptions.... Among them, we shall throw out groups which seem to be affected by a common pattern of errors, for example the entire last section of the text, which seems to be more corrupt than the rest" (Peter Huber, *Astronomical Dating of Babylon I and Ur III* [June 1982], pp. 14-15).

cp123» Huber tries to assure us that he did not ignore or screen some of the text for chronological assumptions. But he writes a few pages later:

"At least 5 of these 8 dates give a poor fit for any chronology fitting the majority of the data. One may wonder whether they belong to Ammisaduqa at all.... Anyway, we cannot gain much by keeping this section in, so we may just as well stay on the safe side and drop it entirely.

..."

This date agrees so poorly with any chronology fitting the majority of the data (it is several days too late) that I decided to drop it, ...

After establishing a particular chronology we may go back and check also the rest of the data against calculation" (Huber, p 19).

cp124» By reading this work by Huber it is obvious that he is changing data to fit chronological assumptions. Huber uses the Venus Tablet as some use the Bible, if the data or scriptures don't fit their assumptions, they change the data or scriptures — "scribal error." One reason the data of the Venus Tablet doesn't fit today's observation of Venus is because Venus may have orbited at that time in a different path and the data in the Venus Tablet was a recording of that different path (see "Astronomical Chaos," CP3).

Suppression of an Eclipse

cp125» Another example of the identification game and of data screening is the blatant ignorance of the eclipse mentioned in the so-called Esarhaddon Chronicle. On the obverse (front) of the clay tablet it reads on the 5th line:

"In the month of Teshri [Sept - Oct] the sun darkened [its] light."

cp126» This is quoted from the English translation found in Sidney Smith's *Babylonian Historical Texts*, page 14. In the "Notes" for this tablet Smith has a footnote for line 5:

- "Sir Frank Watson Dyson, the Astronomer Royal, has kindly informed me that there were three eclipses in 680 B.C., of which only the first could possibly be visible at Babylon; but since this eclipse fell on January 1, 680 B.C. according to the Julian Calendar, this cannot be the phenomenon referred to in the text, which is dealing with September-October. The expression therefore refers to some other phenomenon" (p. 16).

cp127» Line 5 of the obverse side of the tablet indicates a solar eclipse in the first year of Esarhaddon just as clearly as any other note of an eclipse in ancient writings. Of course like the rest of the so-called eclipses mentioned in ancient writings it does not indicate a total or partial eclipse. The only reason, repeat, the *only* reason this apparent eclipse is not used to confirm conventional chronology is because it would not confirm it, but disprove it. Thus the words that expressed that the sun was darkened in the first year of Esarhaddon must therefore refer "to some other phenomenon." When an eclipse in ancient writings confirms the conventional chronology it is an eclipse; when it doesn't it of course is "some other phenomenon." What this tells us is that there is something wrong with the conventional chronology. It is not based on sound thinking or on a solid foundation.

In Conclusion

cp128» Astronomical methods for dating ancient events are not as exact as some think they are:

- **(A)** Present secular and "Biblical" chronologies are based on vague evidence and these chronologies are at variance with the stated chronology of the Bible and that is why some have "corrected" the Biblical chronology so that it would agree with the Assyrian data, Ptolemy's King's List and alleged eclipses. The Biblical chronology is the longest and the better chronology of all the ones available.

- **(B)** There is a vagueness to the records of eclipses, "The principle reason is the paucity [or shortage] of examples of eclipse records which provide adequate data for unequivocal identification of the eclipse record with a calculated eclipse. There is thus always the possibility that the eclipse record has been correlated with the wrong eclipse, thus leading to obscuring the truth rather than establishing it" (Donovan A. Courville, "The Use and Abuse of Astronomy in Dating," p. 201, *Creation Research Society Quarterly*, Vol 12, Number 4,).

- **(C)** "A second factor limiting the value of astronomical data for dating purposes is the fact that only *major* eclipses have any genuine potential for dating. Partial eclipses are of such frequency that the chances for proper correlation are remote, thus leading to erroneous conclusions. Even a total or near total eclipse of the sun can be expected to have occurred within any period of a century or less in a given area" (Courville, p. 201).

Catastrophic-Astronomical Events

cp129» Also, if Velikovsky-like theories of catastrophic events in our solar system in the past are correct, the position of the earth may have been moved in relation to the Sun and Moon in the year -687 and -747 (Velikovsky's dates, but see Sean Mewhinney, "On 'The Year -687'," and "Velikovsky, Mars, and the Eighth Century," *Kronos*, VI:4 [1981] & XII:1 [1987]). This would make calculations before approximately -687 incorrect as far as finding occurrences of eclipses (see Velikovsky, *Worlds in Collision*; see "Astronomical Chaos," CP3). This may be the reason the eclipse of 763 BC gives a false reading and that the suppressed eclipse of the Esarhaddon Chronicle has not found a place in secular chronology. If there were astronomical catastrophic events near -747 and -687, then the solar system before these events would not conform to the present arrangement and thus retrocalculation would not locate a correct date for old eclipses recorded in such old texts as the Assyrian eponym lists.

cp130» Some proof that the solar system changed positions some time between -747 and -687 (Vel. dates) is that about this time Babylon began to gather observation of positions of planets once again.

cp131» Kugler in a later part of his *Sternkunde und Sterndienst in Babel*, had a chapter entitled "Positive Proofs for the Absence of a Scientific Astronomy before the Eighth Century B.C." "These proofs consist of the fact that one finds that after this date Mesopotamian astronomers were concerned with calculating basic data that should have been known for a long time to those who pursue scientific astronomy. They were trying to ascertain such elementary matters as the exact location of the spring equinox and the system of intercalations necessary to obtain a calendar corresponding to the solar year. Furthermore, they would have just begun to keep accurate record of the eclipses... the Chinese record begins at the same moment of time. Kugler observed also that, although the planets had been identified as such for at least one thousand or two thousand years, in the seventh century B.C. the science of planetary motions seems to have been at its very beginning" (Livio C. Stecchini, "Astronomical Theory and Historical Data," *The Velikovsky Affair*, 1967, p. 157).

According to Parker and Dubberstein (*Babylonian Chronology*):

- "Reconstruction before 626 is much too hazardous at present and must await further additions to our knowledge" (p. 2 of the 1956 edition).

Review of Secular Chronology Before 626 BC

cp132» If one believes the Bible is the Word of God, then number (1) above ["Contradicts the Bible"] by itself would disprove any secular chronology before 626 BC that is based on Assyrian chronology that contradicts Biblical evidence because the Bible cannot err (John 10:35). The Bible to Christians is "profitable for doctrine, for reproof, for correction, for instruction" (2 Tim 3:16). Of course to others, number (1) above would mean little. The dubiousness shown in numbers (2) ["Reconstructed Eponym List(s)...,"] and (3) ["Astronomical Calculations,"] above also shows us the unreliability of secular chronology before 626 BC as presently reconstructed from Assyrian eponyms and king lists. The presently accepted chronologies before 626 BC are highly suspect.

Secular Dates from 626 BC to 75 AD

cp133» At one time I thought that the dates of secular history, specifically from 626 BC to 75 AD (conventional dating system), were sound dates because of the apparent evidence shown in the book, *Babylonian Chronology 626 B.C.-A.D. 75* (1956), by Parker and Dubberstein. This book (or one of its earlier versions) is one of the primary books used by chronologists and historians to confirm their dates.

(for example see: A.T. Olmstead, *History of the Persian Empire*, footnotes on pp. 35, 87, 93, etc; D.J. Wiseman, *Nebuchadrezzar and Babylon*, footnotes on pp. 113, 118; D.J. Wiseman, *Chronicles of Chaldaean Kings*, footnotes on pp. 7, 38, 43; John C. Whitcomb, Jr., *Darius The Mede*, footnote on p. 74; Peter J. Huber, *Astronomical Dating of Babylon I and Ur III*, pp. 8, 51)

cp134» But notice what was the basis for this book's chronology:

"The general basis for the chronology of the period here treated is furnished by the **Ptolemaic Canon**, with help from classical sources. Cuneiform chronicles and lists of kings have also been of considerable help in checking and improving on the general framework of chronology. The numerous cuneiform economic texts often furnish an accurate check on the lengths of reigns. Since these texts cover the larger part of the period, from 626 B.C. to the middle of the second century B.C., they are of prime importance. Dates from cuneiform astronomical texts are especially helpful for the chronology of the third and second centuries B.C."

(Parker and Dubberstein, p. 10, my emphasis; also see *The Cambridge Ancient History*, Vol I [1923], p. 149 and Rogers, A *History of Babylonia and Assyria*, 2nd Ed. Vol 1 [1901], p.324 [or p.323, 1900 Ed.])

cp135» Notice the *basis* for the chronology of the period 626 B.C.- 75 A.D. is the Ptolemaic Canon. This canon, called the Royal Canon by Bickerman, is the foundation of ancient chronology for these years *(Chronology of the Ancient World, pp. 81ff)*. As we shall see, this is one problem with secular chronology. I have found other problems.

cp136» **But there are some problems I found with Parker and Dubberstein's book and its documentation:**

(1) the Ptolemaic Canon itself;

(2) juggling of the economic text tablets from one king's reign to another;

(3) reading or projecting or interpolating dates into clay tablets, or suppressing evidence;

(4) and there are about *77 years* where there is *no cuneiform evidence* for the reigns of the later and supposed kings of Persia (Artaxerxes II, Artaxerxes III, Arses, and Darius III).

1: Ptolemaic Canon

cp137» *The Ptolemaic Canon* or Chronology is the work of one man Claudius Ptolemaeus (about 70-161 AD). He was the author of the Ptolemaic System of Astronomy. This is the system where the earth is stationary and all the heavenly bodies rotate around the earth. This theory was king for nearly a millennium and a half. This astronomical system was replaced by the Copernican system in about the 16th Century and thereafter. Ptolemy was apparently also one of the founders of the science of Geography.

cp138» Ptolemy's Canon or Chronology is merely a canon or list of kings with the years of their reigns that was included in his "Handy Tables" (*Ptolemy's Almagest*, 1984, G.J. Toomer, pp. 10-11). It had no explanatory writing with the list to explain the reasons Ptolemy put the list in its form. There is even some contention that the list or Canon was compiled after Ptolemy's death by someone else who then included it with Ptolemy's work, or it was a "list of kings preserved in Theon's [of Alexandria] commentary on Ptolemy's astronomical work. Composed by Alexandrian astronomers for their own calculations" (Bickerman, p. 81ff).

cp139» Ptolemy wrote his list as a late compiler, not as a contemporary historian of the Persian and Babylonian Empire. He is corroborated by *some* evidence found in the book, *Babylonian Chronology 626 B.C. - A.D. 75*, but there are approximately 77 years wherein there are *NO* economic clay tablets (see below).

cp140» He is contradicted by

Canon of Ptolemy

Babylon

Nabonassar (Nabonassaros) [747-734 B.C.]	14 yrs	
Nabu-nadinzir (Nadius)	2	
Ukinzer, Pulu (Chinziros, Poros)	5	
Ululai (Iloulaios)	5	
Marduk-appal-iddin (Mardokempados)		12
First Interregnum	2	
Bel-ibni (Belibos)	3	
Assur-nadin-shum (Aparanadios	6	
Nergal-ushezib (Regebelos)	1	
Mushezib-Marduk (Mesesimordakos)	4	
Second Interregnum	8	
Ashur-akh-iddin (Asaridinos)		13
Shamash-shum-ukin (Saosdouchinos)	20	
Kandalanu (Kineladanos)	22	
Nabopolaassar (Nabopolassaros)	21	
Nebuchadnezzar (Nabocolassaros)	43	
Amel-Marduk (Illaoroudamos)	2	
Nergal-shar-usur (Nerigasolassaros)	4	
Nabonidus (Nabonadios) [554-539 B.C.]	17	

Persia

Cyrus [538-530 B.C.]	9
Cambyses	8
Darius I	36
Xerxes	21
Artaxerxes I	41
Darius II	19
Artaxerxes II	46
Ochus [Artaxerxes III]	21
Arses	2
Darius III [335-332 B.C.]	4

Note: Years are Egyptian years which began on the first of Thoth. B.C. dates are contemporary dates — some are wrong. (list is from E. R. Thiele, *The Mysterious Numbers of the Hebrew Kings*, 1983, Appendix G; and Martin Anstey, *Chronology of the Old Testament*, 1973 reprint, p. 21, which was taken from *Tables Chronologiques des Regnes de C. Ptolemaeus, Theon, etc. par M. L' Abbe Halma*, published in Paris, 1819; also see Toomer's *Ptolemy's Almagest* [84], p. 11 and E.J. Bickerman, *Chronology of the Ancient World*, pp. 107ff, and note 64 on p. 104; F.K Ginzel, *Handbuch Der Mathematischen Und Technischen*, 1906, p. 139)

Persian national traditions preserved by *Firdausi* (about 931-1020 A.D.), by the Jewish national traditions preserved in the *Sedar Olam Rabbah*, and by the writings of *Josephus* (see *Chronology of the Old Testament*, by Martin Anstey, pp 18-19ff).

Ptolemy's Fraud

cp141» In the last several decades Ptolemy has come under some close scrutiny by Robert R. Newton and others. From Newton's *The Crime of Claudius Ptolemy*, 1977:

- "It is possible that Ptolemy has deceived us about what Hipparchus did; we shall find in later chapters that he frequently deceives us about the work of other astronomers" (p. 99).

- "Even if there are such sources, they cannot explain how Ptolemy, by accident, over and over again, happened to make just those errors which allow his erroneous theories to agree with preassigned values, namely values that were accepted from the work of earlier astronomers" (p. 101).

- "In Chapter V. 12 he describes in considerable detail how he built an instrument for measuring the parallax of the moon, how he put it in place and aligned it correctly, and how he made observations with it.... But we showed in Section VIII.5 that Ptolemy did not make this observation at all.... To put the matter bluntly, Ptolemy lies about what he has done, and his elaborate description of his procedures is false. Presumably he inserts the description of the parallactic instrument only to provide convincing detail that will make us think that he did make the claimed observation. I do not know of any principles of science or philosophy, ancient or modern, that justify such conduct" (p. 352).

- "In Chapter VII.4 of the *Syntaxis* [Almagest], Ptolemy says that he has measured the coordinates of all the stars that it is possible to observe, down to stars of the sixth magnitude. He identifies the instrument with which he made the measurements, he describes the procedure that was followed, and he presents the alleged results in his star catalogue. However, we proved in Chapter IX above that the coordinates were not obtained by measurement at all. They were not obtained with the instrument that Ptolemy claims to have used, they were not obtained by the method that he claims to have used, and they were not obtained by any other instrument or procedure of observation. They were fabricated, and Ptolemy lied about what he did" (p. 353).

- "Ptolemy chooses the worst way rather than the best way to get the apparent diameters of the sun and moon" (p. 360).

- "In several places, Ptolemy measures or pretends to measure the same quantity more than once. In spite of this he does not seem to understand the significance of measurement error. We see this because Ptolemy's repeated 'measurements' always agree with almost impossible accuracy" (p. 361).

- "However, Ptolemy does not do this, as we have seen. Instead, he fabricates data in an attempt to make his defective theory seem correct" (p. 362).

- "Since the time of Copernicus, many writers including myself have used Ptolemy's fabricated material in studying the accelerations of the sun, the moon, and the planets. All this work must now be redone" (p. 366).

cp142» You have to study Newton's books and papers to understand why Newton is so angry with Ptolemy. At first Newton did not believe Ptolemy was a fake or a fraud, but someone who just may have fudged his figures a little to prove or explain his "earth is the center of the universe." At first Newton trusted many of Ptolemy's so-called observations and reports of other's observations, but as time went by Newton rejected all of Ptolemy's so-called observations. The more Newton studied Ptolemy the more he saw that Ptolemy was a fake and not even a fair astronomer:

- "The best we can say for him, it seems to me, is that he was mediocre. In view of the summary above, I believe that most readers will have serious reservations about Ptolemy's capacity as an astronomer" (p. 364).

- "Several colleagues with whom I have discussed this work have asked what could be the motive for Ptolemy's fraud.... Another is probably the most likely: Ptolemy wanted to be known as a great astronomer, perhaps as the greatest of all time. He may have found, early in his career, that he did not have the qualifications, and so he turned to the only remaining way of satisfying his ambition, which was to replace ability by fraud" (p. 376).

- "If the *Syntaxis* had not been written, we can be sure that much valid Greek astronomy now lost would have been preserved directly.

  In other words, we do not owe Ptolemy our thanks for the small amount of earlier astronomy that he has preserved. Instead, we owe him our condemnation for the large amount of genuine astronomy that he has caused us to lose....

  We can no longer accept as evidence anything Ptolemy says unless we have independent confirmation, and historians must now confront the task of identifying all historical material that rests upon the unsupported word of Ptolemy. At a guess, the realization of Ptolemy's fraud destroys half of what we have been accepting as Greek astronomy.

  There are many examples of the damage that Ptolemy has done to astronomy by his fabricated data. Because he accepted the observations that Ptolemy used, and because he thus had to reconcile these data with genuine data, *Copernicus* [1543] had to make his heliocentric theory much more complicated than it needed to be.... Since the time of Copernicus, many writers including myself have used Ptolemy's fabricated material in studying the accelerations of the sun, the moon, and the planets. All this work must now be redone" (pp. 365-366).

cp143» Even G.J. Toomer who recently translated Ptolemy's Almagest into English (Pub. 1984) wrote about Ptolemy's "manipulation" of his computations and so-called observations:

- "In the course of making the translation I recomputed all the numerical results in the text, and all the tables... The main purpose of this was to detect scribal errors... But my calculations incidentally revealed a number of computing errors or distortions committed by Ptolemy himself.... I have noted every computing error of a significant amount, and also those cases where the rounding errors are not random, but seem directed towards obtaining some 'neat' result. I hope that this will shed some light on the problem of Ptolemy's manipulation of his material (both computational and observational).." (*Ptolemy's Almagest*, 1984, p. viii).

cp144» Toomer admits, in a roundabout way, that he too found errors that were not random (meaning they were systemic) in both Ptolemy's computations and observations. But he merely calls them "interesting" and protests that Newton's work "tends to bring the whole topic into disrepute" (p. viii). But Newton has good cause to call a spade a spade, or a fraud a fraud: because Ptolemy has done great damage to astronomy. And Toomer has cause not to call a fraud a fraud: because he has spent a great deal of time and energy on his new translation of Ptolemy's *Almagest*. From all appearances Toomer has done a great job on this book: it reads well and it is full of helpful notes and aids. But because of the seriousness of Ptolemy's crime, Newton had just cause to harshly criticize him.

Ptolemy and Chronology

cp145» Ptolemy's work "has been used extensively in two areas of chronology" (Newton, 1977, p. 371). One area has to do with the Athenian calendar:

> • "all seven observations are fabricated. This fact does not in itself mean that the equivalent Athenian and Egyptian dates are incorrect, but it does not give us confidence in the situation.... We cannot accept any statement in the *Syntaxis* [Almagest] as evidence. We can accept only those statements that have confirmation from independent sources, and this means that we are not using the *Syntaxis* itself; we are using only independent sources.... This means that all studies of the Athenian calendar which have been based in whole or in part upon the *Syntaxis* must be redone, so that their dependence upon it can be removed" (p. 372)

This is the only way I use Ptolemy's work — only with other independent confirmation.

No Babylon Calendar Dates

cp146» Furthermore, Ptolemy's work is also used extensively for the Babylonian chronology. But notice what Newton manifests about Ptolemy's use of Babylonian dates and chronology. Ptolemy's reports of Babylonian observations are suspicious:

> "Ptolemy says that he has a copious collection of astronomical observations made in Babylon.... Ptolemy states the dates of seven lunar eclipses with the aid of the Babylonian kings. However, as we point out in Appendix C, he never gives any more of the Babylonian date than the year. This contrasts strongly with his treatment of other calendars. In dealing with any other calendar, Ptolemy gives the full date in that calendar, and he then gives the equivalent in the Egyptian calendar. The exceptions are so few that they can easily be accidental.
>
> His practice with regard to the Babylonian calendar does not arise from defects in the Babylonian records. In all Babylonian astronomical records that I have examined, the year, month, and day are all stated. However... there is a peculiarity about the Babylonian calendar which is not shared by other calendars.... If one has the Babylonian date of a lunar eclipse in the Babylonian calendar, it is easy to find the Egyptian (or Julian) date if one has the list of kings. The converse is not true. If one has the Egyptian date of a lunar eclipse, one can determine the Babylonian

year from the king list. [but not the month or day because of the nature of the Babylonian lunar-solar calendar] ...

Let us see how Ptolemy would go about fabricating a Babylonian record of a lunar eclipse. He would start by determining the Egyptian date of an eclipse that he wants to use, and he would then fabricate the exact circumstances (magnitude and hour) as he wants them. It is important to realize that his process gives the date of an actual eclipse, and that the fabricated circumstances are fairly close to the truth. He then wants to give the date in the Babylonian calendar, but he cannot for the reasons that have been outlined. All he can give is the Babylonian year.

Calculations Does Not Authenticate King's List

cp147» [Continuing quote from Newton]

It is also important to realize that Ptolemy does not need an authentic king list in order to give a year in the Babylonian fashion. Even if his king list is fabricated, he can still use it in order to assign a specific year of a specific king to his fabricated eclipse record.

Now let us see what happens to a modern historian or chronologist who studies Ptolemy's eclipse records. He sees that Ptolemy dates a lunar eclipse in the first year of Mardokempad, for example, on a certain month and day in the Egyptian calendar, at a certain hour on that day, and he states the fraction of the moon that was shadowed during the eclipse. The historian uses Ptolemy's king list to find the year in our calendar and he uses the Egyptian month and day to find the complete date in our calendar. He then finds by astronomical calculations that there was an eclipse on that date, that it came close to the hour that Ptolemy states, and that the stated amount of shadowing is also close to correct. This agreement between Ptolemy and modern astronomy happens not just once but seven times.

The historian or chronologist naturally concludes that there is overwhelming evidence confirming the accuracy of Ptolemy's king list, and he proceeds to use it as the basis for Babylonian chronology. Yet there is no evidence at all. The key point is that there may have been no Babylonian record at all. Ptolemy certainly fabricated many of the aspects of the lunar eclipses, and he may have fabricated all of them. When he fabricated them, it did not matter whether he used a correct king list or not. Any king list he used, regardless of its accuracy, would seem to be verified by eclipses.

For example, according to Ptolemy's king list, Ilulaeus reigned for 5 years and his successor Mardokempad reigned for 12. Suppose that Ptolemy's list had omitted Mardokempad but assigned 17 years to Ilulaeus. Instead of putting an eclipse in the 1st year of Mardokempad, Ptolemy would put the same eclipse in the 6th year of Ilulaaeus. From the altered list, we would still establish that the eclipse was on -720 March 19, and we would still have the same apparent verification of the king list.

It follows that Ptolemy's king list is useless in the study of chronology, and that it must be ignored. What is worse, much Babylonian chronology is based upon Ptolemy's king list. **All relevant chronology must now be reviewed and all dependence upon Ptolemy's list must be removed**" (Newton, 1977, pp. 372-375, my ephasis).

Some independent verification with two clay tablets

cp148» Newton goes on to say that "the later part of his king list has independent verification" because two cuneiform tablets have been found that help to confirm the years of Nebuchadnezzar down to Darius in 522 BC. See CP3 of this book where I discuss this evidence.

cp149» What we are showing you here is the dubiousness of Ptolemy's chronology or king list. I did not follow blindly his list because of the dubiousness of the list. I relied on independent evidence, especially cuneiform tablets that I have studied (see CP3).

Ptolemy's Eclipses: Calculated not Observed

cp150» As just partially documented above, in *The Crime of Claudius Ptolemy* (1977), R.R. Newton writes of Ptolemy fabricating data of so-called ecliptic observations, as far back as the 8th century B.C. Ptolemy used calculations rather than observation for his reported eclipses. Toomer and others disagreed on Newton's strong wording about Ptolemy's shortcomings. But even Toomer agrees that Ptolemy may have fudged on his figures. And Newton in his works definitely gives good evidence that Ptolemy cheated. However, D. Justin Schove in his *Chronology of Eclipses and Comets* says Newton, even if right, doesn't negate Ptolemy's work and that his canon and eclipses may still be good for *historical* dating:

- "The genuineness of the observations reported by Ptolemy has long been suspect. R.R. Newton (The Origins of Ptolemy's Astronomical Parameters, 1982 ...) has examined the matter in detail. He concludes that Ptolemy 'fudged' the observations of the last three eclipses, passing off calculated quantities as observed quantities. However, this investigation, like earlier ones, is concerned with errors of minutes of time; the days and nights remain as we have stated them. Since the times given by Ptolemy, whatever their origin, seem never to be found more than 50 minutes in error, they are as accurate as any times one could hope for from a chronicler at this period, and their chronological usefulness is hardly affected at all" (p. 27; also see above, "Ptolemy's Chronology").

We already quoted from Newton disproof of Schove's idea (See above: "Calculations Does Not Authenticate King's List").

cp151» "For the purposes of the present work, what matters mainly is that the dates are certain (having been confirmed by the calculations of numerous astronomers down the ages)..." (p. 25). Notice these dates or observations are "confirmed by the calculations." Some of Ptolemy's data are only minutes away from modern retrocalculation, but some are 28 hours away and even *weeks* away (see Newton, [1977], pp. 87, 95, etc.; Toomer, pp. 138, 469). And some like the 721 and 720 BC eclipses reported by Ptolemy may never have occurred because the earth may have changed its course since then (see CP3, "Astronomical Chaos"). In Newton's study he has found that Ptolemy's older eclipses are questionable, and most if not all were "fabricated" (Newton, 1977, p. 344-345).

Newton v. Thiele

cp152» Edwin R. Thiele disagrees with Newton and calls Newton's criticism of Ptolemy a "vicious attack" (*The Mysterious Numbers of the Hebrew Kings*, 1983, p.72, footnote #14). Thiele, as we have seen previously, is an author of a chronological system that attempts to synthesize secular and Biblical chronologies, but in fact he changes and "corrects" the Biblical chronology. Thiele thinks he needs Ptolemy to be correct, or his chronology falls apart. This is one reason Thiele calls Newton's critique of Ptolemy a "vicious attack."

cp153» The following examples in (2), (3), and (4) were taken from *Babylonian Chronology* (1971 printing) unless otherwise noted.

2: Juggling of Economic Texts

cp154» *Juggling of economic texts* from one king to another or one year to another is an additional problem for secular chronology for the period 626 BC to 75 AD:

- **(A)** "[9]There remains some question as to whether or not this tablet is correctly placed, as the king's name is not mentioned.." (Parker and Dubberstein, *Babylonian Chronology....*" [1956, 1971 printing], p. 4, footnote #9).

- **(B)** "[10]A broken text ... Kugler, *SSB* II 418, argued that on the basis of elimination this text probably belongs to Nebuchadnezzar; other possibilities were Xerxes, Artaxerxes I, or Artaxerxes II... Since the Addaru II attributed to Xerxes' 5th year in our first edition is now known to belong instead to the 5th year of Artaxerxes l (see below), the present text can fit very nicely in the 4th year of Xerxes, and we have transferred it there" (*Babylonian Chronology....*, p. 4-5, footnote 10).

- **(C)** "No king given, but tablet apparently belongs here" (*Babylonian Chronology....*, p. 5).

- **(D)** "[16]This text was first assigned to Xerxes by Dr. Cameron, but after further study he gives it to Artaxerxes I on the basis of content and seal impression" (*Babylonian Chronology....*, p. 8, footnote 16).

- **(E)** "[4]'We have no published cuneiform records from Alexander the Great; those formerly so attributed come from the reign of his son of the same name.' " (p. 19, footnote 4, quoted by Parker and Dubberstein from Olmstead, *Classical Philology*, 1937)

- **(F)** "The dates given by Strassmaier in *ZA*, IV, pp. 145ff ... and in his *Nabuchodonosor*, No.1 (B.M. 75321), where he reads *ITU.SU*, are wrong for in each case *ITU.DU* is written clearly. This error has resulted in the latter text being wrongly assigned to Nebuchadrezzar III.." (*Chronicles of Chaldaean Kings*, p. 85, note for line 11 of B.M. 21946).

3: Reading Dates into Clay Tablets

cp155» ***Reading dates into the clay tablets*** and suppressing or changing evidence is a third problem with secular chronology:

- **(A)** "Broken date read as 11th year by Kruckmann, but must be read 12th on basis of known materials" (*Babylonian Chronology....*, p. 7).

- **(B)** "Broken date ... must be read as '3' on basis of known intercalated months" (*Babylonian Chronology....*, p. 7).

- **(C)** "By addition of one wedge the year may be read either as '3' or as '12,' or by omission of one wedge it may be read as '1.' Error of either scribe or copyist is evident. Reading as '3' seems preferable to us" (*Babylonian Chronology....*, p. 7, footnote 12).

- **(D)** "Possible dates for this letter are year 2 or 9 of Cyrus or year 3 of Cambyses" (*Babylonian Chronology....* p. 2).

- **(E)** "A collation by Sachs and Wiseman has shown that the text from Sippar (Strassmaier, *loc. cit.*) thought to be from the 4th month is correctly to be dated VII/__/acc. [7th month]" (*Babylonian Chronology....* p.12).

- **(F)** "... line 19 reads VI/6/18 ... year 18 is impossible, so we assume either a scribal error or an error by Contenau" (*Babylonian Chronology....* p. 13). This 18th year pertained to Nabonidus, king of Babylon.

- **(G)** "Clay in *BE* X, page 2, suggests that the last date may incorporate a scribal error, in view of the evidence for the beginning of the reign of Darius II given below... Since there seems to be some confusion, the date from the unpublished text cannot be used" (*Babylonian Chronology....* p. 18).

cp156» In A. K. Grayson's, *Assyrian and Babylonian Chronicles*, the supposed last year of the Babylonian king Nabonidus was added or "restored" to the text (Grayson, p. 109 note for line 5). The last year of king Nabonidus is restored as his 17th year apparently because Ptolemy's list of kings has 17 years for Nabonidus. **There is at least one clay tablet that mentions Nabonidus's 18th year** (Contenau, see "F" above). In the Uruk King List it has "[x] + 15 years" for Nabonidus (James B. Pritchard, *The Ancient Near East Supplementary Texts and Pictures Relating to the Old Testament*, 1969, p.566; for more see below).

cp157» Wiseman in his *Chronicles of Chaldaean Kings* also projects to us juggling of text and the changing of text:

- Concerning British Museum tablet # 21901, "*iqbiuma*. The word, with the sign -*bi*, is written clearly. J. Lewy, *MVAG*, 1924, p. 82 reads *ik-kas-sam-ma...* Landsberger-Bauer (*ZA, XXXVII* (N.F.3), P. 85) object to both readings and propose *ik-sur (!)-u-ma*" (p. 80). This word was "written clearly," yet scholars still changed the word.

- "This restoration is suggested by Oppenheim.." (p. 80).

- "The restoration of this line is very uncertain" (p. 81).

- "Restoration suggested by Lewy... but only the final *MES* is legible.." (p. 81).

- "The name, as restored by Gadd (*FN*, P. 35, n. 2), must have occurred in this line" (p. 82).

Concerning B.M. 21946:

- "This is only one of several possible restorations.." (p. 84).

4: 77 Years of Missing Evidence

cp158» *77 years of missing evidence* for secular chronology is a fourth and major problem:

- "There is no evidence from contemporary business documents for the years 17 to 19 of Darius II, nor are there dated tablets from the accession year of Artaxerxes II ... **The length of the kings' reigns from here on are established chiefly by use of the well known Ptolemaic Canon**" (p. 18, emphasis added).

cp159» There is no evidence that Artaxerxes II followed Darius II because there are no economic texts at the end of Darius II nor the beginning of Artaxerxes II. The Artaxerxes II is only *recognized* as king in 404 BC, that is, *recognized* because of the Ptolemaic Canon states there is a Artaxerxes *after* Darius II. But in fact the texts attributed to Artaxerxes II may be texts for Artaxerxes I.

cp160» The lack of economic or business texts was blamed by Olmstead in his *History of the Persian Empire* on "linguistic decay" rather than on a faulty chronology:

- "No monarch after Darius the Great had attempted a long composition, much less an autobiography. The language of Xerxes' much fewer inscriptions shows the beginning of linguistic decay, and the rare official records from the fourth century indicate almost complete ignorance of grammatical structure.... But an almost complete break in the series of administrative and business documents at the middle of the fourth century implies that its use was more and more confined to the learned" (p. 480).

We also see that other forms of writing mysteriously disappeared during this period.

cp161» Grayson in his *Assyrian and Babylonian Chronicles* speaks of the "complete absence of texts" for this period of Persian rule (p.23). The Persians themselves have no record of the length of kings, or a list of kings for this period. It is because of this "linguistic decay" that the chronology of the period of Artaxerxes II and III, and Darius III is dubious.

cp162» The various systems of Egyptian chronology (Africanus & Eusebius) do not show a Artaxerxes II ruling Egypt after Darius II, but does show a 47 to 64+ years between Darius II and Ochus (Artaxerxes III) when Egypt was ruled by the so-called Dynasties XXVIII-XXX (Budge, *The Book of the Kings of Egypt*, pp lxxi-lxxii).

cp163» In Flavius Josephus's *Antiquities of the Jews*, book XI, chapter VII, according to the contemporary view, Josephus omits the rest of the kings after Artaxerxes II (the "another" Artaxerxes, chapter VII) up until Darius III. But if Ptolemy's king list is wrong, then Josephus did not really omit these kings because they never existed, or more likely because of the lack of historical evidence for this period. The word flow of this part of Josephus's work does not suggest there were any kings between Josephus's "Artaxerxes" of chapter VI and "Darius, the last king" of chapter VII. The "*another*" of "another Artaxerxes" in chapter VII was probably added to the original text by those who, mistakenly or not, thought that there was another Artaxerxes after Artaxerxes I.

cp164» There are NO contemporary cuneiform documents to confirm the reign of Artaxerxes III, Arses, and Darius III (see pp. 18-19). The quote by Olmstead in his *History of the Persian Empire* (p. 437) where king Ochus is identified with king Artaxerxes III is of little value since this is quoted from Smith's *Babylonian Historical Texts* (pp. 148ff) which said the text was corrected or "which after *collation* reads." Smith took this from Strassmaier but does not tell us who made the collation, himself or Strassmaier. The text as quoted by Smith does not identify this king Ochus as Artaxerxes III, but just "Artaxerxes." This Artaxerxes could have been Artaxerxes I. Furthermore, Smith does not say if in the "collation" of the source text(s) that Artaxerxes was added to the text so as to help identify king Ochus. Smith does not give enough detail for us to make an intelligent decision.

Persian Chronology Dubious

cp165» **I do not know the chronology of this period of the Persian empire because** of the lack of sufficient cuneiform texts that mention the supposed later kings of the Persian empire, because the Bible does not give any clear evidence for the kings of this period, and because others, like Ptolemy, have been caught in some fudging of calculations and observations. All this evidence throws a negative light on Ptolemy's list of kings for this period.

Absolute Dates and Edwin R. Thiele

cp166» Points **(1)** to **(4)** of this chapter should cast an enormous shadow on anyone claiming to have an *absolute date* based primarily on Ptolemy's Canon. Furthermore, *absolute dates* based on vague reports of astronomical phenomena, especially reports of only one eclipse or one planet position, are dubious as we saw in the previous section. But Notice the claim made by Edwin R. Thiele:

- "Two eclipses [621 & 568 BC] establish beyond question 605 as the year when Nebuchadnezzar began his reign. The first took place on April 22, 621, in the fifth year of Nabopolassar, which would make 605 the year of his death in his twenty-first year, and the year of Nebuchadnezzar's accession. The second eclipse was on July 4, 568, in the thirty-seventh year of Nebuchadnezzar, which again gives 605 as the year when Nebuchadnezzar began to reign. No date in ancient history is more firmly established than 605 for the commencement of Nebuchadnezzar's reign" (*A Chronology of the Hebrew Kings*, p. 69).

cp167» In part Thiele is wrong, but, in part, he is right. 605 BC is **not** an *absolute date*, it is a secondary date or a date found indirectly through an absolute date. 605 BC is when Nebuchadnezzar took over reign as sole king after his father died. It is his accessional year. The date 605 BC is found indirectly only by subtracting the years of Nebuchadnezzar's regnal years. His official reign, according to the cuneiform tablets called the Babylonian Chronicle and the astronomical clay tablet dated in Nebuchadnezzar's 37th year (568-567 BC), began in 604 BC in the Spring (see Notes CP 5).

cp168» The so-called eclipse of 621 BC is found only in Ptolemy's *Almagest* (G.J. Toomer, p. 253). But the eclipse of 568 BC was found reported on a cuneiform tablet for the 37th year of Nebuchadnezzar. Also on this tablet were reports of other astronomical data. It is the other astronomical data (along with the eclipse) that dates this tablet and helps to prove that Nebuchadnezzar began his official sole reign in 604 BC, while his accessional year began in 605 BC. A single eclipse by itself cannot date an event (see CP3 for more detail on the 37th year tablet).

Nabonidus' Mother's Memorial Tablet

cp169» Two copies of a memorial tablet, one of poor quality found in 1906 and one in much better condition found in 1956, that were written in part by/for the mother of Nabonidus, give the same length of reigns as Ptolemy's list of kings for the years of Nabopolassar through the 9th year of Nabonidus, the year she died (James B. Pritchard, Ed., *The Ancient Near East: Supplementary Texts and Pictures Relating to the Old Testament*, 1969, pp. 560-561 [pp. 124-125]). Contrary to what some writers like Velikovsky think (*Ramses II...*, p. 111 ff), it may have been common practice to have more than one memorial stelae or tablet as it was the case when kings built or restored temples. When kings restored or built temples or other important buildings they made several tablets and spread them around the foundations so that future generations would know who built it:

- "The face of the wall was smoothly rendered with mud plaster; much of this had fallen away and we very soon cleared off the rest, for beneath the plaster there was a dramatic discovery to be made. At regular intervals of 2 feet there appeared the small rounded heads of clay 'nails' driven into the mud mortar between the brick courses; these were 'foundation-cones' and on the "nail's" stem was the inscription... Such cones were familiar enough as objects on museum shelves, but now for the first time we saw them in position just as the builders had set them four thousand years before. That they should be found *in situ* is of course most important scientifically, for we not only learn that a particular king built a particular temple, but ...." "Hidden in the brickwork of the top stage of the tower he found, at each angle of it, cylinders of baked clay on which were long inscriptions giving the history of the building" C.L. Woolley, (*Ur of the Chaldees* [1982], pp. 140, 142, see pp. 105-07, 155-61, 227).

cp170» This clay tablet by the mother of Nabonidus does not give the total length of Nabonidus' reign. Daniel doesn't give the total years of this king either, but tells us it was in the kingship of Belshazzar when Babylon was destroyed (Dan 5:1-31). Belshazzar's co-kingship with Nabonidus is implied by comparing Daniel 5:1 with BM 35382, the Nabonidus Chronicle.

(see Grayson, *Assyrian and Babylonian Chronicles*, pp. 106-108, "prince"; Smith, *BHT*, p. 116, "Crown Prince"; and Grayson & Redford, *Papyrus and Tablet*, p. 120, "the prince, Belshazzar." "Belshazzar" is not in this text, but through restoration is put there by Grayson; see Velikovsky, *Ramses II*, p. 105, note 5; and see Dougherty, *Nabonidus and Belshazzar*; see CP5: Notes)

And this co-kingship of Belshazzar and Nabonidus is further proven by comparing some letters with the Nabonidus Chronicle (see CP5, Notes).

cp171» Through Biblical scripture we can ascertain that there were 70 years between Nebuchadnezzar's co-kingship with his father and the Fall of Babylon (see CP5 years 3365-3435 YM for more details on the 70 years and on Nabonidus' 18th year).

Secular Chronology: Other Problems

Cuneiform Tablets: Excavation and Publication

cp172» "Many an excavation, if not all, had to be stopped before completion or had to restrict itself from the very beginning to a few trenches crossing the ruin in the hope of getting a general insight into the character of the stratification.... Until 1951 not for a single astronomical or mathematical text was its provenance established by excavation. The only apparent exceptions are a number of multiplication tables from Nippur or Sippar but nobody knows where these texts were found in the ruins. Consequently it is, e.g., completely impossible to find out whether these texts came from a temple, a palace, a private house, etc. Not even the stratum is known to give us a more accurate date of the texts.... Thus we are left with the texts alone and must determine their origin form internal evidence, which is often very difficult to interpret...."

cp173» "The Mesopotamian soil has preserved tablets for thousands of years. This will not be the case in our climate. Many tablets are encrusted with salts... A change in moisture produces crystals which break the surface of the tablets, thus rapidly obliterating the writing. I have seen "tablets" which consisted of dust only, carefully kept in showcases.... Many thousands of tablets have been acquired at high cost by big and small collections only to be destroyed without ever being read or recorded in any way."

cp174» "The publication of tablets is a difficult task in itself. First of all, one must find the texts which concern the specific field in question. This is by no means trivial. Only minute fractions of the holdings of collections are catalogued.... I would be surprised if a tenth of all tablets in museums have ever been identified in any kind of catalogue."

cp175» "Tablets are often inscribed not only on both sides but also on the edges. Only multiple photographs taken with variable directions of light would suffice. Thus cost and actual need have resulted in the practice of hand copies."

cp176» "The ideal method of publication would be, of course, direct copying from the text. In practice this is often excluded by the scattering of directly related material all over the world. Even with great experience a text cannot be correctly copied without an understanding of its contents.... Thus repeated collation, joining with other fragments, and comparison with other texts are needed. It requires years of work before a small group of a few hundred tablets is adequately published. And no publication is "final". Invariably a fresh mind will find the solution of a puzzle which escaped the editor, however obvious it might seem afterwards" (O. Neugebauer, *The Exact Sciences in Antiquity*, 2nd Ed., Dover 1969 edition, pp. 59-62).

Roman Historical Gaps

cp177» "The ancient sources of information for certain periods of Roman Imperial history, notably the Third Century, are very poor .... Other periods are much better documented, and I have in the main followed such learned works as the *Cambridge Ancient History* and the *Cambridge Medieval History*" (p. 6, *The Emperors of Rome and Byzantium*, by David R. Sear, Seaby Ltd, London).

cp178» The problem with using these Cambridge historical works for chronology is that their chronological charts have few if any documentation to back up their dates. An unknown number of dates are merely educated guesswork. Of course educated guesswork is better than no chronology.

Era of the Olympiads Rarely Used

cp179» "The old era of Olympiads appears only to have been used by writers, and especially by historians. It does not seem to have been ever adopted by any state in public documents. It is never found on any coins, and scarcely ever on inscriptions." (John J. Bond, *Handy-Book of Rules and Tables for Verifying Dates with the Christian Era*, 1966 [1ˢᵗ Pub. ab. 1866], Russell & Russell, p. 192)

cp180» "A new era of Olympiads however came into use under the Roman Emperors which is found on inscriptions and was used in public documents. This era begins in Ol. 227.3., in which year Hadrian dedicated the Olympieion at Athens..." (Bond, p. 192; also see Samuel and Bickerman's books concerning chronology).

Era of the Foundation of Rome

cp181» "Great doubts have been entertained by historians and chronologists respecting this era" (Bond, p. 195; see CP3).

Public Documents in England

cp182» "Public documents in England, from the time of Richard the First, down to the present day, have been usually dated with the year of the reign of the sovereign, and not with the year of our Lord" (Bond, p. 273).

No Zero Year: Historical v. Astronomical Dating

cp183» "In the historical dating of events there is no year A.D. 0. The year immediately previous to A.D. 1 is always called B.C. 1. This must always be borne in mind in reckoning chronological and astronomical intervals. The sum of the nominal years B.C. and A.D. must be diminished by 1. Thus, from Jan. 1, B.C. 4713 to Jan 1, A.D. 1582, the years elapsed are not 6295, but 6294" (Bond, p. 321).

cp184» In Astronomical dating there is a year 0 and the BC dates are always one short of the historical dating system. Normally, astronomical dates are marked with a minus sign ("-") in front of the date — "-4." And -4 equals 5 B.C. But because some do not understand the difference between the astronomical and the Christian Era system sometimes writers put -4 when they mean 4 B.C. To be correct they should write -3 to indicate 4 B.C (also see Finegan [1964], ¶ 221).

Observed or Calculated Data?

cp185» "Very often it is difficult to decide whether text data were observed or calculated. We know from the diaries of later times that missing observations were filed in by calculation, sometimes without explicit indication of the fact, sometimes with the note 'not observed,' sometimes with a note that the observation gave a different result. In the case of Sirius phenomena an investigation by A. Sachs has shown that calculation was the rule, even when the statement 'not observed' is missing" (*Science Awakening II: The Birth of Astronomy*, by Bartel L. vander Waerden, p. 101, quoted by Rose in *Kronos*, Vol IV, No. 2).

cp186» "... the dates when a planet enters a zodiacal sign are recorded. These texts are based on computations, not on observations, as in evident from the fact that entrances into a zodiacal sign are also noted when the planet is in conjunction with the sun, this being invisible."

cp187» "... one had to assume an extremely high visibility for the horizon in Babylon in order to cover all recorded cases, not realizing that these records contained invisible and visible risings alike" (pp. 90 & 132, *The Exact Sciences in Antiquity*, by Otto Neugebauer, quoted from Rose in *Kronos*, Vol IV, No. 2).

cp188» In *The Crime of Claudius Ptolemy* (1977) R.R. Newton speaks of Ptolemy fabricating data of so-called ecliptic observations, as far back as the 8th century B.C. Ptolemy in many cases used his inaccurate calculations to locate supposed observations of eclipses.

cp189» Also see Robert R. Newton's *Ancient Planetary Observations and the Validity of Ephemeris Time* where he shows other examples of ancient astronomical tablets that in part were calculations and not observations ("goal-year texts," pp. 104ff, 128).

Pottery Dating

The pottery dating method is very complex and many factors are taken into consideration, any of which can be misread. It is very time consuming with years of analysis of categorized findings in order to get approximate dates for the strata and site. Such books as *Pottery in Archaeology, Second Edition*, by Clive Orton [Cambridge University Press, 2013] give explanations as to how pottery is used to date archaeology sites and strata within the sites. To overly simplify, because pottery shapes and styles have changed over the centuries, pottery dating generally has to do with identifying the shapes and styles of the pottery found on a site and comparing it to other pottery found in other sites that have been previously dated by a conventional chronology. The problem with this type of dating is that it relies on conventional chronology. If the conventional dating system is incorrect so will be the pottery dating. Circular thinking plays a part in this dating method. But the major problem with pottery dating, if the analysis of data is correct, is that it will probably identify the century(s), but not the decade or year of the strata or site. The other major problem is that only a small portion of the archaeological site is ever examined, thus the key to the real date may still be buried at the site.

New Techniques for Dating

New techniques such as thermo-luminescence, optically stimulated luminescence, Raman spectrometry and rehydroxylation are beginning to be used in archaeology to date sites.

Luminescence dating refers to a group of methods of determining how long ago mineral grains were last exposed to sunlight or sufficient heating. It is useful to geologists and archaeologists who want to know when such an event occurred. It uses various methods to stimulate and measure luminescence. It includes techniques such as optically stimulated luminescence (OSL), infrared stimulated luminescence (IRSL), and thermoluminescence dating (TL).

CP3: Methods, Chronology, Calendars, Absolute Dates, Chaos, and other Details

Patriarchal Years

Inclusive Counting

Comparing Reigns

Verification of Chronology Periods

Hebrew Calendar

Absolute Dates

Astronomical Chaos

Other Important Information

cp190» As we just saw in this book, Part 2, secular chronology is very difficult and probably incorrect in some cases by hundreds, if not thousands of years. Also the evolutionary time scale may be off billions of years because of its premises (see Appendix). So we turn to the Bible and its chronology. This is also not simple and not obvious. There are several ways, or methods, used to figure the number of years of man, that is, to figure the chronology of man. Remember this is a Biblical chronology. We showed in CP2 why secular chronology cannot be trusted. The Bible used different ways of counting time. We'll show you each method in chronological order. Since these methods are not stated in the Bible, the methods were ascertained by analysis and comparison.

(1)Patriarchal-Year Method of Counting Years

Method used from Creation to Abram

cp191» The beginning of the biblical chronology is figured through the count of years of a patriarch from his first New Year's *day* on which he was alive until (and counting) the birth year of his son. In Adam's case his birth day was the very first year of man (YM), and since there was no patriarchs before him, the first year had to count as his first year, the first year of the patriarchs and the first year in the count of the years of mankind. This patriarchal-year method is the addition of the years (of man) from one patriarch to the next patriarch. For example, "And Adam lived a hundred and thirty years, and begat [Strong's # 3205, 'was born'] ... Seth ... And Seth lived a hundred and five years, and begat [# 3205] Enos" (Gen 5:3, 6). From this we see that Adam lived in 130 years, and in his 130th year Adam's son, Seth, was born, and Seth lived in 105 years and then his son Enos was born in his 105th year.

cp192» Adam was created in the very first year of man (YM) — and since there were no patriarchs before him this very first year had to count as his first year. Adam lived throughout the first year. It was his first year. It was also the first year of man. In the English Old Testament of the Bible the word "man" is translated from the Hebrew word, *adam*. In Hebrew *adam* means "red" or by inference (Gen 2:7), "red clay.": "And LORD God formed man of the dust [Hebrew: Strong's # 6083 - '(red) clay or dirt'] of the ground" (Gen 2:7).

CREATION OF MANKIND	1st YEAR OF MAN
Mankind, ADAM, was created on the first day of the first year of man;	
Adam lived until 930 YM (Gen 5:1-2,5)	
SETH's first year	131 YM
born in 130 YM; died in 1042 YM, son of 912 years (Gen 5:3,8)	
ENOS's first year	236 YM
born in 235 YM; died in 1140 YM,	

Thus the first year of man was counted also as Adam's first year. Sometime in the 130th year of man (130 YM), which was also the 130th year of Adam, Seth was born to Adam. But Seth's first year in the patriarchic count of years was not the year 130 YM, but the year 131 YM *because* Seth was not alive on the first day of the 130th year of mankind. Thus, Seth's patriarchic years are counted from the very beginning of 131 YM. Seth's 105th year was the year 235 YM. Sometime in that year Enos was born. But Enos first year, that is his first New Year's day, was not in the year 235 YM, but the year 236 YM. Enos's years began at the very beginning of 236 YM.

First Day of New Year is Important: Similar to Accessional year system

cp193» The year of the patriarch was counted only if he was alive on the first day of the new year. This method is similar to the accession-year system used by Babylonia, Assyria, and Persia to count the years of kings:

> "In the accession-year system, the portion of a year from the accession of the king to the end of the then current calendar year is only his 'accession year" (and for chronological purposes remains a part of the last numbered regnal year of his predecessor), and the new king's year 1 begins only *on the first day of the new calendar year* after his accession" (paragraph # 161, Jack Finegan, *Handbook of Biblical Chronology*, 1998 Rev. Ed., italics are my emphasis).

Years Old or "Son"

cp194» Many times it speaks of the patriarchs and kings being so many "years old" in such English versions as the King James Version. But in the Hebrew it says: "*a son of* xx years." It is *not* speaking of birthdays, but speaks of how many years of man the patriarch or king were connected to or were "sons" of. The word "son" in English was translated from the Hebrew *ben* (# 1121), which has a broad meaning (see Lexicon).

Long-Lives of Patriarchs?

cp195» Why are the patriarchs registering such long lives in the Bible? 930 years for Adam; 912 years for Seth; 905 years for Enos. Although we cannot be absolutely sure it may be because the atmosphere before the Flood was more protected from radiation from outer space. After the Flood the protection of the "water" above the earth (Gen 1:7) was destroyed when the "windows of heaven"(Gen 7:11) were opened by the catastrophic events around the time of the Flood. The water for the Flood that covered the mountains by 15 cubits, was from the "great deep" and from above the earth (Gen 7:11; 1:7). The seas (Gen 1:10) before the Flood were probably much smaller and the mountains much less higher than today's mountains. Mountains in the pre-Flood period may only have been hills. During and after the catastrophes of the Flood the mountains raised and the valleys fell to form the present great mountain ranges and great ocean floors. (see Psa 104:8, Heb. text) The vast oceans we see today and the high mountains came from the catastrophe of the events of the Flood. Water for the great Flood was kept in store for the Flood under the earth and over the earth (cf. Gen 7:11; 1:7). Our intelligent and extremely complex life-systems come from something that is super intelligent, not from the extremely pretentious yet overly simplistic theory of evolution.

(2) <u>Inclusive Counting</u> Method
Used from Abraham's 75ᵗʰ Year Until Solomon's 4ᵗʰ Year

cp196» There is a method of counting days or years inclusively in which the first day or first year of the count is started at any time within the day or year (see Exo 19:10-11; Lev 7:15-17; 19:5-7; for years see: 2 Ki 19:29; Jer 25:3, 1-3). They could say, for example, today, tomorrow, and the next day. The "next day" being the third day for a count of three days (Exo 19:10-11; Luke 13:32). Today equals the first day, tomorrow the second day, and the next day is the third day. Or they could say, I will meet you the third day. Today being the first day, tomorrow the second day, and the next day the third day. There is a vagueness to this kind of counting because usually when someone counts like this the first day or year of the count and the last day or year of the count need not be full 24 hour days or full years. Today is the first day even if they started their counting from the beginning, middle, or end of the day. Or this year is the first year even if they started their counting from the beginning, middle, or end of the year. The second day or year is the second day or year throughout. The third day or year is the third day or year at any time from the beginning to the end of the day or year. *But there is even a greater vagueness if they started counting the days or years at the very end or very beginning of a day or year.* Were they beginning their count from the very end of the "today/year" or from the very beginning of "tomorrow/year"? This ambivalence is one reason for the confusion about the number of days Christ the man was left in the grave (See GP4).

cp197» Examples of inclusive counting are the 430 years of Israel's sojourning, the 480 years from the Exodus to Solomon's 4ᵗʰ year, the 15 cycles of 49 years (see 3286 YM), and the 23 years of Jeremiah's prophesying (See CP5).

Patriarchal or Regnal Years Not Inclusive Counting

cp198» When they counted the years of a patriarch, they were not counting birthdays, nor were they counting how many years a patriarch *lived in*, but how many years of man that were credited to them starting from the very first New Year's day they lived in. This is different from how many total years they lived in, for the patriarchs (except Adam) "lived in" one more year than was credited to them — the year of birth is not credited to a patriarch, except Adam. When Judah counted the years of the reign of a king, they were counting how many New Year's days he reigned in, not how many years he reigned in. In this method David was counted as reigning for 40 years when in fact he reigned in 41 years. (He reigned for six extra months in Judah.) But David only reigned in 40 New Year's days, thus was counted as reigning for 40 years (2 Sam 5:4-5 compare with 1 Chron 29:27).

Inclusive Count of 430 years of sojourning: Method from Abram to the Exodus
From Abraham's 75ᵗʰ year we count 430 years inclusively to the Exodus.

cp199» The method of adding the years from the birth of one patriarch to the next holds good until Joseph with only a few apparent difficulties, which are explained in the text of our chronology. In the chronology we see that the date of the call of Abram is related to the date of the Exodus. The prophecy of the 430 years of sojourning leads us to the date of the Exodus.

Inclusive Count of 480 years: Method From the Exodus to Solomon
From the Exodus we count 480 years inclusively to the 4th year of Solomon's reign by using the verse, 1 Kings 6:1.

cp200» In our chronology we list other events and their dates between the Exodus and Solomon. The documentation with these other dates should enable you to ascertain how we figured these dates.

Book of Judges

cp201» It is noted that the periods inside the book of Judges cannot be figured because of the overlaps in various time periods within the book of Judges. Unlike the later period of kings for the kingdom of Judah and Israel, the period of Judges gives us nothing to compare the years of reign. The problem being that sometimes reigns overlap and there may even be short periods without kings, but with the given information we cannot figure this out. In other words, the Bible did not give us enough information for us to ascertain the true chronology for this period of judges. But the information on the 480 years in 1 Kings 6:1 allows us to skip this period while still being able to figure the chronology of mankind.

(3) <u>Comparing reigns</u> of Judah v. Israel Kings: Method from Solomon Through the Kingdoms

Method of Counting of Regnal Years
Regnal Years and Accessional Year Method
cp202» The next method of continuing our chronology is used for the period of the kings of Israel and Judah. The method of figuring the chronology of this period is by comparing the reigns of the kings of Judah to the reigns of the kings of Israel and vice versa. But in order to do this we must know *how* they counted regnal years. As shown in (1) above, the count of years for each patriarch begins on the first New Year's day in which he was alive. This is the similar to the count of years for the reign of Judah's kings in the divided kingdom, as well as David and Solomon in the united kingdom. Outside of co-reigns, the *count* of years for Judah's kings began with the first New Year's day in which he reigned. If a son of a king, after his father's death, is crowned king in the 15th year of his late father's reign, then the son's first official regnal year begins in his first New Year's day of his reign, which would be the very next New Year's day after his father's 15th year. That is, he officially begins to reign in what would have been his father's 16th year. This is like:

- the accessional year method explained in Jack Finegan's *Handbook of Biblical Chronology* [1964 & 1998], Paragraph 161
- the method used in Ptolemy's Canon and the method of the Babylonian kings between 626 and 539 BC [*sic*] (Bickerman, p. 66; BM 21946; etc.)
- and like the Patriarchal method explained above under (1)

This is the secret to counting the years of man and counting the years of the kings of Judah.

Confirmation of Judah's Regnal Year
cp203» There is proof that Judah's regnal year always began in the Fall, and that they used the accession-year system to count regnal years of each king of Judah. Some confirmation that the regnal year for the united kingdom and the divided kingdom of Judah started in the fall and that they counted reigns by New Year's days is found in 1 Kings 6:37-38 and Jeremiah 36:1-9. Solomon is reported to have taken seven regnal years to build the house of the LORD (1 Ki 6:38). The foundation of the house began in the 4th year of Solomon the second month, the month of Zif (6:1, 37). It was finished in the 11th year in the eighth month, the month of Bul (6:38). If you understand that the regnal year started in the seventh month, then you understand that he actually took about 6 ½ years to build it, but it included 7 new year's days, thus in this kind of counting it is counted as 7 years. See chart below.

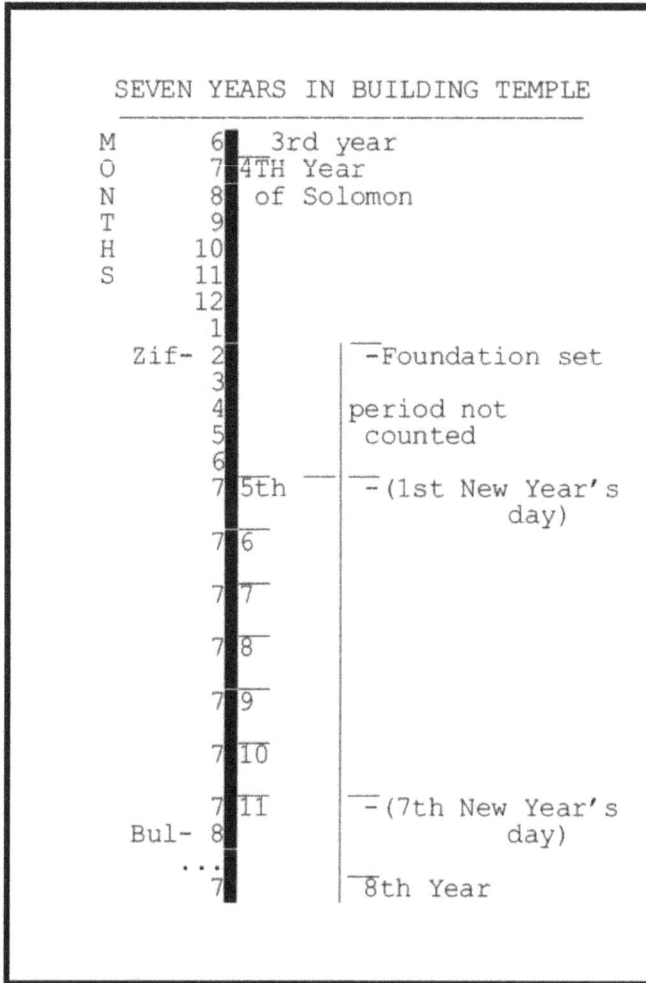

SEVEN YEARS IN BUILDING TEMPLE

```
M        6     3rd year
O        7   4TH Year
N        8    of Solomon
T        9
H       10
S       11
        12
         1
  Zif-   2            -Foundation set
         3
         4          period not
         5          counted
         6
         7 5th      -(1st New Year's
                          day)

         7 6

         7 7

         7 8

         7 9

         7 10

         7 11       -(7th New Year's
  Bul-   8                day)
        ...
         7           8th Year
```

cp204» ***Another proof of the Kingdom of Judah's regnal year:*** In the chronological flow of Jeremiah 36:1-9, Jeremiah, in the 4th year of Jehoiakim (king of Judah), told his scribe Baruch to read from the book (that Jeremiah wrote in the 4th year) in the coming fast day (v. 6). Baruch read the book in the 5th year, in the 9th month (v. 9). This was only two months after the end of the 4th year. Their regnal years were from 7th month to 7th month (Fall to Fall).

Comparing the Different Regnal Systems from Solomon Through the Kingdoms

Regnal Years Started at Different Times

cp205» The method of figuring the chronology of this period is by comparing the reigns of the kings of Judah to the reigns of the kings of Israel and vice versa. Although there was overlapping of reigns in this period much like the period of Judges, this difficulty was overcome by comparing the reigns of the kings of Judah to the kings of Israel. *From this method we learn that the kings of Judah always counted their king's regnal years from fall to fall while Israel also seemed to count their regnal years from the fall to fall of each year up to king Omri and from Jehu up to Hoshea. The other kings of Israel used the spring to spring method of dating regnal years.* The Text of the Biblical Chronology contains the detail of this comparison (See CP5).

Accessional Year System

cp206» If a king never reigned into a New Year's day (Jehoahaz & Jehoiachin), then that king never was counted as reigning for a year. Instead he is counted as reigning, for example, for "three months" versus one year as in the case for Jehoahaz and Jehoiachin (2 Kings 23:31; 24:8). Also Judah figured the last year of each king's total regnal years as being the year in which the king died, that is, the year in which the king did not reach the next New Years day. This is like the accession year method explained in Finegan's *Handbook of Biblical Chronology* [1964 & 1998], Paragraph 161. **This method is similar to the Patriarchal method described above.**

Accession Year Method			
Calender Year		Calender Year	Calender Year
Previous king dies in his 12th year new king is coronated	previous king's 12th year accession period for new king	Year 1 of new king	Year 2 of new king

Israel's Non-Accessional Year System

cp207» Contrary to Judah's system, in most reigns if not all reigns up to Jehu, Israel figured the first year of their kings as beginning in the year that each king took office even though the king hadn't reigned the full year, or had not reigned on the first day of that year. Also Israel counted the year in which a king died as belonging to the dead king. But starting with Jehu Israel did not follow this method. *Consequently, before Jehu Israel counted some years twice: once for the dying king; and once for the succeeding king.* This means that sometimes in the chronology when you compare the total regnal years for Israel's kings with the total regnal years for the kings of Judah you will find that Israel's total regnal years exceeded Judah's. This part of the Chronology is very difficult; some regnal years of Israel in particular may be off the mark by as much as one-half to one year, but not necessarily since there are numerous scriptures that verify the way we have presented this period (see "Verification" below).

Non- Accession Year Method			
Calender Year		Calender Year	Calender Year
Previous king dies in his 12th year new king is coronated	12th year of dead king Year 1 of new king	Year 2 of new king	Year 3 of new king

Interregnal years

cp208» Contrary to many Biblical chronologies, this present Biblical chronology, does not assume that there were interregnal years between Judah's kings Amaziah and Uzziah or between Israel's kings Jeroboam II and Zechariah. This is so because the Bible states that Uzziah (that is Azariah) reigned "instead of" or "in the room of his father" Amaziah, and that Zechariah reigned after Jeroboam II's death "in his stead" (2 Kings 14:21, 29; 2 Chron 26:1). There is a vagueness to these scriptures that does not lead us to a certain conclusion. There seems to be no clear evidence in the Bible that during these periods there were interregnal periods. Yet there may have been interregnal years because of catastrophes or invasions by other nations. *Nevertheless, the count of years is not lost since either Judah or Israel had a king with a continuous reign during any possible interregnal period.*

Co-Reigns

cp209» In the case of the kings of Judah and Israel sometimes more than one king from each kingdom reigned at the same time. This is called co-regencies and usually involved a father and his son: the son being the "crown prince" or co-king. The usual reason for this was that a war was going on or the father-king was ill or injured (See CP5, Chronology Table). It is not apparent how the reign of co-kings are counted. It may have differed from kingdom to kingdom and/or king to king. But in the case of the kings of Judah and Israel's kings how they counted reigns of their kings can be figured out by comparing the starting and ending of their reigns, and by believing the text that gives the number of years each reigned. We believe that by accepting every detail and by knowing how words such as "son" [ben] have a wide meaning, we can correctly figure the chronology. See and study our table for more details.

co-Regnal Year Method during time of war or a sick king (co-king's regnal years count starts in the year crowned)			
Calender Year		Calender Year	Calender Year
Existing King's 12th year	co-King is coronated co-king's 1st year	Existing King's 13th year co-king's 2nd year	Existing King's 14th year co-king's 3rd year

Babylonian (626-539 BC) co-Regnal Year Method during time of war or a sick king (co-king's regnal years count starts in the year after existing king dies)			
Calender Year		Calender Year	Calender Year
Existing King's 12th year	co-king is coronated as prince or king	Existing King's 13th year Existing King dies accession year of co-king	co-king's 1st year as solo King

Changes From One Regnal System to Another

cp210» By studying the scriptures concerning the kings of Judah and kings of Israel in their divided kingdom, we see some kingdoms over the years changed their system from one to another depending on the king's preference. Jeroboam started using the non-accessional year method and this was continued until Jehu, thus his first year was the same as Solomon's last year. Possibly in order for king Omri to make his reign seem older than king Tibni (or for some other reason), he used the non-accessional year method to count his regnal years as well as to change his regnal year from fall to spring (see CP5). But king Jehu in his reforms changed both of these methods that Jeroboam and Omri initiated back to the method of Solomon and the method of the kingdom of Judah (see CP5). Yet under the influence of the Assyrians the system of counting regnal years was changed again under Hoshea (see CP5).

Verification of Chronological Periods

cp211» All the sections of this book show how complex chronology can be. There are numerous ways to make mistakes. In the text of the Biblical chronology there are many scriptures that help to verify or double check the chronology. See and read CP3, CP4, and especially CP5 for more details on our method of ascertaining the Biblical chronology. Follow the shaded columns and rows in the table of the chronology to understand the interconnected dates. The following are the methods/checks for figuring the chronology.

1 YM - 2083 – Patriarchal Years

cp212» **Patriarchal Years:** From Adam to Abraham's call and sojourning. The method of counting years is not the inclusive counting method, but is similar to the accessional year system. The chart on Abraham's age in relation to Isaac and Ishmael helps to verify the Patriarchal counting method for counting the years of the patriarchs (see CP5 chart 2083 YM & thereafter).

2083-2513 YM – 430/400 Years

cp213» **430/400 Years** mentioned in Exodus 12:40-41 and Galatians 3:17. Abraham's call and sojourning to Exodus. *Inclusive method* of counting years applied here.

2513-2992 YM – 480 Years

cp214» **480 Years** is mentioned in 1 Kings 6:1. Exodus to Solomon's 4th year. *Inclusive method* of counting years applied here.

2992-3403 YM – Comparing Regnal years with Jubilee and Absolute Dates

The scriptures that manifest the rulership years of the United Kingdom of Judah and Israel (compared against each other) with the Jubilee Years from the Israel going into the Promised Land (2553 YM) to Hezekiah's 14th year (3287 YM), along with the backward count of years from Absolute Date (3403 YM) back to Hezekiah's 14th year (3287 YM).

3403-4000 YM – From the Absolute Date until the death of Jesus Christ

3073-3114 YM

The 42 Years of Omri's house helps to verify the method of counting the reigns of kings between Omri and Ahaziah. Compare 3073 with 3114 YM.

2553- 3287 YM – Jubilee Year Count Years

cp215» The **Jubilee Year count** is hinted at in 2 Kings 19:29. From Israel's first year in the promised land (beginning in the fall after they came into the land when they first planted their seed) until Hezekiah's 14th and 15th year, or 15 Jubilee periods of 49 years, or thus 735 years. See information under 3287 YM in CP5. The Jubilee Year count (inclusive counting method) mentioned under 3287 YM helps to verify the period between Israel's going into the promised land (2553 YM) and the year 3287 YM.

3287-3345 YM – Problem Period of the Chronology

cp216» The remaining problem is whether or not the beginning/end of the reigns of Hezekiah, Manasseh, Amon, or Josiah overlapped each other. If they did overlap, it means that the overall span of their reign period is shortened, and the period after 523-522 BC must be lengthened. Also if these reigns did overlap, the Christian Era year for the 6000 YM may have to be adjusted. Also our BC dates for the 1 YM will be off by the number of years these kings' reigns overlapped.

3345 - 3367 YM – Jeremiah's 23 Years

cp217» The **23 Years of Jeremiah** (inclusive counting method) helps to verify the count of years for that period (See CP5, 3344 - 3366 YM).

3373½ - 3409 ½ YM 37 Year Captivity of Jehoiachin

The **37 Years of Captivity** (inclusive counting) of Jehoiachin helps to verify the common use of inclusive counting by the Jews but also the counting methods for both Judaean and Babylonian kings for that period (See CP5, 3373 - 3409 YM).

3363 ½ - 3432 ½ YM - 70 Year Prophecy of Jeremiah

The 70 year prophecy of Jeremiah (Jer 27:1-11; Dan 9:2: Jer 25:9, 11; 29:10; see CP Appendix)

The chart on the **seven years in building Solomon's temple** also helps to verify the method of counting regnal years. (see cp203 chart)

cp218» Events dated in the **regnal years of the kings of Judah** and in the **regnal years of the Babylonian king Nebuchadnezzar**, indicate the Judah's regnal years began in the fall, while Babylon's regnal years began in the spring. See CP5 and pertinent scripture. (Example: Jerusalem burned in the 11th year of Zedekiah, which was the 19th year of Nebuchadnezzar.)

See also the "Confirmation of Judah's Regnal Years" above for proof of how Judah counted regnal years.

cp219» **The 25th year of Jehoiachin's captivity** synchronized with the 14th year of the destruction of Jerusalem in Ezekiel 40:1 helps to verify the inclusive count of the years of this period. See 3374-3398/99 YM in chronology table.

Connection to Christian Era System

Connecting Christian Era System to Biblical Dates

cp220» The Bible ties the Babylonian king Nebuchadnezzar to various kings of Judah. There is a clay tablet (VAT 4956) that identifies the 37th year of Nebuchadnezzar's reign with a specific time. By retro-calculation using the astronomical data in the clay tablet (VAT 4956) we know that this tablet is dated in the years 568-567 BC of the Christian Era system. Through the Biblical ties between Nebuchadnezzar and the kings of Judah (Jer 25:1), we can give a Christian Era date to the Biblical Year of Man (YM). Thus by placing the Christian Era date next to our Year of Man date we synchronize both dating systems back to Adam.

Best Absolute Date

568-567 BC

cp221» **Cuneiform Tablet VAT 4956** identifies the 37th year of Nebuchadnezzar as being between 568-567 BC.

Nebuchadnezzar's 37th year. Astronomical calculation is used to verify this period. **Note:** This is a key year since the cuneiform table VAT 4956 is directly connected with the 37th year. Nebuchadnezzar's reign is connected to Judah's kings through such scripture as Jeremiah 25:1. This then establishes an absolute date for connecting secular chronology with Biblical chronology. See *Absolute Dates* in CP3.

cp222» In order to better understand our book you must have the knowledge found in Parts 2, 3, and 4. You must thus have more knowledge of the Hebrew calendar and other methods of keeping time.

YM not A.M. Method

cp223» When we say "in 236 YM," it means "in the 236th year of man." It indicates that 235 full years have passed and that we are referring to the time *in* the next year after the first 235 full years of mankind. This is like the method used for the reigns of kings: When you say, "in the 4th year of Solomon," you mean in the year following 3 full years. This method is *different* from those who use *anno mundi* (A.M.). Our year "131 YM" corresponds to their 130 A.M. Our YM method is like the method used for the reign of kings, and not like the A.M. method used by others.

Hebrew Calendar
Observation and Calculation

cp224» At first the Hebrew calendar was one of observation, "the beginnings of the months were determined by direct observation of the moon" (*The Comprehensive Hebrew Calendar*, by A. Spier, p. 1-2). This was so because the Sun, Moon, and stars were "to divide the day from the night; and let them be for signs, and for appointed times [*moed*], and for days, and years" (Gen 1:14). Later this observation system may have been helped by calculation ("Calendar," *Ency. Brit.*, 11th ed., p. 1000; A. Spier, pp. 1-2, 217ff). But in *The International Standard Bible Encyclopaedia* (1915) it states:

> "We have lately learned from the discovery of a number of Aram.[aic] papyri at Syene [Egypt] that there was a colony of Jews there who used a calendar constructed, not from observation, but from calculation based upon a very exact luni-solar cycle ... This cycle, known to us by the name of its supposed discoverer, Meton, is one of 19 years, which is only two hours short of 235 complete months. As this Jewish colony appears to have been founded after Nebuchadnezzar's destruction of Jerus[alem] by some of the refugees who fled into Egypt with Johanan the son of Kareah (Jer 40-44), this acquaintance with the Metonic cycle cannot have been due to Bab[ylonian] influence. Nor can it have been due to Egypt, since the Egyptians did not use or require any such cycle, their year being a solar one of 365 days. Indeed no other nation appears to have been aware of it until, a generation later, Meton, the Athenian, won immortal fame by announcing it. The evidence of these Syene papyri renders it probable that Meton did not himself discover the cycle but learned it from Jewish sources"
>
> ("Astronomy," p. 305).

cp225» According to this article, and according to information in Finegan's book (¶ 76), Jews used calculation to help with ascertaining their New Moons. In fact, out of necessity of having their holy days at the proper times, even in the event of cloudy skies, the Jews in all probability discovered the so-called Metonic cycle before Meton. If I were to guess it was through Daniel that Nebuchadnezzar and Babylon learned further details of the so-called Metonic cycle (Dan 1:17-21; 2:48; 5:11-12).

Waning Moon Method

cp226» There is also another method of figuring the new moon without calculation when it is cloudy on the new moon evening. When the moon is waning, that is the light of the moon after the full moon is decreasing, when there is just a small crescent of light left on the moon, it is a day or at most two days before the conjunction of the moon and the sun. You can see the last light of the waning moon about one hour before sunrise the day or two before the conjunction. You can thus figure the first day of the new moon as figured by the Hebrews (the first new crescent of light on the new moon after the conjunction is the new moon, the beginning of the new month) will occur about three or four days after you have seen the last light of the waning moon. Even if on the new moon the sky is cloudy, you thus will know that it is the evening of the new moon. In 1 Samuel 20:5 it states, David said unto Jonathan, Behold, tomorrow is the new moon." David knew a day ahead that the new moon was going to appear. He may have known this without calculation or knowledge of calculation, because like others in his time, he knew the "waning moon method." They watched the heavens for their calendar. On September 24, 1992, 5:15 am PDT in California, near Stockton, I saw the last crescent light of the waning moon (.05 phase). I didn't see the crescent in the early mourning of September 25 even though the moon was in a .01 phase because its position in the sky was too close to the sun near sunrise. I didn't see the first light of the new moon on the night of September 27 (.03 phase) even though it was clear because the sunset was too close to the moon set. The new moon for the Stockton, California area was thus on September 28 (.09 phase) even though it was too cloudy that day after sunset to see the new moon. It was thus 4 days after the last waning moon crescent that the new moon occurred.

Postponements of Holy Days

cp227» Today the Jews adjust their calendar so as to have their holy days fall on certain week days:

- "But some slight adjustments will occasionally be needed for the reasons before assigned, viz. to avoid certain festivals falling on incompatible days of the week. Whenever the computed conjunction falls on a Sunday, Wednesday or Friday, the new year is in such case to be fixed on the day after .... If the computed new moon be after 18 hours, the following day is to be taken, and if that happens to be Sunday, Wednesday or Friday, it must be further postponed one day .... The Jews, to avoid celebrating 'Passover' on Monday, Wednesday, or Friday, observe 'New Moon' one day earlier or later than the date indicated by the Golden Number" (*Ency. Brit.*, 11th Ed., p. 1000; A. Spier, pp. 218-219; Bond, p. 264).

- "Further, — the Jews, to avoid celebrating 'Passover' on Monday, Wednesday, or Friday, observe 'New Moon' one day earlier or later than the date indicated by the Golden Number... With these notes concerning the Hebrew Calendar, it will be obvious that a calendar to serve perpetually cannot be easily produced; but if we take the date of the new moon of the vernal equinox indicated by the Golden Number, according to the following tables, we shall be able to determine the date of the Jewish civil year, within a day, for the modern Jewish Calendar" (Bond, pp. 264-265).

- The postponements according to *The Jewish Encyclopedia* "were introduced to provide that the Day of Atonement should not be on Sunday or Friday ... and that the seventh day of Tabernacles should not be on Saturday" ("Calendar").

- "The second complication is introduced to prevent certain dates from falling on the Sabbath. To provide the required flexibility, two months (*Cheshwan* and *Kislew*) may both have 29 days" (*Jewish Chrononomy*, by Leo Levi, p. 6, 1967).

- Spier lists four postponements of the calculated new year's day from the calendar's new year's day (p. 219).

Notice from the above that there seems to be no consistent explanation for the postponements. There is something superstitious about manipulating a calendar so that festival days only appear on certain days. We reject this as non-Biblical and we will not use it in order to determine Biblical dates. During Christ's time there were no postponements, for the festival of the Passover "could fall on any day of the week..." (Solomon Zeitlin, "The Judean Calendar During the Second Commonwealth, and the Scrolls," *Jewish Quarterly Review*, July 1966).

Difference Between Astronomical, Golden Number's, and Observational New Moon

cp228» "The date of a new moon, indicated by any number of the Dionysian Cycle, or of the other cycles, differ from the date of the appearance of the new moon of the heavens..." (Bond p. 122, the date of Golden Numbers "indicate the *Calendar* New Moon").

cp229» And "it ought to be remarked that the new moons, determined in this manner [Golden Number method], may differ from the astronomical new moons sometimes as much as two days" ("Calendar," *Ency. Brit.*, 11th ed.).

Difference Between Observational New Moons and Calculated New Moons

cp230» Most of today's new moon calculations and calendar new moons are based on calculations of the astronomical conjunction between the moon and the sun. The conjunction is about one to two days before the time the new moon's new crescent is observable by human eyes from the earth. "The most common termination / beginning point is the first visibility of the crescent in the evening; on observation of the crescent, the old month is deemed to have ended and the new month to have begun. So far as we can determine, all Greek calendars used first visibility of the crescent, as did, *inter alia*, Babylonian, Hebrew, and Moslem calendars" (see p. 14 *Greek and Roman Chronology*, Alan E. Samuel). The new moon can be observed at the very earliest about 18 hours after the astronomical conjunction, while many say the *earliest* it can be seen is 22-24 hours after the conjunction. Jacob O. Meyer of the Assemblies of Yahweh, has based his churches' calendar on observation for many years and it is his belief based on his experience,

- "that the new moon can rarely be seen less than 24 hours after the conjunction. Especially around the time of the spring equinoctial points, the length of time between conjunction to possible observation is greatly reduced. However, in the summer and fall of the year the length from the conjunction to the sighting of the moon is greatly lengthened.... Many factors enter into the subject of the new moon visibility...There must be sufficient light in the moon to mark its visibility as a crescent, the necessary length of time after sunset, with satisfactory twilight (darkness), and distance from the earth, etc.... Pinpointing the correct day when the new crescent visibility should occur is no easy matter..." ("How to Keep Time By Yahweh's Calendar in the Heavens," by Jacob O. Meyer, p. 7).

In many cases the new crescent is seen 1 to 2 days after the astronomical conjunction. In the July 11, 1991 conjunction, which was also an eclipse of the sun at about 11:20 AM (PDT), the new crescent wasn't seen in Tracy, California until about 8:50 PM (PDT) on July 12, or about 34 hours later, less than an hour after sunset. According to the *EZCosmos* PC program the moon was at the .02 phase. Of course, in other parts of the world this new moon may have been seen a little earlier or a little later than when I saw it near Tracy, California.

First Month

cp231» The Bible says that the month of Abib was for the beginning of the months of the year for Israel:

- "This month shall be unto you the beginning of months; it shall be the first month of the year to you.... This day you came out (of Egypt) in the month of Abib." (Ex 12:2; 13:4; & see 23:15; 34:18; Deu 16:1)

cp232» It was *not* the beginning of the year cycle, because other scriptures tell us that the year began and ended in the Fall at harvest time (Ex 23:16; 34:22). The month of Abib was the beginning of the *count of months* for the new year of Israel that pointed to and celebrated Israel's coming out of Egypt before entering the holy land, the promised land. In other words, the first month was not at the beginning of the year but someplace within the yearly cycle; the first month pointed to the first month of Israel escaping from their slavery in Egypt. This may be confusing at first, but do read on to better understand this (see New Year's Day below).

cp233» Notice Deuteronomy 16:1:

> Observe [watch for] the month of Abib and celebrate the Passover to the LORD your God,
> for in the month of Abib the LORD your God brought you out of Egypt by night.

This scripture asked Israel to watch for and observe the month of Abib, that is the new moon of Abib, for the word "month" was translated from the Hebrew word, *kodesh*, that meant, *new* moon or month depending on context. The word "Abib" means young ears or fresh ears, and from the context where it was first used, it means the time of the young ears of barley: "For barley was in the ear" (Ex 9:31-32). "In the ear" is a translation of the Hebrew word, *abib*, which is the name of the first month of Israel's calendar mentioned in the book of Exodus. In context, it means young or fresh ears of barley. At the time Israel came out of Egypt the wheat and the rye had not yet ripened enough to be destroyed by the plagues (Ex 9:32, 31). What this means is that the beginning of the first month for Israel was when the barley was beginning to become ripe. Since barley becomes ripen enough to harvest in the southern parts of Israel in early April, then the young ears appeared a week or so before this. Therefore Abib or the first month of Israel's calendar should not start before about March 20-21. There is room for some interpretation here, so we must be careful when we attempt to translate the start of the year in the old days or for that matter predict the start of the year in the future. Because twelve months of lunar-calendar year is shorter than the solar-calendar year, the beginning of Israel's months moved forward about eleven days each year until about every third year they had to add a second twelfth month. See video on how to figure when the first month (Abib or Nisan) starts and what part the ripening of barley plays in this process. (https://youtu.be/v0nR2XgaG4k)

New Year's Day

cp234» In order for Moses's new count of months for the year to be *new* there must have been a different Hebrew or Israelite count of months before this one (Ex 12:1-3). The old year began in the fall (Sept-Oct). Even today the Jews celebrate the New Year as beginning on *Rosh Hashanah* or the first of Tishri (Spier, p. 10). The month *Tishri* is the seventh month of Moses' *new* count of months. But before Moses the count of months started in the Fall. The month "Tishri" corresponds to our September-October period. This is confusing. The New Year's day for the year is the first day of the *seventh* month of Moses' new Hebrew Calendar, not the first day of the first month of Moses' new calendar. But before Moses the New Year's day was the first day of the first month (Gen 8:13 cf 7:6, 11 & Biblical Chronology under "1656 YM"), and began in the Fall. But from Moses onward, because Moses changed the months, the New Year's day was the first day of the seventh month of the Sacred Calendar. The confusion is caused because Moses initiated the Sacred Calendar or Religious Calendar while Israel still kept its old civil calendar, but only used it for counting years. The table below may help you to understand this.

Civil Years and the Religious Calendar

cp235» There is a distinction between the Old Testament's Hebrew Civil or Regnal year and their Religious or Sacred year. Civil years are from Tishri to Tishri (Fall to Fall), that is, from the seventh month to seventh month. But the seventh month is the seventh month of the religious calendar. The religious calendar was from the first month (Abib or Nisan) to the first month of each religious year, or more correctly from the first day of the first month through the last day of the last month. The civil year or regnal year for the Old Testament's Jews started from the first year of man, but the religious calendar started from Moses (Exo 12:1-3). This Old Testament civil year should not be confused with the contemporary civil year of many Jews — the Julian-Gregorian calendar year — which begins on January the first (also see *The International Standard Bible Ency.* [1915], under "Calendar"; Unger's *Bible Dict*, "Calendar"; etc).

Names of Months

cp236» In Moses' time this first month was called, *Abib* (Exo 13:4; 23:15; 34:18; Deut 16:1). But in the time of Nehemiah and Esther the first month was called, *Nisan* (Neh 2:1; Est 3:7). Most of time the first month was called not by name but by the number of the month, the *first* month (Exo 12:2, 18; Lev 23:5; Num 9:1; 33:3; Josh 4:19; 1 Chr 12:15; 27:2; 2 Chr 29:17; 35:1; Ezra 6:19; Est 3:12; Ezek 29:17; Dan 10:4). In the book 1 Chronicles chapter 27 the twelve months are not called by their names but by their numbers: first month, second month, third month, etc. This first month of Moses' year corresponds to the Julian-Gregorian calendar's March-April (see Unger's *Bible Dict*, "Calendar"). This first month is the same first month, *Nisan*, that the Jews today observe (*The Comprehensive Hebrew Calendar*, by A. Spier).

JULIAN- GREGORIAN MONTHS	PRE- MOSES MONTHS	SACRED YEAR MONTHS	
Sept-Oct	1st	7th	Tishri/Ethanim
Oct-Nov	2nd	8th	Marcheshvan/Bul
Nov-Dec	3rd	9th	Kislev
Dec-Jan	4th	10th	Tebeth
Jan-Feb	5th	11th	Shebat/Sebat
Feb-Mar	6th	12th	Adar
Mar-Apr	7th	1st	Nisan/Abib
Apr-May	8th	2nd	Iyar/Zif
May-June	9th	3rd	Sivan
June-July	10th	4th	Tammuz
July-Aug	11th	5th	Ab
Aug-Sept	12th	6th	Elul

Patriarchal/Regnal/Chronological Years = Sept-Oct
to Sept-Oct
New Year's Day = 1st Day of Regnal Year
New Year's Day = 1st Day of 7th Month of Sacred Calendar

Significance of the New Year's Day

cp237» The count of years for the patriarchs and the kings of Judah started with the first New Year's day they ruled on. This New Year's day is Israel's Civil New Year's day, not their religious year. It was on this day that Israel had a festival — Feast of Trumpets (Num 29:1ff; see Unger's *Bible Dict*, "Festivals"). But Israel did not have a festival for the beginning of the Sacred Calendar. In most if not all ancient cultures there was a festival or holiday for New Year's day (*Ency. Brit.*, 15th Ed., 1985, "Rites and Ceremonies: Feasts and Festivals," Vol 26, p. 881ff). In some of these cultures the king was sanctified by the high priest for the new year on the New Year's day festival (see D.J. Wiseman, *Nebuchadrezzar and Babylon*, pp. 19, 21; A.T. Olmstead, *History of the Persian Empire*, pp. 36, 86-87).

Cardinal v. Ordinal Numbers

cp238» Some make a clarification between the cardinal numbers and ordinal numbers. They say that cardinal numbers are such numbers as "one," "ten," or "one-hundred." They say they have full value. Thus if a king is said to rule five years, because "five" is a cardinal number, then this king must have ruled five full years. But ordinal numbers such as "first," "tenth," or "one-Hundredth" do not have full value. According to this theory, the tenth year of a king means he has only ruled nine full years and is in his tenth year.

cp239» But it should be noted here that some numbers in Hebrew are used as either cardinal or ordinal numbers:

- "In numbering days of the month and years, the cardinals are very frequently used instead of the ordinals even for the numbers from 1 to 10,"...
- "The *ordinals* above 10 have no special forms, but are expressed by the corresponding cardinals," ...
  (Gesenius' *Hebrew Grammar*, 2nd Eng Tran, 1910, 1980 reprint, Section 128*p* & 128*o*)

cp240» For example in 1 Kings 6:1 it reads in the Hebrew, "in the eighty year and four hundred year," and not in the eightie*th* year and four hundred*th* year, or in the four hundred and eightie*th* year. It has been translated by English translators as, "in the four hundred and eightieth year." Thus the 480 years (cardinal number in Hebrew) was translated in English as an ordinal number: 480th. Why? Because it sounded better; it was better English; or because of context. So to make a great deal about ordinal or cardinal numbers in chronology is projecting one's lack of knowledge of the Hebrew text: "the *ordinals* above 10 have no special forms, but are expressed by the corresponding cardinals."

Absolute Dates

Economic Cuneiform Tablets

cp241» Although economic or business cuneiform clay tablets (legal documents) had dates of kings ("in the 21st year of Nabopolassar" or only, "in the xxth year," with no king's name), they in most cases did not mention the year of reign of another king of another kingdom because most of these legal documents of business were only pertinent to one kingdom in one year of reign of some king of that kingdom. They also did not give the total years of reign of the kings mentioned. Thus when using cun

cp242» eiform business tablets as evidence for chronology, it becomes a game of which king follows which king, and only some supposed correct list of kings such as Ptolemy's gives conventional chronologists the idea they *know* which king follows which king (note *Babylonian Chronology 626 B.C.-A.D. 75*, by Parker and Dubberstein, pp. 10, 18, 24, note 10 pp 4-5).

cp243» It is on very rare occasions such as in the Bible where the reigns of the kings of Judah and Israel are sometimes both mentioned (books of Kings and Chronicles) or the place in the Bible where the year of reign of both Nebuchadnezzar and Jehoiakim are mentioned (Jer 25:1) that a real chronology can be built. It is through this scripture that we can connect the Biblical chronology with Babylonian chronology, thus to secular chronology.

Connection Between Biblical and BC-AD Dates

From the End of Judah's Kingdom

cp244» *Secular Evidence Used*. The 11th year of Zedekiah marked the end of the kingdom of Judah. From this point to Christ's time and the Christian Era system of dating we must rely on secular evidence, especially astronomical cuneiform tablets and retro-calculation of past celestial movements.

cp245» Before we can even attempt to find the date of Christ's birth or find out which year of man (YM) we now live in, we need to connect the Year of Man system of dating to the Christian Era system. The method of connection is principally through two astronomical cuneiform tablets. One can be dated 568 to 567 BC and the other can be dated from 523 to 522 BC.

cp246» Both of these tablets note a year of a king and both mention certain dates, month and day, and various astronomical events that happened on these dates. These tablets mention moon positions, eclipses of the moon, and both mention position of planets. I have studied these tablets and I have used computer programs to calculate the various years in which the position of the planets and the eclipses could have occurred in the past. I have found that the astronomical tablets can only describe the year in which they have been assigned by the experts. Because of the number of planets mentioned, because of the eclipses mentioned, because of the dates mentioned, and because there is no proof of a major realignment of the paths of the planets, sun, and moon since the time of the tablets, I believe these two tablets do identify ancient **absolute dates** and do connect our system of dating to the Biblical and Babylonian system of dating. (See following sections)

cp247» If I had to trust the few experts alone to calculate and identify these tablets, I would be less assured that these tablets were identifying absolute dates. It is because the latest methods of calculating past position of astronomical bodies are available on personal computers, because I spent weeks using my computer checking every conceivable way of disproving these dates, and because I examined the translation of these tablets, I have changed my opinion and now believe that the Biblical chronology can be linked to secular chronology through the use of these absolute dates.

Two Clay Tablets

cp248» After years of studying chronology since 1969, and after I had come to the conclusion about 1979 that Ptolemy's chronology was too dubious to rely on, I was at a loss for a method to connect my Biblical chronology with the Christian Era system (BC-AD system). I had studied eclipses and I had found that you could not identify a date with only one eclipse, especially the vague historical eclipses found in various texts (see, CP2). I had also studied various astronomical cuneiform tablets, but the ones I was aware of did not seem to hold the answer to finding an absolute date. In my studies I had read several books by Robert R. Newton and had found them very helpful. But in 1987 I read *The Crime of Claudius Ptolemy*, first published in 1977. In it Newton mentions two clay tablets. One is dated 523-522 BC, in the 7th year of Cambyses, and the other dated 568-567 BC, in the 37th year of Nebuchadnezzar. They were identified with these dates because of the astronomical information included within these tablets.

cp249» Concerning the tablets dated 568-567 BC, Newton said, "I find that the times of moonrise and moonset agree with calculated values within 10 minutes. The longitudes of the moon and planets inferred from the conjunctions agree with calculated values within 1 degree or less for most observations, although there is a discrepancy of 3 degrees for one lunar conjunction" (*Crime of* ..., p. 375).

cp250» Although Newton wasn't as satisfied with the tablet for the 7th year of Kambyses (Cambyses), he stated:

- "Thus we have quite strong confirmation that Ptolemy's list is correct for Nebuchadrezzar, and reasonable confirmation for Kambyses" (*Crime of* ..., p. 375).

cp251» After reading this I began my search for copies and/or translations of these tablets. I wrote Newton for any further information he might have, but he could not supply any except to note that he believed that the tablets were correctly dated and that they could not describe any other date within decades of the identified ones (letter, Dec 23, 1987).

cp252» I finally obtained copies of these tablets and used several computer programs to check them. **In my studies I have found that they could not have been any other date: the position of the planets were unique to the years assigned to them.**

Clay Tablet # 1: Tablet VAT 4956
37th Year, 568-567 BC

cp253» The tablet that describes the 37th year of Nebuchadnezzar and various planet positions within that year is the cuneiform tablet known as VAT 4956. I have a copy of the autograph of this tablet made by E. Weidner which is found as Plate XVII in *Archiv Fur Orientforschung*, Band XVI, 1953. It is also transcribed and discussed by P.V. Neugebauer and E. Weidner in *Ber. Sachs. Akad. 67* (Leipzig 1915) and is cataloged in A.J. Sachs' *Late Babylonian Astronomical And Related Texts*, 1955, page xii. The "VAT" before the number of the tablet (VAT 4956) means this tablet is in Berlin in the Staatliche Museen (Sachs, p. xxxix). I also obtained an English copy of VAT 4956 from the University of California at Berkeley in 1997 from the book, *Astronomical Diaries and Related Texts From Babylonia*, by Abraham J. Sachs, Volume I. Also on various pages in Robert R. Newton's 1976 book, *Ancient Planetary Observations ...*, Newton has information on the data from this tablet (*Ancient Planetary Observations ...*, Newton; pp. 110, 131-141, 145, 336, 345, 348, 352, 503, 511, 513, 519, 524).

cp254» This document records among other things, "9 measurements of the times of moonrise or moonset, 5 times of conjunctions of the moon with specified stars, plus 1 conjunction of Mercury, 2 of Venus, and 3 of Mars, all with specified stars" (Newton, 1977, p. 375).

Names of Kings in Clay Tablets

cp255» This document *does* mention Nebuchadnezzar by his full name. It begins with "year thirty seven [of] Nebukadnezar" The tablet uses word-signs or Ideograms for Nebuchadnezzar's name. These word-signs are not from the Akkadian language, but from the Sumerian language. Before April 7, 1997, when I obtained an English copy of VAT 4956, I could not identify Nebuchadnezzar's name in the tablet because I was only looking for Akkadian words in my copy of the clay tablet. I thought wrongly that some abbreviation was used in the tablet, and thus the reason I could not find the king's name. Abbreviations were used often in ancient texts:

- "The scribe uses, with the exception of writings A-lik-sa-an-dar and Pi-lip-su, abbreviations to refer to the kings. Thus Seleucus is consistently written Si and Antiochus An, Demetrius Di and Arsaces, probably, Ar; in line 5 Alexander is rendered by A-lik. The translation uses the full names with the ordinals and the identifying Greek by-names for the convenience of the reader" (*The Ancient Near East: Supplementary Texts and Pictures Relating to the Old Testament*, Edited by James B. Pritchard, 1969, page 131 [567] footnote 1).

37th Year

Yrs BC		Year of King	Year of Man	Hebrew Months
	Oct		?	7
	Nov			8
	Dec			9
568	Jan			10
	Feb			11
	Mar			12
	Apr	37		1
	May			2
	Jun			3
	Jul			4
	Aug			5
	Sep			6
	Oct		?	7
	Nov			8
	Dec			9
567	Jan			10
	Feb			11
	Mar			12
	Apr	38		1

Note: Because the first month of the Hebrew Calendar is either March or April, the above alignment is only approximate.

But Nebuchadnezzar's name is in the tablet as an ideogram: at least four times. On an edge of the tablet it also mentions the 37th year and the 38th year of Nebuchadnezzar. In astronomical tablets, one will more than likely not find the name of the king: you would find the year of the king, but not the name of the king. Many astronomical tablets are and were identified as to BC-AD year by the astronomical information within the tablet and through calculation (Sachs, 1955, p. vi), not by any king's name within it.

Clay Tablet # 2

7th Year, 523-522 BC

cp256» The tablet that describes the 7th year of Kambyses (Cambyses) and various astronomical positions is found in Franz Xaver Kugler's *Sternkunde und Sterndienst in Babel*, published in 1907, pages 70-71. Some information on this tablet is found in Newton's 1976 book (pp. 110, 131, 135, 139, 144, 503, 513, 523, 711-715).

cp257» I have a copy of Kugler's work on this tablet. On page 70 is the transliteration, and on page 71 is the German translation. This tablet lists two eclipses of the moon, conjunctions or near conjunctions of Mercury and Venus, Saturn and Venus, Mars and Jupiter, Saturn and Jupiter, Venus and Jupiter, Moon and Mercury, Moon and Jupiter, and positions of Jupiter, Venus, Saturn, and Mars in relationship to stars or star constellations (Virgo, Leo, etc.).

Identification Process
Software and Books

cp258» I used the following computer programs for an IBM PC computer to analyze the information on these two tablets:

- *Tables for the Motion of the Sun and the Five Bright Planets from -4000 to + 2800*, Supplemental Programs (Willmann-Bell, Pub.), by Pierre Bretagnon and Jean-Louis Simon, 1986.
- *Newcomb* and *Gnewcomb*, David Eagle, 1988 (Willmann-Bell).
- *EclipseMaster*, 1987, Zephyr Services.

I used the following to further analyze the information:

- *Canon of Lunar Eclipses -2002 to +2526*, by Jean Meeus and Hermann Mucke, 1979.
- *Smithsonian Contributions to Astrophysics, 5,000 and 10,000 year Star Catalogs*, by Gerald S. Hawkins and Shoshana K. Rosenthal, 1967.
- *Ancient Planetary Observations and the Validity of Ephemeris Time*, by Robert R. Newton, 1976.

Findings of Study

cp259» First I found both tablets to be properly dated, not because of the lunar eclipses, but because of the numerous planet positions. One lunar eclipse would be too vague to date any event (see CP2). Two lunar eclipses would help more to identify a year. But the numerous planet positions were the clincher. The position of planets as seen from the earth repeat themselves every so many months or years. This is called the synodic period of planets.

Planets' Orbits Repeat

cp260» Mercury returns every .31726 years or 3.9241 months to the same place in the background of the same stars as seem from the earth. Venus repeats every 1.59872 years or 19.7742 months. Mars repeats every 2.13539 years or 26.4121 months. Jupiter repeats every 1.09211 years or 13.5080 months. Saturn repeats every 1.03518 years or 12.8039 months (Newton, 1976, p. 101). 145 synodic periods of Mercury comes to an almost even 46 years (46.003). Five synodic periods of Venus comes to an almost even 8 years (7.994). 22 or 37 snyodic periods of Mars comes to an almost even 47 years or 79 years (46.979 or 79.009). 65 or 76 snyodic periods of Jupiter comes to an almost even 71 or 83 years (70.987 or 83.000). 57 snyodic periods of Saturn comes to an almost even 59 years (59.005).

Synodic Periods

cp261» Both tablets list a date, month and day, with the year. In order to identify the year of the tablets in the Christian Era system, we need to understand the pattern or synodic period that repeats itself in whole years. Venus returns every 8 (7.994) years to the same apparent position among the stars of the sky as seen from the earth on a specific date of the solar year. Thus, if we know a Julian or Gregorian (not a Babylonian) date (month and day) in a clay tablet where Venus was observed near "x" star, but do not know which Julian year it is, we know that Venus will return each 8 solar years to the same position in the sky.

King Lists

cp262» If we have other information in the tablet such as a year of a king along with a reliable king's list we can by a hit and miss method move this sighting eight years at a time until we fit this tablet into its proper place in history. But if the tablets we are studying do not list the name of the king with the year, it will be more difficult. One of these tablets did not name the king, but it did mention the year (7th) of some unknown king. The most used kings list for this period is Ptolemy's. We can not absolutely trust Ptolemy's kings list (CP2). Therefore we can only use his list tentatively. But there are also the Assyrian king list, the Uruk King list, and the Seleucid King list, as well as the tablet of the mother of Nabonidus (*The Ancient Near East: Supplementary Texts and Pictures Relating to the Old Testament*, James B. Pritchard, 1969, pp. 560-562, 564-567; see CP2). Using all these lists helps us to get a good idea of the length of years of the kings of this period.

Tablet Contents & King Lists

cp263» We know by the language of the clay tablets, the way they were written, in context with previously found astronomical tablets, that these two tablets can roughly be dated (A.J. Sachs, *Late Babylonian Astronomical and Related Texts*, p. xii ff; A.K. Grayson, *Assyrian and Babylonian Chronicles*, pp. 12, col 2). Furthermore, we can know specifically the date of the tablets by the astronomical information within them (see below). One tablet has the name of the king, Nebuchadnezzar. To find the name of the other king we can use the various king lists of this period and the Assyrian and Babylonian Chronicles to ascertain how many kings reigned for at least 7 years. By this method we narrow down the possible kings that the tablets may belong to only Cambyses.

cp264» As mentioned before these tablets contain planet positions for specific dates. Since the position of planets like Venus repeat their position every so many years, by knowing these synodic periods in whole years, we can further narrow down the years.

Lunar Eclipses

cp265» These tablets also contain reports of lunar eclipses, and since eclipses only repeat themselves every so often, this information also enables us to narrow down the year of the tablet (CP2).

Planet Positions

cp266» But not only did these tablets report on lunar eclipses, and one planet position with specific dates (month and day), these tablets report on *many* planet positions. By ascertaining through retro-calculation the position of these planets on certain dates, we narrow the dates down to the exact year in the Christian Era system. For example the 523-522 BC tablet contains several positions of the planets Jupiter, Venus, Saturn, and Mars during this time period. Jupiter repeats its synodic period every 71 (70.987) or 83 solar years. Venus repeats itself every eight years. Saturn repeats itself every 59 years. And Mars repeats itself every 47 (46.979) years. These four planets will all be in the same position in relation to themselves and the stars on the same solar date approximately every 1,575,064 years. But this tablet also contained seven reports of near conjunctions of two planets. This would also greatly increase the odds that the astronomical phenomena reported on the tablet would be unique in history.

Babylonian Calendar

cp267» It also should be remembered that the dates given were from the Babylonian calendar, which was a lunar-solar calendar. It does not correspond to our solar calendar. This again would increase the odds of finding another year in history that would have the same planet positions as reported in the tablets.

Other Planet Conjunction Patterns

cp268» In the 523-522 tablet it mentions seven near conjunctions of two bodies:

- Moon and Mercury; Moon and Jupiter; Venus and Jupiter; Saturn and Jupiter; Mars and Jupiter; Saturn and Venus; and Mercury and Venus.

cp269» The tablet speaks of these pairs of planets being so many degrees (*ammat* or *uban* which equal about 2 to 2 ½ degrees) away from each other. Concerning these conjunctions, the tablet does not report the position of the planets in relationship to the stars. These conjunctions have only to do with the nearing of the two planets together irrespective of their position among the stars at the time of their conjunction. This gives us a different possible period of repetition. Using the computer programs I found that the periods that these conjunctions repeated themselves to be *approximately*:

- Venus and Jupiter
  13 months; 11 months; 26 months; 30 months, 40 months; 10 & 14 months; 20 months; 15 months; etc.
- Saturn and Jupiter
  20 years
- Mars and Jupiter
  26 months
- Saturn and Venus
  14 months; 10 months; 14 months; 13 months; 10 months; 14 months; 11 months; 14 months; 11 months; etc.

- Mercury and Venus
    1 year; 2 years; 19 months; 8 months; 9 months; 28 months; etc.

cp270» Because of the apparent non-synchronizing of these conjunctions, it adds more weight to the identification of the dates of the tablets.

cp271» By using and comparing the length of king's reigns in the Uruk King list, the king list in the tablet of Nabonidus's mother, the Babylonian chronicle, the Ptolemy's king list between Nabopolassar and Darius II (because of the economic tablets found in this time period), various other tablets and monuments concerning the Persian kings (Anstey, pp. 260 ff), and because of the 70 years prophecy (see CP5), we can conclude that the tablets dated astronomically and dated through the comparison of king lists and lengths of kings reigns, are correctly dated to the right Julian years and to the right Kings.

cp272» Also the Seleucid King list (Pritchard, 1969, pp. 566 ff), the dated astronomical diaries (Sachs, pp. xii ff), the so-called "goal-year" texts (Sachs, pp. xxv ff), and other texts give us the rough information on the years of the kings.

cp273» Our contention with Ptolemy's list is not the *general* number of years between Nebuchadnezzar's time to Darius II, but his king list before Nabopolassar, and the kings after Darius II, because of the lack of pertinent cuneiform tablets between Nebuchadnezzar and Christ's time. It is not clear from the Bible the names of the kings and the order of their reigns after Cyrus (see the Bible books: Ezra, Nehemiah, Esther, Daniel).

Astronomical Chaos

cp274» Another aspect to consider is astronomical chaos. There was a book published in 1950 that caused an emotional outburst from many who called themselves scientists. The book was by Immanuel Velikovsky. The book's name was *Worlds in Collision*. It told the story of apparent astronomical chaos, worlds in collision, planets or planet-comets off their present orbits. Some felt Velikovsky's book was somewhat convincing in parts, but not very scientific in whole. Velikovsky used many sources of information, synthesizing them into a story of astronomical chaos. He took information from cuneiform tablets and classical historians. But he also took information from literature classified as myth, and from the Bible. We don't classify the Bible as myth, but some unknowingly do.

Gods, Stars and Chaos

cp275» What Velikovsky reported was the numerous stories in ancient sources about astronomical chaos, of war in the heavens between planets or planets and comets. Some stories were open and obvious; some were hidden in poetry. Homer in his *Iliad* wrote poetically about the gods and their fights in the heavens. In the Sumerian and Akkadian languages the word or sign for god (*an* or DINGIR) was used in front of the names of stars. This indicates that stars were gods according to their mindset. According to Plato stars were gods, "stars which are living creatures divine and eternal" (Plato, *Timaeus* Loeb Classical Lib, No. 234, p. 85). It was common for Greeks to call all heavenly bodies "stars" (Gk. *aster*) even the sun and moon. Planets were the wandering stars, and what we call stars they called "fixed stars" (Newton [1977] p. 2-3; Ptolemy's *Almagest*, trans. Toomer, p. 21). Plato called the stars, "gods" (*Timaeus* p. 87, & footnote 3). Thus, the gods warring in the heavens were the planet-stars warring against each other in the heavens.

cp276» In Plato's own words:

- "There have been and there will be many and divers destructions of mankind, of which the greatest are by fire and water, and lesser ones by countless other means. For in truth the story that is told in your country as well as ours, how once upon a time Phaethon, son of Helios, yoked his father's chariot, and, because he was unable to drive it along the course taken by his father, burnt up all that was upon the earth and himself perished by a thunderbolt,—that story, as it is told, has the fashion of a legend, **but the truth of it lies in the occurrence of a shifting of the bodies in the heaven which move round the earth**, and a destruction of the things on the earth by fierce fire, which recurs at long intervals" (Plato, *Timaeus*, pp. 33-35, my emphasis).

cp277» Ancient sources told the story of an unstable universe. In the past people were aware of the previous periods of the unstable universe. Ancient writers openly and poetically wrote of this universe. Velikovsky and others gave evidence of changes in ancient calendars (Velikovsky, *Worlds....*, Chap. 8; E.A. Wallis Budge, *The Book of the Kings of Egypt*, Vol 1, p. XLV ff). What this means is that the orbits of the moon and the earth have changed; the calendars changed to reflect the orbit changes. At least two to four major changes have occurred in the past. Because of these changes astronomical retro-calculation before these orbit changes are impossible. We will not analyze the pros and cons of astronomical chaos. It would be too long and complicated for this paper. We will refer you to some books and journals. They make for interesting and informative reading:

- Immanuel Velikovsky, *Worlds in Collision*;
  Earth in Upheaval;
  Ages in Chaos;
- Alfred de Grazia, Ralph E. Juergens, and Livio C. Stecchini, *The Velikovsky Affair*;
- Donald W. Patten, Ronald R. Hatch and Loren C. Steinhauer, *The Long Day of Joshua and Six Other Catastrophes*;
- Donald W. Patten, *Catastrophism and the Old Testament (Seattle: Pacific Meridian Pub., 1988)*;
- Donald Wesley Patten, *The Biblical Flood and the Ice Epoch*;
- *Kronos*, a journal, all volumes;
- *Pensee*, a journal, all 10 volumes;
- *Cosmos and Chronos*, a journal, all volumes;
- *Creation Research Society Quarterly*, a journal, various articles from time to time;
- William H. Stiebing, Jr., *Ancient Astronauts; Cosmic Collisions*, pp. 57-80, a critique of Velikovsky's work.

cp278» In our chronology we rely on Biblical and secular sources, with Biblical sources given the upper hand. In the Bible there are many references to catastrophic events that were from astronomical chaos. Reading these catastrophic scriptures with the point of view that they may be astronomical in nature makes many of these puzzling scriptures come alive. I am inclined to believe there has been astronomical chaos, with the flood, the Exodus, and other events being a part of this chaos.

Israel's God did All: Good and Bad

cp279» **The people of Israel interpret all events as coming from God, the good ones and the bad ones** (see *God Papers*; "God's Wrath" papers). To the Hebrews good events happen because people were good; bad events happen because they were bad. But Christ, Paul, and Peter said this was not necessarily so (Luke 13:1-4; Rom 11; 8:17; 1 Pet 2:21-22; 3:14, 17 ff; 4:1; see "Joy" section in NM18). To the Hebrews when the skies rained fire and brimstone it wasn't because of astronomical chaos, it was because God was punishing the bad. When the sun apparently went down 10 degrees, it wasn't because of astronomical chaos, it was a sign from God. See the *God Papers* and "God's Wrath Papers" to understand more about the Hebrews attributing almost all things good and bad to God.

cp280» The assumption that present orbits have been stable for a long time is not scientific, especially in light of historical writings to the contrary. The present "laws" of orbits are nothing but *mathematical descriptions* of the present orbits with small adjustments (secular terms) for past variations. They tell us little about orbits 3,000 years ago. The theory of astronomical science that the orbits were stable thousands of years ago is based on linear thinking. But a new branch of science called the science of chaos is projecting the naivete of linear thinking (James Gleick, *Chaos: Making a New Science*, 1987; see my *Science Papers*).

cp281» Hailstones and brimstones mixed with fire falling from heaven or the sky are reported in the Bible. These stones came out of the sky either from a comet or planet-comet that came close enough to the earth to cause chaos on the earth and in some cases to cause great earthquakes and cause our volcanoes to erupt. They may even have caused the earth to stand still or appear to stand still, or in some way, have turned the earth upside down, reversed temporarily the apparent movement of the cosmic bodies, or caused a reversal in the magnetic polarity, etc. [The Hale-Bopp comet coming our way (this was written on 9-23-95) was last here about 3000 to 4000 years ago. Was it this comet or others like it that caused the chaos thousands of years ago?]

Examples of Past Chaos

cp282» *Brimstone and/or hailstones and fire from heaven*
Genesis 19:24-29; Exodus 9:18-19,22-25; Joshua 10:11-14; Isa 28:2; Isaiah 30:30 cf 37:36 with Isa 38:8 and see Velikovsky *World's ...* Part 2, Chap 2;

Great earthquakes
Isaiah 24:13, 18-20; Amos 1:1; Zech 14:5;

Sun, Moon, and Earth in chaos
Joshua 10:11-14; Isaiah 24:1, 20, 23; 2 Kings 20:8-11; Isa 38:8;

Mountains and valleys lifted up and down
Psalm 104:8 see Hebrew or margin in Bible; an effect of the Flood and astronomical chaos;

The Flood and collapse of the waters above the earth
Genesis 1:6-7 compare with Genesis chaps. 7 & 8; see CP5 under "1656 YM"; an effect of cosmic bodies coming too close to the earth;

Rocks. You can travel through the land in and around Israel and through various parts of the United States, especially the desert area between California and Texas and see rocks that look just like the rocks seen on Mars (same sizes, same color, same texture) as photographed by the Viking 2 lander (*Science News*, Vol. 110. No. 11, Sept 11, 1976, "Viking 2's View of Utopia: A Rock-Strewn Martian Plain," pp. 164 ff; Time-Life Books [editors], *The Near Planets*, 1989, pp. 122-124; etc.) Some of these may be the "hailstones" or "brimstones" of the

Bible caused by the interaction of Mars and/or Venus or a comet or a shattered cosmic body with the Moon and the Earth.

Moon's Craterous Face. The past chaos in the solar system is revealed by the moon's surface: crater-like formations.

Rocks from Moon and Mars. "Scattered across the frozen plains of Antarctica lie thousands of mysterious rocks, some as small as olives, others as large as grapefruits. Geologists believe that many of the stones are from the moon and some perhaps from Mars.

> 'We are certain that these samples are from the moon,' University of Pittsburgh geologist William Cassidy said at a recent International Geological Congress session. The chemical composition of many of the rocks matches that of moon rocks gathered by the Apollo astronauts....
>
> In all scientists have gathered more than 12,000 Antarctic rocks, and two in particular, known as shurgities, remain especially puzzling. Cassidy says they might have come from Mars but notes that no one will know for sure until scientists can compare them with rocks brought back from that planet" (*Insight*, August 21, 1989, p. 50).

Reversal of the Magnetic Poles. There is evidence of reversals of the magnetic poles of the Earth, moon, and even Mars. These reversals indicate past cosmic chaos (Kenneth A. Hoffman, "Ancient Magnetic Reversals," *Scientific American*, May, 1988, pp.76-83, 126; Arthur Fisher, "What Flips Earth's Field," *Popular Science*, Jan. 1988, pp. 71ff; S.K. Runcorn, "The Moon's Ancient Magnetism," *Scientific American*, Dec. 1987, pp. 60ff; Thomas G. Barnes, *Origin And Destiny of The Earth's Magnetic Field*, 1973, ICR, San Diego; J.A. Jacobs, *Reversals of The Earth's Magnetic Field*, Adam Hilger, Ltd., 1984; David Gubbins, "Mechanism For Geomagnetic Polarity Reversals," *Nature*, March 12, 1987, Vol 326, No. 6109, pp. 167-169). For example, "the moon once had its own magnetic field, and a remarkably strong one. At one time the moon's field may have been nearly twice as strong as the present-day magnetic field of the earth...it seems that the body of the moon as a whole, has shifted several times in relation to its own axis of spin. The spin axis has preserved its orientation and position in space, but the moon itself has rotated in such a way that regions that were once at the poles (where the spin axis intersects the surface) are now closer to the equator" (pp 60-61, "The Moon's Ancient Magnetism," *Scientific American*, Dec 1987).

Other Important Information

Names: Kings Who Had More Than One Name
Different Kings With The Same Name

cp283» The Judaean king Jehoiachin of the Bible is also called Jeconiah and Coniah (2 Kings 24:8; 1 Chron 3:16; Jer 24:1; Jer 22:24). The Judaean king Eliakim's name was changed to Jehoiakim (2 Kings 23:34). The Judaean king Mattaniah had his named changed to Zedekiah (2 Kings 24:17). Daniel and Abram, although not kings, had their names changed to Belteshazzar and Abraham. Most Egyptian kings had at least five names: a throne name, a personal name, and epithets (*Ages in Chaos*, p. 234; see "Kings Names" in CP2 of this paper). Furthermore, the cuneiform tablets can be read both ideographically and syllabically: Nergil can become Muwatallis (Velikovsky, *Ramses II and his Time*, pp. 101-102; quoting from Delaporte, *Les Hittites*; see *An Akkadian Grammar*, 1984 printing, p. 10).

cp284» Also each country or language had it own name for the other nation's kings: Nabopolassar was called Belesys (Diodorus, II, 24) and Bussalossor (Abydenus) by Greek authors, Merosar by Egyptians, and in Babylonian Bel-shum-ishkun and Nabopolassar (*Ramses*, p. 102). For "Darius, King of the Persians — Darayawaush, Dorejawosch, Dara, Darab, Dareios are variation of his name in different languages..." "I have learned from the Zend-Avesta (a collective term for the sacred Persian writings) that the name Hystaspes was pronounced Goschasp, Gustasp, Kistasp, or Wistasp in Persian" (*Gods, Graves and Scholars*, by C.W. Ceram, pp. 268, 266; see Chap. 19 & 20).

cp285» Furthermore, kings of different nations had kings with the same name in the same time period: in the same time period there were two kings called Jehoram for both Judah and Israel and two kings called Ahaziah for both Judah and Israel.

cp286» Also some nations had their kings *apparently* alternating the throne names of their kings almost every other generation: Darius, Cyrus, Cambyses, Xerxes, and Artaxerxes of the Median and Persian empire (James B. Pritchard, *The Ancient Near East* [1958], p. 207; Martin Anstey, *Chronology of the Old Testament*, p. 260 ff).

Akkadian Language: Different Language signs = Same Sound; Same Language Sign = Different Sounds

cp287» The language called today, Akkadian, which earlier this century was called Assyrian or Babylonian-Assyrian, was like an international language in the Middle Eastern region. Thus from king lists or chronicles written in Akkadian on clay tablets found in the last two centuries, we today learn about the history of Egypt and the other nations of the region. But there is a great vagueness to the Akkadian script. In one sense it was like a shorthand script. Many signs in Akkadian represent the same sound: these are "homophonous signs."; and one cuneiform sign or symbol can represent a number of different values: these signs are called "polyphonous signs" (*A Manual of Akkadian*, David Marcus, 1978, p. 4 & 15). "When dealing with a polyphonous sign the correct value must be selected for the transliteration. This is determined by elimination based on vowel and consonantal harmony, and on a knowledge of the grammar and the lexicon" (p. 15). "Cuneiform uses word-signs frequently and many of its syllable-signs have several possible phonetic values. Only the advanced student, with the help of his grammatical knowledge, can select the correct reading from a plethora of possibilities by eliminating what is grammatically possible" (*An Akkadian Grammar*, 1975, p. ii, see pp. 9-11).

cp288» One cuneiform sign can be translated as *pe*, or *pi*, or *wa*, or *we*, or *wi*, or *wu*. "The above list [in King's book] will be somewhat simplified by observing that the same signs are employed for *ab*, *ib*, *ub* and for *ap*, *ip*, *up* respectively; that the same signs are employed for *ag*, *ig*, *ug*, for *ak*, *ik*, *uk* and for *ak*, *ik*, *uk*; that the same signs are employed for *ad*, *id*, *ud*, for *at*, *it*, *ut*, and for *at*, *it*, *ut*; and that the same signs are employed for *az*, *iz*, *uz*, for *as*, *is*, *us* and for *as*, *is*, *us*" (L.W. King, *Assyrian Language*, p. 57, pub. 1901). What applies to the Babylonian-Assyrian languages (Akkadian) also applied to other languages written in cuneiform:

- "The principle of using several signs to represent the same sound (gu) is called homophony, and giving one sign several values (like KA) is called polyphony. Both principles are fundamental features of cuneiform writing throughout its 3,000 year history" (*Cuneiform*, C.B.F. Walker, 1987, p. 12).

Thus concerning Woolley's book on Ur, "A similar advance has occurred in the understanding of the Sumerian language and the names given today to the persons whose tombs Woolley excavated are no longer those he used in his text. Shub-ab is actually Pu-abi and the later Neo-Sumerian kings Dungi and Bur-Sin are Shulgi and Amar-sin" (Shirley Glubok, *Discovering the Royal Tombs at Ur*, pub. 1969, 'Foreword').

cp289» In other words there is great variety of choice in translating cuneiform script. This adds to the uncertainty about the name of kings in king lists and for comparing Biblical names with cuneiform names. This causes confusion when we try to decipher ancient documents.

Pul and Tiglath-Pileser

cp290» Pul is mentioned in the Bible as being a separate king from Tiglath-pileser (2 Kings 15:19-20, 29; 1 Chron 5:26, the "he" in this text refers to God not to Tiglath-Pileser or Pul; see CP5 in Text). Ptolemy's list of kings does have a "Pulu" reigning in Babylon after Ukin-zer. One Assyrian King list has "Pulu" reigning for two years in Babylon after Ukin-zer reigned three years while another list has Tiglath-Pileser reigning for two years in Babylon after Ukin-zer reigned for three years (Grayson, *Assyrian and Babylonian Chronicles*, p. 248). Some say that Pul and Tiglath-Pileser are the same king. There may have been a co-kingship of Pul and Tiglath-Pileser or some other explanation. Or merely that the same king used different names for some of his kingdoms, depending on custom.

[Grayson, p. XXI, see pp. 29 paragraphs 172 & 173, p. 36 paragraph 222, p. 50 paragraph 323, and p. 83 footnote 178; and see Grayson's "Problematical Battles in Mesopotamian History" in Studies Landsberger pp. 337-342]

Non-Accessional versus Accessional System of Counting

cp291» There is the non-accessional year method of counting regnal years where the first year is not counted from the first New Year's day, but from the year they became king (see above under "Israel's Non-Accessional Year System"). Thus, it is important to know if a kingdom used the accessional year system or the non-accessional year system when trying to ascertain the count of years for kings of different kingdoms.

"Began to Reign"

cp292» The phrase "began to reign" in about 284 cases in the King James Version and other English version of the Bible comes from the Hebrew word *malak*. This word means, "to reign, or to be king." This is Strong's number 4427, found in Strong's concordance.

cp293» From my personal study of the words "began to reign" in the Bible concerning the united kingdom and the divided kingdom, I found that the phrase indicated the king's *first* year of reign, whether the accessional year or non-accessional year method was used, if the king was counted as ruling for at least one year. But in the case of those kings who used the accession year method, but never ruled on a New Year's day (and therefore were not officially counted as ruling for a year or more), thus were counted as ruling only for months or days; they "began to reign" in the last official year of the king that preceded them. This was the case of Jehoahaz and Jehoiachin.

cp294» In the case of 2 Kings 25:27, the phrase "he began to reign" comes from the Hebrew word *malak*, but with the Hebrew suffix for "he" added. In this case *malak* becomes, *malekhow*. If you count Jehoiachin years of captivity inclusively, as we have in this edition, then Evil-Merodach let Jehoiachin go from his captivity in his first year.

Mistakes in Other Chronologies

cp295» Because of the mistakes in the Greek translation of the original Hebrew text, because of misunderstanding of figures of speech in the Bible, because of the misunderstanding of the broad meaning of some Hebrew words, because of the lack of knowledge of the culture and laws of the Old Testament Jews, and because of the use of excuses such as "copyist error," there have been many mistakes in previous attempts at forming a correct Biblical chronology.

Chaos

cp296» The Bible projects again and again astronomical chaos: hailstones and fire from the heavens; great earthquakes; the Sun, Moon, and Earth in chaos; mountains and valleys lifted up and down; the great Flood; the 360 day year versus today's year length, and so forth. The craterous face of the moon, rocks from the Moon and Mars on the face of the earth, reversals of the earth's magnetic poles, and so forth also project great upheaval in the past (see later in cp129ff).

Co-reigns

cp297» As in the case of the kings of Judah and Israel, sometimes more than one king reigned at the same time, co-regencies. Both Nabonidus and Belshazzar of Babylon ruled at the same time (see CP5). Both Darius the Mede and Cyrus the Persian reigned at the same time in the same kingdom. (See the book of Daniel and the Text of our chronology for more details.)

Dating Methods Differ

cp298» Sometimes there was confusion as to when the start of a king's reign began: "Alexander was recognized in Egypt probably shortly after his invasion, late in 332. He was recognized in Babylon after Gaugamela in October, 331. Cuneiform evidence for the period of Alexander is confused, since two systems of dating were used. One system reckoned year 1 of Alexander as beginning April 3, 330; the other counted from his Macedonian accession, with year 1 as 336..." (*Babylonian Chronology 626 B.C.-A.D. 75*, by Parker and Dubberstein, p. 19).

cp299» Some nations start the reigns of their kings in the fall or spring or other times of the year (*Handbook of Biblical Chronology* [1964], by Jack Finegan, pp. 77-100). Some nations changed their system over the years (see cp216).

cp300» Some nations used the non-accessional year system for regnal years, others used the accessional year system. Some switched from one system to another (see cp211ff).

Artificially Longer Reigns

cp301» Kings changed the length of their reigns in their chronicles in order to make themselves more important in history or in the case of non-contemporary chronicles to fill interregnum periods (p. 11 Parker and Dubberstein; pp 25ff Anstey).

Non-Contemporary Evidence

cp302» Claudius Ptolemaeus (Ptolemy) wrote his Canon more than half a millennium after the time of the Babylonian empire. Berosus, a Chaldean priest at Babylon wrote a history of Babylon a quarter of a millennium after the Babylonian empire and only partial copies or translations or quotes of his work remain. The writings of Josephus which mention the Babylonian empire were written more than half a millennium after the Babylonian empire. The *Sedar Olam Rabbah*, containing the chronology of the world as reckoned by Jews was written after the destruction of Jerusalem and thus after the pertinent chronological documents were hidden away or destroyed by the Romans' attack on the city and temple. Some say the *Sedar Olam Rabbah* was written in the 2nd Century after Christ; there seems to be no real proof of its date. Many other works quoted by chronologists are made up of non-contemporary evidence (see Anstey's Chronology).

Different Meaning of the Hebrew *Ben*

cp303» "A male son," but "The name of son, like those of father and brother ... is of wide extent in Hebrew, and is variously applied. It is used — (1) Of a *grandson* ... also *descendants* .. (2). It is a name of age, for *boy, youth* .. (3). is applied to a *subject*, rendering obedience to a king or lord, as to a father, 2 Ki 16:7.. (4). a *foster son*, who is brought up like a son ... and a *disciple* .. (5). Followed by a gen. *of place*, it denotes *a man there born*, or *brought up*, 'sons of Zion,' .. (6). Followed by a gen. *of time*, it denotes *a person* or *thing*, either *born* or *appearing in that time* or as *having existed during that time*. Thus, 'son of his old age,' .. (7). Followed by a genitive denoting *virtue, vice* or *condition of life*; it denotes *a man who has that virtue or vice*, or who *has been brought up in that condition* ..." (Gesenius' *Hebrew-Chaldee Lexicon of the Old Testament*).

cp304» ***Other Hebrew words*** translated into such English words as *daughter* (# 1323), *sister* (# 269), *brother* (# 251), and *mother* (# 517) have also broad meaning in Hebrew. Some of the confusion in other Biblical chronologies exists because some have not understood the broad meaning of these and other Hebrew words.

CP4: Chronology and Christ

Methods for Finding Christ's Birth, Baptism, and Death

cp305» We have connected our Biblical chronology to the Christian Era system through the information in the Bible on kings in the last stages of Judah and the Babylonian king Nebuchadnezzar, and because there is an astronomical cuneiform tablet that connects Nebuchadnezzar's 37th year with the Christian Era date 568-567 BC. (See CP3) This allows us to call the 37th year of Nebuchadnezzar (568-567 BC) an absolute date. Because this was the 37th year of Nebuchadnezzar, because of the scripture that connects the first official year of Nebuchadnezzar to the 4th year Jehoiakim (Jer 25:1), and because of other scriptures and cuneiform tablets that connect various events in Nebuchadnezzar's reign and events in Judah and the surrounding areas, we are assured of the connection between the Christian Era system (BC-AD dates) and the years of many events in the Old Testament of the Bible. Although this connects events in the Old Testament to the BC-AD dates, it does *not* tell us exactly which Christian Era year Christ was born on or died on or how long Christ lived.

Christian Era

cp306» To date from Christ's time onward most modern historians use the system of secular chronology that Dionysius helped to establish sometime in the sixth century AD. This is sometimes called the "Christian Era" system.

cp307» Even more sacred to some than Ptolemy's chronology is the Dionysius's chronological system, or the B.C. - A.D. system, or Christian Era system. "BC" or "B.C." means "before Christ." While "AD" or "A.D." means *Anno Domini* in Latin or "in the year of the Lord" in English. Almost all chronologists today use this system. There is a slight difference between the Christian Era system and the astronomical system (see CP2, "No Zero Year").

Dionysius Exiguus

cp308» To help us understand the Christian Era system, we will look first at Dionysius and his system.

- Dionysius Exiguus (Dionysius the "Little") was a "Roman monk, chronologist, and scholar, a transmitter of Greek thought to the Middle Ages. He made collections of 5th century papal decrees and the canonical documents of the early church councils. Dionysius, in an attempt to improve the reckoning of the date of Easter, was the first (525) to use our present system of reckoning a date from the time of the birth of Christ" (p. 767, *The New Columbia Encyclopedia*, 4th Ed., 1975).

- "It was not until the year A.D. 532 that the Christian Era was invented by Dionysius Exiguus, a Scythian by birth, and a Roman Abbot. He flourished in the reign of Justinian (A.D. 527-565). He was unwilling to connect his cycles of dates with the era of the impious tyrant and persecutor Diocletian, which began with the year A.D. 284, but chose rather to date the times of the years from the incarnation of our Lord Jesus Christ '**to the end that the commencement of our hope might be better known to us and that the cause of man's restoration, namely, our redeemer's passion, might appear with clearer evidence**.' The year following that in which Dionysius Exiguus wrote these words to Bishop Petronius was the year 248 of the Diocletian Era. Hence the new Era of the Incarnation as it was then reckoned was 284 + 248 = A.D. 532" (Martin Anstey, *Chronology of the Old Testament*, p. 33 [p. 19]).

Here it says Dionysius dated his system from "the birth of Christ" or "to date the times of the years from the incarnation of our Lord Jesus Christ." This is what is credited to him now.

cp309» Dionysius' "new chronology [dating system] was not regarded as a major discovery by its author; Dionysius' own letters are all dated by the indiction... The indiction was a cycle of 15 years originally based on the interval between imperial tax assessments but during the Middle ages always reckoned from the accession of Constantine, in 312" (*Encyclopedia Britannia*, 15th Ed., 1985, Vol. 20, p. 651, under heading, "History," and subheading, "Christian: The Christian Era"; see CP2 & 3).

cp310» This system credited to Dionysius (although in his own letters he does not use the system) is said to be called by some the "Era of the Incarnation." This Era of the Incarnation "was used in Italy in the sixth century, in France in the seventh century, and in England also in the seventh century, but not universally adopted in England until the ninth century.." (John J. Bond, *Handy Book of Rules and Tables for Verifying Dates with the Christian Era*, p. 212).

cp311» According to the *Greek Harmony of the Gospels*, "this era was first used in historical works by Venerable Bede early in the 8th century" (as quoted in *Unger's Bible Dictionary*, 3rd ed., p. 198).

Therefore Dionysius did *not* in the truest sense introduce the B.C. - A.D. dating system! The dating system began to be used later by others long after Dionysius' death.

What System did Dionysius Introduce?

cp312» What Dionysius introduced was a system or table to identify the Passover each year and from that to identify the Easter date each year; it was a system to determine the Paschal Cycle.

cp313» "The Orient and the West were divided on the question of the way to determine the date of Easter. The council of Nicaea had commanded the adoption of the Alexandrine rule, based on the 19-year cycle. At Rome, a tradition had been adopted that declared Easter should not be celebrated before March 25 or after April 21, and the basis for calculation was the old 84-year cycle. Tables for the dates of Easter had been prepared in the Orient by Theophilus of Alexandria, and St. Cyril had continued his work. In the West tables were drawn up by Victorius of Aquitaine. They terminated with the year A.D. 531, **and had as their respective points of departure the reign of Diocletian, for the Orient; and the Passion, for the West**. In the *Liber de Paschate* (PL 67:483-508), Dionysius recommended the adoption of the Alexandrine cycle, as required by the Council of Nicaea, whose decisions were universally respected. He established a **table of Paschal dates** up to the year 626, which was a continuation of the table of Cyril of Alexandria..." (p. 877, "Dionysius Exiguus." *The New Catholic Encyclopedia*, 1967).

cp314» What Dionysius did was to create a table of Passover dates or Easter dates, but he dated from the year *one* "to the end that the commencement of our hope might be better known to us and that the cause of man's restoration, namely, our Redeemer's *passion*, might appear with clearer evidence" (Anstey, p. 33). And "we have been unwilling to connect our cycle with the name of an impious persecutor, but have chosen rather to note the years from the *incarnation* of our Lord Jesus Christ" (Finegan [1964], sec 218).

cp315» Our Redeemer Jesus Christ's *passion* was his suffering and death on the day the Jews' killed their Passover lamb, the 14th of Nisan (John 19:14, 31, 42; Num 9:1-14; see CP4).

cp316» The table of the Paschal Cycle, or the Passover Cycle, or the Easter Cycle was written, according to Anstey, to make "better known to us ... our Redeemer's *passion*." But according to Finegan the cycle started "from the *incarnation* of our Lord Jesus Christ."

March 25th: the Confusion

cp330» Dionysius started his system not from December 25th or late Summer to the early Fall when Christ was **born**, but March 25th, the Julian date that some believe Christ probably **died** on.

cp331» "The system of reckoning the Christian era, now in use, was introduced by Dionysius Exiguus A.D. 533, **commencing with the 25th of March**, but subsequently reckoned from Christmas-day, in some countries, was reckoned from the 1st of January according to the year of the Julian era..." (Bond, p. 21).

cp332» "The system of commencing the year on the 25th of March was observed in various countries during several centuries; and in England, where it has been known as the English legal year, it was in use until 1751 A.D., after which date the year in England was reckoned from the 1st of January, according to the Julian form of year introduced 45 years before 1 *Anno Domini* of the Dionysian reckoning.

cp333» "Particular attention should be given to the system of writing dates according to the English legal year, as it was called, mistakes having been made by confusing that form of year with the Julian year commencing on the 1st of January. There are not many historians who recognize the English legal system, and we are not aware that it has been noticed in any correct list of regnal years of the English Sovereigns, in modern works, before the first edition of this work was published...

cp334» "The reign of James the First furnishes an illustration of the '*historical*' confusion of dates, as that reign began on the 24th of March, 1602, according to the English system, the next day being called the 25th of March, 1603. While in Scotland, the date of the Accession of James to the English throne was 1603, the Julian form of year having been ordered to be used in Scotland in the year 1600, by proclamation, dated the 17th of December, 1599" (Bond pp. xvi & xvii).

cp335» "It was not until 1752 A.D. that the year in England commenced on the 1st of January, and the 29th of February was written so as to accord entirely with the form of the Julian year" (Bond, p. xx).

cp336» Today many interpret that Dionysius started his system on March 25th because at that time the 25th of March was felt to be the annunciation to Mary (see Finegan [1964], ¶ 219).

cp337» Dionysius system from the beginning started from March 25th. Over a period of time it was changed to various times until finally today it mostly begins on January 1st of each year. But from the beginning it was March 25th:

- Anastasius, a Bishop of Antioch, states, that our Lord suffered, in his 33rd year, on the 14th day of the moon, the 29th of Phamenoth (see Bond p. 222f). The month "Phamenoth" is from the Egyptian Civil Calendar (Finegan [1964], ¶ 49 & Table 8). This month had 30 days corresponding to the Julian year dates of Feb 25th (or 26th for intercalary years) for the 1st of Phamenoth to March 26th for the 30th of Phamenoth. Even in intercalary years the 29th of Phamenoth was always March 25th. **Therefore the 29th of Phamenoth was March 25th.**
- The 25th of March was when Jesus Christ suffered or was "crucified" (Bond p. 222, quoted by Anastasius from a fragment of the *Apostolic Constitutions*).
- The 25th of March was when the system of Dionysius began (Bond, p. 21).
- England began its year from the 25th of March "after the sixth century, until 1066. 1 January to 31 December, 1067 to 1155. 25 March to 24 March, 1155 to 1750-1" (Bond, p. 91).
- In Scotland the year was reckoned from March 25th to March 24th until 1599 (Bond, p. 92).
- In France the year was from March 25th to March 24th until 1564. Many other countries also dated their year from March 25th to March 24 (see Bond, p. 91 to 101).

March 25ᵗʰ: Incarnation & Birth Confusion

cp338» According to Augustine (c.354-430 A.D.), Bishop of Hippo:

- "For He [Christ] is believed to have been conceived on the twenty-fifth of March, upon which day also he suffered .... But he was born, according to tradition, upon December the twenty-fifth." [Finegan [1964], ¶ 407; *On the Trinity*, Book IV, Chap 5 found in the *Christian Classics Ethereal Library* on the Wheaton College web page.]

Paschal Cycle

cp339» The Dionysius system is also called the Paschal Cycle: "The cycle is composed of 532 years, on the completion of which, the Easter-days recur in the same order as before, if the cycle of Golden Numbers be not changed. The solar cycle 28, and the Lunar cycle 19, multiplied together make the cycle of 532 years" (Bond p. 125).

cp340» "A.D. 532 *Dionysius Exiguus* commenced his cycle of 19 years [the lunar cycle] with Golden Number I. ... And further, — Dionysius by making Golden Number I of his cycle of 19 years fall to 532, made Number II fall to 1 A.D" (Bond, p xli, & see p. 223).

cp341» Thus, the year just before A.D. 1 had the same Golden Number as A.D. 532, which is I (Bond, p. 127). *If* Dionysius dated from the passion, then A.D. 1 was the first anniversary of the passion, the year 532 being the 532nd anniversary, and the year 1987 being the 1,987th anniversary of Christ's passion, thus "to the end that the commencement of our hope might be better known to us and that the cause of man's restoration, namely, **our Redeemer's passion, might appear with clearer evidence**" (Dionysius, as translated from Migne's *Patrologiae*).

cp342» "And further, — Dionysius by making Golden Number I of his cycle of 19 years fall to 532, made Number II fall to 1 A.D. of his reckoning, as well as to 533 with the year-Letter B, and thus the 27th of March was the date of Easter-day for 533 A.D. while the 25th of March, the date of 'the annunciation' was commemorated for Good Friday; hence we have the supposititious statement of some writers, that our Lord suffered on the 25th of March" (Bond, p. xli).

cp343» We disagree that the Lord suffered on a Friday (See CP4). But we quote here from Bond so you can see some of the thinking of those trying to ascertain the date of Christ's "annunciation" and or "passion," and to show you again the mixing together of Christ's conception and his death in the thinking of some.

When was Christ Born?

cp344» "But the modern chronologist is confronted with no inconsiderable difficulty at the very outset to fix the *exact date* of the nativity of Jesus Christ ... This is due to the fact that he is compelled to base his computation on dateless documents written in a remote antiquity. For neither sacred nor profane authors in those times were at all accustomed to record historical facts under distinct dates. All demands were satisfied when known occurrences were referred to definite periods, as within a certain generation, or under a specific dynasty, or within the reign of a given ruler already familiar to the contemporaries addressed" (*Unger's Bible Dict.*, p. 197, col. 2).

A.U.C. Date

cp345» Modern writers state that Dionysius connected the start of his table with the year 754 A.U.C. [*A.U.C.* stands for *anno urbis conditae* or "in the year of the founded city." The founded city being Rome.] They then state that he made a mistake and that the year was really 750 A.U.C (Bond, pp. x-xi; Unger, *Dict.* p. 198; etc.). Thus, today many believe that Dionysius made an error in dating Christ's birth of from 4 to 7 years (p. 877, *The New Catholic Encyclopedia*). "The *common consensus* of eminent biblicists is that he [Dionysius] erred in his conclusion by at least four years" (*Unger's Bible Dict.* p. 198, col. 1). But nowhere in Dionysius' document does he even mention A.U.C. or any thing to do with any date about the foundation of the city of Rome.

Diverse Dating Methods and Assumptions

cp346» Dionysius' *letter* in which he set forth his system, was called "Epistolae Duae De Ratione Paschae." A copy is found in *Patrologiae*, LXVII, 19 ff. It was *not* dated by the A.U.C. system, or the Era of Olympiads, or the Era of Seleucid. It was *not* dated according to the rule of some king. It only indirectly dated through the BC-AD system. He is said to have dated his letters by the indiction (*Ency. Brit.*, 15th Ed., Vol 20, p. 681, 15th Ed., 1985). Copies of papyri letters in such books as C.K. Barrett's *The New Testament Background* are dated by the year of the reign of kings, not the so-called era of Augustus. Furthermore, it was only in about the last 200 years that most nations started dating with BC-AD system. Their old methods and dates may have been wrong, thus when they converted their history to BC-AD dates mistakes may have been made. Dionysius, himself, did not use the BC-AD system. Others after Dionysius started to date by the AD system, but not commonly until the 18th century. And it was only in the 18th century that writers started to date events happening before Christ by using "B.C" (before Christ) in connection with the date (Finegan [1964], ¶ 220).

cp347» Many writers assume that Dionysius dated Christ's birth from 1 AD with this being the first year of Christ. This is only an assumption since nowhere does Dionysius state clearly the date of Christ's birth or conception. Dionysius, himself, did not use or invent the BC-AC terminology. His table was a Passover table. His cycle is a cycle of 532 years. The cycle is made up of the 28 year solar cycle and the 19 year lunar cycle. 28 times 19 is 532 years. Each year of Dionysius' 532 year cycle is numbered from 1 to 19. When the year number reaches 19, the next number is 1. These numbers indicate the year of the 19 year lunar cycle. His cycle supposedly began on March 25th, 532 AD. If this date is correct, the evidence does not point to 1 AD, but to 1 BC. This is so since the first year of his lunar-solar cycle of 19 years can be retro-calculated to 1 BC, because it began in 532 BC, which is one cycle of 532 years since 1 BC (Bond, p. 127 ff; *PL*, LXVII, p. 493 ff).

To Review

cp348» By reviewing the beginning of the Christian Era system we again manifest the difficulty of chronology. What Dionysius *apparently* did was to connect his Passover Table to Christ's conception, March 25th 1 BC (see above). In some manner he also connected his table to the Passion or death of Christ, which he supposed was also March 25th. Dionysius' Passover Table was a continuation of two other tables before his. One of them in the West dated from the Passion. But there are other problems with some of the assumptions and lack of clear evidence for some dates.

Christ's Possible Birth Dates
Using Dionysius' System

cp349» As we just saw, Dionysius Exiguus is the one who is credited with inventing the Christian Era system. Dionysius' system was a continuation of two older systems that supposedly went back to 297 AD and 284 AD and even to the Passion (Bickerman, pp. 78-79, 72-73, 81). We just learned that the date that Dionysius started his system was March 25th. March 25th was the date he assumed Christ was conceived on and/or died on. Most today, through various methods, date Christ's birth from about 7 BC to 1 AD with one at 13-12 BC. Jack Finegan in his *Handbook of Biblical Chronology* [1964] gives a review of pertinent information on this subject (pp. 215-258) cp350» According to Finegan, most dates from early Christian sources give dates for Christ's birth that *translate* from 4/3 BC to 1 AD (Finegan [1964], Table 107; etc.). The following gives a date between 3 to 2 BC, and two at c. 13-12 BC:

- Tertullian, *An Answer to the Jews* (c. 198 AD)
- Julius Africanus, *Chronographies* (c. 170-240 AD)
- Hippolytus of Rome, *Chronicle*, (c. 170-236 AD)
- Origen, *Homilies on Luke*, (c. 185-253 AD)
- Eusebius of Caesarea *Church History*, (c. 325 AD)
- Epiphanius, *Panarion*, (c. 315-403 AD)
- Vardaman & Nikos Kokkinos give a date of Christ's birth at 12 BC:
Jerry Vardaman, *New Chronology of the New Testament* (1998); See Vardaman's *Chronology and early Church History in the New Testament*, 1998 Lectures, Hong Kong Bapist Theological Seminary [Web Link located just before Endnotes: www.catholicplanet.com/articles/article108.htm; and see Finegan [1998], ¶ 521 & 543.
- If you look at our 6000 year chronology table in this book, you will see **that Jesus was crucified [died] in April, 31 AD** on Wednesday at a full moon, and that an eclipse of the moon had occurred on April 10, 1 BC (Julian Cal.) about 12 weeks before Herod died and about a year and a half after Christ was born (ab. 3 BC).

Eclipse: Days of Herod – Some Proof for JC Birth Date

cp351» Matthew 2:1 says that Jesus was born "in the days of Herod the King." There are different ways of dating Herod's reign (Finegan [1964], ¶ 432; Finegan [1998], ¶ 521 & 543). Herod died sometime after Christ's birth maybe as much as two years (Matt Chap 2).

cp352» Josephus in his *Antiquities of the Jews* mentions an eclipse of the moon before Herod's death (Bk. 17, Chap. 6, ¶ 4). This is the only eclipse mentioned by Josephus in his known works. According to Josephus, this eclipse happened on the very night that the leader of a sedition against Herod was burnt alive (Josephus, *Antiquities of the Jews*, book 17, chap. 6, ¶ 4; see Josephus, *War of the Jews*, book 1, chap. 33, ¶ 2-4).

cp353» This eclipse may have been the total eclipse that happened on April 10, 1 BC on the Julian calendar **or** the eclipse on March 29, 4 BC.

cp354» Before Herod died he killed the youths of Bethlehem and the surrounding area from two years and under in accordance to the time the wise men's star appeared (Mat 2:16). Herod died sometime after Christ was a "young child." Therefore Christ *may* have been up to one or two years old just before the eclipse. In our table in CP5, we have Christ being in His first year at the time of the March 29th eclipse in 4 BC.

cp355» **The Bible does not mention an eclipse**, so there is no Biblical evidence one way or another concerning an eclipse near Christ's birth. Because of what we learn about the "identification game" in CP2, we cannot identify any event in the past by only one eclipse: *thus this eclipse is not definitive*. Although, an eclipse along with other evidence could help in identifying Christ birth, death, and resurrection.

Rule of Caesar Augustus

cp356» In Luke 2:1 it says that Christ was born under the rule of Caesar Augustus. There are various ways to date the reign of Augustus. Finegan in his *Handbook of Biblical Chronology* [1964] shows 5 different ways of counting Augustus' reign (Finegan [1964] Table 96, [1998] table 128). Depending on which method is used the date for Christ's birth varies. (Finegan [1964], pp. 215 ff) One way of dating Augustus' reign is to assume that Eusebius of Caesarea (c. 325 AD) is correct in dating Christ's birth in the "twenty-eighth year after the submission of Egypt and the death of Antony and Cleopatra" (Finegan, p. 226; see Table 96, col. 3, 4, 5). But the Bible does not mention the regnal year of Augustus in connection with the birth of Christ. In the data alone concerning Augustus's connection to Christ's birth there is no absolute evidence for the BC-AD date of his birth.

Governor Cyrenius/Quirinius

cp357» Luke 2:1-5 speaks of the enrollment for taxation when Cyrenius or Quirinius was governor of Syria. This was at the time Mary the mother of Christ was pregnant. She gave birth during this time (v. 6-7). "Tertullian says in fact that the census at the time of the birth of Jesus was 'taken in Judea by Sentius Saturninus.' A study of the possible year(s) when Quirinius was governor of Syria shows there is no absolute way of dating his governorship, thus there is no absolute evidence of the BC-AD date for Christ's birth through the Quirinius connection.

Fall Birth Date

cp358» The part of the year Christ may have been born in was the Fall. It is traditional for many to say that Christ was born on Dec 25 or Jan 6. Because of evidence that indicate that Christ's ministry lasted three and one-half years after he was about 30 years old (see below), and because Christ died in the Spring on the Passover, then Christ was born in the Fall.

Star

cp359» In Matthew 2:1-2 it mentions a "star" in connection with Christ's birth. Since we do not know for sure what was meant by this star (planet, star, group of stars, new star, comet, conjunction, etc.), the reference in the Bible does not really help us identify Christ's birth in relation to BC-AD dates.

Baptism & Death

cp360» The approximate date of Christ's baptism and the length of Christ's life may be ascertained through scripture and through secular evidence, if any reliable secular evidence can be found.

Tiberius' 15th Year

cp361» In Luke 3:1-3 it connects the beginning of the preaching of John the Baptist in the 15th year of "Tiberius Caesar, Pontius Pilate being governor of Judea, and Herod being tetrarch of Galilee, and his brother Philip tetrarch of Ituraea and of the region of Trachonitis, and Lysanias the tetrarch of Abilene, Annas and Caiaphas being the high priests."

cp362» There are at least 4 different ways of counting Tiberius Caesar's reign. (See Finegan [1964], Table 115, and paragraph 409 [1998] Table 150) It should be noted that Luke 3:1-3 is speaking about *when* John the Baptist began to teach. Through scripture it can be shown that John began his ministry 6 months before Christ started his own ministry, and six months before his water baptism (Luke 1:11-33; cf. Num 4:2, 3; Luke 3:23).

cp363» There is also dubiousness about the time of the year that Tiberius started his count of years, and dubiousness about the method Luke used to count Tiberius's years. This again gives no absolute way of dating Christ's life in BC-AD dates.

30 Years Old

cp364» From Luke 3:23 we see that Christ began to be about 30 in the 15ᵗʰ [16th] year of Tiberius. But in this time he was baptized by John who was teaching in the wilderness (Luke 3:1-23). This time was also the 15th (or 16th year depending on method of counting regnal years and remembering that Christ was baptized six months after John first went into the wilderness to teach) of Tiberius Caesar. In this time period Christ also started his teaching (Luke 3:23; 4:1-16).

46 Years of the Temple

cp365» In John 2:20, at the time of one of Christ's passovers during his 3 ½ years of teaching (John 2:13), some Jews said that the Temple in Jerusalem was in its 46th year of building, or it was 46 years after it was rebuilt. Josephus states in his *Wars of the Jews* that in the "fifteenth year of his reign, Herod rebuilt the temple" (Book 1, Chap XXI, ¶ 1). But in Josephus' *Antiquities of the Jews* he says, "Herod, in the eighteenth year of his reign, and after the acts already mentioned, undertook a very great work, that is, to build of himself the temple of God" (Book 15, Chap XI, ¶ 1). And Josephus said in his *Wars of the Jews*, "So, Herod, having survived the slaughter of his son five days, died, having reigned thirty-four years since he had caused Antigonus to be slain, and obtained his kingdom; but thirty-seven years since he had been made king by the Romans" (Book 1, Chap XXIII, ¶ 8). According to Finegan "there is a difference of three years between the two possible beginning points for the reign of Herod ... when he was named king, and ... when he actually took Jerusalem" (¶ 432). Finegan's dates for Herod are in his [1964] Table 108 [1998] Table 140.

So in his 15ᵗʰ/18th year, Herod after he took Jerusalem, began to rebuild or restore the temple. At the time of John 2:20 , the temple had been in its 46ᵗʰ year of restoration.

Olympiads & Seleucid Years

cp366» By comparing Josephus *Ant.* Book 14 Chap XIV, ¶ 8 with Book 16, Chap V, ¶ 1, we see that Herod received his reign in the 184th Olympiad, year 4, his first year being the 185th Olympiad and his 28th year the 191st Olympiad, 4th year. If Josephus counted the Era of the Olympiads correctly, and if we could correctly place Josephus' count of the Olympiads in the Christian Era system we would have the correct years of Herod the Great. But as Bond indicates in his *Handy Book ...*, "the old era of Olympiads appears only to have been used by writers, and especially by historians. It does not seem to have been ever adopted by any state in public documents. It is never found on any coins, and scarcely ever on inscriptions" (p. 192, Bond). There is no hard connection between the Era of Olympiads and the Christian Era system. In Josephus' work there is a connection between the Era of Olympiads and the Era of Seleucid (*Ant.* Book 12, V, ¶ 4; book 12, VII, ¶ 6). But as we will see in CP2, there are two starting points to the Era of Seleucid, one in Egypt and one elsewhere. 1 AD is only "said to coincide with Ol. 195.1" (p. 193, Bond) if Dionysius dated his table's start from Christ's birth.

Length of Life

cp367» Irrespective of this confusion, as stated above, we see that Christ began to be about 30 years old when he began to teach. He died according to scripture after his few 3 ½ years of ministry. We ascertain the length of his ministry by how many Passovers he taught on. Finegan [1964] gives a somewhat detailed explanation on how to ascertain the length (¶ 436-443 [596-603]). What it comes down to are the 3 Passovers mentioned (2:13; 6:4; 11:55) in the book of John and the one implied in John 5:1, or between 4:35 and 5:1. Also depending on how you interpret Dan 9:27 and the weeks of years, this scripture indicates a 7 year period with Christ being cut off in the middle of the 7 years: 3 ½ years (See William E. Biederwolf, *The Second Coming Bible*, p. 224). See our chronology table.

To Review

cp368» What connects Christ to Roman history is that he was born in the rule of Augustus, at the time of the taxation by Quirinius, in the last days of Herod the Great, just before an eclipse (up to two years before). He was 30 years old in the 15th/16th year of Tiberius (see above). He died on the 14th of Nisan on a Wednesday three and one-half years after he turned 30 years old. But scripture does not give which regnal year of Augustus Christ was born on, yet others state in the 28th year. Because of the confusion for the beginning of certain key Roman rulers, because of the uncertainty of the way these rulers' years were counted (by local methods, by Roman methods, accession year or non-accession year method, etc.), there is a 3 to 4 year uncertainty concerning the years of certain key rulers of the Roman Empire.

Difficulty of Connecting the Christian Era With Other Systems

cp369» *Connection Between Christ's Time and Other Systems.* There are methods to translate the years of Roman leaders into the Christian Era dates (Bickerman, *Chronology of the Ancient World*, 1968, pp. 80 ff; Finegan, pp 215 ff). But we must be careful here:

- "A casual glance at the texts of Livy or Diodorus Siculus will suggest the validity of Bickerman's conclusion that the Romans dated by consuls ... The system like the Athenian archon list, was cumbersome and inefficient. Although the Romans could have tied their chronography to Olympiads or to an early event like the fall of Troy ... they chose to try to create a system with an epoch that of the founding date of Rome.... A number of such systems were devised, but as Roman scholarship never reached a consensus in the founding date, each of the systems was at variance with the others..." (Alan E. Samuel, *Greek and Roman Chronology* [1972], pp. 249-50).

Ptolemy: The king list of Ptolemy which is used by some for chronology purposes is just that a list of kings with what Ptolemy thought was the length of their reigns. His testimony cannot be compared with continuous records of contemporary witnesses because there are gaps in records and other problems (Also see CP2 & CP3).

Censorinus: Censorinus was a Latin writer who according to contemporary dates wrote or published a work called *De die Natali* in the year A.D. 238. He fixed the date of the last Sothic period before his own time. This "fix" is used by Egyptologers in translating the Egyptian Vague year of 365 days into the Julian year of 365 1/4 days. Also he helped to set contemporary dates for the first Olympiad by placing the 1014th year since the first Olympic before the consulship of Ulpius and Pontianus. This makes the first Olympiad occurring in about B.C. 776. Censorinus admits that "there was also some disagreement among different writers, though it is confined within a period of only six or seven years" (*Cory's Ancient Fragments*). But the date 776 BC depends on how Dionysius dated his table. And, remember Dionysius wrote his table 500 years after the fact, leaving him centuries away from the best evidence.

Eusebius' Influence

cp370» Eusebius, who is a father of Ecclesiastical history, relied on others for his chronology:

> • "It was Eusebius who first adopted the hypothetical Era of the Greek Olympiads, and assuming its truth, equated the years there given to the annals of the Old Testament.... The importance of Eusebius lies in the fact that the example which he set, and the figures which he gave, have been followed ever since" (Anstey, *Chron. Old Testament*, p. 45 [25]).

Eusebius assumed something to be true and ever since chronologies have copied his numbers as fact. These assumptions are probably not true.

Christ's Time Identified Through His Death

cp371» Now we will turn to the *death* of Christ and the prophecy as to when He would appear in time. It is his death on a Passover which may help us to identify his year of death and thus his birth and the years of His ministry. Later in CP4 we show that Christ, was killed at the end of a Wednesday near or at sunset on a Jewish Passover, the 14th of Nisan when the lamb was killed. **We look for a Jewish Passover, 14th of Nisan, that occurs on a Wednesday to find out which year Christ died on.** This Passover should be about 2000 years prior to the end of the age in order for the antitype of the three days and three nights to come true. I will not explain this in detail here, but remember the antitypical day is equal to 1000 years, and remember the duality of Daniel 9:26-27.

cp372» Today most believe that Christ died between 27 and 34 AD (Finegan ¶ 455, p. 292 [1964]), with many thinking his death was between 30 and 33 **As of March, 2026 my best educated estimate is that he died on a Wednesday in April 5, 30 AD using the Julian calender.**

Seven Day Patterns in the Bible	
Before the beginning of creation – Planning and Predestination	
Typical or physical Days 24 hours	Anti-typical or Spiritual Days 1000 yrs
1st Day creation of light & darkness	1st Day of 1000 yrs Both God & Satan appeared on earth
2nd Day	2nd Day of 1000 yrs
3rd Day	3rd Day of 1000 yrs
4th Day Sun & Moon's bodies manifested the light on this day	4th Day of 1000 yrs The Messiah manifested in his flesh the True light inside him as the moon manifests the light from the sun. At the end of the 4th day in the week (Wednesday), which was the 4th day of the Passover week, he was killed.
5th Day	5th Day of 1000 yrs
6th Day	6th Day of 1000 yrs
7th Day physical day of rest	7th Day of 1000 yrs The Kingdom of God, a day of rest from evil for mankind. The Messiah is King of kings.

This pattern above is one piece of evidence that the Messiah must have concluded his days on earth in the 4th Millennium, and this is the reason our Chronology must be in harmony with this pattern. Also study NM15 and NM16 to understand better the patterns.

Summary
Christ died on?
cp373» Although we have found no absolute clear evidence for the date of Christ's birth and death, yet we can be reasonably sure because of the Biblical evidence herein that Christ's death in His 33th year (33 ½ years old), as Judah counted her kings' years, in the last year of the 4th millennium: thus fulfilling the antitype for the fourth physical day of creation (Genesis 1:14-19) when the sun, moon, and stars were created. Christ is symbolized by the Sun and Moon (see gp514ff). See our chronology table.

Three Days and Three Nights

cp374» Jesus Christ said the only sign he would give, "an evil and adulterous generation seeks after a sign; and there shall be no sign given to it, but the sign of the prophet Jonah: For as Jonah was three days and three nights in the whale's belly; so shall the Son of man be *three days and three nights* in the heart of the earth" (Matt 12:39-40).

cp375» Read these words again. To the world no other sign would be given to it except that Jesus Christ would be in the grave for "three days and three nights." The sign that proved that Jesus Christ was the Messiah was the sign of him being in the grave for three days and three nights and thereafter being resurrected as other parallel scriptures indicate.

cp376» Jesus Christ said he would be in his tomb for exactly three days and three nights, **not** from about 6 PM Friday to about 6 AM Sunday morning (36 hours) as tradition has it ("But from the evening of the burial to the dawn of the resurrection are thirty-six hours..." *On the Trinity*, by Augustine, Book IV, Chap. 6). Jesus Christ did not make a mistake, he knew his fate. When you examine *all* the scriptures on the duration of Christ's time in the grave it can only be three full days and three full nights. In this paper we will examine these scriptures.

cp377» This is very important. This is not something to give little weight to. Jesus Christ knew he was going to be in the grave for 3 days and 3 nights as scripture indicates, and as we will prove in the remainder of this section.

cp378» Christ did not make a mistake, but traditionalists are making a mistake teaching their misunderstanding of scripture. Why believe anything that Jesus Christ said, if he was wrong about the time he was going to be in the grave, he was probably wrong about other things he said. Jesus Christ said he was going to be in the grave ("heart of the earth") for three days and three nights. He did not say he was going to be in the grave for two nights and one day or any other combination except — three days and three nights. There are scriptures that show how Jesus was in the grave for three full days. Why not believe these scriptures? Why do many still doggedly hold to the mistaken tradition? Is tradition that strong?

cp379» In *The NIV Study Bible*, Zondervan — 1985, it says in its notes concerning Matt 12:40:

- "12:40 *three days and three nights.* Including at least part of the first day and part of the third day, a common Jewish reckoning of time."

This is a mix of two truths. It is a common Hebrew reckoning of time to include part of the first day and part of the last day when counting days inclusively. When the Hebrews used such statements as, "today, tomorrow, and the next day," they meant in some cases not full 24 hour days (Exo 19:10-16; Lev 7:16-18; 19:6-7; Luke 13:32). Depending on what time of the day David spoke in 1 Samuel 20:5, the phrase 'the third day,' may indicate three full days (see verses 20:5, 12, 18-19, 24, 27, 34-35; 21:5; see Esther 4:16; 5:1) because David qualified the third day by saying "the third *day* at evening." Just because it is *possible* in scripture for the phrase "three days and three nights" to mean less than three full 24 hour days, does not mean this is what Christ meant, especially considering all the scriptures pertaining to this event.

cp380» In another work, *The Narrated Bible*, Harvest House published in 1984, it says:

"Traditionally the last supper is believed to have occurred on Thursday evening, followed by the crucifixion on Friday afternoon and the resurrection on Sunday morning. However, such reckoning raises at least two questions. First, in an action-packed final week, what reason is there to believe that there would be a whole day of either actual inactivity or activity which is left unrecorded? Second, and far more important — if Jesus is crucified on Friday afternoon and thereafter hurriedly put into the tomb, how can there be sufficient time to match Jesus' own prediction that he would remain in the tomb for three days and three nights before being resurrected? Even if one stretches imagination within the traditional time frame in order to find parts of three days, it is not possible to find three nights. The resolution of both questions appears to be found in recognizing that the last supper took place on Wednesday evening, followed by the crucifixion and burial on Thursday. Acceptance of that assumption requires an understanding of the Passover, the Feast of Unleavened Bread, and the way in which the Jews reckon time. As for the reckoning of time, the Jewish day begins at sunset on the previous evening. This means, for example, that our Wednesday night is actually [the Jews'] Thursday ..." (pp. 1454-1455).

This opinion is closer to the truth, but not close enough, for if the crucifixion was on Thursday instead of Friday, there still would **not** be three full days and nights between when Jesus was put in the grave and when he was resurrected.

cp381» The resurrection did *not* occur on Sunday morning at sunrise as commonly taught today. Yes, as we will see, Jesus was resurrected at the very end of the week. But he was resurrected *on* the very late evening of Saturday — the Sabbath, the seventh day, not on Sunday morning (see below)

Jews' Day Started After Sunset

cp382» To the Jew the new 24 hour day period started at sunset, not at midnight (Lev 23:27, 32; Deut 16:6, cf Neh 13:19 & Lev 22:6-7; see God's Appointed Times and Seasons, under "Passover"). It begins to get dark or deep shadowing appear before a new day begins (Neh 13:19, see Hebrew). Shortly after the sun goes down it gets dark (Gen 15:17; 28:11, see Hebrew; see John 20:1 in context with Matthew, Mark and Luke, see Greek text). A Jewish day is from evening to evening (Lev 23:32, 27). And it is the evening time when the sun goes down (Deut 16:6). Even today, the Jews celebrate their Sabbath (Saturday) each week beginning after sunset Friday (see *Comprehensive Hebrew Calendar*, by Spier, p. 3).

Counting Days

cp383» There is a method of counting days inclusively in which the first day of the count is started at any time within the day (see Exo 19:10-11; Lev 7:15-17; 19:5-7; for years see: 2 Kings 19:29; Jer 25:3). They could say, for example, today, tomorrow, and the next day. The "next day" being the third day for a count of three days (Exo 19:10-11; Luke 13:32). Today equals the first day, tomorrow the second day, and the next day is the third day. Or they could say, I will meet you the third day. Today being the first day, tomorrow the second day, and the next day the third day. There is a vagueness to this kind of counting because usually when someone counts like this the first day of the count and the last day of the count need not be full 24 hour days. Today is the first day even if they started their counting from the beginning, middle, or end of it. The second day is the second day throughout. The third day is the third day at any time from the beginning to the end of the day. *But there is even a greater vagueness if they started counting the days at the very end or very beginning of a day.* Were they beginning their count from the very end of the "today" or from the very beginning of "tomorrow"? This is what happened to the three days in which Christ was buried: the count of the three days began at exactly the end/beginning of a day. Although when they counted three days they could have meant less than three full days, in no way was the count of three days more that 72 hours.

cp384» There are counts of days that seem to indicate full days (Num 29:12, 17, 20, 23, 26, 29, 32, 35; Est 4:16-5:1; Jonah 1:17; Matt 12:40; Gen 42:17-18; 1Sam 30:12-13).

More Than 36 Hours

cp385» Today most think that Christ died on a Friday afternoon and was resurrected to life on the next Sunday morning at or near sunrise. If this tradition is correct then Christ was only in the grave for about 36 hours. But Christ was very emphatic about his foreknowledge that he would be in the grave for three days and three nights. Most who believe that Christ was in the grave for only about 36 hours also believe that Jesus Christ is God. Can God make a mistake? Can Jesus Christ make a mistake? Concerning the three days and three nights in the grave Christ was most emphatic. In fact he was more emphatic about his time in the grave than about any other statement or any other belief he spoke on.

Death and Resurrection, Scriptures

cp386» Let's look to see how scripture for close to 2,000 years has been manifesting the truth concerning Jesus's statement that he was to be buried for three days and three nights and then be resurrected to life.

cp387» Note the scriptural proof that Jesus Christ the man died about 3PM to 4 PM and was buried at the very last part of the evening just before a Sabbath day:

cp388» (A) Time and Day Buried

- It was the evening of the day (day light time and the 24 hour day) when Jesus died (Mark 15:42; Luke 27:57), about the ninth hour of the day light time (Mark 15:33ff; Matt 27:45ff; Luke 23:44ff). There are 12 hours[2] in the day light time (John 11:9), thus it was about 3PM to 4 PM in the afternoon when Jesus died. It was the evening time, about two to three hours before the sunset. They took down Jesus' body, prepared it and buried it (Mark 15:43ff; Matt 27:57ff; Luke 23:50ff; John 19:38ff), just at the very end of the Jews' Preparation day (John 19:14, 31, 42; cf Matt 27:62) as a Sabbath drew near (Luke 23:54).
- John 19:33ff with Deut 21:23 (see Josh 8:29; 10:26-27) indicate that the body of Jesus could not remain on the cross (tree, stake) during the night, but must be removed that very day before sunset.

cp389» *But what Sabbath?* The Preparation day of the Passover week (note John 19:14) is the day just before the seven days of the Passover Festival of Unleavened Bread. It is the day when the Passover lamb is killed. It is the 14th of Nisan according to the Jewish Calendar. It is just before the first annual Sabbath of the Passover week (see "Passover" in our paper called "God's Appointed Times and Seasons" [NM16]).

---

[2] The length of hours of the day and night are not necessarily equal

cp390» The Passover week had two special or annual Sabbaths besides the regular weekly one: one of these annual Sabbaths was on the 15th of Nisan while the other was on the 21st of Nisan (Num 28:17-18, 25; Deut 16:8; Exo 12:18; see "First Passover week with two Sabbaths" below, and "God's Appointed Times and Seasons" paper [NM16]). Of course there was a regular weekly Sabbath within the Passover week. At the time of Jesus Christ the man's death the 14th day was the Passover day when the lamb was killed (Christ is the antitypical Lamb — the real Passover — 1 Pet 1:19; Heb 9:14; 1 Cor 5:7), it was also the Preparation day (for the Passover lamb and meal), and as scripture projects it was on a Wednesday the year Christ died. Therefore Thursday (15th) was the first annual Sabbath, and Saturday (17th of Nisan) was the regular weekly Sabbath.

Review of "(A) Time and Day Buried." Jesus Christ the man died on the evening of the 14th of Nisan, a Wednesday, which was the Preparation day of the Passover festival. According to the Law, the Passover was sacrificed in the evening, at the going down of the sun (Deut 16:6). Because Christ fulfilled this scripture, Christ was sacrificed in the evening, at the going down of the sun. He was buried just before sunset, or at sunset, just before the 15th of Nisan, an annual Sabbath of the Passover week. Three days later was the very late part of the regular weekly Sabbath, Saturday, the 17th of Nisan.

Note some of the important scriptures concerning the *length* of time that Jesus would spend in the grave:

cp391» (B) Length of Time Buried

- Matt 12:40 — "in the heart of the earth three days and three nights" (Thus He was 'buried' for three days and nights or 72 hours, but He died two to three hours before He was buried.)
- Mark 8:31 (9:31) — "and be killed and *after* three days to rise up. (Notice He was 'killed' and after three days He was to be raised up from the grave. He died about 3 PM on a Wednesday. The first day after He was killed was Thursday, the second day was Friday, the third day was Saturday. He was resurrected near the end of Saturday, the Sabbath. See 1 Samuel 20:5-21:5 for counting method.)
- Matt 16:21 (17:23) — "and be killed and *the* third day be raised up."
- Luke 9:22 — "and be killed and *the* third day to be raised up."
- John 2:19, 21 — "destroy this temple, and *in* three days I will raise it up ... but he spoke about the temple of his body."

These last three verses speak about being *raised up*on the third day. He was *laid down* into the earth at the very end of Wednesday. Thus the first day was Thursday; the second day was Friday; the third day was Saturday. He was *raised up* near the end of the third day, Saturday – the Jews' Sabbath after three full days in the earth.

Three Days and Three Nights									
Wednesday		Thursday		Friday		Saturday		Sunday	
24 hour day		24 hour day		24 hour day		24 hour day		24 hour day	
night	day	night	day	night	day	night	day	night	day
14 Nisan Preparation day for the Passover		**Passover** an annual Sabbath		Women buy spices (Mark 16:1)		**Sabbath** a weekly Sabbath			
Buried at sunset >		*First Day*		*Second Day*		*Third Day* **Resurrected** at sunset>		**Christ** (sheaf of first-fruits - Lev 23:9-14)	
Resurrected after three days in the grave near the end of the 3rd day, before the 4th day of the count									

cp392» In order to fulfill all these scriptures in (A) & (B) above (cp388 & cp391):

(1) According to Matt 12:40; John 2:19, 21, Jesus *must* have been resurrected in three days and nights after he was placed in the grave.

(2) According to point (1) and with Matt 16:21; 17:23; and Luke 9:22, Jesus *must* have been resurrected near the end of the third day (1= Thur.; 2= Fri.; 3=Saturday — the Sabbath).

(3) According to points (1) and (2) and with Mark 8:31 and 9:31, Jesus *must* have been resurrected three days after His death towards the very beginning of the fourth day (Sunday — first day of the new week).

cp393» Therefore in order to fulfill the very word of Christ about his burial for the three days and nights, and to fulfill the scriptures of the account of Jesus's death, burial, and resurrection, Jesus would have to have been buried[3] Wednesday just before sunset, and he would have to be resurrected right after the three days and three nights later near the last part of Saturday (see Collation of Scriptures below). And scripture does indicate that Jesus died near the end of Wednesday (4th day of the week), was buried before sunset, and was in the grave three days (5th, 6th, & 7th day).

Christ's Ascension

cp394» It was only the angel of the Lord who came (Matt 28:2). One angel came to the tomb. This is important, very important, for the women saw visions of two angels (John 20:12) or two men (Luke 24:4) or one young man (Mark 16:5) or one angel (Matt 28:5). Now we see that *one* angel came out of heaven to resurrect Christ the dead *man* (Matt 28:2). From here let's see how and when Jesus ascended to his Father.

---

[3] Stone closing the tomb

Two Men; Two Angels?

cp395» The next "morning" after 7th day Sabbath (after sunset), the women (Mary Magdalene; Mary; Joanna; and other women, John 20:l; Luke 24:9-10) came to the tomb and saw **two men**, according to Luke 24:4; or **an angel** according to Matthew 28:5; or **a young man** according to Mark 16:5. (See Robertson's Harmony of the Gospel, or our notes.) In Luke's account it says the two men spoke ("they said"). In the Matthew account it says the angel spoke. In the Mark account it says a young man spoke (Mark 16:6). Each of these renditions have the two men, the angel, and the young man, saying about the same thing. Surely this proves the Bible contradicts itself? Absolutely not!

cp396» Notice in Luke 24:5, "*they* said." Two spoke, for just before (v. 4), Luke said there were two men in the tomb. In Mark it says a young man was on the *right*, on the right there was a young man. Who was next to this young man? It was the angel (who looked like a man) who was next to the young man (Matt 28:5). Who came to resurrect Christ? It was the angel of the Lord (Matt 28:2-4). As we have shown you before (*God Papers* [GP3]) the angel of the Lord could either manifest himself as looking like a man, or like a flaming-fire. When he came to resurrect Christ, he came *looking* like a man. Thus, the young man (Christ) was on the right of the two who looked like men, and both spoke at once. There is no contradiction here. The scripture says merely that there were two who both looked like men, but one was a young man (Christ), and the other "man" was the angel of the Lord, who looked like a man.

cp397» After this event, the women went to the disciples (Luke 24:9-11; John 20:2; Luke 24:22-24) to tell them what had happened. With Peter and another disciple the women went back to the tomb that very Sunday, just after sunset on Saturday evening – the morning of the new day. But on reaching the tomb they found nothing, but some linen cloths of Christ (John 20:6-7; Luke 24:12). Then the two disciples returned to the house of the disciples where they were meeting (John 20:10). But Mary Magdalene tarried behind, she was crying outside the tomb. Then she looked inside and saw two angels, according to John 20:11-13.

cp398» Now notice the two disciples had examined the tomb and did not see the two "men" that the women had seen, but they did see Christ's body was gone (Luke 24:22-24; John 20:6-9). Then these disciples left the tomb and headed back to the house again, but Mary stayed behind crying outside the tomb. Next she looked in and saw two angels. But the texts about the resurrection say only *one* angel came to resurrect Christ. Notice they were clothed in white. But so was the young man clothed in a white robe (Mark 16:5). Thus, as Luke (Luke 24:4) called the angel of the Lord (Matt 28:5) and the resurrected Christ (Mark 16:5) two "men," so also did John (John 20::11-13) call Christ and the angel of the Lord, two "angels." These two looked like men, but with their bright or white robes they also looked like angels. What do angels look like? They looked like burning flames (Heb 1:7; Acts 7:30). The bright, white light of their robes made them look like fire, thus, they looked like angels, and like men.

cp399» Mary, after the "angels" spoke to her, turned around "and beholds [that] the Jesus *had* stood, and she not known it was Jesus [standing as one of the two angels]" (John 20:14). Examine the King James Version, it implies she turned around and *then* saw Jesus. This is wrong. For in Greek the word translated "standing" and the words "knew not" are: one, a perfect tense participle, and two, a pluperfect tense verb in the indicative mood (in the 3rd person). Perfect tense words in Greek indicate *past* or *complete* action. Jesus was not standing after she turned, he *had* stood there before she turned. In other words, Jesus *had* stood with the angel of the Lord (as two "angels"), but Mary did not comprehend it. Further, a pluperfect tense word ("knew not" KJV) indicates a "*past state* resulting from *previous action*" (*Exegetical Grammar*, by J. Harold Greenlee, Eerdmans Pub, 1963). What was the previous action? It was the act of Mary turning. Thus, *before* this action Mary had seen Jesus, but "knew not" it was Jesus.

cp400» Fine. Mary had turned away from the two "angels" (one being Jesus, but she realized it not), and "Jesus says to her, why ... she supposing him to be the gardener" (John 20:15). She had turned away from the two "angels," then Jesus spoke to her, but she only thought it was a gardener. She must have been upset; this was an emotional evening, they didn't realize Christ was to be resurrected. They thought someone had stolen the body (V. 13). Mary had just seen two "angels" and talked to them. She turns away still crying and Jesus (now behind her, for she had turned away) spoke to her, but she believed it was a gardener. By the unbelievable events and her tears, one must conclude that she was somewhat upset. Now what?

Ascension & Fulfillment of Sheaf of the First Fruits

cp401» "Jesus said unto her [from behind], Mary. She turned herself [she turned now back to Jesus], and said to him, Rabboni, which is to say, Master. Jesus said unto her, *Touch me not*; for I am not yet ascended to my Father: but go to the brethren, and say unto them, I ascend unto my Father, and your Father; and to my God, and your God."(John 20:16-17)

cp402» Notice, Jesus would not let Mary touch him, for he hadn't ascended yet to his Father. Now notice *when* he ascended. "And behold! Jesus met them, saying, All hail. And they came and took hold of his feet, and worshiped him" (Matt 28:9). Who took hold of Christ's feet? — the women leaving the tomb, the *second* time. Remember these women went to the tomb in the morning at sunrise, and saw two "men." They went to the disciples and told them of it. The disciples rushed to the tomb. On seeing nothing they returned to their house. While they (the two disciples) returned, Mary tarried crying and Christ the resurrected man appeared to her. Then Mary went to tell the disciples about seeing Christ (John 20:18; Mark 16:10). Through a little comparison, we can see that Matthew 28:9-10 is Mary and the women returning home the *second* time from the tomb (see scripture below).

cp403» Right after Mary had spoken to Christ, Jesus ascended, for as they (Mary and the women, Matt 28:9-10) were returning Christ appeared to them again. But this time he allowed them to touch him. Yet what was his excuse for not allowing Mary to touch him (John 20:17)? — he hadn't yet ascended to his Father. Thus, because seconds or minutes later he did allow Mary and the other women to touch him, he *must* have ascended to his Father. This ascension of Christ fulfilled Spiritually Lev 23:9-14, which occurs on a Sunday, the morrow after the Sabbath:

> Lev 23:9 Then the LORD spoke to Moses, saying, 10 "Speak to the sons of Israel and say to them, 'When you enter the land which I am going to give to you and reap its harvest, then you shall bring in **the sheaf of the first fruits of your harvest** to the priest. 11 'He shall wave the sheaf before the LORD for you to be accepted; **on the day <u>after</u> the Sabbath the priest shall wave it.**

Read "Sheaf of the First Fruits" in the NM 16, "God's Appointed Times," for more information on the sheaf of first fruits.
Also see *Prophecy Papers* 7 [PP7] under "Sheaf of the First Fruits," and in this book, Part 4 [CP4] under "Christ's Ascension."

Collation of Scriptures Pertaining to Christ's Burial and Resurrection

cp404» The Biblical scriptures concerning Christ's death were written by four: Matthew, Mark, Luke, and John. They each only wrote just part of the story. In order to understand all that went on at the time of Christ's death; we must put all the scriptures together; we must collate them. The following collation shows Christ's pre-death words were true, he would be in the grave for three full days and nights. The scriptures quoted below are from the BCB translation unless otherwise stated.

Comments	Scripture	Matt	Mark	Luke	John
Wednesday, 14th of Nisan Christ died on the day of Preparation as the day drew on towards the first annual Sabbath (High day -- John 19:31) of the Passover festival. The True Passover (Christ) was killed on the 14th day of the first month of the Hebrew's Calendar (Ex 12:6; Num 28:16).	Lk 23:54 And it was preparation day [before the annual Sabbath day], and [the] Sabbath was coming on. Lk 23:55 And women, who had come along with him out of Galilee, having followed, saw the tomb and how his body was placed.			23:54-55	
Thursday, 15th of Nisan; *First Day* The first annual Sabbath of the Passover after Christ died was Thursday the 15th of Nisan on the Hebrew or Jewish Calendar (Num 28:17-18).	This being the Sabbath (an annual Sabbath) spoken about in Luke 23:54.			23:54 ("Sab. drew near")	
Friday, 16th of Nisan; *Second Day* After the **annual Sabbath** on the 15th of Nisan, the women buy spices and prepare them for Christ's body on the day *after* the annual Sabbath, for no Jew was allowed to buy such items on a Sabbath (Neh 10:31). This Sabbath was a High day of the festival, not the weekly Sabbath.	Mark 16:1 And the Sabbath being [now] past, Mary of Magdalene, and Mary the [mother] of James, and Salome, bought aromatic spices that they might come and embalm him. Lk 23:56 And having returned they prepared aromatic spices and ointments,		16:1	23:56a	
Saturday, 17th of Nisan, a weekly Sabbath day ; *The Third Day* The women rest on the regular weekly Sabbath	Lk 23:56b and rested on the Sabbath[7th day], according to the commandment.			23:56b	
Late on the Sabbath, on Saturday	Mat 28:1 Now late [on the	28:1			

Comments	Scripture	Matt	Mark	Luke	John
late evening of the **17th of NISAN**, the women begin to travel to the tomb with the spices for the body of Christ.	Sabbath evening] it dawning toward the first day of the week [Sunday], came Mary the Magdala and the other Mary to look at the tomb				
The resurrection occurs on the late evening of the 17th of NISAN, when the angel of the Lord resurrects Christ at the end of the 3rd day.	Mat 28: 2 And behold, there was a **great earthquake**; for an angel of [the] Lord, descending out of heaven, came and rolled away the stone and sat upon it 3 And his look was as lightning, and his clothing white as snow 4 And for fear of him the guards trembled and became as dead men **Note**: The resurrection of the dead saints occurred with the resurrection of Christ at the end of the 7th day Sabbath when an **earthquake** happened. (Matt 27:51-54)	28:2-4			

Comments	Scripture	Matt	Mark	Luke	John
On Sunday, 18th of Nisan, in dawning of a new day, right at or after sunset the women come to the tomb. **Jesus is the antitypical Sheaf** of the Passover festival. Read nm594 in context. Study the original text.	John 20:1a And toward the first of the [day] of the week [Sunday], Mary of Magdalene comes early morning [the morning of a new day for the Jews came at sunset] (darkness even now taken place) to the tomb, Mark 16:2 And very early [after *sunset*] on the first day of the week [Sunday], they came to the tomb, the [antitype] sun having risen. 3 And they said to one another, Who shall roll us away the stone out of the door of the tomb? Lk 24:1 But on the first [day] of the week [Sunday], very early indeed in the dawning of the new day, they came to the tomb, bringing the aromatic spices which they had prepared.		16:2-3	24:1	20:1a
Sunday, 18th Nisan On reaching the tomb, after sunset, they see the stone in front of the tomb was moved.	Mark 16:4 And when they looked, they see that the stone has been rolled [away] for it was very great. Lk 24:2 And they found the stone rolled away from the tomb. John 20:1b and sees the stone taken away from the tomb.		16:4	24:2	20:1b
They then enter the tomb; the body is gone.	Lk 24:3 And when they had entered they found not the body of the Lord Jesus. Mark 16:5a And entering into the tomb,		16:5a	24:3	
Sunday, early after Saturday's sunset, they see two "men," one angel [Matt 28:5] and one man [Mark 16:5]; both looked like they were either an angel or a man in bright-white clothes, see CP4.	Lk 24:4 And it came to pass as they were in perplexity about it, that behold, two men suddenly stood by them in shining raiment.			24:4	

Comments	Scripture	Matt	Mark	Luke	John
One of these two was a young man on the right.	**Mark 16:5** And entering into the tomb, they saw a young man sitting on the right, clothed in a white robe, and they were amazed and alarmed;		16:5		
The two "men" said, "Why seek ..."	**Lk 24:5** And as they were filled with fear and bowed their faces to the ground, they said to them, Why seek you the living one among the dead?			24:5	
The "angel," "he," "they" continue to speak	**Mat 28:5** And the angel answering said to the women, Fear not, for I know that you seek Jesus the crucified one 6 He is not here, for he is risen, as he said. Come, see the place where the Lord lay 7 And go quickly and say to his disciples that he is risen from the dead; and behold, he goes before you into Galilee, there shall you see him. Behold, I have told you **Mark 16:6** but he says to them, Be not alarmed. You seek Jesus, the Nazarene, the crucified one. He is risen, he is not here; behold the place where they had put him. 7 But go, tell his disciples and Peter, he goes before you into Galilee; there shall you see him, as he said to you. **Lk 24:6** He is not here, but is risen: remember how he spoke to you, being yet in Galilee, 7 saying, The Son of man must be delivered up into the hands of sinners, and be crucified, and rise the third day. 8 And they remembered his words;	28:5-7	16:6-7	24:6-8	

Comments	Scripture	Matt	Mark	Luke	John
The women flee the tomb astonished	Mat 28:8 And going out quickly from the tomb with fear and great joy, they ran to bring his disciples word Mark 16:8 And they went out, and fled from the tomb. And trembling and excessive amazement possessed them, and they said nothing to any one, for they were afraid.	28:8	16:8		
The women speak about what they saw to the disciples	Lk 24:9 and, returning from the tomb, related all these things to the eleven and to all the rest. 10 Now it was Mary of Magdalene, and Johanna, and Mary the [mother] of James, and the others with them, who told these things to the apostles. John 20:2 She runs therefore and comes to Simon Peter, and to the other disciple, to whom Jesus was attached, and says to them, They have taken away the Lord out of the tomb, and we know not where they have laid him.			24:9-10	20:2
Their words seemed as foolish talk to the disciples	Lk 24:11 And their words appeared in their eyes as an idle tale, and they disbelieved them.			24:11	
Yet Peter went with the women back to the tomb, but another disciple outran Peter to the tomb; both saw that the body of Christ was gone. They departed wondering, for they didn't understand that Christ must first suffer then be resurrected after three days.	Lk 24:12 But Peter, rising up, ran to the tomb, and stooping down he sees the linen clothes lying there alone, and went away home, wondering at what had happened. John 20:3 Peter therefore went forth, and the other disciple, and came to the tomb. 4 And the two ran together, and the other disciple ran			24:12	20:3-10

Comments	Scripture	Matt	Mark	Luke	John
	forward faster than Peter, and came first to the tomb, 5 and stooping down he sees the linen cloths lying; he did not however go in. 6 Simon Peter therefore comes, following him, and entered into the tomb, and sees the linen cloths lying, 7 and the handkerchief which was upon his head, not lying with the linen cloths, but folded up in a distinct place by itself. 8 Then entered in therefore the other disciple also who came first to the tomb, and he saw and believed; 9 for they had not yet known the scripture, that he must rise from among [the] dead. 10 The disciples therefore went away again to their own home.				
BUT Mary Magdalene and others (John 20:1 & Matt 28:1) tarried behind; Jesus then appeared to Mary (but Jesus said she couldn't touch him until he ascended to his Father).	Mark 16:9 Now when he had risen, very early the first [day] of the week, he appeared first to Mary of Magdalene, out of whom he had cast seven daemons. John 20:11 But Mary stood at the tomb weeping outside. As therefore she wept, she stooped down into the tomb, 12 and beholds two angels sitting in white [garments] one at the head and one at the feet, where the body of Jesus had lain. 13 And they say to her, Woman, why do you weep? She says to them, Because they have taken away my Lord, and I know not where		16:9		20:11-17

Comments	Scripture	Matt	Mark	Luke	John
	they have laid him. 14 Having said these things she turned backward and beholds Jesus standing [there] and knew not that it was Jesus. 15 Jesus says to her, Woman, why do you weep? Whom do you seek? She, supposing that it was the gardener, says to him, Sir, if you have borne him hence, tell me where you have laid him, and I will take him away. 16 Jesus says to her, Mary. She, turning round, says to him in Hebrew, Rabboni, which means Teacher. 17 Jesus says to her, Touch me not, for I have not yet ascended towards my Father; but go to my brethren and say to them, I ascend towards the Father of me and Father of you, and [to] my God and your God.				
Moments later Jesus appeared to the women (Mary Magdalene and the others who tarried with her) as they were going back from the tomb to the disciples the second time (this time Jesus allows them to touch him, thus, he in this short time had ascended to his Father).	Mat 28:9 And as they went to bring his disciples word, behold also, Jesus met them, saying, Hail! And they coming up took him by the feet, and did him homage. 10 Then Jesus says to them, Fear not; go, bring word to my brethren that they go into Galilee, and there they shall see me.	28:9-10			
Sunday, after Sabbath sunset While the women continue to the disciples, the guards tell the chief priests a lie when they were explaining what had occurred (see, Matt 28:2-4). Please read these verse to see what they said and how	Mat 28:11 And as they went, behold, some of the watch went into the city, and brought word to the chief priests of all that had taken	28:11-15			

Comments	Scripture	Matt	Mark	Luke	John
they lied.	place. 12 And having assembled with the elders, and having taken counsel, they gave a large sum of money to the soldiers, 13 saying, Say that his disciples coming by night stole him [while] we [were] sleeping. 14 And if this should come to the hearing of the governor, we will persuade him, and save you from all anxiety. 15 And they took the money and did as they had been taught. And this report is current among the Jews until this day.				
The women (Matt 28:8,9,11) continue to the house where the disciples were staying at. Mary tells the disciples that they saw Jesus and they held him and they relate what He said, but the disciples didn't believe.	Mark 16:10 She went and brought word to those that had been with him, [who were] grieving and weeping. 11 And when these heard that he was alive and had been seen of her, they disbelieved [it]. John 20:18 Mary of Magdalene comes bringing word to the disciples that she had seen the Lord, and [that] he had said these things to her.		16:10 - 11		20:18
Sunday, during the day light and before sunset Christ manifests Himself in another form (different from Mark 16:9 & John 20:17; but probably like Matt 28:9 & Luke 24:39) to two disciples going to a village of Emmaus. On reaching it they perceived it was Christ who was walking and talking with them. Then Christ vanished out of sight.	Mark 16:12 And after these things he was manifested in another form to two of them as they walked, going into the country; 13 and they went and brought word to the rest; neither did they believe them. Lk 24:13 And behold, two of them were going on that same day [Sunday] to a village distant sixty stadia [few miles] from Jerusalem,		16:12 - 13	24:13- 32	

Comments	Scripture	Matt	Mark	Luke	John
	called Emmaus; 14 and they conversed with one another about all these things which had taken place. 15 And it came to pass as they conversed and reasoned, that Jesus himself drawing near, went with them; 16 but their eyes were holden so as not to know him. 17 And he said to them, What discourses are these which pass between you as you walk, and are downcast? 18 And one [of them] named Cleopas, answering said to him, Are you alone sojourning in Jerusalem, and do not know what has taken place in it in these days? 19 And he said to them, What things? And they said to him, The things concerning Jesus the Nazarene, who was a prophet mighty in deed and word before the God and all the people; 20 and how the chief priests and our rulers delivered him up to [the] judgment of death and crucified him. 21 But we had hoped that he was [the one] who is about to redeem Israel. Yes, and along with all this, this brings on *the* third day since these things [v. 20] took place. 22 And certain women from among us astonished us, having been very early at the tomb [on this third day], [The women went to the tomb at the very end of the third reaching the tomb right after Jesus was resurrected on the very beginning of the fourth day, that is, the first day of the new week. See Part 4 of this book]				

Comments	Scripture	Matt	Mark	Luke	John
	23 and, not having found his body [right after sunset on the fourth day], came, saying that they also had seen a vision of angels, who say that he is living. 24 And some of those with us went to the tomb, and found it so, as the women also had said, but him they saw not. 25 And he [Jesus] said to them, O senseless and slow of heart to believe in all that the prophets have spoken! 26 Ought not the Christ to have suffered these things and to enter into his glory? 27 And having begun from Moses and from all the prophets, he interpreted to them in all the scriptures the things concerning himself. 28 And they drew near to the village where they were going, and he made as though he would go farther. 29 And they constrained him, saying, Stay with us, for it is toward evening and the day is declining. And he entered in to stay with them. 30 And it came to pass as he was at table with them, having taken the bread, he blessed, and having broken it, gave it to them. 31 And their eyes were opened, and they recognized him. And he disappeared from them. 32 And they said to one another, Was not our heart burning in us as he spoke to us on the way, [and] as he opened the scriptures to us?				

Comments	Scripture	Matt	Mark	Luke	John
After this, the two who were going to the village, returned to Jerusalem and grouped with the disciples, and told the disciples that Jesus appeared to them (the two being Simon and Cleopas (Luke 24:18, 34).	Mark 16:14a Afterwards as they lay at table he was manifested to the eleven, Lk 24:33 And rising up the same hour, they returned to Jerusalem. And they found the eleven, and those with them, gathered together, 34 saying, The Lord is indeed risen and has appeared to Simon. 35 And they related what [had happened] on the way, and how he was made known to them in the breaking of bread. 1CO 15:5 KJV And that he was seen of Cephas,		16:14 a	24:33-35	
At this time, Christ manifested Himself to eleven disciples, but without Thomas (Luke 24:33; John 20:24).	Mark 16:14 Afterwards as they lay at table he was manifested to the eleven, and reproached [them with] their unbelief and hardness of heart, because they had not believed those who had seen him risen. John 20:19 When therefore it was evening on that day, which was first [day] of the week, and the doors shut where the disciples were, through fear of the Jews, Jesus came and stood in the midst, and says to them, Peace [be] to you.		16:14		20:19
The disciples feared this appearance of Christ who seemed to come from nowhere -- they thought He was a spirit.	Lk 24:36 And as they were saying these things, he himself stood in their midst, and says to them, Peace [be] unto you. 37 But they, being confounded and being frightened, supposed they			24:36-37	

Comments	Scripture	Matt	Mark	Luke	John
	beheld a spirit.				
Jesus questioned their unbelief	Mark 16:14b and reproached [them with] their unbelief and hardness of heart, because they had not believed those who had seen him risen. Lk 24:38 And he said to them, Why are you troubled? and why are thoughts rising in your hearts?		16:14 b	24:38	
Christ shows the disciples He is flesh and blood	Lk 24:39 behold my hands and my feet, that it is I myself. Handle me and see, for a spirit has not flesh and bones as you see me having. 40 And having said this he showed them his hands and his feet. John 20:20 And having said this, he showed to them his hands and his side. The disciples rejoiced therefore, having seen the Lord.			24:39-40	20:20
He eats with them also	Lk 24:41 But while they yet did not believe for joy, and were wondering, he said to them, Have you anything here to eat? 42 And they gave him part of a broiled fish and of a honeycomb; 43 and he took it and ate before them.			24:41-43	
Jesus Christ explains scripture about His death and gives a commission; Thomas is not with them, and Thomas doesn't believe Christ appeared.	Lk 24:44 And he said to them, These [are] the words which I spoke to you while I was yet with you, that all that is written concerning me in the law of Moses and prophets			24:44-49	20:21-25

Comments	Scripture	Matt	Mark	Luke	John
	and psalms must be fulfilled.				
	45 Then he opened their understanding to understand the scriptures,				
	46 and said to them, Thus it is written, and thus it behooved the Christ to suffer, and to rise from among the dead the third day;				
	47 and that repentance and forgiveness of sins should be preached in his name to all the nations beginning at Jerusalem.				
	48 And you are witnesses of these things.				
	49 And behold, I send the promise of my Father upon you; but do you remain in the city till you be clothed with power from on high.				
	John 20:21 [Jesus] said therefore again to them, Peace [be] to you: as the Father sent me forth, I also send you.				
	22 And having said this, he breathed into [them] and says to them, Receive [the] Holy Spirit:				
	23 whose sins you remit, they are remitted to them; whose sins you retain, they are retained.				
	24 But Thomas, one of the twelve, called Didymus, was not with them when Jesus came.				
	25 The other disciples therefore said to him, We have seen the Lord. But he said to them, Unless I see in his hands the mark of the nails, and put my finger into the mark of the nails, and put my hand into his side, I will not believe.				

Comments	Scripture	Matt	Mark	Luke	John
	ACT 1:4a KJV And, being assembled together with them, commanded them that they should not depart from Jerusalem, but wait for the promise of the Father ... 5 For John truly baptized with water; but ye shall be baptized with the Holy Ghost not many days hence.				
Eight Days Later Jesus appears eight days later to the 12 disciples; Thomas sees Christ and believes -- calls Him his Lord and his God.	John 20:26 And eight days after, his disciples were again within, and Thomas with them. Jesus comes, the doors being shut, and stood in the midst and said, Peace [be] to you. 27 Then he says to Thomas, Bring your finger here and see my hands; and bring your hand and put it into my side; and be not unbelieving, but believing. 28 Thomas answered and said to him, The Lord of me and the God of me. 29 Jesus says to him, Because you have seen me you have believed: blessed they who have not seen and have believed. 30 Many other signs therefore also Jesus did before his disciples, which are not written in this book; 31 but these are written that you may believe that Jesus is the Christ, the Son of the God, and that believing you might have life in his name.				20:26-31
Thereafter Christ later appeared again near the sea of Galilee (Tiberias) as he said he would appear to all the brethren (Mark 16:7; Matt 28:7;Luke 24:6-7; Matt 28:9-10; etc.)	John 21:1 After these things Jesus manifested himself again to the disciples at the sea of Tiberias. And he manifested [himself] thus.				21:1-23

Comments	Scripture	Matt	Mark	Luke	John
	2 There were together Simon Peter, and Thomas called Didymus, and Nathanael who was of Cana of Galilee, and the [sons] of Zebedee, and two others of his disciples.				
	3 Simon Peter says to them, I go to fish. They say to him, We also come with you. They went forth, and went on board, and that night took nothing.				
	4 And early morn already breaking, Jesus stood on the shore; the disciples however did not know that it was Jesus.				
	5 Jesus therefore says to them, Children, have you anything to eat? They answered him, No.				
	6 And he said to them, Cast the net at the right side of the ship and you will find. They cast therefore, and they could no longer draw it, from the multitude of fishes.				
	7 That disciple therefore whom Jesus loved says to Peter, It is the Lord. Simon Peter therefore, having heard that it was the Lord, girded his overcoat [on him] for he was naked, and cast himself into the sea;				
	8 and the other disciples came in the small boat, for they were not far from the land, but somewhere about two hundred cubits, dragging the net of fishes.				
	9 When therefore they went out on the land, they see a fire of coals there, and fish laid on it, and bread.				
	10 Jesus says to them, Bring				

Comments	Scripture	Matt	Mark	Luke	John
	of the fishes which you have now taken.				
	11 Simon Peter went up and drew the net to the land full of great fishes, a hundred and fifty-three; and though there were so many, the net was not rent.				
	12 Jesus says to them, Come [and] dine. But none of the disciples dared inquire of him, Who are you? knowing that it was the Lord.				
	13 Jesus comes and takes the bread and gives it to them, and the fish in like manner.				
	14 This is already the third time that Jesus had been manifested to the disciples, being risen from among [the] dead.				
	15 When therefore they had dined, Jesus says to Simon Peter, Simon, [son] of Jonas, do you love me more than these? He says to him, Yes, Lord; you know that I am attached to you. He says to him, Feed my lambs.				
	16 He says to him again a second time, Simon, [son] of Jonas, do you love you me? He says to him, Yes, Lord; you know that I am attached to you. He says to him, Shepherd my sheep.				
	17 He says to him the third time, Simon, [son] of Jonas, are you attached to me? Peter was grieved because he said to him the third time, Are you attached to me? and said to him, Lord, you know all things; you know that I am attached to you. Jesus says to him, Feed my sheep.				
	18 Truly, truly, I say to you,				

Comments	Scripture	Matt	Mark	Luke	John
	When you were young, you girded yourself, and walked where you desired; but when you shall be old, you shall stretch forth your hands, and another shall gird you, and bring you where you do not desire. 19 But he said this signifying by what death he should glorify the God. And having said this, he says to him, Follow me. 20 Peter, turning round, sees the disciple whom Jesus loved following, who also leaned at supper on his breast, and said, Lord, who is it that delivers you up? 21 Peter, seeing him, says to Jesus, Lord, and what [of] this [man] 22 Jesus says to him, If I wish that he abide until I come, what [is that] to you? You follow me. 23 This word therefore went out among the brethren, That disciple does not die. And Jesus did not say to him, He does not die; but, If I wish that he abide until I come, what [is that] to you?				
Christ at this same time appeared in Galilee to 500 as he promised.	1CO 15:6 KJV After that, he was seen of above five hundred brethren at once; of whom the greater part remain unto this present, but some are fallen asleep.				
Christ then leads them over against Bethany into the appointed mountain.	Mat 28:16 But the eleven disciples went into Galilee to the mountain which Jesus had appointed them 17 And when they saw him, they did homage to him: but	28:16-17		24:50	

Comments	Scripture	Matt	Mark	Luke	John
	some doubted Lk 24:50 And he led them out as far as Bethany, and having lifted up his hands, he blessed them.				
Jesus in the mountain teaches that the knowledge of the end of the age was in his Father's hand.	ACT 1:6 KJV When they therefore were come together, they asked of him, saying, Lord, wilt thou at this time restore again the kingdom to Israel? 7 And he said unto them, It is not for you to know the times or the seasons, which the Father hath put in his own power.				
BUT he notes all power was given to Him. ["All things that the Father has are mine; therefore I said, that He shall take of mine, and shall show it unto you" (John 16:15).]	Mat 28:18 And Jesus coming up spoke to them, saying, All power has been given me in heaven and upon earth	28:18			
Jesus says they will receive the power of the Spirit. ["Howbeit when he the Spirit of Truth, is come, he will guide you into all truth" (John 16:13).]	ACT 1:8a KJV But ye shall receive power, after that the Holy Ghost is come upon you:				
He then tells them to preach the gospel to ALL and baptize "them into the NAME of the Father, and of the Son, and of the Holy Spirit."	Mat 28:19 Go [therefore] and make disciples of all the nations, baptizing them into the name of the Father, and of the Son, and of the Holy Spirit 20 teaching them to observe all things whatsoever I have enjoined you. And behold, I am with you all the days, until the completion of the age [aeon]. Mark 16:15 And he said to them, Go into all the world, and preach the good news to all the creation. ACT 1:8b KJV and ye shall be witnesses unto me both in Jerusalem, and in all Judaea, and in Samaria, and unto the uttermost part of the earth.	28:19-20	16:15		

Comments	Scripture	Matt	Mark	Luke	John
Christ further gives them power	Mark 16:16 He that believes and is baptized shall be saved, and he that disbelieves shall be condemned. 17 And these signs shall follow those that have believed: in my name they shall cast out daemons; they shall speak with new tongues; 18 they shall take up serpents; and if they should drink any deadly thing it shall not injure them; they shall lay hands upon the infirm, and they shall be well.		16:16 - 18		
and he said He would be with the Church until the end of the age.	Mat 28:20b And behold, I am with you all the days, until the completion of the age [aeon].	28:20 b			
After this commission was given to the apostles by Christ on the mountain, He then ascends into heaven.	Mark 16:19 The Lord therefore, after he had spoken to them, was taken up into heaven, and sat at the right hand of the God. Lk 24:51 And it came to pass as he was blessing them, he was separated from them and was carried up into heaven. ACT 1:9 KJV And when he had spoken these things, while they beheld, he was taken up; and a cloud received him out of their sight.		16:19	24:51	
But lo! two others were there.	ACT 1:10 KJV And while they looked stedfastly toward heaven as he went up, behold, two men stood by them in white apparel; 11 Which also said, Ye men of Galilee, why stand ye gazing up into heaven? this same Jesus, which is taken up from you into heaven, shall so				

Comments	Scripture	Matt	Mark	Luke	John
	come in like manner as ye have seen him go into heaven.				
A list of those on the hill is given.	ACT 1:13 KJV And when they were come in, they went up into an upper room, where abode both Peter, and James, and John, and Andrew, Philip, and Thomas, Bartholomew, and Matthew, James the son of Alphaeus, and Simon Zelotes, and Judas the brother of James. 14 These all continued with one accord in prayer and supplication, with the women, and Mary the mother of Jesus, and with his brethren.				
The disciples returned to Jerusalem from the appointed mountain.	Lk 24:52 And they, having done him homage, returned to Jerusalem with great joy, ACT 1:12 KJV Then returned they unto Jerusalem from the mount called Olivet, which is from Jerusalem a Sabbath day's journey.			24:52	
The disciples teach in the temple.	Mark 16:20 And they, going forth, preached everywhere, the Lord working with [them] and confirming the word by the signs following upon Lk 24:53 and were continually in the temple praising and blessing the God.		16:20	24:53	

Passover Scriptures Reiteration

cp405» The chief priests of the Jews had a meeting wherein they took counsel to kill Christ (John 11:47-53; Luke 22:2). Because of those out to kill him, Christ no more could walk openly. (John 11:54)

cp406» Now the passover wherein Christ was killed was near, and many had come to Jerusalem for the festival and were wondering among themselves whether Christ would show up at the festival. The chief priests had given direction that if any knew where Christ was that they should point him out to them so the priests could take Jesus. (John 11:55-57)

9th of Nisan, a Friday

cp407» Then six days before the Passover (the 9th of Nisan), Christ came to Bethany which is only a few miles from Jerusalem. (John 12:1; 11:17)

At that time they had a supper wherein Mary anointed the feet of Jesus, and wiped his feet with her hair. (John 12:2-3; Mark 14:3; Matt 26:6-7)

Now some of the disciples had indignation inside their minds at this act, and one named Judas Iscariot, said: "Why was not this ointment sold for three hundred pence, and given to the poor?" (Mark 14:4-5; Matt 26:8-9; John 12:4-6)

Then when Jesus understood what was being said, he spoke saying, "let her alone: that of the day of my burial may she keep it" (John 12:7). The Mary that anointed Christ was Mary Magdalene, who later brought this ointment to Christ's tomb on the day of his resurrection along with some spices she and others had bought and prepared the day before Christ's resurrection (Luke 23:56-24:1; Mark 16:1; Matt 28:1). (John 12:7-8; Mark 14:6-9; Matt 26:10-13)

10th of Nisan, a Saturday

cp408» Now right after this supper, right after sunset, thus on the 10th of Nisan, Judas the betrayer of Christ went to the chief priests and said he would help them take Jesus in the absence of a great crowd. Because of this the priests were glad that Judas would betray Christ, and agreed to give him 30 pieces of silver. Further, they consulted if they shouldn't also put Lazarus to death since many of the Jews believed in Jesus because Christ had previously resurrected Lazarus from the dead. (Mark 14:10-11; Matt 26:14-16; Luke 22:3-6; John 12:9-11)

On the next day after Christ came to Bethany, which was the daylight hours of the same 24 hour day that Judas had agreed to betray Christ to the priests, Christ came into Jerusalem — 10th day of Nisan (John 12:12).

Christ rode on an ass into Jerusalem, and the people cried, "Hosanna; Blessed is he that comes in the name of the Lord." This was the 10th day of the Jews 1st month — Nisan. (Mark 11:1-10; Matt 21:1-11; Luke 19:28-40)

Now in the 10th day of Nisan after he entered into Jerusalem, Jesus went into the temple (Mark 11:11).

Then in the evening just before sunset, Christ went into Bethany, a town about two miles from Jerusalem. (Mark 11:11)

First Week with Two Sabbaths

11th of Nisan, a Sunday

cp409» Now in the morrow (the next day, that is the 11th of Nisan), Christ came from Bethany back into Jerusalem. (Mark 11:12-15)

Now it was the 11th, and again Christ goes into the temple in Jerusalem. (Mark 11:15; Luke 19:45; Matt 21:12)

At this time Christ put the money changers out of the temple (Matt 21:12-16; Mark 11:15-18; Luke 19:45-46).

During this time period just before the Passover, Christ was teaching daily in the temple. (Luke 19:47)

Then in the evening of the 11th he went out of Jerusalem again and went into Bethany. (Mark 11:19; Matt 21:17)

12th of Nisan, a Monday

cp410» After he stayed in Bethany, he came back into Jerusalem on the next day, the 12th. (Mark 11:20; Matt 21:18)

Now when they returned into Jerusalem, the disciples with Christ noticed the tree Christ cursed the previous day (Mark 11:13-14), and how it already had dried up (Mark 11:21; Matt 21:19-20).

At this time on the 12th Christ entered again into the temple (Matt 21:23; Mark 11:27; Luke 20:1).

At this time on the 12th, Christ taught various parables (Matt 21:23-23:39; Mark 11:27-12:44; Luke 20:1-21:4).

Then Christ went out of the temple, and taught his disciples on the mount of Olives about the time of the end of the age (Mark 13:1-33; Luke 21:5-36: Matt 24:1-25:46).

At that time on the 12th of Nisan, Christ noted that after two days would be the feast of unleavened bread, which some call the Passover festival (Luke 22:1). (Matt 26:1-2; Mark 14:1)

At this time Christ mentioned that he is betrayed (for on the 10th remember Judas went to the chief priests to betray Jesus) (Matt 26:2).

The chief priests had decided at that time that Christ shouldn't be taken on the feast day (the 15th, Num 28:17), because there might be an uproar among the people. (Matt 26:3-5; Mark 14:1-2)

But remember on the 10th Judas had come to the chief priests, and said he would betray Jesus (John 12:1-11; Luke 22:3-6; Mark 14:3-11; Matt 26:6-16).

After Christ had returned from the temple on the 12th, after he taught many parables (see above), and after he on Mount Olives had spoken of the end of the age that late evening of the 12th (or early on the 13th after sunset), he then stayed on Mount Olives in Bethany (note Luke 24:50 with Acts 1:12). (Luke 21:37)

13th of Nisan, a Tuesday

cp411» The next day on the 13th, Jesus taught in the temple again after he abode in Bethany the night of the 13th, for at this time Jesus was teaching daily in the temple (Luke 19:47) (Luke 21:38).

Now before the feast of the passover, on the evening of the 13th, after Christ had taught during the daylight of the 13th in the temple, he was again in Bethany, and was eating his supper, as he had been doing each evening since he had began teaching in the temple on the 10th (John 13:1).

The home he was staying in was that of Mary Magdalene, Martha, and Lazarus (John 12:1).

Now Jesus on the 13th had instructed the apostles to get a room and make it ready for the passover meal, which was to occur on the 14th (Matt 26:17-19; Mark 14:12-16; Luke 22:7-13).

cp412» [[Let's correct a few verses that may be a mistranslated in many English translations of the Bible. These corrections were made by a Greek text. Matt 26:17 should read: "now *towards* the first [day] of unleavened [bread] approaches the disciples to Jesus ..." And Mark 14:12 should read: "and *towards* the first day of the unleavened [bread], when they kill the passover, his disciples say to him...." And Luke 22:7 should read: "now it came *towards* the day of unleavened [bread], in which was needful to be killed the passover." Therefore what these verses are saying is that *towards* or near the 14th day when the passover was to be killed, the disciples had asked Christ where they would eat the passover the next day. Now in Matthew 26:19, Mark 14:16, and Luke 22:13 the Greek verbal word translated "they made ready" is an aorist word that indicates an action without indicating the time of the action. Thus, it can mean action in the past, present, or future. According to the context of this verse this Greek word should have been rendered in the following manner: "were to make ready" the Passover in the certain house where Christ said to prepare it. Christ had ordered them to prepare for the Passover, but the events surrounding Christ's betrayal made it impossible to go and eat the Passover.]]

cp413» Now the evening of the 13th came and Christ was in Bethany at supper with his disciples. "And supper taking place..." (John 13:2; Matt 26: 20-21; Mark 14:17-18; Luke 22:14).

cp414» Christ time after time taught the disciples that the greatest thing was to serve others (Luke 9:46-48; Mark 10:42-44). And again on the evening of the 13th he again by using the example of washing their feet, said that the greatest thing was to serve, not to lord over others. "It is more blessed to give then to receive" (Acts 20:35). The washing of the feet was a reiteration of the principle of giving and serving. We try our best to follow this principle always, not just on one day of the year.

cp415» Now during this meal Jesus broke the bread, and passed it around, and said he could "not eat it," the passover, with them until it was fulfilled in the kingdom of God. (Luke 22:15-20; Mark 14:22-24; Matt 26:26-29)

cp416» And during this meal, Christ revealed who would deliver him up that night (14th, after sunset; after the supper they were eating on the 13th before sunset). (Matt 26:21-25; Mark 14:18-21; Luke 22:21-23; John 13:21-29)

14th of Nisan, a Wednesday

cp417»

(1) It was Judas Iscariot, and right after he took the piece of bread, which pointed him out as the betrayer (yet the apostles didn't understand), Judas immediately went out, "and it was night." That is, right after sunset Judas went out to bring the chief priests to take Jesus. (John 13:30) They were in Bethany, which is on the side of Mount Olives, when they were eating this meal (see above).

(2) After they sang a hymn, they went onto Mount Olives, and brought two swords with them so scripture could be fulfilled (Mark 14:26; Matt 26:30; Luke 22:35-39).

(3) On Mount Olives Christ speaks of various matters to the apostles. (The scripture is vague as to whether these things were spoke still in the house in Bethany, or near the house, or somewhere on the mount of Olives.) (Mark 14:26-31; Matt 26:31-35; John 13:31-17:36)

(4) At Gethsemane (probably on the mount of Olives) he enters into a garden to pray. (Matt 26:36-46; Mark 14:32-42; Luke 22:40-46; John 18:1)

(5) Now Judas knew where this garden was, for Jesus came often to it to pray (John 18:2).

(6) It was in this garden that Judas came with the chief priests and Pharisees, who came with lanterns and torches because it was at night on the 14th after sunset (John 18:3; Luke 22:47; Mark 14:43; Matt 26:47).

(7) At this time Judas revealed Christ by greeting him with a kiss. Peter cut off an ear of a guard, but Christ healed the ear. Then *all* the disciples "forsook him, and fled." (Matt 26:47-56; Mark 14:43-52; Luke 22:47-53; John 18:4-11)

(8) Then the band of men with the chief priests bound Christ and brought him, and let him away to Annas *first*, for he was the father-in-law to Caiaphas, who was the high priest that same year (John 18:12-13).

(9) Then they took Christ to Caiaphas the high priest (John 18:24).

(10) During that time Peter denied Christ three times as Jesus foretold (John 18:15-27; Luke 22:54-65; Mark 14:66-72; Matt 26:69-75). The rooster crowed in early morning. [5-6AM]

["Morning was come" (Matt 27:l; Mark 15:1); "and as it was morning, the elders of the people and the chief priests" (Luke 22:66). Or, "and it was morning; and they themselves went not into the judgment hall" (John 18:28)]

(11) In this morning part of the day, the chief priests and the elders came to take Christ, and right after they had him briefly before the high priest, they brought him to the judgement hall to Pilate (John 18:28-29; Luke 22:66-71; 23:1; Mark 15:1; Matt 27:1-2). Pilate sent Jesus to Herod Antipas because "he knew that he was of Herod's jurisdiction" (Luke 23:6-7). But Herod after mocking Jesus sent him back to Pilate (Luke 23:8-12).

(12) Then Jesus was tried and sent to be crucified (John 18:29-19:16; Luke 23:2-25; Mark 15:2-20; Matt 27:2-31).

(13) Now during that day Judas the Betrayer killed himself (Matt 27:3-10; Acts 1:16-20).

(14) Then they crucified Christ. (Matt 27:32-56; Mark 15:21-41; Luke 23:26-49; John 19:16-37)

(15) Now the Passover was prepared and killed on the 14th of Nisan, and also the 14th was a day to prepare for the 15th, which was an annual Sabbath wherein no work was to be done. Thus, because of a law that a body could not hang or remain on a tree (stake or wood cross) during the night, but must be taken down the very same day (Deut 21:23; cf Josh 8:29; 10:26-27). "The Jews therefore ... besought Pilate ... that he might be taken away." (John 19:31)

(16) Therefore Christ was quickly buried before sunset, before the annual Sabbath of the 15th. (John 19:40-42; Luke 23:53-55; Mark 15:42; Matt 27:57-61)

(17) Right after the burial "they returned" to their houses (Luke 23:56, 1st part of verse).

15th of Nisan, a Thursday, Annual Sabbath, 1st Sabbath of the Week

cp418» This was day of the annual Sabbath, a "high day" or festival Sabbath for Jews (John 19:31; Mark 15:42; Luke 23:54).

16th of Nisan, a Friday

cp419» After this one annual Sabbath (the 15th) some women bought spices, and they prepared these spices and the ointments that Mary Magdalene had saved (John 12:7). (Mark 16:1; Luke 23:56, middle part of verse)

17th of Nisan, a Saturday, 7th day Sabbath, 2nd Sabbath of the Week

cp420» Jesus was then resurrected on the last of the evening, just before or at sunset, on the second Sabbath. He laid in the tomb from late Wednesday evening to late Saturday evening, three days and three nights as he said he would in Matthew (Matt 28:2-4; 12:38-40; Matthew 27:63; and Mark 9:31). Read nm594.

Note: The resurrection of the dead saints happened with the resurrection of Christ at the end of the 7th day Sabbath when an earthquake happened. (Matt 27:51-54)

Second Week with two Sabbaths

18th of Nisan, a Sunday

Mat 28:1 "Now **after** the Sabbaths [15th & 17th of Nisan], it being minutes after sunset on Sunday, Jesus **ascends** to His Father. Read nm594.

19th of Nisan, a Monday, 2nd day of week

20th of Nisan, a Tuesday, 3rd day of week

21st of Nisan, a Wednesday, 4th day of week, an annual Sabbath, 1st Sabbath of the next Week

22nd of Nisan, a Thursday, 5th day of week,

23rd of Nisan, a Friday, 5th day of week

24th of Nisan, a Saturday, 7th day Sabbath, 2nd Sabbath of the Week

CP5: Chronology Table

cp421» **YM** = "Year of Man"; **BC** = "Before Christ" or **BCE** "before the common era"; **AD** = "Anno Domini" or "year of our Lord".

Note: The years below may be off a few years because of the complexity. See qualifications for dates in CP3 ("Verification of Chronology Periods"– cp211) and cp190ff, cp216 and 10 Nations to 7 (at the end of the Table).

Note: The following table was taken from a PDF file that has each and every year on it. But because it would add about 100 more pages to this book, we had to reduce its size by cutting thousands of rows off the table. All of the rows of years cut had no real data on them except for the count of years. See below for a link to the full PDF file.

For the full 6000 year chronology table
with each year included and latest updates
Go to

https://becoming-one.org/resources/6000yeartable.pdf

Accession Year Method

Calender Year		Calender Year	Calender Year
Previous king dies	accession period is when new king is coronated	Year 1 of new king	Year 2 of new king

Non- Accession Year Method

Calender Year		Calender Year	Calender Year
Previous king dies	Year 1 of new king new king is coronated	Year 2 of new king	Year 3 of new king

co-Regnal Year Method
during time of war or a sick king
(co-king's regnal years count starts in the year crowned)

Calender Year		Calender Year	Calender Year
Existing King's 12th year	co-King is coronated co-king's 1st year	Existing King's 13th year co-king's 2nd year	Existing King's 14th year co-king's 3rd year

Babylonian (626-539 BC) co-Regnal Year Method
during time of war or a sick king
(co-king's regnal years count starts in the year after existing king dies)

Calender Year		Calender Year	Calender Year
Existing King's 12th year	co-king is coronated as prince or king	Existing King dies in his 13th year accession year of co-king	co-king's 1st year as solo King

To understand better the above table you must read our book called the,
***6000 Years of Mankind*, published in 2024**

[Top | Flood | Abram | Exodus | David | Hezekiah | Jerusalem | JC | End Time | End Notes]

BC AD Years + or -		YM Years		6000 Years of Mankind Copyright © 2024 by Walter R. Dolen **Biblical Chronology Details** YM = Year of Mankind Begins in Sept/Oct 3 months before BC/AD dates	Additional Details	# of yrs	# of yrs	# of yrs
3971	BC	0	Y M	Note: the seven days of the week is a type of the seven millenniums. Type and antitype. See NM15.				
3970	BC	1	Y M	(Begins in Sept/Oct 3 months before BC/AD) Mankind created; **Adam** lived until 930 YM (Gen 5:1-2, 5) [next] Note: This year began in 3971 BC Sept/October. The patriarchs of Israel year one of their lives start on the first New Year day (Sep/Oct) they live in. See text.	[5] So all the days that Adam lived were nine hundred and thirty years, and he died. (Gen 5:5 BCB) "And Adam lived 130 years and begat a son [Seth]" (Gn 5:3)	1		
3969	BC	2	Y M			2		
3968	BC	3	Y M			3		
3967	BC	4	Y M			4		
3966	BC	5	Y M			5		
3965	BC	6	Y M			6		
3964	BC	7	Y M			7		
3963	BC	8	Y M			8		
3962	BC	9	Y M			9		
3961	BC	10	Y M			10		
3960	BC	11	Y M			11		
3959	BC	12	Y M			12		
3958	BC	13	Y M			13		
3957	BC	14	Y M			14		
3956	BC	15	Y M			15		
3955	BC	16	Y M			16		
3954	BC	17	Y M			17		
3953	BC	18	Y M			18		
3952	BC	19	Y M			19		

[Top | Flood | Abram | Exodus | David | Hezekiah | Jerusalem | JC | End Time | End Notes]							
BC AD Years + or -		YM Years		**6000 Years of Mankind** Copyright © 2024 by Walter R. Dolen **Biblical Chronology Details** YM = Year of Mankind Begins in Sept/Oct 3 months before BC/AD dates	**Additional Details**	# of yrs	# of yrs	# of yrs
3951	BC	20	YM			20		
3950	BC	21	YM			21		
3949	BC	22	YM			22		
3948	BC	23	YM			23		
3947	BC	24	YM			24		
3946	BC	25	YM			25		
3945	BC	26	YM			26		
3944	BC	27	YM			27		
3943	BC	28	YM			28		
3942	BC	29	YM			29		
3941	BC	30	YM			30		
3940	BC	31	YM			31		
3939	BC	32	YM			32		
3938	BC	33	YM			33		
3937	BC	34	YM			34		
3936	BC	35	YM			35		
3935	BC	36	YM			36		
3934	BC	37	YM			37		
3933	BC	38	YM			38		
3932	BC	39	YM			39		
3931	BC	40	YM			40		

[Top | Flood | Abram | Exodus | David | Hezekiah | Jerusalem | JC | End Time | End Notes]

BC AD Years + or -		YM Years		6000 Years of Mankind Copyright © 2024 by Walter R. Dolen Biblical Chronology Details YM = Year of Mankind Begins in Sept/Oct 3 months before BC/AD dates	Additional Details	# of yrs	# of yrs	# of yrs
3930	BC	41	Y M			41		
3929	BC	42	Y M			42		
3928	BC	43	Y M			43		
3927	BC	44	Y M			44		
3926	BC	45	Y M			45		
3925	BC	46	Y M			46		
3924	BC	47	Y M			47		
3923	BC	48	Y M			48		
3922	BC	49	Y M			49		
3921	BC	50	Y M			50		
3920	BC	51	Y M			51		
3919	BC	52	Y M			52		
3918	BC	53	Y M			53		
3917	BC	54	Y M			54		
3916	BC	55	Y M			55		
3915	BC	56	Y M			56		
3914	BC	57	Y M			57		
3913	BC	58	Y M			58		
3912	BC	59	Y M			59		
3911	BC	60	Y M			60		
3910	BC	61	Y M			61		

BC AD Years + or -		YM Years		6000 Years of Mankind Copyright © 2024 by Walter R. Dolen **Biblical Chronology Details** YM = Year of Mankind Begins in Sept/Oct 3 months before BC/AD dates	Additional Details	# of yrs	# of yrs	# of yrs
3909	BC	62	YM			62		
3908	BC	63	YM			63		
3907	BC	64	YM			64		
3906	BC	65	YM			65		
3905	BC	66	YM			66		
3904	BC	67	YM			67		
3903	BC	68	YM			68		
3902	BC	69	YM			69		
3901	BC	70	YM			70		
3900	BC	71	YM			71		
3899	BC	72	YM			72		
3898	BC	73	YM			73		
3897	BC	74	YM			74		
3896	BC	75	YM			75		
3895	BC	76	YM			76		
3894	BC	77	YM			77		
3893	BC	78	YM			78		
3892	BC	79	YM			79		
3891	BC	80	YM			80		
3890	BC	81	YM			81		
3889	BC	82	YM			82		

[Top | Flood | Abram | Exodus | David | Hezekiah | Jerusalem | JC | End Time | End Notes]

BC AD Years + or -		YM Years		**6000 Years of Mankind** Copyright © 2024 by Walter R. Dolen **Biblical Chronology Details** YM = Year of Mankind Begins in Sept/Oct 3 months before BC/AD dates	**Additional Details**	# of yrs	# of yrs	# of yrs
3888	BC	83	YM			83		
3887	BC	84	YM			84		
3886	BC	85	YM			85		
3885	BC	86	YM			86		
3884	BC	87	YM			87		
3883	BC	88	YM			88		
3882	BC	89	YM			89		
3881	BC	90	YM			90		
3880	BC	91	YM			91		
3879	BC	92	YM			92		
3878	BC	93	YM			93		
3877	BC	94	YM			94		
3876	BC	95	YM			95		
3875	BC	96	YM			96		
3874	BC	97	YM			97		
3873	BC	98	YM			98		
3872	BC	99	YM			99		
3871	BC	100	YM			100		
3870	BC	101	YM			101		
3869	BC	102	YM			102		
3868	BC	103	YM			103		

[Top	Flood	Abram	Exodus	David	Hezekiah	Jerusalem	JC	End Time	End Notes]							
BC AD Years + or -		YM Years	**6000 Years of Mankind** Copyright © 2024 by Walter R. Dolen **Biblical Chronology Details** YM = Year of Mankind Begins in Sept/Oct 3 months before BC/AD dates		**Additional Details**	# of yrs	# of yrs	# of yrs
3867	BC	104	Y M			104		
3866	BC	105	Y M			105		
3865	BC	106	Y M			106		
3864	BC	107	Y M			107		
3863	BC	108	Y M			108		
3862	BC	109	Y M			109		
3861	BC	110	Y M			110		
3860	BC	111	Y M			111		
3859	BC	112	Y M			112		
3858	BC	113	Y M			113		
3857	BC	114	Y M			114		
3856	BC	115	Y M			115		
3855	BC	116	Y M			116		
3854	BC	117	Y M			117		
3853	BC	118	Y M			118		
3852	BC	119	Y M			119		
3851	BC	120	Y M			120		
3850	BC	121	Y M			121		
3849	BC	122	Y M			122		
3848	BC	123	Y M			123		
3847	BC	124	Y M			124		

BC AD Years + or -		YM Years		6000 Years of Mankind Copyright © 2024 by Walter R. Dolen **Biblical Chronology Details** YM = Year of Mankind Begins in Sept/Oct 3 months before BC/AD dates	Additional Details	# of yrs	# of yrs	# of yrs
3846	BC	125	Y M			125		
3845	BC	126	Y M			126		
3844	BC	127	Y M			127		
3843	BC	128	Y M			128		
3842	BC	129	Y M			129		
3841	BC	130	Y M	Seth born		130		
3840	BC	131	Y M	**Seth** first year[1]; died in 1042 YM, son of 912 years (Gen 5:3,8) [Next] "And Seth lived 105 years and begat Enosh" (Gen 5:6)	[8] So all the days of Seth were nine hundred and twelve years, and he died. (Gen 5:8 BCB)	1		
3839	BC	132	Y M			2		
3838	BC	133	Y M			3		
3837	BC	134	Y M			4		
3836	BC	135	Y M			5		
3835	BC	136	Y M			6		
3834	BC	137	Y M			7		
3833	BC	138	Y M			8		
3832	BC	139	Y M			9		
3831	BC	140	Y M			10		
3830	BC	141	Y M			11		
3829	BC	142	Y M			12		
3828	BC	143	Y M			13		
3827	BC	144	Y M			14		

[Top | Flood | Abram | Exodus | David | Hezekiah | Jerusalem | JC | End Time | End Notes]

BC AD Years + or -		YM Years		6000 Years of Mankind Copyright © 2024 by Walter R. Dolen **Biblical Chronology Details** YM = Year of Mankind Begins in Sept/Oct 3 months before BC/AD dates	Additional Details	# of yrs	# of yrs	# of yrs
3826	BC	145	Y M			15		
3825	BC	146	Y M			16		
3824	BC	147	Y M			17		
3823	BC	148	Y M			18		
3822	BC	149	Y M			19		
3821	BC	150	Y M			20		
3820	BC	151	Y M			21		
3819	BC	152	Y M			22		
3818	BC	153	Y M			23		
3817	BC	154	Y M			24		
3816	BC	155	Y M			25		
3815	BC	156	Y M			26		
3814	BC	157	Y M			27		
3813	BC	158	Y M			28		
3812	BC	159	Y M			29		
3811	BC	160	Y M			30		
3810	BC	161	Y M			31		
3809	BC	162	Y M			32		
3808	BC	163	Y M			33		
3807	BC	164	Y M			34		
3806	BC	165	Y M			35		

BC AD Years + or -		YM Years		**6000 Years of Mankind** Copyright © 2024 by Walter R. Dolen **Biblical Chronology Details** YM = Year of Mankind Begins in Sept/Oct 3 months before BC/AD dates	**Additional Details**	# of yrs	# of yrs	# of yrs
3805	BC	166	Y M			36		
3804	BC	167	Y M			37		
3803	BC	168	Y M			38		
3802	BC	169	Y M			39		
3801	BC	170	Y M			40		
3800	BC	171	Y M			41		
3799	BC	172	Y M			42		
3798	BC	173	Y M			43		
3797	BC	174	Y M			44		
3796	BC	175	Y M			45		
3795	BC	176	Y M			46		
3794	BC	177	Y M			47		
3793	BC	178	Y M			48		
3792	BC	179	Y M			49		
3791	BC	180	Y M			50		
3790	BC	181	Y M			51		
3789	BC	182	Y M			52		
3788	BC	183	Y M			53		
3787	BC	184	Y M			54		
3786	BC	185	Y M			55		
3785	BC	186	Y M			56		

[Top | Flood | Abram | Exodus | David | Hezekiah | Jerusalem | JC | End Time | End Notes]

BC AD Years + or -		YM Years		**6000 Years of Mankind** Copyright © 2024 by Walter R. Dolen **Biblical Chronology Details** YM = Year of Mankind Begins in Sept/Oct 3 months before BC/AD dates	**Additional Details**	# of yrs	# of yrs	# of yrs
3784	BC	187	Y M			57		
3783	BC	188	Y M			58		
3782	BC	189	Y M			59		
3781	BC	190	Y M			60		
3780	BC	191	Y M			61		
3779	BC	192	Y M			62		
3778	BC	193	Y M			63		
3777	BC	194	Y M			64		
3776	BC	195	Y M			65		
3775	BC	196	Y M			66		
3774	BC	197	Y M			67		
3773	BC	198	Y M			68		
3772	BC	199	Y M			69		
3771	BC	200	Y M			70		
3770	BC	201	Y M			71		
3769	BC	202	Y M			72		
3768	BC	203	Y M			73		
3767	BC	204	Y M			74		
3766	BC	205	Y M			75		
3765	BC	206	Y M			76		
3764	BC	207	Y M			77		

[Top | Flood | Abram | Exodus | David | Hezekiah | Jerusalem | JC | End Time | End Notes]

BC AD Years + or -		YM Years		**6000 Years of Mankind** Copyright © 2024 by Walter R. Dolen **Biblical Chronology Details** YM = Year of Mankind Begins in Sept/Oct 3 months before BC/AD dates	**Additional Details**	# of yrs	# of yrs	# of yrs
3763	BC	208	Y M			78		
3762	BC	209	Y M			79		
3761	BC	210	Y M			80		
3760	BC	211	Y M			81		
3759	BC	212	Y M			82		
3758	BC	213	Y M			83		
3757	BC	214	Y M			84		
3756	BC	215	Y M			85		
3755	BC	216	Y M			86		
3754	BC	217	Y M			87		
3753	BC	218	Y M			88		
3752	BC	219	Y M			89		
3751	BC	220	Y M			90		
3750	BC	221	Y M			91		
3749	BC	222	Y M			92		
3748	BC	223	Y M			93		
3747	BC	224	Y M			94		
3746	BC	225	Y M			95		
3745	BC	226	Y M			96		
3744	BC	227	Y M			97		
3743	BC	228	Y M			98		

[Top | Flood | Abram | Exodus | David | Hezekiah | Jerusalem | JC | End Time | End Notes]

BC AD Years + or -		YM Years		6000 Years of Mankind Copyright © 2024 by Walter R. Dolen **Biblical Chronology Details** YM = Year of Mankind Begins in Sept/Oct 3 months before BC/AD dates	Additional Details	# of yrs	# of yrs	# of yrs
3742	BC	229	Y M			99		
3741	BC	230	Y M			100		
3740	BC	231	Y M			101		
3739	BC	232	Y M			102		
3738	BC	233	Y M			103		
3737	BC	234	Y M			104		
3736	BC	235	Y M	Enos born		105		
3735	BC	236	Y M	**Enosh** first year; died in 1140 YM, son of 905 years (Gen 5:6, 11) [Next] "And Enosh lived 90 years and begat Cainan" (Gen 5:9)	[11] So all the days of Enosh were nine hundred and five years, and he died. (Gen 5:11 BCB)	1		
3734	BC	237	Y M			2		
3733	BC	238	Y M			3		
3732	BC	239	Y M			4		
3731	BC	240	Y M			5		
3730	BC	241	Y M			6		
3729	BC	242	Y M			7		
3728	BC	243	Y M			8		
3727	BC	244	Y M			9		
3726	BC	245	Y M			10		
3725	BC	246	Y M			11		
3724	BC	247	Y M			12		
3723	BC	248	Y M			13		

[Top | Flood | Abram | Exodus | David | Hezekiah | Jerusalem | JC | End Time | End Notes]

BC AD Years + or -		YM Years		**6000 Years of Mankind** Copyright © 2024 by Walter R. Dolen **Biblical Chronology Details** YM = Year of Mankind Begins in Sept/Oct 3 months before BC/AD dates	**Additional Details**	# of yrs	# of yrs	# of yrs
3722	BC	249	Y M			14		
3721	BC	250	Y M			15		
3720	BC	251	Y M			16		
3719	BC	252	Y M			17		
3718	BC	253	Y M			18		
3717	BC	254	Y M			19		
3716	BC	255	Y M			20		
3715	BC	256	Y M			21		
3714	BC	257	Y M			22		
3713	BC	258	Y M			23		
3712	BC	259	Y M			24		
3711	BC	260	Y M			25		
3710	BC	261	Y M			26		
3709	BC	262	Y M			27		
3708	BC	263	Y M			28		
3707	BC	264	Y M			29		
3706	BC	265	Y M			30		
3705	BC	266	Y M			31		
3704	BC	267	Y M			32		
3703	BC	268	Y M			33		
3702	BC	269	Y M			34		

[Top | Flood | Abram | Exodus | David | Hezekiah | Jerusalem | JC | End Time | End Notes]

BC AD Years + or -		YM Years		6000 Years of Mankind Copyright © 2024 by Walter R. Dolen Biblical Chronology Details YM = Year of Mankind Begins in Sept/Oct 3 months before BC/AD dates	Additional Details	# of yrs	# of yrs	# of yrs
3701	BC	270	Y M			35		
3700	BC	271	Y M			36		
3699	BC	272	Y M			37		
3698	BC	273	Y M			38		
3697	BC	274	Y M			39		
3696	BC	275	Y M			40		
3695	BC	276	Y M			41		
3694	BC	277	Y M			42		
3693	BC	278	Y M			43		
3692	BC	279	Y M			44		
3691	BC	280	Y M			45		
3690	BC	281	Y M			46		
3689	BC	282	Y M			47		
3688	BC	283	Y M			48		
3687	BC	284	Y M			49		
3686	BC	285	Y M			50		
3685	BC	286	Y M			51		
3684	BC	287	Y M			52		
3683	BC	288	Y M			53		
3682	BC	289	Y M			54		
3681	BC	290	Y M			55		

[Top | Flood | Abram | Exodus | David | Hezekiah | Jerusalem | JC | End Time | End Notes]

BC AD Years + or -		YM Years		**6000 Years of Mankind** Copyright © 2024 by Walter R. Dolen **Biblical Chronology Details** YM = Year of Mankind Begins in Sept/Oct 3 months before BC/AD dates	**Additional Details**	# of yrs	# of yrs	# of yrs
3680	BC	291	Y M			56		
3679	BC	292	Y M			57		
3678	BC	293	Y M			58		
3677	BC	294	Y M			59		
3676	BC	295	Y M			60		
3675	BC	296	Y M			61		
3674	BC	297	Y M			62		
3673	BC	298	Y M			63		
3672	BC	299	Y M			64		
3671	BC	300	Y M			65		
3670	BC	301	Y M			66		
3669	BC	302	Y M			67		
3668	BC	303	Y M			68		
3667	BC	304	Y M			69		
3666	BC	305	Y M			70		
3665	BC	306	Y M			71		
3664	BC	307	Y M			72		
3663	BC	308	Y M			73		
3662	BC	309	Y M			74		
3661	BC	310	Y M			75		
3660	BC	311	Y M			76		

BC AD Years + or -		YM Years		6000 Years of Mankind Copyright © 2024 by Walter R. Dolen **Biblical Chronology Details** YM = Year of Mankind Begins in Sept/Oct 3 months before BC/AD dates	**Additional Details**	# of yrs	# of yrs	# of yrs
3659	BC	312	Y M			77		
3658	BC	313	Y M			78		
3657	BC	314	Y M			79		
3656	BC	315	Y M			80		
3655	BC	316	Y M			81		
3654	BC	317	Y M			82		
3653	BC	318	Y M			83		
3652	BC	319	Y M			84		
3651	BC	320	Y M			85		
3650	BC	321	Y M			86		
3649	BC	322	Y M			87		
3648	BC	323	Y M			88		
3647	BC	324	Y M			89		
3646	BC	325	Y M	Cainan born		90		
3645	BC	326	Y M	**Cainan** (Kenan) first year; died in 1235 YM, son of 910 years (Gen 5:9, 14) [Next] "And Cainan lived 70 years and begat Mahalalel" Gen 5:12)	[14] So all the days of Kenan were nine hundred and ten years, and he died. (Gen 5:14 BCB)	1		
3644	BC	327	Y M			2		
3643	BC	328	Y M			3		
3642	BC	329	Y M			4		
3641	BC	330	Y M			5		
3640	BC	331	Y M			6		

[Top | Flood | Abram | Exodus | David | Hezekiah | Jerusalem | JC | End Time | End Notes]								
BC AD Years + or -		YM Years		**6000 Years of Mankind** Copyright © 2024 by Walter R. Dolen **Biblical Chronology Details** YM = Year of Mankind Begins in Sept/Oct 3 months before BC/AD dates	**Additional Details**	# of yrs	# of yrs	# of yrs
3639	BC	332	Y M			7		
3638	BC	333	Y M			8		
3637	BC	334	Y M			9		
3636	BC	335	Y M			10		
3635	BC	336	Y M			11		
3634	BC	337	Y M			12		
3633	BC	338	Y M			13		
3632	BC	339	Y M			14		
3631	BC	340	Y M			15		
3630	BC	341	Y M			16		
3629	BC	342	Y M			17		
3628	BC	343	Y M			18		
3627	BC	344	Y M			19		
3626	BC	345	Y M			20		
3625	BC	346	Y M			21		
3624	BC	347	Y M			22		
3623	BC	348	Y M			23		
3622	BC	349	Y M			24		
3621	BC	350	Y M			25		
3620	BC	351	Y M			26		
3619	BC	352	Y M			27		

[Top | Flood | Abram | Exodus | David | Hezekiah | Jerusalem | JC | End Time | End Notes]

BC AD Years + or -		YM Years		**6000 Years of Mankind** Copyright © 2024 by Walter R. Dolen **Biblical Chronology Details** YM = Year of Mankind Begins in Sept/Oct 3 months before BC/AD dates	**Additional Details**	# of yrs	# of yrs	# of yrs
3618	BC	353	Y M			28		
3617	BC	354	Y M			29		
3616	BC	355	Y M			30		
3615	BC	356	Y M			31		
3614	BC	357	Y M			32		
3613	BC	358	Y M			33		
3612	BC	359	Y M			34		
3611	BC	360	Y M			35		
3610	BC	361	Y M			36		
3609	BC	362	Y M			37		
3608	BC	363	Y M			38		
3607	BC	364	Y M			39		
3606	BC	365	Y M			40		
3605	BC	366	Y M			41		
3604	BC	367	Y M			42		
3603	BC	368	Y M			43		
3602	BC	369	Y M			44		
3601	BC	370	Y M			45		
3600	BC	371	Y M			46		
3599	BC	372	Y M			47		
3598	BC	373	Y M			48		

BC AD Years + or -		YM Years		**6000 Years of Mankind** Copyright © 2024 by Walter R. Dolen **Biblical Chronology Details** YM = Year of Mankind Begins in Sept/Oct 3 months before BC/AD dates	**Additional Details**	# of yrs	# of yrs	# of yrs
3597	BC	374	Y M			49		
3596	BC	375	Y M			50		
3595	BC	376	Y M			51		
3594	BC	377	Y M			52		
3593	BC	378	Y M			53		
3592	BC	379	Y M			54		
3591	BC	380	Y M			55		
3590	BC	381	Y M			56		
3589	BC	382	Y M			57		
3588	BC	383	Y M			58		
3587	BC	384	Y M			59		
3586	BC	385	Y M			60		
3585	BC	386	Y M			61		
3584	BC	387	Y M			62		
3583	BC	388	Y M			63		
3582	BC	389	Y M			64		
3581	BC	390	Y M			65		
3580	BC	391	Y M			66		
3579	BC	392	Y M			67		
3578	BC	393	Y M			68		
3577	BC	394	Y M			69		

BC AD Years + or -		YM Years		6000 Years of Mankind Copyright © 2024 by Walter R. Dolen **Biblical Chronology Details** YM = Year of Mankind Begins in Sept/Oct 3 months before BC/AD dates	Additional Details	# of yrs	# of yrs	# of yrs
3576	BC	395	YM	Mahalaleel born		70		
3575	BC	396	YM	**Mahalaleel** first year; died in 1290 YM, son of 895 years (Gen 5:12, 17) [Next] "And lived Mahalalel 65 years and begat Jarred" (Gen 5:15)	[17] So all the days of Mahalalel were eight hundred and ninety-five years, and he died. (Gen 5:17 BCB)	1		
3574	BC	397	YM			2		
3573	BC	398	YM			3		
3572	BC	399	YM			4		
3571	BC	400	YM			5		
3570	BC	401	YM			6		
3569	BC	402	YM			7		
3568	BC	403	YM			8		
3567	BC	404	YM			9		
3566	BC	405	YM			10		
3565	BC	406	YM			11		
3564	BC	407	YM			12		
3563	BC	408	YM			13		
3562	BC	409	YM			14		
3561	BC	410	YM			15		
3560	BC	411	YM			16		
3559	BC	412	YM			17		
3558	BC	413	YM			18		
3557	BC	414	YM			19		

				6000 Years of Mankind Copyright © 2024 by Walter R. Dolen **Biblical Chronology Details** YM = Year of Mankind Begins in Sept/Oct 3 months before BC/AD dates	**Additional Details**	# of yrs	# of yrs	# of yrs
				[Top | Flood | Abram | Exodus | David | Hezekiah | Jerusalem | JC | End Time | End Notes]				
BC AD Years + or -		YM Years						
3556	BC	415	YM			20		
3555	BC	416	YM			21		
3554	BC	417	YM			22		
3553	BC	418	YM			23		
3552	BC	419	YM			24		
3551	BC	420	YM			25		
3550	BC	421	YM			26		
3549	BC	422	YM			27		
3548	BC	423	YM			28		
3547	BC	424	YM			29		
3546	BC	425	YM			30		
3545	BC	426	YM			31		
3544	BC	427	YM			32		
3543	BC	428	YM			33		
3542	BC	429	YM			34		
3541	BC	430	YM			35		
3540	BC	431	YM			36		
3539	BC	432	YM			37		
3538	BC	433	YM			38		
3537	BC	434	YM			39		
3536	BC	435	YM			40		

BC AD Years + or -		YM Years		**6000 Years of Mankind** Copyright © 2024 by Walter R. Dolen **Biblical Chronology Details** YM = Year of Mankind Begins in Sept/Oct 3 months before BC/AD dates	**Additional Details**	# of yrs	# of yrs	# of yrs
3535	BC	436	Y M			41		
3534	BC	437	Y M			42		
3533	BC	438	Y M			43		
3532	BC	439	Y M			44		
3531	BC	440	Y M			45		
3530	BC	441	Y M			46		
3529	BC	442	Y M			47		
3528	BC	443	Y M			48		
3527	BC	444	Y M			49		
3526	BC	445	Y M			50		
3525	BC	446	Y M			51		
3524	BC	447	Y M			52		
3523	BC	448	Y M			53		
3522	BC	449	Y M			54		
3521	BC	450	Y M			55		
3520	BC	451	Y M			56		
3519	BC	452	Y M			57		
3518	BC	453	Y M			58		
3517	BC	454	Y M			59		
3516	BC	455	Y M			60		
3515	BC	456	Y M			61		

[Top | Flood | Abram | Exodus | David | Hezekiah | Jerusalem | JC | End Time | End Notes]

BC AD Years + or -		YM Years		**6000 Years of Mankind** Copyright © 2024 by Walter R. Dolen **Biblical Chronology Details** YM = Year of Mankind Begins in Sept/Oct 3 months before BC/AD dates	**Additional Details**	# of yrs	# of yrs	# of yrs
3514	BC	457	Y M			62		
3513	BC	458	Y M			63		
3512	BC	459	Y M			64		
3511	BC	460	Y M	Jared born		65		
3510	BC	461	Y M	**Jared** first year; died in 1422 YM, son of 962 years (Gen 5:15, 20) [Next] "And Jared lived 162 years and begat Enoch" (Gen 5:18)	[20] So all the days of Jared were nine hundred and sixty-two years, and he died. (Gen 5:20 BCB)	1		
3509	BC	462	Y M			2		
3508	BC	463	Y M			3		
3507	BC	464	Y M			4		
3506	BC	465	Y M			5		
3505	BC	466	Y M			6		
3504	BC	467	Y M			7		
3503	BC	468	Y M			8		
3502	BC	469	Y M			9		
3501	BC	470	Y M			10		
3500	BC	471	Y M			11		
3499	BC	472	Y M			12		
3498	BC	473	Y M			13		
3497	BC	474	Y M			14		
3496	BC	475	Y M			15		
3495	BC	476	Y M			16		

[Top | Flood | Abram | Exodus | David | Hezekiah | Jerusalem | JC | End Time | End Notes]

BC AD Years + or -		YM Years		6000 Years of Mankind Copyright © 2024 by Walter R. Dolen **Biblical Chronology Details** YM = Year of Mankind Begins in Sept/Oct 3 months before BC/AD dates	Additional Details	# of yrs	# of yrs	# of yrs
3494	BC	477	Y M			17		
3493	BC	478	Y M			18		
3492	BC	479	Y M			19		
3491	BC	480	Y M			20		
3490	BC	481	Y M			21		
3489	BC	482	Y M			22		
3488	BC	483	Y M			23		
3487	BC	484	Y M			24		
3486	BC	485	Y M			25		
3485	BC	486	Y M			26		
3484	BC	487	Y M			27		
3483	BC	488	Y M			28		
3482	BC	489	Y M			29		
3481	BC	490	Y M			30		
3480	BC	491	Y M			31		
3479	BC	492	Y M			32		
3478	BC	493	Y M			33		
3477	BC	494	Y M			34		
3476	BC	495	Y M			35		
3475	BC	496	Y M			36		
3474	BC	497	Y M			37		

BC AD Years + or -		YM Years		6000 Years of Mankind Copyright © 2024 by Walter R. Dolen **Biblical Chronology Details** YM = Year of Mankind Begins in Sept/Oct 3 months before BC/AD dates	Additional Details	# of yrs	# of yrs	# of yrs
3473	BC	498	Y M			38		
3472	BC	499	Y M			39		
3471	BC	500	Y M			40		
3470	BC	501	Y M			41		
3469	BC	502	Y M			42		
3468	BC	503	Y M			43		
3467	BC	504	Y M			44		
3466	BC	505	Y M			45		
3465	BC	506	Y M			46		
3464	BC	507	Y M			47		
3463	BC	508	Y M			48		
3462	BC	509	Y M			49		
3461	BC	510	Y M			50		
3460	BC	511	Y M			51		
3459	BC	512	Y M			52		
3458	BC	513	Y M			53		
3457	BC	514	Y M			54		
3456	BC	515	Y M			55		
3455	BC	516	Y M			56		
3454	BC	517	Y M			57		
3453	BC	518	Y M			58		

[Top | Flood | Abram | Exodus | David | Hezekiah | Jerusalem | JC | End Time | End Notes]

[Top | Flood | Abram | Exodus | David | Hezekiah | Jerusalem | JC | End Time | End Notes]

BC AD Years + or -		YM Years		**6000 Years of Mankind** Copyright © 2024 by Walter R. Dolen **Biblical Chronology Details** YM = Year of Mankind Begins in Sept/Oct 3 months before BC/AD dates	**Additional Details**	# of yrs	# of yrs	# of yrs
3452	BC	519	Y M			59		
3451	BC	520	Y M			60		
3450	BC	521	Y M			61		
3449	BC	522	Y M			62		
3448	BC	523	Y M			63		
3447	BC	524	Y M			64		
3446	BC	525	Y M			65		
3445	BC	526	Y M			66		
3444	BC	527	Y M			67		
3443	BC	528	Y M			68		
3442	BC	529	Y M			69		
3441	BC	530	Y M			70		
3440	BC	531	Y M			71		
3439	BC	532	Y M			72		
3438	BC	533	Y M			73		
3437	BC	534	Y M			74		
3436	BC	535	Y M			75		
3435	BC	536	Y M			76		
3434	BC	537	Y M			77		
3433	BC	538	Y M			78		
3432	BC	539	Y M			79		

BC AD Years + or -		YM Years		**6000 Years of Mankind** Copyright © 2024 by Walter R. Dolen **Biblical Chronology Details** YM = Year of Mankind Begins in Sept/Oct 3 months before BC/AD dates	**Additional Details**	# of yrs	# of yrs	# of yrs
3431	BC	540	Y M			80		
3430	BC	541	Y M			81		
3429	BC	542	Y M			82		
3428	BC	543	Y M			83		
3427	BC	544	Y M			84		
3426	BC	545	Y M			85		
3425	BC	546	Y M			86		
3424	BC	547	Y M			87		
3423	BC	548	Y M			88		
3422	BC	549	Y M			89		
3421	BC	550	Y M			90		
3420	BC	551	Y M			91		
3419	BC	552	Y M			92		
3418	BC	553	Y M			93		
3417	BC	554	Y M			94		
3416	BC	555	Y M			95		
3415	BC	556	Y M			96		
3414	BC	557	Y M			97		
3413	BC	558	Y M			98		
3412	BC	559	Y M			99		
3411	BC	560	Y M			100		

BC AD Years + or -		YM Years		**6000 Years of Mankind** Copyright © 2024 by Walter R. Dolen **Biblical Chronology Details** YM = Year of Mankind Begins in Sept/Oct 3 months before BC/AD dates	**Additional Details**	# of yrs	# of yrs	# of yrs
3410	BC	561	Y M			101		
3409	BC	562	Y M			102		
3408	BC	563	Y M			103		
3407	BC	564	Y M			104		
3406	BC	565	Y M			105		
3405	BC	566	Y M			106		
3404	BC	567	Y M			107		
3403	BC	568	Y M			108		
3402	BC	569	Y M			109		
3401	BC	570	Y M			110		
3400	BC	571	Y M			111		
3399	BC	572	Y M			112		
3398	BC	573	Y M			113		
3397	BC	574	Y M			114		
3396	BC	575	Y M			115		
3395	BC	576	Y M			116		
3394	BC	577	Y M			117		
3393	BC	578	Y M			118		
3392	BC	579	Y M			119		
3391	BC	580	Y M			120		
3390	BC	581	Y M			121		

BC AD Years + or -		YM Years		6000 Years of Mankind Copyright © 2024 by Walter R. Dolen **Biblical Chronology Details** YM = Year of Mankind Begins in Sept/Oct 3 months before BC/AD dates	Additional Details	# of yrs	# of yrs	# of yrs
				[Top | Flood | Abram | Exodus | David | Hezekiah | Jerusalem | JC | End Time | End Notes]				
3389	BC	582	YM			122		
3388	BC	583	YM			123		
3387	BC	584	YM			124		
3386	BC	585	YM			125		
3385	BC	586	YM			126		
3384	BC	587	YM			127		
3383	BC	588	YM			128		
3382	BC	589	YM			129		
3381	BC	590	YM			130		
3380	BC	591	YM			131		
3379	BC	592	YM			132		
3378	BC	593	YM			133		
3377	BC	594	YM			134		
3376	BC	595	YM			135		
3375	BC	596	YM			136		
3374	BC	597	YM			137		
3373	BC	598	YM			138		
3372	BC	599	YM			139		
3371	BC	600	YM			140		
3370	BC	601	YM			141		
3369	BC	602	YM			142		

[Top | Flood | Abram | Exodus | David | Hezekiah | Jerusalem | JC | End Time | End Notes]

BC AD Years + or -		YM Years		**6000 Years of Mankind** Copyright © 2024 by Walter R. Dolen **Biblical Chronology Details** YM = Year of Mankind Begins in Sept/Oct 3 months before BC/AD dates	**Additional Details**	# of yrs	# of yrs	# of yrs
3368	BC	603	Y M			143		
3367	BC	604	Y M			144		
3366	BC	605	Y M			145		
3365	BC	606	Y M			146		
3364	BC	607	Y M			147		
3363	BC	608	Y M			148		
3362	BC	609	Y M			149		
3361	BC	610	Y M			150		
3360	BC	611	Y M			151		
3359	BC	612	Y M			152		
3358	BC	613	Y M			153		
3357	BC	614	Y M			154		
3356	BC	615	Y M			155		
3355	BC	616	Y M			156		
3354	BC	617	Y M			157		
3353	BC	618	Y M			158		
3352	BC	619	Y M			159		
3351	BC	620	Y M			160		
3350	BC	621	Y M			161		
3349	BC	622	Y M	Enoch born		162		

BC AD Years + or -		YM Years		6000 Years of Mankind Copyright © 2024 by Walter R. Dolen **Biblical Chronology Details** YM = Year of Mankind Begins in Sept/Oct 3 months before BC/AD dates	**Additional Details**	# of yrs	# of yrs	# of yrs
3348	BC	623	Y M	**Enoch** first year; "took" in 987 YM, son of 365 years (Gen 5:18, 23) [Next] "And Enoch lived 65 years and begat Methuselah" (Gen 5:21)	[23] So all the days of Enoch were three hundred and sixty-five years. (Gen 5:23 BCB)	1		
3347	BC	624	Y M			2		
3346	BC	625	Y M			3		
3345	BC	626	Y M			4		
3344	BC	627	Y M			5		
3343	BC	628	Y M			6		
3342	BC	629	Y M			7		
3341	BC	630	Y M			8		
3340	BC	631	Y M			9		
3339	BC	632	Y M			10		
3338	BC	633	Y M			11		
3337	BC	634	Y M			12		
3336	BC	635	Y M			13		
3335	BC	636	Y M			14		
3334	BC	637	Y M			15		
3333	BC	638	Y M			16		
3332	BC	639	Y M			17		
3331	BC	640	Y M			18		
3330	BC	641	Y M			19		
3329	BC	642	Y M			20		

[Top | Flood | Abram | Exodus | David | Hezekiah | Jerusalem | JC | End Time | End Notes]

BC AD Years + or -		YM Years		6000 Years of Mankind Copyright © 2024 by Walter R. Dolen Biblical Chronology Details YM = Year of Mankind Begins in Sept/Oct 3 months before BC/AD dates	Additional Details	# of yrs	# of yrs	# of yrs
3328	BC	643	Y M			21		
3327	BC	644	Y M			22		
3326	BC	645	Y M			23		
3325	BC	646	Y M			24		
3324	BC	647	Y M			25		
3323	BC	648	Y M			26		
3322	BC	649	Y M			27		
3321	BC	650	Y M			28		
3320	BC	651	Y M			29		
3319	BC	652	Y M			30		
3318	BC	653	Y M			31		
3317	BC	654	Y M			32		
3316	BC	655	Y M			33		
3315	BC	656	Y M			34		
3314	BC	657	Y M			35		
3313	BC	658	Y M			36		
3312	BC	659	Y M			37		
3311	BC	660	Y M			38		
3310	BC	661	Y M			39		
3309	BC	662	Y M			40		
3308	BC	663	Y M			41		

[Top | Flood | Abram | Exodus | David | Hezekiah | Jerusalem | JC | End Time | End Notes]

BC AD Years + or -		YM Years		6000 Years of Mankind Copyright © 2024 by Walter R. Dolen **Biblical Chronology Details** YM = Year of Mankind Begins in Sept/Oct 3 months before BC/AD dates	Additional Details	# of yrs	# of yrs	# of yrs
3307	BC	664	Y M			42		
3306	BC	665	Y M			43		
3305	BC	666	Y M			44		
3304	BC	667	Y M			45		
3303	BC	668	Y M			46		
3302	BC	669	Y M			47		
3301	BC	670	Y M			48		
3300	BC	671	Y M			49		
3299	BC	672	Y M			50		
3298	BC	673	Y M			51		
3297	BC	674	Y M			52		
3296	BC	675	Y M			53		
3295	BC	676	Y M			54		
3294	BC	677	Y M			55		
3293	BC	678	Y M			56		
3292	BC	679	Y M			57		
3291	BC	680	Y M			58		
3290	BC	681	Y M			59		
3289	BC	682	Y M			60		
3288	BC	683	Y M			61		
3287	BC	684	Y M			62		

BC AD Years + or -		YM Years		6000 Years of Mankind Copyright © 2024 by Walter R. Dolen Biblical Chronology Details YM = Year of Mankind Begins in Sept/Oct 3 months before BC/AD dates	Additional Details	# of yrs	# of yrs	# of yrs
3286	BC	685	Y M			63		
3285	BC	686	Y M			64		
3284	BC	687	Y M	Methuselah born		65		
3283	BC	688	Y M	**Methuselah** first year; died in 1656 YM, son of 969 years (Gen 5:21, 27) [Next] "And lived Methuselah 187 years and begat Lamech" (Gen 5:25)	[27] So all the days of Methuselah were nine hundred and sixty-nine years, and he died. (Gen 5:27 BCB)	1		
3282	BC	689	Y M			2		
3281	BC	690	Y M			3		
3280	BC	691	Y M			4		
3279	BC	692	Y M			5		
3278	BC	693	Y M			6		
3277	BC	694	Y M			7		
3276	BC	695	Y M			8		
3275	BC	696	Y M			9		
3274	BC	697	Y M			10		
3273	BC	698	Y M			11		
3272	BC	699	Y M			12		
3271	BC	700	Y M			13		
3270	BC	701	Y M			14		
3269	BC	702	Y M			15		
3268	BC	703	Y M			16		
3267	BC	704	Y M			17		

BC AD Years + or -		YM Years		**6000 Years of Mankind** Copyright © 2024 by Walter R. Dolen **Biblical Chronology Details** YM = Year of Mankind Begins in Sept/Oct 3 months before BC/AD dates	**Additional Details**	# of yrs	# of yrs	# of yrs
3266	BC	705	Y M			18		
3265	BC	706	Y M			19		
3264	BC	707	Y M			20		
3263	BC	708	Y M			21		
3262	BC	709	Y M			22		
3261	BC	710	Y M			23		
3260	BC	711	Y M			24		
3259	BC	712	Y M			25		
3258	BC	713	Y M			26		
3257	BC	714	Y M			27		
3256	BC	715	Y M			28		
3255	BC	716	Y M			29		
3254	BC	717	Y M			30		
3253	BC	718	Y M			31		
3252	BC	719	Y M			32		
3251	BC	720	Y M			33		
3250	BC	721	Y M			34		
3249	BC	722	Y M			35		
3248	BC	723	Y M			36		
3247	BC	724	Y M			37		
3246	BC	725	Y M			38		

BC AD Years + or -		YM Years		*6000 Years of Mankind* Copyright © 2024 by Walter R. Dolen **Biblical Chronology Details** YM = Year of Mankind Begins in Sept/Oct 3 months before BC/AD dates	**Additional Details**	# of yrs	# of yrs	# of yrs
3245	BC	726	Y M			39		
3244	BC	727	Y M			40		
3243	BC	728	Y M			41		
3242	BC	729	Y M			42		
3241	BC	730	Y M			43		
3240	BC	731	Y M			44		
3239	BC	732	Y M			45		
3238	BC	733	Y M			46		
3237	BC	734	Y M			47		
3236	BC	735	Y M			48		
3235	BC	736	Y M			49		
3234	BC	737	Y M			50		
3233	BC	738	Y M			51		
3232	BC	739	Y M			52		
3231	BC	740	Y M			53		
3230	BC	741	Y M			54		
3229	BC	742	Y M			55		
3228	BC	743	Y M			56		
3227	BC	744	Y M			57		
3226	BC	745	Y M			58		
3225	BC	746	Y M			59		

| | [Top | Flood | Abram | Exodus | David | Hezekiah | Jerusalem | JC | End Time | End Notes] | | | | |

BC AD Years + or -		YM Years		**6000 Years of Mankind** Copyright © 2024 by Walter R. Dolen **Biblical Chronology Details** YM = Year of Mankind Begins in Sept/Oct 3 months before BC/AD dates	**Additional Details**	# of yrs	# of yrs	# of yrs
3224	BC	747	Y M			60		
3223	BC	748	Y M			61		
3222	BC	749	Y M			62		
3221	BC	750	Y M			63		
3220	BC	751	Y M			64		
3219	BC	752	Y M			65		
3218	BC	753	Y M			66		
3217	BC	754	Y M			67		
3216	BC	755	Y M			68		
3215	BC	756	Y M			69		
3214	BC	757	Y M			70		
3213	BC	758	Y M			71		
3212	BC	759	Y M			72		
3211	BC	760	Y M			73		
3210	BC	761	Y M			74		
3209	BC	762	Y M			75		
3208	BC	763	Y M			76		
3207	BC	764	Y M			77		
3206	BC	765	Y M			78		
3205	BC	766	Y M			79		
3204	BC	767	Y M			80		

[Top | Flood | Abram | Exodus | David | Hezekiah | Jerusalem | JC | End Time | End Notes]

BC AD Years + or -		YM Years		6000 Years of Mankind Copyright © 2024 by Walter R. Dolen **Biblical Chronology Details** YM = Year of Mankind Begins in Sept/Oct 3 months before BC/AD dates	**Additional Details**	# of yrs	# of yrs	# of yrs
3203	BC	768	Y M			81		
3202	BC	769	Y M			82		
3201	BC	770	Y M			83		
3200	BC	771	Y M			84		
3199	BC	772	Y M			85		
3198	BC	773	Y M			86		
3197	BC	774	Y M			87		
3196	BC	775	Y M			88		
3195	BC	776	Y M			89		
3194	BC	777	Y M			90		
3193	BC	778	Y M			91		
3192	BC	779	Y M			92		
3191	BC	780	Y M			93		
3190	BC	781	Y M			94		
3189	BC	782	Y M			95		
3188	BC	783	Y M			96		
3187	BC	784	Y M			97		
3186	BC	785	Y M			98		
3185	BC	786	Y M			99		
3184	BC	787	Y M			100		
3183	BC	788	Y M			101		

[Top | Flood | Abram | Exodus | David | Hezekiah | Jerusalem | JC | End Time | End Notes]

BC AD Years + or -		YM Years		**6000 Years of Mankind** Copyright © 2024 by Walter R. Dolen **Biblical Chronology Details** YM = Year of Mankind Begins in Sept/Oct 3 months before BC/AD dates	**Additional Details**	# of yrs	# of yrs	# of yrs
3182	BC	789	Y M			102		
3181	BC	790	Y M			103		
3180	BC	791	Y M			104		
3179	BC	792	Y M			105		
3178	BC	793	Y M			106		
3177	BC	794	Y M			107		
3176	BC	795	Y M			108		
3175	BC	796	Y M			109		
3174	BC	797	Y M			110		
3173	BC	798	Y M			111		
3172	BC	799	Y M			112		
3171	BC	800	Y M			113		
3170	BC	801	Y M			114		
3169	BC	802	Y M			115		
3168	BC	803	Y M			116		
3167	BC	804	Y M			117		
3166	BC	805	Y M			118		
3165	BC	806	Y M			119		
3164	BC	807	Y M			120		
3163	BC	808	Y M			121		
3162	BC	009	Y M			122		

[Top | Flood | Abram | Exodus | David | Hezekiah | Jerusalem | JC | End Time | End Notes]

BC AD Years + or -		YM Years		6000 Years of Mankind Copyright © 2024 by Walter R. Dolen **Biblical Chronology Details** YM = Year of Mankind Begins in Sept/Oct 3 months before BC/AD dates	Additional Details	# of yrs	# of yrs	# of yrs
3161	BC	810	Y M			123		
3160	BC	811	Y M			124		
3159	BC	812	Y M			125		
3158	BC	813	Y M			126		
3157	BC	814	Y M			127		
3156	BC	815	Y M			128		
3155	BC	816	Y M			129		
3154	BC	817	Y M			130		
3153	BC	818	Y M			131		
3152	BC	819	Y M			132		
3151	BC	820	Y M			133		
3150	BC	821	Y M			134		
3149	BC	822	Y M			135		
3148	BC	823	Y M			136		
3147	BC	824	Y M			137		
3146	BC	825	Y M			138		
3145	BC	826	Y M			139		
3144	BC	827	Y M			140		
3143	BC	828	Y M			141		
3142	BC	829	Y M			142		
3141	BC	830	Y M			143		

[Top | Flood | Abram | Exodus | David | Hezekiah | Jerusalem | JC | End Time | End Notes]

BC AD Years + or -		YM Years		6000 Years of Mankind Copyright © 2024 by Walter R. Dolen **Biblical Chronology Details** YM = Year of Mankind Begins in Sept/Oct 3 months before BC/AD dates	Additional Details	# of yrs	# of yrs	# of yrs
3140	BC	831	YM			144		
3139	BC	832	YM			145		
3138	BC	833	YM			146		
3137	BC	834	YM			147		
3136	BC	835	YM			148		
3135	BC	836	YM			149		
3134	BC	837	YM			150		
3133	BC	838	YM			151		
3132	BC	839	YM			152		
3131	BC	840	YM			153		
3130	BC	841	YM			154		
3129	BC	842	YM			155		
3128	BC	843	YM			156		
3127	BC	844	YM			157		
3126	BC	845	YM			158		
3125	BC	846	YM			159		
3124	BC	847	YM			160		
3123	BC	848	YM			161		
3122	BC	849	YM			162		
3121	BC	850	YM			163		
3120	BC	851	YM			164		

[Top	Flood	Abram	Exodus	David	Hezekiah	Jerusalem	JC	End Time	End Notes]

BC AD Years + or -		YM Years		**6000 Years of Mankind** Copyright © 2024 by Walter R. Dolen **Biblical Chronology Details** YM = Year of Mankind Begins in Sept/Oct 3 months before BC/AD dates	**Additional Details**	# of yrs	# of yrs	# of yrs
3119	BC	852	Y M			165		
3118	BC	853	Y M			166		
3117	BC	854	Y M			167		
3116	BC	855	Y M			168		
3115	BC	856	Y M			169		
3114	BC	857	Y M			170		
3113	BC	858	Y M			171		
3112	BC	859	Y M			172		
3111	BC	860	Y M			173		
3110	BC	861	Y M			174		
3109	BC	862	Y M			175		
3108	BC	863	Y M			176		
3107	BC	864	Y M			177		
3106	BC	865	Y M			178		
3105	BC	866	Y M			179		
3104	BC	867	Y M			180		
3103	BC	868	Y M			181		
3102	BC	869	Y M			182		
3101	BC	870	Y M			183		
3100	BC	871	Y M			184		
3099	BC	872	Y M			185		

BC AD Years + or -		YM Years		6000 Years of Mankind Copyright © 2024 by Walter R. Dolen **Biblical Chronology Details** YM = Year of Mankind Begins in Sept/Oct 3 months before BC/AD dates	**Additional Details**	# of yrs	# of yrs	# of yrs
3098	BC	873	Y M			186		
3097	BC	874	Y M	Lamech born		187		
3096	BC	875	Y M	**Lamech** first year; died in 1651 YM, son of 777 years (Gen 5:25, 31) [Next] "And lived Lamech 182 years and begat a son [Noah]" Gen 5:28)	[31] So all the days of Lamech were seven hundred and seventy-seven years, and he died. (Gen 5:31 BCB)	1		
3095	BC	876	Y M			2		
3094	BC	877	Y M			3		
3093	BC	878	Y M			4		
3092	BC	879	Y M			5		
3091	BC	880	Y M			6		
3090	BC	881	Y M			7		
3089	BC	882	Y M			8		
3088	BC	883	Y M			9		
3087	BC	884	Y M			10		
3086	BC	885	Y M			11		
3085	BC	886	Y M			12		
3084	BC	887	Y M			13		
3083	BC	888	Y M			14		
3082	BC	889	Y M			15		
3081	BC	890	Y M			16		
3080	BC	891	Y M			17		
3079	BC	892	Y M			18		

[Top | Flood | Abram | Exodus | David | Hezekiah | Jerusalem | JC | End Time | End Notes]

BC AD Years + or -		YM Years		**6000 Years of Mankind** Copyright © 2024 by Walter R. Dolen **Biblical Chronology Details** YM = Year of Mankind Begins in Sept/Oct 3 months before BC/AD dates	Additional Details	# of yrs	# of yrs	# of yrs
3078	BC	893	Y M			19		
3077	BC	894	Y M			20		
3076	BC	895	Y M			21		
3075	BC	896	Y M			22		
3074	BC	897	Y M			23		
3073	BC	898	Y M			24		
3072	BC	899	Y M			25		
3071	BC	900	Y M			26		
3070	BC	901	Y M			27		
3069	BC	902	Y M			28		
3068	BC	903	Y M			29		
3067	BC	904	Y M			30		
3066	BC	905	Y M			31		
3065	BC	906	Y M			32		
3064	BC	907	Y M			33		
3063	BC	908	Y M			34		
3062	BC	909	Y M			35		
3061	BC	910	Y M			36		
3060	BC	911	Y M			37		
3059	BC	912	Y M			38		
3058	BC	913	Y M			39		

[Top | Flood | Abram | Exodus | David | Hezekiah | Jerusalem | JC | End Time | End Notes]

BC AD Years + or -		YM Years		6000 Years of Mankind Copyright © 2024 by Walter R. Dolen **Biblical Chronology Details** YM = Year of Mankind Begins in Sept/Oct 3 months before BC/AD dates	Additional Details	# of yrs	# of yrs	# of yrs
3057	BC	914	Y M			40		
3056	BC	915	Y M			41		
3055	BC	916	Y M			42		
3054	BC	917	Y M			43		
3053	BC	918	Y M			44		
3052	BC	919	Y M			45		
3051	BC	920	Y M			46		
3050	BC	921	Y M			47		
3049	BC	922	Y M			48		
3048	BC	923	Y M			49		
3047	BC	924	Y M			50		
3046	BC	925	Y M			51		
3045	BC	926	Y M			52		
3044	BC	927	Y M			53		
3043	BC	928	Y M			54		
3042	BC	929	Y M			55		
3041	BC	930	Y M	**Adam dies in this year** (b, 1)		56		
3040	BC	931	Y M			57		
3039	BC	932	Y M			58		
3038	BC	933	Y M			59		
3037	BC	934	Y M			60		

[Top | Flood | Abram | Exodus | David | Hezekiah | Jerusalem | JC | End Time | End Notes]

BC AD Years + or -		YM Years		6000 Years of Mankind Copyright © 2024 by Walter R. Dolen **Biblical Chronology Details** YM = Year of Mankind Begins in Sept/Oct 3 months before BC/AD dates	**Additional Details**	# of yrs	# of yrs	# of yrs
3036	BC	935	Y M			61		
3035	BC	936	Y M			62		
3034	BC	937	Y M			63		
3033	BC	938	Y M			64		
3032	BC	939	Y M			65		
3031	BC	940	Y M			66		
3030	BC	941	Y M			67		
3029	BC	942	Y M			68		
3028	BC	943	Y M			69		
3027	BC	944	Y M			70		
3026	BC	945	Y M			71		
3025	BC	946	Y M			72		
3024	BC	947	Y M			73		
3023	BC	948	Y M			74		
3022	BC	949	Y M			75		
3021	BC	950	Y M			76		
3020	BC	951	Y M			77		
3019	BC	952	Y M			78		
3018	BC	953	Y M			79		
3017	BC	954	Y M			80		
3016	BC	955	Y M			81		

[Top | Flood | Abram | Exodus | David | Hezekiah | Jerusalem | JC | End Time | End Notes]

BC AD Years + or -		YM Years		6000 Years of Mankind Copyright © 2024 by Walter R. Dolen **Biblical Chronology Details** YM = Year of Mankind Begins in Sept/Oct 3 months before BC/AD dates	Additional Details	# of yrs	# of yrs	# of yrs
3015	BC	956	YM			82		
3014	BC	957	YM			83		
3013	BC	958	YM			84		
3012	BC	959	YM			85		
3011	BC	960	YM			86		
3010	BC	961	YM			87		
3009	BC	962	YM			88		
3008	BC	963	YM			89		
3007	BC	964	YM			90		
3006	BC	965	YM			91		
3005	BC	966	YM			92		
3004	BC	967	YM			93		
3003	BC	968	YM			94		
3002	BC	969	YM			95		
3001	BC	970	YM			96		
3000	BC	971	YM			97		
2999	BC	972	YM			98		
2998	BC	973	YM			99		
2997	BC	974	YM			100		
2996	BC	975	YM			101		
2995	BC	976	YM			102		

BC AD Years + or -		YM Years		6000 Years of Mankind Copyright © 2024 by Walter R. Dolen **Biblical Chronology Details** YM = Year of Mankind Begins in Sept/Oct 3 months before BC/AD dates	Additional Details	# of yrs	# of yrs	# of yrs
2994	BC	977	Y M			103		
2993	BC	978	Y M			104		
2992	BC	979	Y M			105		
2991	BC	980	Y M			106		
2990	BC	981	Y M			107		
2989	BC	982	Y M			108		
2988	BC	983	Y M			109		
2987	BC	984	Y M			110		
2986	BC	985	Y M			111		
2985	BC	986	Y M			112		
2984	BC	987	Y M	Enoch "took" (b. 623)		113		
2983	BC	988	Y M			114		
2982	BC	989	Y M			115		
2981	BC	990	Y M			116		
2980	BC	991	Y M			117		
2979	BC	992	Y M			118		
2978	BC	993	Y M			119		
2977	BC	994	Y M			120		
2976	BC	995	Y M			121		
2975	BC	996	Y M			122		
2974	BC	997	Y M			123		

[Top | Flood | Abram | Exodus | David | Hezekiah | Jerusalem | JC | End Time | End Notes]

BC AD Years + or -		YM Years		**6000 Years of Mankind** Copyright © 2024 by Walter R. Dolen **Biblical Chronology Details** YM = Year of Mankind Begins in Sept/Oct 3 months before BC/AD dates	**Additional Details**	# of yrs	# of yrs	# of yrs
2973	BC	998	YM			124		
2972	BC	999	YM			125		
2971	BC	1000	YM			126		
2970	BC	1001	YM			127		
2969	BC	1002	YM			128		
2968	BC	1003	YM			129		
2967	BC	1004	YM			130		
2966	BC	1005	YM			131		
2965	BC	1006	YM			132		
2964	BC	1007	YM			133		
2963	BC	1008	YM			134		
2962	BC	1009	YM			135		
2961	BC	1010	YM			136		
2960	BC	1011	YM			137		
2959	BC	1012	YM			138		
2958	BC	1013	YM			139		
2957	BC	1014	YM			140		
2956	BC	1015	YM			141		
2955	BC	1016	YM			142		
2954	BC	1017	YM			143		
2953	BC	1018	YM			144		

[Top | Flood | Abram | Exodus | David | Hezekiah | Jerusalem | JC | End Time | End Notes]

BC AD Years + or -		YM Years		6000 Years of Mankind Copyright © 2024 by Walter R. Dolen **Biblical Chronology Details** YM = Year of Mankind Begins in Sept/Oct 3 months before BC/AD dates	Additional Details	# of yrs	# of yrs	# of yrs
2952	BC	1019	Y M			145		
2951	BC	1020	Y M			146		
2950	BC	1021	Y M			147		
2949	BC	1022	Y M			148		
2948	BC	1023	Y M			149		
2947	BC	1024	Y M			150		
2946	BC	1025	Y M			151		
2945	BC	1026	Y M			152		
2944	BC	1027	Y M			153		
2943	BC	1028	Y M			154		
2942	BC	1029	Y M			155		
2941	BC	1030	Y M			156		
2940	BC	1031	Y M			157		
2939	BC	1032	Y M			158		
2938	BC	1033	Y M			159		
2937	BC	1034	Y M			160		
2936	BC	1035	Y M			161		
2935	BC	1036	Y M			162		
2934	BC	1037	Y M			163		
2933	BC	1038	Y M			164		
2932	BC	1039	Y M			165		

[Top | Flood | Abram | Exodus | David | Hezekiah | Jerusalem | JC | End Time | End Notes]

BC AD Years + or -		YM Years		6000 Years of Mankind Copyright © 2024 by Walter R. Dolen **Biblical Chronology Details** YM = Year of Mankind Begins in Sept/Oct 3 months before BC/AD dates	Additional Details	# of yrs	# of yrs	# of yrs
2931	BC	1040	Y M			166		
2930	BC	1041	Y M			167		
2929	BC	1042	Y M	**Seth died, son of 912 years (b. 130)**		168		
2928	BC	1043	Y M			169		
2927	BC	1044	Y M			170		
2926	BC	1045	Y M			171		
2925	BC	1046	Y M			172		
2924	BC	1047	Y M			173		
2923	BC	1048	Y M			174		
2922	BC	1049	Y M			175		
2921	BC	1050	Y M			176		
2920	BC	1051	Y M			177		
2919	BC	1052	Y M			178		
2918	BC	1053	Y M			179		
2917	BC	1054	Y M			180		
2916	BC	1055	Y M			181		
2915	BC	1056	Y M	Noah born		182		
2914	BC	1057	Y M	**Noah** first year; died in 2006 YM, son of 950 years (Gen 5:28-29; 9:28-29) 1st yr of 600 (Gen 7:11) until the flood [Next] [28] Lamech lived one hundred and eighty-two years, and became the father of a son. [29] Now he called his name Noah, saying, This one will give us rest from our work and from the toil of our hands [arising] from the ground which the BeComingOne has cursed. (Gen 5:28-29 BCB)	[28] Noah lived three hundred and fifty years after the flood. [29] So all the days of Noah were nine hundred and fifty years, and he died. (Gen 9:28-29 BCB)			1 of 600

[Top	Flood	Abram	Exodus	David	Hezekiah	Jerusalem	JC	End Time	End Notes]						

BC AD Years + or -		YM Years		**6000 Years of Mankind** Copyright © 2024 by Walter R. Dolen **Biblical Chronology Details** YM = Year of Mankind Begins in Sept/Oct 3 months before BC/AD dates	**Additional Details**	# of yrs	# of yrs	# of yrs
2913	BC	1058	Y M					2
2912	BC	1059	Y M					3
2911	BC	1060	Y M					4
2910	BC	1061	Y M					5
2909	BC	1062	Y M					6
2908	BC	1063	Y M					7
2907	BC	1064	Y M					8
2906	BC	1065	Y M					9
2905	BC	1066	Y M					10
2904	BC	1067	Y M					11
2903	BC	1068	Y M					12
2902	BC	1069	Y M					13
2901	BC	1070	Y M					14
2900	BC	1071	Y M					15
2899	BC	1072	Y M					16
2898	BC	1073	Y M					17
2897	BC	1074	Y M					18
2896	BC	1075	Y M					19
2895	BC	1076	Y M					20
2894	BC	1077	Y M					21
2893	BC	1078	Y M					22

				6000 Years of Mankind Copyright © 2024 by Walter R. Dolen **Biblical Chronology Details** YM = Year of Mankind Begins in Sept/Oct 3 months before BC/AD dates	**Additional Details**	# of yrs	# of yrs	# of yrs
BC AD Years + or -		YM Years						
2892	BC	1079	Y M					23
2891	BC	1080	Y M					24
2890	BC	1081	Y M					25
2889	BC	1082	Y M					26
2888	BC	1083	Y M					27
2887	BC	1084	Y M					28
2886	BC	1085	Y M					29
2885	BC	1086	Y M					30
2884	BC	1087	Y M					31
2883	BC	1088	Y M					32
2882	BC	1089	Y M					33
2881	BC	1090	Y M					34
2880	BC	1091	Y M					35
2879	BC	1092	Y M					36
2878	BC	1093	Y M					37
2877	BC	1094	Y M					38
2876	BC	1095	Y M					39
2875	BC	1096	Y M					40
2874	BC	1097	Y M					41
2873	BC	1098	Y M					42
2872	BC	1099	Y M					43

BC AD Years + or -		YM Years		**6000 Years of Mankind** Copyright © 2024 by Walter R. Dolen **Biblical Chronology Details** YM = Year of Mankind Begins in Sept/Oct 3 months before BC/AD dates	**Additional Details**	# of yrs	# of yrs	# of yrs
2871	BC	1100	Y M					44
2870	BC	1101	Y M					45
2869	BC	1102	Y M					46
2868	BC	1103	Y M					47
2867	BC	1104	Y M					48
2866	BC	1105	Y M					49
2865	BC	1106	Y M					50
2864	BC	1107	Y M					51
2863	BC	1108	Y M					52
2862	BC	1109	Y M					53
2861	BC	1110	Y M					54
2860	BC	1111	Y M					55
2859	BC	1112	Y M					56
2858	BC	1113	Y M					57
2857	BC	1114	Y M					58
2856	BC	1115	Y M					59
2855	BC	1116	Y M					60
2854	BC	1117	Y M					61
2853	BC	1118	Y M					62
2852	BC	1119	Y M					63
2851	BC	1120	Y M					64

BC AD Years + or -		YM Years		6000 Years of Mankind Copyright © 2024 by Walter R. Dolen **Biblical Chronology Details** YM = Year of Mankind Begins in Sept/Oct 3 months before BC/AD dates	Additional Details	# of yrs	# of yrs	# of yrs
2850	BC	1121	Y M					65
2849	BC	1122	Y M					66
2848	BC	1123	Y M					67
2847	BC	1124	Y M					68
2846	BC	1125	Y M					69
2845	BC	1126	Y M					70
2844	BC	1127	Y M					71
2843	BC	1128	Y M					72
2842	BC	1129	Y M					73
2841	BC	1130	Y M					74
2840	BC	1131	Y M					75
2839	BC	1132	Y M					76
2838	BC	1133	Y M					77
2837	BC	1134	Y M					78
2836	BC	1135	Y M					79
2835	BC	1136	Y M					80
2834	BC	1137	Y M					81
2833	BC	1138	Y M					82
2832	BC	1139	Y M					83
2831	BC	1140	Y M	**Enos Died son of 905 years (b. 235)**				84
2830	BC	1141	Y M					85

[Top | Flood | Abram | Exodus | David | Hezekiah | Jerusalem | JC | End Time | End Notes]

BC AD Years + or -		YM Years		**6000 Years of Mankind** Copyright © 2024 by Walter R. Dolen **Biblical Chronology Details** YM = Year of Mankind Begins in Sept/Oct 3 months before BC/AD dates	**Additional Details**	# of yrs	# of yrs	# of yrs
2829	BC	1142	Y M					86
2828	BC	1143	Y M					87
2827	BC	1144	Y M					88
2826	BC	1145	Y M					89
2825	BC	1146	Y M					90
2824	BC	1147	Y M					91
2823	BC	1148	Y M					92
2822	BC	1149	Y M					93
2821	BC	1150	Y M					94
2820	BC	1151	Y M					95
2819	BC	1152	Y M					96
2818	BC	1153	Y M					97
2817	BC	1154	Y M					98
2816	BC	1155	Y M					99
2815	BC	1156	Y M					100
2814	BC	1157	Y M					101
2813	BC	1158	Y M					102
2812	BC	1159	Y M					103
2811	BC	1160	Y M					104
2810	BC	1161	Y M					105
2809	BC	1162	Y M					106

BC AD Years + or -		YM Years		**6000 Years of Mankind** Copyright © 2024 by Walter R. Dolen **Biblical Chronology Details** YM = Year of Mankind Begins in Sept/Oct 3 months before BC/AD dates	**Additional Details**	# of yrs	# of yrs	# of yrs
2808	BC	1163	Y M					107
2807	BC	1164	Y M					108
2806	BC	1165	Y M					109
2805	BC	1166	Y M					110
2804	BC	1167	Y M					111
2803	BC	1168	Y M					112
2802	BC	1169	Y M					113
2801	BC	1170	Y M					114
2800	BC	1171	Y M					115
2799	BC	1172	Y M					116
2798	BC	1173	Y M					117
2797	BC	1174	Y M					118
2796	BC	1175	Y M					119
2795	BC	1176	Y M					120
2794	BC	1177	Y M					121
2793	BC	1178	Y M					122
2792	BC	1179	Y M					123
2791	BC	1180	Y M					124
2790	BC	1181	Y M					125
2789	BC	1182	Y M					126
2788	BC	1183	Y M					127

[Top | Flood | Abram | Exodus | David | Hezekiah | Jerusalem | JC | End Time | End Notes]

BC AD Years + or -		YM Years		6000 Years of Mankind Copyright © 2024 by Walter R. Dolen **Biblical Chronology Details** YM = Year of Mankind Begins in Sept/Oct 3 months before BC/AD dates	Additional Details	# of yrs	# of yrs	# of yrs
2787	BC	1184	YM					128
2786	BC	1185	YM					129
2785	BC	1186	YM					130
2784	BC	1187	YM					131
2783	BC	1188	YM					132
2782	BC	1189	YM					133
2781	BC	1190	YM					134
2780	BC	1191	YM					135
2779	BC	1192	YM					136
2778	BC	1193	YM					137
2777	BC	1194	YM					138
2776	BC	1195	YM					139
2775	BC	1196	YM					140
2774	BC	1197	YM					141
2773	BC	1198	YM					142
2772	BC	1199	YM					143
2771	BC	1200	YM					144
2770	BC	1201	YM					145
2769	BC	1202	YM					146
2768	BC	1203	YM					147
2767	BC	1204	YM					148

BC AD Years + or -		YM Years		**6000 Years of Mankind** Copyright © 2024 by Walter R. Dolen **Biblical Chronology Details** YM = Year of Mankind Begins in Sept/Oct 3 months before BC/AD dates	**Additional Details**	# of yrs	# of yrs	# of yrs
2766	BC	1205	Y M					149
2765	BC	1206	Y M					150
2764	BC	1207	Y M					151
2763	BC	1208	Y M					152
2762	BC	1209	Y M					153
2761	BC	1210	Y M					154
2760	BC	1211	Y M					155
2759	BC	1212	Y M					156
2758	BC	1213	Y M					157
2757	BC	1214	Y M					158
2756	BC	1215	Y M					159
2755	BC	1216	Y M					160
2754	BC	1217	Y M					161
2753	BC	1218	Y M					162
2752	BC	1219	Y M					163
2751	BC	1220	Y M					164
2750	BC	1221	Y M					165
2749	BC	1222	Y M					166
2748	BC	1223	Y M					167
2747	BC	1224	Y M					168
2746	BC	1225	Y M					169

BC AD Years + or -		YM Years		**6000 Years of Mankind** Copyright © 2024 by Walter R. Dolen **Biblical Chronology Details** YM = Year of Mankind Begins in Sept/Oct 3 months before BC/AD dates	**Additional Details**	# of yrs	# of yrs	# of yrs
2745	BC	1226	Y M					170
2744	BC	1227	Y M					171
2743	BC	1228	Y M					172
2742	BC	1229	Y M					173
2741	BC	1230	Y M					174
2740	BC	1231	Y M					175
2739	BC	1232	Y M					176
2738	BC	1233	Y M					177
2737	BC	1234	Y M					178
2736	BC	1235	Y M	Cainan dies on of 910 years (b. 325)				179
2735	BC	1236	Y M					180
2734	BC	1237	Y M					181
2733	BC	1238	Y M					182
2732	BC	1239	Y M					183
2731	BC	1240	Y M					184
2730	BC	1241	Y M					185
2729	BC	1242	Ẏ M					186
2728	BC	1243	Y M					187
2727	BC	1244	Y M					188
2726	BC	1245	Y M					189
2725	BC	1246	Y M					190

[Top | Flood | Abram | Exodus | David | Hezekiah | Jerusalem | JC | End Time | End Notes]

BC AD Years + or -		YM Years		**6000 Years of Mankind** Copyright © 2024 by Walter R. Dolen **Biblical Chronology Details** YM = Year of Mankind Begins in Sept/Oct 3 months before BC/AD dates	**Additional Details**	# of yrs	# of yrs	# of yrs
2724	BC	1247	YM					191
2723	BC	1248	YM					192
2722	BC	1249	YM					193
2721	BC	1250	YM					194
2720	BC	1251	YM					195
2719	BC	1252	YM					196
2718	BC	1253	YM					197
2717	BC	1254	YM					198
2716	BC	1255	YM	.				199
2715	BC	1256	YM					200
2714	BC	1257	YM					201
2713	BC	1258	YM					202
2712	BC	1259	YM					203
2711	BC	1260	YM					204
2710	BC	1261	YM					205
2709	BC	1262	YM					206
2708	BC	1263	YM					207
2707	BC	1264	YM					208
2706	BC	1265	YM					209
2705	BC	1266	YM					210
2704	BC	1267	YM					211

BC AD Years + or -		YM Years		6000 Years of Mankind Copyright © 2024 by Walter R. Dolen Biblical Chronology Details YM = Year of Mankind Begins in Sept/Oct 3 months before BC/AD dates	Additional Details	# of yrs	# of yrs	# of yrs
2703	BC	1268	Y M					212
2702	BC	1269	Y M					213
2701	BC	1270	Y M					214
2700	BC	1271	Y M					215
2699	BC	1272	Y M					216
2698	BC	1273	Y M					217
2697	BC	1274	Y M					218
2696	BC	1275	Y M					219
2695	BC	1276	Y M					220
2694	BC	1277	Y M					221
2693	BC	1278	Y M					222
2692	BC	1279	Y M					223
2691	BC	1280	Y M					224
2690	BC	1281	Y M					225
2689	BC	1282	Y M					226
2688	BC	1283	Y M					227
2687	BC	1284	Y M					228
2686	BC	1285	Y M					229
2685	BC	1286	Y M					230
2684	BC	1287	Y M					231
2683	BC	1288	Y M					232

BC AD Years + or -		YM Years		6000 Years of Mankind Copyright © 2024 by Walter R. Dolen **Biblical Chronology Details** YM = Year of Mankind Begins in Sept/Oct 3 months before BC/AD dates	Additional Details	# of yrs	# of yrs	# of yrs
2682	BC	1289	Y M					233
2681	BC	1290	Y M	Mahalaleel died son of 895 years (b. 395)				234
2680	BC	1291	Y M					235
2679	BC	1292	Y M					236
2678	BC	1293	Y M					237
2677	BC	1294	Y M					238
2676	BC	1295	Y M					239
2675	BC	1296	Y M					240
2674	BC	1297	Y M					241
2673	BC	1298	Y M					242
2672	BC	1299	Y M					243
2671	BC	1300	Y M					244
2670	BC	1301	Y M					245
2669	BC	1302	Y M					246
2668	BC	1303	Y M					247
2667	BC	1304	Y M					248
2666	BC	1305	Y M					249
2665	BC	1306	Y M					250
2664	BC	1307	Y M					251
2663	BC	1308	Y M					252
2662	BC	1309	Y M					253

BC AD Years + or -		YM Years		6000 Years of Mankind Copyright © 2024 by Walter R. Dolen Biblical Chronology Details YM = Year of Mankind Begins in Sept/Oct 3 months before BC/AD dates	Additional Details	# of yrs	# of yrs	# of yrs
2661	BC	1310	Y M					254
2660	BC	1311	Y M					255
2659	BC	1312	Y M					256
2658	BC	1313	Y M					257
2657	BC	1314	Y M					258
2656	BC	1315	Y M					259
2655	BC	1316	Y M					260
2654	BC	1317	Y M					261
2653	BC	1318	Y M					262
2652	BC	1319	Y M					263
2651	BC	1320	Y M					264
2650	BC	1321	Y M					265
2649	BC	1322	Y M					266
2648	BC	1323	Y M					267
2647	BC	1324	Y M					268
2646	BC	1325	Y M					269
2645	BC	1326	Y M					270
2644	BC	1327	Y M					271
2643	BC	1328	Y M					272
2642	BC	1329	Y M					273
2641	BC	1330	Y M					274

[Top | Flood | Abram | Exodus | David | Hezekiah | Jerusalem | JC | End Time | End Notes]

BC AD Years + or -		YM Years		**6000 Years of Mankind** Copyright © 2024 by Walter R. Dolen **Biblical Chronology Details** YM = Year of Mankind Begins in Sept/Oct 3 months before BC/AD dates	**Additional Details**	# of yrs	# of yrs	# of yrs
2640	BC	1331	Y M					275
2639	BC	1332	Y M					276
2638	BC	1333	Y M					277
2637	BC	1334	Y M					278
2636	BC	1335	Y M					279
2635	BC	1336	Y M					280
2634	BC	1337	Y M					281
2633	BC	1338	Y M					282
2632	BC	1339	Y M					283
2631	BC	1340	Y M					284
2630	BC	1341	Y M					285
2629	BC	1342	Y M					286
2628	BC	1343	Y M					287
2627	BC	1344	Y M					288
2626	BC	1345	Y M					289
2625	BC	1346	Y M					290
2624	BC	1347	Y M					291
2623	BC	1348	Y M					292
2622	BC	1349	Y M					293
2621	BC	1350	Y M					294
2620	BC	1351	Y M					295

BC AD Years + or -		YM Years		6000 Years of Mankind Copyright © 2024 by Walter R. Dolen **Biblical Chronology Details** YM = Year of Mankind Begins in Sept/Oct 3 months before BC/AD dates	Additional Details	# of yrs	# of yrs	# of yrs
2619	BC	1352	Y M					296
2618	BC	1353	Y M					297
2617	BC	1354	Y M					298
2616	BC	1355	Y M					299
2615	BC	1356	Y M					300
2614	BC	1357	Y M					301
2613	BC	1358	Y M					302
2612	BC	1359	Y M					303
2611	BC	1360	Y M					304
2610	BC	1361	Y M					305
2609	BC	1362	Y M					306
2608	BC	1363	Y M					307
2607	BC	1364	Y M					308
2606	BC	1365	Y M					309
2605	BC	1366	Y M					310
2604	BC	1367	Y M					311
2603	BC	1368	Y M					312
2602	BC	1369	Y M					313
2601	BC	1370	Y M					314
2600	BC	1371	Y M					315
2599	BC	1372	Y M					316

[Top	Flood	Abram	Exodus	David	Hezekiah	Jerusalem	JC	End Time	End Notes]							
BC AD Years + or -		YM Years		**6000 Years of Mankind** Copyright © 2024 by Walter R. Dolen **Biblical Chronology Details** YM = Year of Mankind Begins in Sept/Oct 3 months before BC/AD dates	**Additional Details**	# of yrs	# of yrs	# of yrs
2598	BC	1373	Y M					317
2597	BC	1374	Y M					318
2596	BC	1375	Y M					319
2595	BC	1376	Y M					320
2594	BC	1377	Y M					321
2593	BC	1378	Y M					322
2592	BC	1379	Y M					323
2591	BC	1380	Y M					324
2590	BC	1381	Y M					325
2589	BC	1382	Y M					326
2588	BC	1383	Y M					327
2587	BC	1384	Y M					328
2586	BC	1385	Y M					329
2585	BC	1386	Y M					330
2584	BC	1387	Y M					331
2583	BC	1388	Y M					332
2582	BC	1389	Y M					333
2581	BC	1390	Y M					334
2580	BC	1391	Y M					335
2579	BC	1392	Y M					336
2578	BC	1393	Y M					337

[Top | Flood | Abram | Exodus | David | Hezekiah | Jerusalem | JC | End Time | End Notes]

BC AD Years + or -		YM Years		6000 Years of Mankind Copyright © 2024 by Walter R. Dolen **Biblical Chronology Details** YM = Year of Mankind Begins in Sept/Oct 3 months before BC/AD dates	Additional Details	# of yrs	# of yrs	# of yrs
2577	BC	1394	Y M					338
2576	BC	1395	Y M					339
2575	BC	1396	Y M					340
2574	BC	1397	Y M					341
2573	BC	1398	Y M					342
2572	BC	1399	Y M					343
2571	BC	1400	Y M					344
2570	BC	1401	Y M					345
2569	BC	1402	Y M					346
2568	BC	1403	Y M					347
2567	BC	1404	Y M					348
2566	BC	1405	Y M					349
2565	BC	1406	Y M					350
2564	BC	1407	Y M					351
2563	BC	1408	Y M					352
2562	BC	1409	Y M					353
2561	BC	1410	Y M					354
2560	BC	1411	Y M					355
2559	BC	1412	Y M					356
2558	BC	1413	Y M					357
2557	BC	1414	Y M					358

[Top | Flood | Abram | Exodus | David | Hezekiah | Jerusalem | JC | End Time | End Notes]

BC AD Years + or -		YM Years		6000 Years of Mankind Copyright © 2024 by Walter R. Dolen Biblical Chronology Details YM = Year of Mankind Begins in Sept/Oct 3 months before BC/AD dates	Additional Details	# of yrs	# of yrs	# of yrs
2556	BC	1415	YM					359
2555	BC	1416	YM					360
2554	BC	1417	YM					361
2553	BC	1418	YM					362
2552	BC	1419	YM					363
2551	BC	1420	YM					364
2550	BC	1421	YM					365
2549	BC	1422	YM	Jared died son of 962 years (b. 460)				366
2548	BC	1423	YM					367
2547	BC	1424	YM					368
2546	BC	1425	YM					369
2545	BC	1426	YM					370
2544	BC	1427	YM					371
2543	BC	1428	YM					372
2542	BC	1429	YM					373
2541	BC	1430	YM					374
2540	BC	1431	YM					375
2539	BC	1432	YM					376
2538	BC	1433	YM					377
2537	BC	1434	YM					378
2536	BC	1435	YM					379

[Top | Flood | Abram | Exodus | David | Hezekiah | Jerusalem | JC | End Time | End Notes]							

BC AD Years + or -		YM Years		**6000 Years of Mankind** Copyright © 2024 by Walter R. Dolen **Biblical Chronology Details** YM = Year of Mankind Begins in Sept/Oct 3 months before BC/AD dates	**Additional Details**	# of yrs	# of yrs	# of yrs
2535	BC	1436	Y M					380
2534	BC	1437	Y M					381
2533	BC	1438	Y M					382
2532	BC	1439	Y M					383
2531	BC	1440	Y M					384
2530	BC	1441	Y M					385
2529	BC	1442	Y M					386
2528	BC	1443	Y M					387
2527	BC	1444	Y M					388
2526	BC	1445	Y M					389
2525	BC	1446	Y M					390
2524	BC	1447	Y M					391
2523	BC	1448	Y M					392
2522	BC	1449	Y M					393
2521	BC	1450	Y M					394
2520	BC	1451	Y M					395
2519	BC	1452	Y M					396
2518	BC	1453	Y M					397
2517	BC	1454	Y M					398
2516	BC	1455	Y M					399
2515	BC	1456	Y M					400

[Top | Flood | Abram | Exodus | David | Hezekiah | Jerusalem | JC | End Time | End Notes]

BC AD Years + or -		YM Years		6000 Years of Mankind Copyright © 2024 by Walter R. Dolen Biblical Chronology Details YM = Year of Mankind Begins in Sept/Oct 3 months before BC/AD dates	Additional Details	# of yrs	# of yrs	# of yrs
2514	BC	1457	Y M					401
2513	BC	1458	Y M					402
2512	BC	1459	Y M					403
2511	BC	1460	Y M					404
2510	BC	1461	Y M					405
2509	BC	1462	Y M					406
2508	BC	1463	Y M					407
2507	BC	1464	Y M					408
2506	BC	1465	Y M					409
2505	BC	1466	Y M					410
2504	BC	1467	Y M					411
2503	BC	1468	Y M					412
2502	BC	1469	Y M					413
2501	BC	1470	Y M					414
2500	BC	1471	Y M					415
2499	BC	1472	Y M					416
2498	BC	1473	Y M					417
2497	BC	1474	Y M					418
2496	BC	1475	Y M					419
2495	BC	1476	Y M					420
2494	BC	1477	Y M					421

BC AD Years + or -		YM Years		6000 Years of Mankind Copyright © 2024 by Walter R. Dolen Biblical Chronology Details YM = Year of Mankind Begins in Sept/Oct 3 months before BC/AD dates	Additional Details	# of yrs	# of yrs	# of yrs
2493	BC	1478	Y M					422
2492	BC	1479	Y M					423
2491	BC	1480	Y M					424
2490	BC	1481	Y M					425
2489	BC	1482	Y M					426
2488	BC	1483	Y M					427
2487	BC	1484	Y M					428
2486	BC	1485	Y M					429
2485	BC	1486	Y M					430
2484	BC	1487	Y M					431
2483	BC	1488	Y M					432
2482	BC	1489	Y M					433
2481	BC	1490	Y M					434
2480	BC	1491	Y M					435
2479	BC	1492	Y M					436
2478	BC	1493	Y M					437
2477	BC	1494	Y M					438
2476	BC	1495	Y M					439
2475	BC	1496	Y M					440
2474	BC	1497	Y M					441
2473	BC	1498	Y M					442

[Top | Flood | Abram | Exodus | David | Hezekiah | Jerusalem | JC | End Time | End Notes]

BC AD Years + or -		YM Years		6000 Years of Mankind Copyright © 2024 by Walter R. Dolen Biblical Chronology Details YM = Year of Mankind Begins in Sept/Oct 3 months before BC/AD dates	Additional Details	# of yrs	# of yrs	# of yrs
2472	BC	1499	YM					443
2471	BC	1500	YM					444
2470	BC	1501	YM					445
2469	BC	1502	YM					446
2468	BC	1503	YM					447
2467	BC	1504	YM					448
2466	BC	1505	YM					449
2465	BC	1506	YM					450
2464	BC	1507	YM					451
2463	BC	1508	YM					452
2462	BC	1509	YM					453
2461	BC	1510	YM					454
2460	BC	1511	YM					455
2459	BC	1512	YM					456
2458	BC	1513	YM					457
2457	BC	1514	YM					458
2456	BC	1515	YM					459
2455	BC	1516	YM					460
2454	BC	1517	YM					461
2453	BC	1518	YM					462
2452	BC	1519	YM					463

BC AD Years + or -		YM Years		6000 Years of Mankind Copyright © 2024 by Walter R. Dolen Biblical Chronology Details YM = Year of Mankind Begins in Sept/Oct 3 months before BC/AD dates	Additional Details	# of yrs	# of yrs	# of yrs
2451	BC	1520	Y M					464
2450	BC	1521	Y M					465
2449	BC	1522	Y M					466
2448	BC	1523	Y M					467
2447	BC	1524	Y M					468
2446	BC	1525	Y M					469
2445	BC	1526	Y M					470
2444	BC	1527	Y M					471
2443	BC	1528	Y M					472
2442	BC	1529	Y M					473
2441	BC	1530	Y M					474
2440	BC	1531	Y M					475
2439	BC	1532	Y M					476
2438	BC	1533	Y M					477
2437	BC	1534	Y M					478
2436	BC	1535	Y M					479
2435	BC	1536	Y M					480
2434	BC	1537	Y M					481
2433	BC	1538	Y M					482
2432	BC	1539	Y M					483
2431	BC	1540	Y M					484

[Top | Flood | Abram | Exodus | David | Hezekiah | Jerusalem | JC | End Time | End Notes]

BC AD Years + or -		YM Years		**6000 Years of Mankind** Copyright © 2024 by Walter R. Dolen **Biblical Chronology Details** YM = Year of Mankind Begins in Sept/Oct 3 months before BC/AD dates	**Additional Details**	# of yrs	# of yrs	# of yrs
2430	BC	1541	Y M					485
2429	BC	1542	Y M					486
2428	BC	1543	Y M					487
2427	BC	1544	Y M					488
2426	BC	1545	Y M					489
2425	BC	1546	Y M					490
2424	BC	1547	Y M					491
2423	BC	1548	Y M					492
2422	BC	1549	Y M					493
2421	BC	1550	Y M					494
2420	BC	1551	Y M					495
2419	BC	1552	Y M					496
2418	BC	1553	Y M					497
2417	BC	1554	Y M					498
2416	BC	1555	Y M					499
2415	BC	1556	Y M					500
2414	BC	1557	Y M					501
2413	BC	1558	Y M	Shem born				502

BC AD Years + or -		YM Years		**6000 Years of Mankind** Copyright © 2024 by Walter R. Dolen **Biblical Chronology Details** YM = Year of Mankind Begins in Sept/Oct 3 months before BC/AD dates	**Additional Details**	# of yrs	# of yrs	# of yrs

2412	BC	1559	Y M	**Shem** first year; died in 2158 YM, son of 600 years (Gen 5:32; with 11:10-11; 9:28-29; 7:6; note Gen 10:21) [Next]
				
				   In Genesis 5:32 it says Noah "was was a son of five hundred years: and Noah begat Shem, Ham, and Japheth." But Genesis 10:21 tells us that Japheth was "*the* elder" (see Hebrew text). Therefore, Genesis 5:32 does not give the chronological order that Noah had his three children. **Genesis 11:10 informs us that Shem was a 100 years old** *two years after the flood*, **when he begot Arphaxad. From Genesis 7:6 we learn that Noah was 600 years old at the time of the Flood.** **This means that Shem was 98 years old at the Flood, and that Shem was 98 years old when Noah was 600.** Therefore Shem was born when Noah was 502 (see *Chronology of the Old Testament*, by Martin Anstey, 1973, pp. 35-36 & page 16 of Ozanne's *The First 7000 Years*).
				
				More Proof:
				   The phrase "**after the flood**" doesn't mean after the *full* duration of the flood, but after the *beginning* of the flood (compare Genesis 11:10 with Genesis 7:6; 9:28-29; 8:13). "Noah was 600 years old, and the flood of waters was on the earth" (Gen 7:6; see 7:10-11). "And Noah lived 350 years **after the flood**. And all the days of Noah were 950 years" (Gen 9:28-29). These verses tell us that Noah was 600 when the flood *began* and died 350 years "*after* the flood." His total years being 950. This absolutely proves that "after the flood" means after the very beginning of the flood of waters. *If* "after the flood" meant after the full duration of the flood, then Noah would have been 951 years when he died, for the flood ended when Noah was 601 years (Gen 8:13).
				   The **order of Noah's sons** in Genesis 5:32 is not from the oldest to the youngest. The true order though can be ascertained from other scripture. Genesis 9:24 implies that Ham is Noah's youngest son, and Genesis 10:21 speaks of "Japheth *the* eldest" (see Hebrew text). The order of birth, then, was Japheth, Shem, and Ham. Genesis 11:26 is similar: "And Terah lived seventy years, and begat Abram, Nahor, and Haran." By this it does not mean that Abram was the eldest, for Abram was born when Terah was 130 years old as we shall see below. "In Genesis 5:32 and 11:26, therefore, the most important son is put first, and in neither case was he the eldest" (*The First 7000 Years*, p. 16). "Similarly Isaac is placed before Ishmael in 1 Chron. 1:28, 'The sons of Abraham, Isaac and Ishmael,' though Isaac was not the older, but the younger of the two" (Anstey, p. 36).
					[32] Noah was five hundred years old, and Noah became the father of Shem, Ham, and Japheth. (Gen 5:32 BCB)
					
					[10] These are [the records of] the generations of Shem. Shem was one hundred years old, and became the father of Arpachshad two years after the flood; [11] and Shem lived five hundred years after he became the father of Arpachshad, and he had [other] sons and daughters. (Gen 11:10-11 BCB)
					
					[28] Noah lived three hundred and fifty years after the flood. [29] So all the days of Noah were nine hundred and fifty years, and he died. (Gen 9:28-29 BCB)
					
					[6] Now Noah was six hundred years old when the flood of water came upon the earth. (Gen 7:6 BCB)
					
					[21] Also to Shem, the father of all the children of Eber, [and] the older brother of Japheth, children were born. (Gen 10:21 BCB)
						1 of 98 S h e m		503

2411	BC	1560	Y M			2		504
2410	BC	1561	Y M			3		505
2409	BC	1562	Y M			4		506
2408	BC	1563	Y M			5		507

BC AD Years + or -		YM Years		6000 Years of Mankind Copyright © 2024 by Walter R. Dolen Biblical Chronology Details YM = Year of Mankind Begins in Sept/Oct 3 months before BC/AD dates	Additional Details	# of yrs	# of yrs	# of yrs
2407	BC	1564	YM			6		508
2406	BC	1565	YM			7		509
2405	BC	1566	YM			8		510
2404	BC	1567	YM			9		511
2403	BC	1568	YM			10 Shem		512
2402	BC	1569	YM			11		513
2401	BC	1570	YM			12		514
2400	BC	1571	YM			13		515
2399	BC	1572	YM			14		516
2398	BC	1573	YM			15		517
2397	BC	1574	YM			16		518
2396	BC	1575	YM			17		519
2395	BC	1576	YM			18		520
2394	BC	1577	YM			19		521
2393	BC	1578	YM			20		522
2392	BC	1579	YM			21		523
2391	BC	1580	YM			22		524
2390	BC	1581	YM			23		525
2389	BC	1582	YM			24		526

				6000 Years of Mankind Copyright © 2024 by Walter R. Dolen **Biblical Chronology Details** YM = Year of Mankind Begins in Sept/Oct 3 months before BC/AD dates	**Additional Details**	# of yrs	# of yrs	# of yrs
BC AD Years + or -		YM Years						
2388	BC	1583	Y M			25		527
2387	BC	1584	Y M			26		528
2386	BC	1585	Y M			27		529
2385	BC	1586	Y M			28		530
2384	BC	1587	Y M			29		531
2383	BC	1588	Y M			30 S h e m		532
2382	BC	1589	Y M			31		533
2381	BC	1590	Y M			32		534
2380	BC	1591	Y M			33		535
2379	BC	1592	Y M			34		536
2378	BC	1593	Y M			35		537
2377	BC	1594	Y M			36		538
2376	BC	1595	Y M			37		539
2375	BC	1596	Y M			38		540
2374	BC	1597	Y M			39		541
2373	BC	1598	Y M			40		542
2372	BC	1599	Y M			41		543
2371	BC	1600	Y M			42		544
2370	BC	1601	Y M			43		545

[Top | Flood | Abram | Exodus | David | Hezekiah | Jerusalem | JC | End Time | End Notes]

[Top | Flood | Abram | Exodus | David | Hezekiah | Jerusalem | JC | End Time | End Notes]

BC AD Years + or -		YM Years		6000 Years of Mankind Copyright © 2024 by Walter R. Dolen **Biblical Chronology Details** YM = Year of Mankind Begins in Sept/Oct 3 months before BC/AD dates	Additional Details	# of yrs	# of yrs	# of yrs
2369	BC	1602	Y M			44		546
2368	BC	1603	Y M			45		547
2367	BC	1604	Y M			46		548
2366	BC	1605	Y M			47		549
2365	BC	1606	Y M			48		550
2364	BC	1607	Y M			49		551
2363	BC	1608	Y M			50 S h e m		552
2362	BC	1609	Y M			51		553
2361	BC	1610	Y M			52		554
2360	BC	1611	Y M			53		555
2359	BC	1612	Y M			54		556
2358	BC	1613	Y M			55		557
2357	BC	1614	Y M			56		558
2356	BC	1615	Y M			57		559
2355	BC	1616	Y M			58		560
2354	BC	1617	Y M			59		561
2353	BC	1618	Y M			60		562
2352	BC	1619	Y M			61		563
2351	BC	1620	Y M			62		564

[Top	Flood	Abram	Exodus	David	Hezekiah	Jerusalem	JC	End Time	End Notes]						

BC AD Years + or -		YM Years		**6000 Years of Mankind** Copyright © 2024 by Walter R. Dolen **Biblical Chronology Details** YM = Year of Mankind Begins in Sept/Oct 3 months before BC/AD dates	Additional Details	# of yrs	# of yrs	# of yrs
2350	BC	1621	Y M			63		565
2349	BC	1622	Y M			64		566
2348	BC	1623	Y M			65		567
2347	BC	1624	Y M			66		568
2346	BC	1625	Y M			67		569
2345	BC	1626	Y M			68		570
2344	BC	1627	Y M			69		571
2343	BC	1628	Y M			70 S h e m		572
2342	BC	1629	Y M			71		573
2341	BC	1630	Y M			72		574
2340	BC	1631	Y M			73		575
2339	BC	1632	Y M			74		576
2338	BC	1633	Y M			75		577
2337	BC	1634	Y M			76		578
2336	BC	1635	Y M			77		579
2335	BC	1636	Y M			78		580
2334	BC	1637	Y M			79		581
2333	BC	1638	Y M			80		582
2332	BC	1639	Y M			81		583

				6000 Years of Mankind Copyright © 2024 by Walter R. Dolen **Biblical Chronology Details** YM = Year of Mankind Begins in Sept/Oct 3 months before BC/AD dates	**Additional Details**	# of yrs	# of yrs	# of yrs
				[Top	Flood	Abram	Exodus	David	Hezekiah	Jerusalem	JC	End Time	End Notes]				
BC AD Years + or -		YM Years						
2331	BC	1640	Y M			82		584
2330	BC	1641	Y M			83		585
2329	BC	1642	Y M			84		586
2328	BC	1643	Y M			85		587
2327	BC	1644	Y M			86		588
2326	BC	1645	Y M			87		589
2325	BC	1646	Y M			88		590
2324	BC	1647	Y M			89		591
2323	BC	1648	Y M			90 S h e m		592
2322	BC	1649	Y M			91		593
2321	BC	1650	Y M			92		594
2320	BC	1651	Y M	Lamech died son of 777 years (b. 874)		93		595
2319	BC	1652	Y M			94		596
2318	BC	1653	Y M			95		597
2317	BC	1654	Y M			96		598
2316	BC	1655	Y M	World population before the flood ?		97		599

[Top | Flood | Abram | Exodus | David | Hezekiah | Jerusalem | JC | End Time | End Notes]

BC AD Years + or -		YM Years		**6000 Years of Mankind** Copyright © 2024 by Walter R. Dolen **Biblical Chronology Details** YM = Year of Mankind Begins in Sept/Oct 3 months before BC/AD dates	**Additional Details**	# of yrs	# of yrs	# of yrs

2315	BC	1656	Y M	**Flood** (1656-1657) 2ⁿᵈ month
				
				The Flood began in the 17th day, 2nd month of the 1656th Year of Man and lasted until the 27th day, 2nd month of the year 1657 YM. (Gen 7:6, 11-14; see under "Shem")
				  Scripture here indicates **30 day months**. In the 17th day of the 2nd month the flood started. On this day "the fountains of the great deep" were "broken up, and the windows of heaven were opened. And rain was upon the earth forty days and forty nights" (Gen 7:11b-12). The rain and the water from "the fountains of the great deep" caused the water to cover the mountains by 15 cubits (7:20). These pre-Flood mountains were smaller than now and the oceans were much smaller: the effects of the flood catastrophe caused the mountains to rise and the valleys to fall (Psa 104:8, NASB & Hebrew text). "And the waters are mighty on the earth a hundred and fifty days" (7:24, Young's *Literal Trans.*, see Heb. text). The waters were on or over the earth for a total of 150 days. But before these 150 days ended, "the fountains also of the deep and the windows of heaven were stopped, and the rain from heaven was restrained" (8:2). At the end of these 150 days the waters had receded enough so that the ark was able to rest on the mountains of Ararat (8:3-4). This day was "in the seventh month, on the seventeenth day of the month" (8:4). Thus, from the 17 day of the 2nd month to the 17th day of the 7th month is exactly five months and a total of 150 days. This indicates that each month had 30 days. Unlike today's Jewish Calendar with alternating 30 day and 29 day months, the months of Noah's time had 30 days. From the 17th day of the 2nd month in the 600th year of Noah (1656 YM) until the 27th day of the 2nd month in the 601st year of Noah is 370 days with 30 day months. There is no reason not to believe that at the time of the flood the year was 360 days long. The flood or other natural catastrophes could have changed the time of orbit for the earth around the sun (see CP3 under "Astronomical Chaos"). There is other evidence of 360 day calendars in ancient times.(Budge, *The Book of the Kings of Egypt*, Vol 1, p XLV ff ; Budge, *The Gods of the Egyptians* Vol 2 p. 186; A.T. Olmstead *History of the Persian Empire*, p.209; Velikovsky, *Worlds in Collision*, Part II, Chapter 8)
				  There is a theory that the flood lasted one solar year (365 days) and that the present Jewish calendar fits the scriptural evidence. But this theory misplaces the 150th day until after the ark rested (see William G. Lowe's, "Discovering the Calendar of the Creation," in *Science and Scripture*, Sept-Oct, 1971). This is impossible since the waters were prevailing on the earth for the 150 days and it was only "after the end of the hundred and fifty days that the waters abated" enough for the ark to rest on the land (Gen 7:24; 8:3-4). At the beginning of the flood the fountains of water of the great deep, the "windows of heaven," and the rain of 40 days flooded the earth until the waters were 15 cubits over the mountains (Gen 7:11-12, 17-20). But sometime after the 40 days "the water receded steadily from the earth. At the end of the hundred and fifty days the water had gone down." (Gen 8:3, NIV; see Heb text) It was only after the 150 days that it was possible for the ark to rest on the earth. See "Flood Chart."
					⁶ Now Noah was six hundred years old when the flood of water came upon the earth.
					⁷ Then Noah and his sons and his wife and his son's wives with him entered the ark because of the water of the flood. (Gen 7:6-7 BCB)
					
					¹¹ In the six hundredth year of Noah's life, in the second month, on the seventeenth day of the month, on the same day all the fountains of the great deep burst open, and the floodgates of the sky were opened. [9:29]
					¹² The rain fell upon the earth for forty days and forty nights.
					¹³ On the very same day Noah and Shem and Ham and Japheth, the sons of Noah, and Noah's wife and the three wives of his sons with them, entered the ark,
					¹⁴ they and every beast after its kind, and all the cattle after their kind, and every creeping thing that creeps on the earth after its kind, and every bird after its kind, all sorts of birds. (Gen 7:11-14 BCB)
					
					Methuselah died son of 969 years (b. 688)
						S H E M i s 98		600

[Top | Flood | Abram | Exodus | David | Hezekiah | Jerusalem | JC | End Time | End Notes]

BC AD Years + or -		YM Years		**6000 Years of Mankind** Copyright © 2024 by Walter R. Dolen **Biblical Chronology Details** YM = Year of Mankind Begins in Sept/Oct 3 months before BC/AD dates	**Additional Details**	# of yrs	# of yrs	# of yrs
2314	BC	1657	Y M	**Flood** to 2nd month (370 days) **World population was 8 after the flood**	Population growth after the flood	99		
2313	BC	1658	Y M	Arphaxad born **Shem is 100** "two years after the flood" (Gen 11:10)	[10] These are [the records of] the generations of Shem. Shem was one hundred years old, and became the father of Arphaxad two years after the flood; (Gen 11:10 BCB)	100		
2312	BC	1659	Y M	Arphaxad first year; died in 2096 YM, son of 438 years (Gen 11:10, 12-13) [Next]	[12] **Arphaxad lived thirty-five years**, and became the father of Shelah; [13] and Arphaxad lived four hundred and three years after he became the father of **Salah**, and he had [other] sons and daughters. (Gen 11:12-13 BCB)	1 of 35		
2311	BC	1660	Y M			2		
2310	BC	1661	Y M			3		
2309	BC	1662	Y M			4		
2308	BC	1663	Y M			5		
2307	BC	1664	Y M			6		
2306	BC	1665	Y M			7		
2305	BC	1666	Y M			8		
2304	BC	1667	Y M			9		
2303	BC	1668	Y M			10		
2302	BC	1669	Y M			11		
2301	BC	1670	Y M			12		
2300	BC	1671	Y M			13		
2299	BC	1672	Y M			14		

BC AD Years + or -		YM Years		6000 Years of Mankind Copyright © 2024 by Walter R. Dolen **Biblical Chronology Details** YM = Year of Mankind Begins in Sept/Oct 3 months before BC/AD dates	Additional Details	# of yrs	# of yrs	# of yrs
2298	BC	1673	Y M			15		
2297	BC	1674	Y M			16		
2296	BC	1675	Y M			17		
2295	BC	1676	Y M			18		
2294	BC	1677	Y M			19		
2293	BC	1678	Y M			20		
2292	BC	1679	Y M			21		
2291	BC	1680	Y M			22		
2290	BC	1681	Y M			23		
2289	BC	1682	Y M			24		
2288	BC	1683	Y M			25		
2287	BC	1684	Y M			26		
2286	BC	1685	Y M			27		
2285	BC	1686	Y M			28		
2284	BC	1687	Y M			29		
2283	BC	1688	Y M			30		
2282	BC	1689	Y M			31		
2281	BC	1690	Y M			32		
2280	BC	1691	Y M			33		
2279	BC	1692	Y M			34		
2278	BC	1693	Y M	Salah born		35		

[Top	Flood	Abram	Exodus	David	Hezekiah	Jerusalem	JC	End Time	End Notes]							

BC AD Years + or -		YM Years		**6000 Years of Mankind** Copyright © 2024 by Walter R. Dolen **Biblical Chronology Details** YM = Year of Mankind Begins in Sept/Oct 3 months before BC/AD dates	**Additional Details**	# of yrs	# of yrs	# of yrs
2277	BC	1694	Y M	**Salah** first year; died in 2126 YM, son of 433 years (Gen 11:12, 14-15) [Next]	[14] **Salah lived thirty years**, and became the father of Eber; [15] and **Salah** lived four hundred and three years after he became the father of Eber, and he had [other] sons and daughters. (Gen 11:14-15 BCB)	1 of 30		
2276	BC	1695	Y M			2		
2275	BC	1696	Y M			3		
2274	BC	1697	Y M			4		
2273	BC	1698	Y M			5		
2272	BC	1699	Y M			6		
2271	BC	1700	Y M			7		
2270	BC	1701	Y M			8		
2269	BC	1702	Y M			9		
2268	BC	1703	Y M			10		
2267	BC	1704	Y M			11		
2266	BC	1705	Y M			12		
2265	BC	1706	Y M			13		
2264	BC	1707	Y M			14		
2263	BC	1708	Y M			15		
2262	BC	1709	Y M			16		
2261	BC	1710	Y M			17		
2260	BC	1711	Y M			18		

BC AD Years + or -		YM Years		6000 Years of Mankind Copyright © 2024 by Walter R. Dolen Biblical Chronology Details YM = Year of Mankind Begins in Sept/Oct 3 months before BC/AD dates	Additional Details	# of yrs	# of yrs	# of yrs
2259	BC	1712	YM			19		
2258	BC	1713	YM			20		
2257	BC	1714	YM			21		
2256	BC	1715	YM			22		
2255	BC	1716	YM			23		
2254	BC	1717	YM			24		
2253	BC	1718	YM			25		
2252	BC	1719	YM			26		
2251	BC	1720	YM			27		
2250	BC	1721	YM			28		
2249	BC	1722	YM			29		
2248	BC	1723	YM	Eber born		30		
2247	BC	1724	YM	Eber first year; died in 2187 YM, son of 464 years (Gen 11:14, 16-17) [Next]	[14] Salah lived thirty years, and became the father of Eber; [15] and Salah lived four hundred and three years after he became the father of Eber, and he had [other] sons and daughters. [16] Eber lived thirty-four years, and became the father of Peleg; [17] and Eber lived four hundred and thirty years after he became the father of Peleg, and he had [other] sons and daughters. (Gen 11:14-17 BCB)	1		
2246	BC	1725	YM			2		
2245	BC	1726	YM			3		
2244	BC	1727	YM			4		

BC AD Years + or -		YM Years		6000 Years of Mankind Copyright © 2024 by Walter R. Dolen **Biblical Chronology Details** YM = Year of Mankind Begins in Sept/Oct 3 months before BC/AD dates	Additional Details	# of yrs	# of yrs	# of yrs
2243	BC	1728	Y M			5		
2242	BC	1729	Y M			6		
2241	BC	1730	Y M			7		
2240	BC	1731	Y M			8		
2239	BC	1732	Y M			9		
2238	BC	1733	Y M			10		
2237	BC	1734	Y M			11		
2236	BC	1735	Y M			12		
2235	BC	1736	Y M			13		
2234	BC	1737	Y M			14		
2233	BC	1738	Y M			15		
2232	BC	1739	Y M			16		
2231	BC	1740	Y M			17		
2230	BC	1741	Y M			18		
2229	BC	1742	Y M			19		
2228	BC	1743	Y M			20		
2227	BC	1744	Y M			21		
2226	BC	1745	Y M			22		
2225	BC	1746	Y M			23		
2224	BC	1747	Y M			24		
2223	BC	1748	Y M			25		

[Top | Flood | Abram | Exodus | David | Hezekiah | Jerusalem | JC | End Time | End Notes]

[Top | Flood | Abram | Exodus | David | Hezekiah | Jerusalem | JC | End Time | End Notes]								
BC AD Years + or -		YM Years		**6000 Years of Mankind** Copyright © 2024 by Walter R. Dolen **Biblical Chronology Details** YM = Year of Mankind Begins in Sept/Oct 3 months before BC/AD dates	**Additional Details**	# of yrs	# of yrs	# of yrs
2222	BC	1749	Y M			26		
2221	BC	1750	Y M			27		
2220	BC	1751	Y M			28		
2219	BC	1752	Y M			29		
2218	BC	1753	Y M			30		
2217	BC	1754	Y M			31		
2216	BC	1755	Y M			32		
2215	BC	1756	Y M			33		
2214	BC	1757	Y M	Peleg born		34		
2213	BC	1758	Y M	**Peleg** first year; died in 1996 YM, son of 239 years (Gen 11:16, 18-19) [Next]	[18] **Peleg lived thirty years, and became the father of Reu**; [19] and Peleg lived two hundred and nine years after he became the father of Reu, and he had [other] sons and daughters. (Gen 11:18-19 BCB)	1 of 30		
2212	BC	1759	Y M		**Babylonian Rebellion?**[2]	2		
2211	BC	1760	Y M			3		
2210	BC	1761	Y M			4		
2209	BC	1762	Y M			5		
2208	BC	1763	Y M			6		
2207	BC	1764	Y M			7		
2206	BC	1765	Y M			8		
2205	BC	1766	Y M			9		

[Top | Flood | Abram | Exodus | David | Hezekiah | Jerusalem | JC | End Time | End Notes]

BC AD Years + or -		YM Years		6000 Years of Mankind Copyright © 2024 by Walter R. Dolen **Biblical Chronology Details** YM = Year of Mankind Begins in Sept/Oct 3 months before BC/AD dates	Additional Details	# of yrs	# of yrs	# of yrs
2204	BC	1767	YM			10		
2203	BC	1768	YM			11		
2202	BC	1769	YM			12		
2201	BC	1770	YM			13		
2200	BC	1771	YM			14		
2199	BC	1772	YM			15		
2198	BC	1773	YM			16		
2197	BC	1774	YM			17		
2196	BC	1775	YM			18		
2195	BC	1776	YM			19		
2194	BC	1777	YM			20		
2193	BC	1778	YM			21		
2192	BC	1779	YM			22		
2191	BC	1780	YM			23		
2190	BC	1781	YM			24		
2189	BC	1782	YM			25		
2188	BC	1783	YM			26		
2187	BC	1784	YM			27		
2186	BC	1785	YM			28		
2185	BC	1786	YM			29		
2184	BC	1787	YM	Reu born		30		

BC AD Years + or -		YM Years		6000 Years of Mankind Copyright © 2024 by Walter R. Dolen **Biblical Chronology Details** YM = Year of Mankind Begins in Sept/Oct 3 months before BC/AD dates	Additional Details	# of yrs	# of yrs	# of yrs
2183	BC	1788	Y M	**Reu** first year; died in 2026 YM, son of 239 years (Gen 11:18, 20-21) [Next]	[20] **Reu lived thirty-two years, and became the father of Serug;** [21] and Reu lived two hundred and seven years after he became the father of Serug, and he had [other] sons and daughters. (Gen 11:20-21 BCB)	1 of 32		
2182	BC	1789	Y M			2		
2181	BC	1790	Y M			3		
2180	BC	1791	Y M			4		
2179	BC	1792	Y M			5		
2178	BC	1793	Y M			6		
2177	BC	1794	Y M			7		
2176	BC	1795	Y M			8		
2175	BC	1796	Y M			9		
2174	BC	1797	Y M			10		
2173	BC	1798	Y M			11		
2172	BC	1799	Y M			12		
2171	BC	1800	Y M			13		
2170	BC	1801	Y M			14		
2169	BC	1802	Y M			15		
2168	BC	1803	Y M			16		
2167	BC	1804	Y M			17		
2166	BC	1805	Y M			18		

[Top | Flood | Abram | Exodus | David | Hezekiah | Jerusalem | JC | End Time | End Notes]

BC AD Years + or -		YM Years		6000 Years of Mankind Copyright © 2024 by Walter R. Dolen **Biblical Chronology Details** YM = Year of Mankind Begins in Sept/Oct 3 months before BC/AD dates	Additional Details	# of yrs	# of yrs	# of yrs
2165	BC	1806	Y M			19		
2164	BC	1807	Y M			20		
2163	BC	1808	Y M			21		
2162	BC	1809	Y M			22		
2161	BC	1810	Y M			23		
2160	BC	1811	Y M			24		
2159	BC	1812	Y M			25		
2158	BC	1813	Y M			26		
2157	BC	1814	Y M			27		
2156	BC	1815	Y M			28		
2155	BC	1816	Y M			29		
2154	BC	1817	Y M			30		
2153	BC	1818	Y M			31		
2152	BC	1819	Y M	Serug born		32		
2151	BC	1820	Y M	**Serug** first year; died in 2049 YM, son of 230 years (Gen 11:20, 22-23) [Next]	[22] **Serug lived thirty years, and became the father of Nahor;** [23] and Serug lived two hundred years after he became the father of Nahor, and he had [other] sons and daughters. (Gen 11:22-23 BCB)	1		
2150	BC	1821	Y M			2		
2149	BC	1822	Y M			3		
2148	BC	1823	Y M			4		

			6000 Years of Mankind Copyright © 2024 by Walter R. Dolen Biblical Chronology Details YM = Year of Mankind Begins in Sept/Oct 3 months before BC/AD dates	Additional Details	# of yrs	# of yrs	# of yrs
BC AD Years + or -		YM Years						
2147	BC	1824	Y M			5		
2146	BC	1825	Y M			6		
2145	BC	1826	Y M			7		
2144	BC	1827	Y M			8		
2143	BC	1828	Y M			9		
2142	BC	1829	Y M			10		
2141	BC	1830	Y M			11		
2140	BC	1831	Y M			12		
2139	BC	1832	Y M			13		
2138	BC	1833	Y M			14		
2137	BC	1834	Y M			15		
2136	BC	1835	Y M			16		
2135	BC	1836	Y M			17		
2134	BC	1837	Y M			18		
2133	BC	1838	Y M			19		
2132	BC	1839	Y M			20		
2131	BC	1840	Y M			21		
2130	BC	1841	Y M			22		
2129	BC	1842	Y M			23		
2128	BC	1843	Y M			24		
2127	BC	1844	Y M			25		

[Top | Flood | Abram | Exodus | David | Hezekiah | Jerusalem | JC | End Time | End Notes]

BC AD Years + or -		YM Years		6000 Years of Mankind Copyright © 2024 by Walter R. Dolen **Biblical Chronology Details** YM = Year of Mankind Begins in Sept/Oct 3 months before BC/AD dates	**Additional Details**	# of yrs	# of yrs	# of yrs
2126	BC	1845	Y M			26		
2125	BC	1846	Y M			27		
2124	BC	1847	Y M			28		
2123	BC	1848	Y M			29		
2122	BC	1849	Y M	Nabor born		30		
2121	BC	1850	Y M	**Nabor** first year; died in 1997 YM, son of 148 years (Gen 11:22, 24-25) [Next]	[24] **Nahor lived twenty-nine years, and became the father of Terah;** [25] and Nahor lived one hundred and nineteen years after he became the father of Terah, and he had [other] sons and daughters. (Gen 11:24-25 BCB)	1 of 29		
2120	BC	1851	Y M			2		
2119	BC	1852	Y M			3		
2118	BC	1853	Y M			4		
2117	BC	1854	Y M			5		
2116	BC	1855	Y M			6		
2115	BC	1856	Y M			7		
2114	BC	1857	Y M			8		
2113	BC	1858	Y M			9		
2112	BC	1859	Y M			10		
2111	BC	1860	Y M			11		
2110	BC	1861	Y M			12		
2109	BC	1862	Y M			13		

[Top | Flood | Abram | Exodus | David | Hezekiah | Jerusalem | JC | End Time | End Notes]

BC AD Years + or -		YM Years		6000 Years of Mankind Copyright © 2024 by Walter R. Dolen **Biblical Chronology Details** YM = Year of Mankind Begins in Sept/Oct 3 months before BC/AD dates	Additional Details	# of yrs	# of yrs	# of yrs
2108	BC	1863	Y M			14		
2107	BC	1864	Y M			15		
2106	BC	1865	Y M			16		
2105	BC	1866	Y M			17		
2104	BC	1867	Y M			18		
2103	BC	1868	Y M			19		
2102	BC	1869	Y M			20		
2101	BC	1870	Y M			21		
2100	BC	1871	Y M			22		
2099	BC	1872	Y M			23		
2098	BC	1873	Y M			24		
2097	BC	1874	Y M			25		
2096	BC	1875	Y M			26		
2095	BC	1876	Y M			27		
2094	BC	1877	Y M			28		
2093	BC	1878	Y M	Terah born		29		
2092	BC	1879	Y M	**Terah first year; died in 2083 YM, son of 205 years** (Gen 11:24, 32) Terah dies in Haran at 205 when Abram is Called and when he leaves Haran for the Promised land after Terah dies. (Acts 7:4) To Abram 1st yr. [Next]	[32] **The days of Terah were two hundred and five years; and Terah died in Haran.** (Gen 11:32 BCB)		1 of 205	
2091	BC	1880	Y M				2	
2090	BC	1881	Y M				3	
2089	BC	1882	Y M				4	

[Top | Flood | Abram | Exodus | David | Hezekiah | Jerusalem | JC | End Time | End Notes]

BC AD Years + or -		YM Years		6000 Years of Mankind Copyright © 2024 by Walter R. Dolen Biblical Chronology Details YM = Year of Mankind Begins in Sept/Oct 3 months before BC/AD dates	Additional Details	# of yrs	# of yrs	# of yrs
2088	BC	1883	Y M				5	
2087	BC	1884	Y M				6	
2086	BC	1885	Y M				7	
2085	BC	1886	Y M				8	
2084	BC	1887	Y M				9	
2083	BC	1888	Y M				10	
2082	BC	1889	Y M				11	
2081	BC	1890	Y M				12	
2080	BC	1891	Y M				13	
2079	BC	1892	Y M				14	
2078	BC	1893	Y M				15	
2077	BC	1894	Y M				16	
2076	BC	1895	Y M				17	
2075	BC	1896	Y M				18	
2074	BC	1897	Y M				19	
2073	BC	1898	Y M				20	
2072	BC	1899	Y M				21	
2071	BC	1900	Y M				22	
2070	BC	1901	Y M				23	
2069	BC	1902	Y M				24	

[Top | Flood | Abram | Exodus | David | Hezekiah | Jerusalem | JC | End Time | End Notes]

BC AD Years + or -		YM Years		6000 Years of Mankind Copyright © 2024 by Walter R. Dolen **Biblical Chronology Details** YM = Year of Mankind Begins in Sept/Oct 3 months before BC/AD dates	Additional Details	# of yrs	# of yrs	# of yrs
2068	BC	1903	Y M				25	
2067	BC	1904	Y M				26	
2066	BC	1905	Y M				27	
2065	BC	1906	Y M				28	
2064	BC	1907	Y M				29	
2063	BC	1908	Y M				30	
2062	BC	1909	Y M				31	
2061	BC	1910	Y M				32	
2060	BC	1911	Y M				33	
2059	BC	1912	Y M				34	
2058	BC	1913	Y M				35	
2057	BC	1914	Y M				36	
2056	BC	1915	Y M				37	
2055	BC	1916	Y M				38	
2054	BC	1917	Y M				39	
2053	BC	1918	Y M				40	
2052	BC	1919	Y M				41	
2051	BC	1920	Y M				42	
2050	BC	1921	Y M				43	
2049	BC	1922	Y M				44	

[Top	Flood	Abram	Exodus	David	Hezekiah	Jerusalem	JC	End Time	End Notes]								
BC AD Years + or -		YM Years		**6000 Years of Mankind** Copyright © 2024 by Walter R. Dolen **Biblical Chronology Details** YM = Year of Mankind Begins in Sept/Oct 3 months before BC/AD dates	**Additional Details**	# of yrs	# of yrs	# of yrs
2048	BC	1923	Y M				45	
2047	BC	1924	Y M				46	
2046	BC	1925	Y M				47	
2045	BC	1926	Y M				48	
2044	BC	1927	Y M				49	
2043	BC	1928	Y M				50	
2042	BC	1929	Y M				51	
2041	BC	1930	Y M				52	
2040	BC	1931	Y M				53	
2039	BC	1932	Y M				54	
2038	BC	1933	Y M				55	
2037	BC	1934	Y M				56	
2036	BC	1935	Y M				57	
2035	BC	1936	Y M				58	
2034	BC	1937	Y M				59	
2033	BC	1938	Y M				60	
2032	BC	1939	Y M				61	
2031	BC	1940	Y M				62	
2030	BC	1941	Y M				63	
2029	BC	1942	Y M				64	

[Top | Flood | Abram | Exodus | David | Hezekiah | Jerusalem | JC | End Time | End Notes]						

BC AD Years + or -		YM Years		**6000 Years of Mankind** Copyright © 2024 by Walter R. Dolen **Biblical Chronology Details** YM = Year of Mankind Begins in Sept/Oct 3 months before BC/AD dates	**Additional Details**	# of yrs	# of yrs	# of yrs
2028	BC	1943	Y M				65	
2027	BC	1944	Y M				66	
2026	BC	1945	Y M				67	
2025	BC	1946	Y M				68	
2024	BC	1947	Y M				69	
2023	BC	1948	Y M				70	
2022	BC	1949	Y M				71	
2021	BC	1950	Y M				72	
2020	BC	1951	Y M				73	
2019	BC	1952	Y M				74	
2018	BC	1953	Y M				75	
2017	BC	1954	Y M				76	
2016	BC	1955	Y M				77	
2015	BC	1956	Y M				78	
2014	BC	1957	Y M				79	
2013	BC	1958	Y M				80	
2012	BC	1959	Y M				81	
2011	BC	1960	Y M				82	
2010	BC	1961	Y M				83	
2009	BC	1962	Y M				84	

[Top | Flood | Abram | Exodus | David | Hezekiah | Jerusalem | JC | End Time | End Notes]

BC AD Years + or -		YM Years		6000 Years of Mankind Copyright © 2024 by Walter R. Dolen **Biblical Chronology Details** YM = Year of Mankind Begins in Sept/Oct 3 months before BC/AD dates	Additional Details	# of yrs	# of yrs	# of yrs
2008	BC	1963	Y M				85	
2007	BC	1964	Y M				86	
2006	BC	1965	Y M				87	
2005	BC	1966	Y M				88	
2004	BC	1967	Y M				89	
2003	BC	1968	Y M				90	
2002	BC	1969	Y M				91	
2001	BC	1970	Y M				92	
2000	BC	1971	Y M				93	
1999	BC	1972	Y M				94	
1998	BC	1973	Y M				95	
1997	BC	1974	Y M				96	
1996	BC	1975	Y M				97	
1995	BC	1976	Y M				98	
1994	BC	1977	Y M				99	
1993	BC	1978	Y M				100	
1992	BC	1979	Y M				101	
1991	BC	1980	Y M				102	
1990	BC	1981	Y M				103	
1989	BC	1982	Y M				104	

BC AD Years + or -		YM Years		**6000 Years of Mankind** Copyright © 2024 by Walter R. Dolen **Biblical Chronology Details** YM = Year of Mankind Begins in Sept/Oct 3 months before BC/AD dates	**Additional Details**	# of yrs	# of yrs	# of yrs
1988	BC	1983	YM				105	
1987	BC	1984	YM				106	
1986	BC	1985	YM				107	
1985	BC	1986	YM				108	
1984	BC	1987	YM				109	
1983	BC	1988	YM				110	
1982	BC	1989	YM				111	
1981	BC	1990	YM				112	
1980	BC	1991	YM				113	
1979	BC	1992	YM				114	
1978	BC	1993	YM				115	
1977	BC	1994	YM				116	
1976	BC	1995	YM				117	
1975	BC	1996	YM	Peleg dies			118	
1974	BC	1997	YM	**Nabor dies**			119	
1973	BC	1998	YM				120	
1972	BC	1999	YM				121	
1971	BC	2000	YM				122	
1970	BC	2001	YM				123	
1969	BC	2002	YM				124	

[Top | Flood | Abram | Exodus | David | Hezekiah | Jerusalem | JC | End Time | End Notes]

BC AD Years + or -		YM Years		6000 Years of Mankind Copyright © 2024 by Walter R. Dolen **Biblical Chronology Details** YM = Year of Mankind Begins in Sept/Oct 3 months before BC/AD dates	Additional Details	# of yrs	# of yrs	# of yrs
1968	BC	2003	Y M				125	
1967	BC	2004	Y M				126	
1966	BC	2005	Y M				127	
1965	BC	2006	Y M	**Noah dies** in this year			128	
1964	BC	2007	Y M				129	
1963	BC	2008	Y M	**Abram born** **World's population: from ab. 8,000** [2%35yrs] **to 262,000** [4.7%15yrs] **Note:** 2% is extremely fast growth; 4.7% growth is ultra extreme growth	10th generation since Arphaxad		130	
1962	BC	2009	Y M	**Abram** first year; died in 2184 YM, son of 175 years (Gen 11:26-32; with 12:4; 25:7)	[7] These are all the years of Abraham's life that he lived, one hundred and seventy-five years. (Gen 25:7 BCB)	1	131	
1961	BC	2010	Y M			2	132	
1960	BC	2011	Y M			3	133	
1959	BC	2012	Y M			4	134	
1958	BC	2013	Y M			5	135	
1957	BC	2014	Y M			6	136	
1956	BC	2015	Y M			7	137	
1955	BC	2016	Y M			8	138	
1954	BC	2017	Y M	Sarah born (Gen 17:17)		9	139	
1953	BC	2018	Y M	**Sarah** first year Ten years younger than Abram	[17] Then Abraham fell on his face and laughed, and said in his heart, Will a child be born to a man one hundred years old? And will Sarah, who is ninety years old, bear [a child]? (Gen 17:17 BCB)	10	140	

[Top | Flood | Abram | Exodus | David | Hezekiah | Jerusalem | JC | End Time | End Notes]

BC AD Years + or -		YM Years		6000 Years of Mankind Copyright © 2024 by Walter R. Dolen **Biblical Chronology Details** YM = Year of Mankind Begins in Sept/Oct 3 months before BC/AD dates	Additional Details	# of yrs	# of yrs	# of yrs
1952	BC	2019	Y M			11	141	
1951	BC	2020	Y M			12	142	
1950	BC	2021	Y M			13	143	
1949	BC	2022	Y M			14	144	
1948	BC	2023	Y M			15	145	
1947	BC	2024	Y M			16	146	
1946	BC	2025	Y M			17	147	
1945	BC	2026	Y M	**Reu dies**		18	148	
1944	BC	2027	Y M			19	149	
1943	BC	2028	Y M			20 - Abram	150	
1942	BC	2029	Y M			21	151	
1941	BC	2030	Y M			22	152	
1940	BC	2031	Y M			23	153	
1939	BC	2032	Y M			24	154	
1938	BC	2033	Y M			25	155	
1937	BC	2034	Y M			26	156	
1936	BC	2035	Y M			27	157	
1935	BC	2036	Y M			28	158	
1934	BC	2037	Y M			29	159	

BC AD Years + or -		YM Years		6000 Years of Mankind Copyright © 2024 by Walter R. Dolen Biblical Chronology Details YM = Year of Mankind Begins in Sept/Oct 3 months before BC/AD dates	Additional Details	# of yrs	# of yrs	# of yrs
1933	BC	2038	Y M			30 - Abram	160	
1932	BC	2039	Y M			31	161	
1931	BC	2040	Y M			32	162	
1930	BC	2041	Y M			33	163	
1929	BC	2042	Y M			34	164	
1928	BC	2043	Y M			35	165	
1927	BC	2044	Y M			36	166	
1926	BC	2045	Y M			37	167	
1925	BC	2046	Y M			38	168	
1924	BC	2047	Y M			39	169	
1923	BC	2048	Y M			40 - Abram	170	
1922	BC	2049	Y M	Serug dies		41	171	
1921	BC	2050	Y M			42	172	
1920	BC	2051	Y M			43	173	
1919	BC	2052	Y M			44	174	
1918	BC	2053	Y M			45	175	
1917	BC	2054	Y M			46	176	
1916	BC	2055	Y M			47	177	
1915	BC	2056	Y M			48	178	

BC AD Years + or -		YM Years		**6000 Years of Mankind** Copyright © 2024 by Walter R. Dolen **Biblical Chronology Details** YM = Year of Mankind Begins in Sept/Oct 3 months before BC/AD dates	Additional Details	# of yrs	# of yrs	# of yrs
1914	BC	2057	Y M			49	179	
1913	BC	2058	Y M			50 - Abr am	180	
1912	BC	2059	Y M			51	181	
1911	BC	2060	Y M			52	182	
1910	BC	2061	Y M			53	183	
1909	BC	2062	Y M			54	184	
1908	BC	2063	Y M			55	185	
1907	BC	2064	Y M			56	186	
1906	BC	2065	Y M			57	187	
1905	BC	2066	Y M			58	188	
1904	BC	2067	Y M			59	189	
1903	BC	2068	Y M			60 - Abr am	190	
1902	BC	2069	Y M			61	191	
1901	BC	2070	Y M			62	192	
1900	BC	2071	Y M			63	193	
1899	BC	2072	Y M			64	194	
1898	BC	2073	Y M			65	195	
1897	BC	2074	Y M			66	196	
1896	BC	2075	Y M			67	197	

[Top | Flood | Abram | Exodus | David | Hezekiah | Jerusalem | JC | End Time | End Notes]

BC AD Years + or -		YM Years		6000 Years of Mankind Copyright © 2024 by Walter R. Dolen **Biblical Chronology Details** YM = Year of Mankind Begins in Sept/Oct 3 months before BC/AD dates	Additional Details	# of yrs	# of yrs	# of yrs
1895	BC	2076	Y M			68	198	
1894	BC	2077	Y M			69	199	
1893	BC	2078	Y M			70	200	
1892	BC	2079	Y M			71	201	
1891	BC	2080	Y M			72	202	
1890	BC	2081	Y M			73	203	
1889	BC	2082	Y M	**Worlds population about 24,000 to the very high 750,000** Re: high numbers in OT go to https://beone.ws/exodusnumbers.html	(About 426 years since the flood)	74	204	
1888		2083	Y M	**Abram's Call** **430 years of sojourning begins** (Exo 12:40-41; Acts 7:2-4; Gal 3:17) In this year, Abram, who was 75, leaves his home land moves to Canaan	Now Abram was seventy-five years old when he departed from Haran. (Gen 12:4 BCB)	75	205 T e r a h	
1887	BC	2084	Y M	Abram in Canaan moves to Egypt and back to Canaan in the same year (Gen 12:1-5; 12:10; 13:1). See "Ur of the Chaldeans" in this book, *6000 years of Mankind: Chronology Papers*, 2025 version.	**First year in Canaan** & Egypt, begins the inclusive count of the 430 years (Exodus 12:40-41). **1 of 430**	1 of 430		
1886	BC	2085	Y M	76 - Abram **World's population:** about 24,000 to 750,000 at about 1.5% increase per year since 2008 YM, without wars, diseases and droughts being prevalent.		2		
1885	BC	2086	Y M	77 Abram's 3rd year in Canaan		3		
1884	BC	2087	Y M	78		4		
1883	BC	2088	Y M	79		5		
1882	BC	2089	Y M	80 Abram		6		
1881	BC	2090	Y M	81		7		
1880	BC	2091	Y M	82		8		

[Top | Flood | Abram | Exodus | David | Hezekiah | Jerusalem | JC | End Time | End Notes]

BC AD Years + or -		YM Years		6000 Years of Mankind Copyright © 2024 by Walter R. Dolen **Biblical Chronology Details** YM = Year of Mankind Begins in Sept/Oct 3 months before BC/AD dates	Additional Details	# of yrs	# of yrs	# of yrs
1879	BC	2092	Y M	83		9		
1878	BC	2093	Y M	84 10th year in Canaan		10		
1877	BC	2094	Y M	85 Ishmael conceived thru Hagar		11		
1876	BC	2095	Y M	86 - Ishmael born: "Abram was 86 when Hagar bore Ishmael to Abram" (Gen 16:16)	[16] Abram was eighty-six years old when Hagar bore Ishmael to him. (Gen 16:16 BCB)	12		
1875	BC	2096	Y M	87 **Ishmael** first year born in in 2094, but this year counted as his first year		13		1
1874	BC	2097	Y M	88 **Arphaxad dies**		14		2
1873	BC	2098	Y M	89		15		3
1872	BC	2099	Y M	90 Abram		16		4
1871	BC	2100	Y M	91		17		5
1870	BC	2101	Y M	92		18		6
1869	BC	2102	Y M	93		19		7
1868	BC	2103	Y M	94		20		8
1867	BC	2104	Y M	95		21		9
1866	BC	2105	Y M	96		22		10
1865	BC	2106	Y M	97		23		11
1864	BC	2107	Y M	98		24		12

[Top | Flood | Abram | Exodus | David | Hezekiah | Jerusalem | JC | End Time | End Notes]

BC AD Years + or -		YM Years		6000 Years of Mankind Copyright © 2024 by Walter R. Dolen **Biblical Chronology Details** YM = Year of Mankind Begins in Sept/Oct 3 months before BC/AD dates	Additional Details	# of yrs	# of yrs	# of yrs
1863	BC	2108	Y M	99 - **Abram's circumcised and name changed to Abraham** (Gen 17:24-25) (Gen 17:1, 24, 21; 21:2; 17:17; 21:5) Ishmael's 13 year (Gen 17:25)	Ishmael's 13th year [24] Now Abraham was ninety-nine years old when he was circumcised in the flesh of his foreskin. [25] And Ishmael his son was thirteen years old when he was circumcised in the flesh of his foreskin. (Gen 17:24-25 BCB) [17] Then Abraham fell on his face and laughed, and said in his heart, Will a child be born to a man one hundred years old? And will Sarah, who is ninety years old, bear [a child]? (Gen 17:17 BCB) [21] But my covenant I will establish with Isaac, whom Sarah will bear to you at this season next year. (Gen 17:21 BCB)	25 of 430		13
1862	BC	2109	Y M	100 - Abraham **Isaac born** (Gen 17:1; 17:17, 21; 21:5)		26		
1861	BC	2110	Y M	**Isaac's first year** Isaac lived 180 years (Gen 35:28). Isaac was born on a Feast day (Gen 17:21; see Hebrew text). [Next] 101 - Abraham	[28] Now the days of Isaac were one hundred and eighty years. (Gen 35:28 BCB)	27		1st I s a a c of 180
1860	BC	2111	Y M	102		28		2
1859	BC	2112	Y M	103 - Abraham		29		3
1858	BC	2113	Y M			30 of 430		4

[Top | Flood | Abram | Exodus | David | Hezekiah | Jerusalem | JC | End Time | End Notes]

BC AD Years + or -		YM Years		**6000 Years of Mankind** Copyright © 2024 by Walter R. Dolen **Biblical Chronology Details** YM = Year of Mankind Begins in Sept/Oct 3 months before BC/AD dates	**Additional Details**	# of yrs	# of yrs	# of yrs
1857	BC	2114	Y M	**When the 400 of Affliction started for Abraham and his offspring (Israel)** Isaac grew up and was weaned on his birthday (about 4 years old) (Gen 21:8). And Sarah [mother of Isaac] saw the son of Hagar, the Egyptian," mocking Issac (Gen 21:9) – a mild beginning for the affliction. **The 400 years of affliction begins for Abram's seed** (Gen 15:13; Acts 7:6) Genesis 15:13 speaks of Abram's seed ("thy seed") being *strangers* in a land that is not for them, that Abraham's seed would serve them of this land, and that the people of this land would afflict the seed for 400 years (see Hebrew text). Notice that it was the affliction that would last for 400 years, not the slavery. **400 years ended at the Exodus.** In Genesis 15:14 it identifies the nation that the Seed would serve or be in slavery to, and that God would judge this nation. After this judgment the Seed would come out with great substance. In context this nation can only be Egypt (note Ex 6:6-7; 12:36; etc). It so happened that the beginning of the affliction of 400 years was caused by a son (Ishmael) of an *Egyptian* woman. ***When 400 Years Began.*** The 400 years of affliction for the Seed of Abraham began in the year of Isaac's feast when he was weaned. At that time Isaac was mocked or persecuted [Gal 4:29] by "the son [Ishmael] of Hagar the *Egyptian*" (Gen 21:8-9; Gal 4:29). It was also at that time that God said: "for in Isaac shall your [Abraham's] seed be called" (Gen 21:12; 17:19; Gal 4:28; see "Seed Paper" [PP1]). Sarah breastfed Isaac for 4 full years (or 5 inclusive counting years) in celebration because it took her so long to conceive (90 years). 105- Abraham	Isaac's 5th year inclusive count since he was born on the 1st day of the year *Fourth Generation.* In Genesis 15:16 it speaks of "the fourth generation" coming to the land of Canaan again. The fourth generation that returned to Canaan was that of Joseph and his brothers who returned to the land of Canaan to bury Jacob (Gen 50:1-13). The first generation was **Abram**; the second was **Isaac**; the third was **Jacob**; and the fourth was **Joseph** and his brothers.	31 of 430	1 of 400	5
1856	BC	2115	Y M	106		32	2	6
1855	BC	2116	Y M	107		33	3	7
1854	BC	2117	Y M	108		34	4	8
1853	BC	2118	Y M	109		35	5	9
1852	BC	2119	Y M	110 - Abraham		36	6	10
1851	BC	2120	Y M	111 - Abraham		37	7	11
1850	BC	2121	Y M	112		38	8	12
1849	BC	2122	Y M	113		39	9	13

[Top | Flood | Abram | Exodus | David | Hezekiah | Jerusalem | JC | End Time | End Notes]

BC AD Years + or -		YM Years		6000 Years of Mankind Copyright © 2024 by Walter R. Dolen **Biblical Chronology Details** YM = Year of Mankind Begins in Sept/Oct 3 months before BC/AD dates	Additional Details	# of yrs	# of yrs	# of yrs
1848	BC	2123	YM	114		40	10	14
1847	BC	2124	YM	115		41	11	15
1846	BC	2125	YM	116		42	12	16
1845	BC	2126	YM	117		43	13	17
1844	BC	2127	YM	118 **Salah died son of 433 years (b. 1693)**		44	14	18
1843	BC	2128	YM	119		45	15	19
1842	BC	2129	YM	120 - Abraham		46	16	20
1841	BC	2130	YM	121		47	17	21
1840	BC	2131	YM	122		48	18	22
1839	BC	2132	YM	123		49	19	23
1838	BC	2133	YM	124		50	20	24
1837	BC	2134	YM	125		51	21	25
1836	BC	2135	YM	126		52	22	26
1835	BC	2136	YM	127		53	23	27
1834	BC	2137	YM	128		54	24	28
1833	BC	2138	YM	129		55	25	29
1832	BC	2139	YM	130 - Abraham		56	26	30
1831	BC	2140	YM	131		57	27	31
1830	BC	2141	YM	132 - Abraham		58	28	32
1829	BC	2142	YM	133		59	29	33

BC AD Years + or -		YM Years		6000 Years of Mankind Copyright © 2024 by Walter R. Dolen **Biblical Chronology Details** YM = Year of Mankind Begins in Sept/Oct 3 months before BC/AD dates	Additional Details	# of yrs	# of yrs	# of yrs
1828	BC	2143	Y M	134		60	30	34
1827	BC	2144	Y M	135		61	31	35
1826	BC	2145	Y M	136 - Abraham		62	32	36
1825	BC	2146	Y M	137 - Abraham **Sarah** dies in her 127th year (Gen 23:1) She was born 10 years after Abram. (Gen 17:17)	BCB **Genesis 23:1** Now Sarah lived one hundred and twenty-seven years; [these were] the years of the life of Sarah. (Gen 23:1 BCB) 17 Then Abraham fell on his face and laughed, and said in his heart, Will a child be born to a man one hundred years old? And will Sarah, who is ninety years old, bear [a child]? (Gen 17:17 BCB)	63 of 430	33 of 400	37 of 180 I s a a c
1824	BC	2147	Y M			64	34	38
1823	BC	2148	Y M			65	35	39
1822	BC	2149	Y M	**Issac marries Rebekah** in Isaac's 40th year (Gen 25:20)		66	36	40
1821	BC	2150	Y M			67	37	41
1820	BC	2151	Y M			68	38	42
1819	BC	2152	Y M			69	39	43
1818	BC	2153	Y M			70	40	44
1817	BC	2154	Y M			71	41	45
1816	BC	2155	Y M			72	42	46
1815	BC	2156	Y M			73	43	47
1814	BC	2157	Y M			74	44	48
1813	BC	2158	Y M	**Shem dies** in his 600th year (Gen 11:10-11)		75	45	49

[Top | Flood | Abram | Exodus | David | Hezekiah | Jerusalem | JC | End Time | End Notes]

BC AD Years + or -		YM Years		6000 Years of Mankind Copyright © 2024 by Walter R. Dolen **Biblical Chronology Details** YM = Year of Mankind Begins in Sept/Oct 3 months before BC/AD dates	Additional Details	# of yrs	# of yrs	# of yrs
1812	BC	2159	YM			76	46	50
1811	BC	2160	YM			77	47	51
1810	BC	2161	YM			78	48	52
1809	BC	2162	YM			79	49	53
1808	BC	2163	YM			80	50	54
1807	BC	2164	YM			81	51	55
1806	BC	2165	YM			82	52	56
1805	BC	2166	YM			83	53	57
1804	BC	2167	YM			84	54	58
1803	BC	2168	YM			85	55	59
1802	BC	2169	YM	**Jacob (Israel) and Esau born** in Isaac's 60th year (Gen 25:26)		86	56	60 I s a a c
1801	BC	2170	YM	**Jacob** first year	1 -Jacob	87	57	61
1800	BC	2171	YM		2	88	58	62
1799	BC	2172	YM		3	89	59	63
1798	BC	2173	YM		4	90	60	64
1797	BC	2174	YM		5	91	61	65
1796	BC	2175	YM		6	92	62	66
1795	BC	2176	YM		7	93	63	67
1794	BC	2177	YM		8	94	64	68

[Top | Flood | Abram | Exodus | David | Hezekiah | Jerusalem | JC | End Time | End Notes]

BC AD Years + or -		YM Years		**6000 Years of Mankind** Copyright © 2024 by Walter R. Dolen **Biblical Chronology Details** YM = Year of Mankind Begins in Sept/Oct 3 months before BC/AD dates	**Additional Details**	# of yrs	# of yrs	# of yrs
1793	BC	2178	Y M		9	95	65	69
1792	BC	2179	Y M		10	96	66	70
1791	BC	2180	Y M		11	97	67	71
1790	BC	2181	Y M		12	98	68	72
1789	BC	2182	Y M		13	99	69	73
1788	BC	2183	Y M		14	100	70	74
1787	BC	2184	Y M	**Abraham dies** (175th year) (Gen 25:7)	15	101 of 430	71 of 400	75 I s a a c
1786	BC	2185	Y M		16	102	72	76
1785	BC	2186	Y M		17	103	73	77
1784	BC	2187	Y M		18	104	74	78
1783	BC	2188	Y M	**Eber dies** in his 464th year (Gen 11:16-17, 14)	19	105	75	79
1782	BC	2189	Y M		20 - Jacob	106	76	80
1781	BC	2190	Y M		21	107	77	81
1780	BC	2191	Y M		22	108	78	82
1779	BC	2192	Y M		23	109	79	83
1778	BC	2193	Y M		24	110	80	84
1777	BC	2194	Y M		25	111	81	85
1776	BC	2195	Y M		26	112	82	86
1775	BC	2196	Y M		27	113	83	87

BC AD Years + or -		YM Years		**6000 Years of Mankind** Copyright © 2024 by Walter R. Dolen **Biblical Chronology Details** YM = Year of Mankind Begins in Sept/Oct 3 months before BC/AD dates	**Additional Details**	# of yrs	# of yrs	# of yrs
1774	BC	2197	YM		28	114	84	88
1773	BC	2198	YM		29	115	85	89
1772	BC	2199	YM		30	116	86	90
1771	BC	2200	YM		31	117	87	91
1770	BC	2201	YM		32	118	88	92
1769	BC	2202	YM		33	119	89	93
1768	BC	2203	YM		34	120	90	94
1767	BC	2204	YM		35	121	91	95
1766	BC	2205	YM		36	122	92	96
1765	BC	2206	YM		37	123	93	97
1764	BC	2207	YM		38	124	94	98
1763	BC	2208	YM		39	125	95	99
1762	BC	2209	YM		40 - Jacob	126	96	100
1761	BC	2210	YM		41	127	97	101
1760	BC	2211	YM		42	128	98	102
1759	BC	2212	YM		43	129	99	103
1758	BC	2213	YM		44	130	100	104
1757	BC	2214	YM		45	131	101	105
1756	BC	2215	YM		46	132	102	106
1755	BC	2216	YM		47	133	103	107

[Top | Flood | Abram | Exodus | David | Hezekiah | Jerusalem | JC | End Time | End Notes]

BC AD Years + or -		YM Years	**6000 Years of Mankind** Copyright © 2024 by Walter R. Dolen **Biblical Chronology Details** YM = Year of Mankind Begins in Sept/Oct 3 months before BC/AD dates	**Additional Details**	# of yrs	# of yrs	# of yrs
1754	BC	2217	Y M	48	134	104	108
1753	BC	2218	Y M	49	135	105	109
1752	BC	2219	Y M	50	136	106	110
1751	BC	2220	Y M	51	137	107	111
1750	BC	2221	Y M	52	138	108	112
1749	BC	2222	Y M	53	139	109	113
1748	BC	2223	Y M	54	140	110	114
1747	BC	2224	Y M	55	141	111	115
1746	BC	2225	Y M	56	142	112	116
1745	BC	2226	Y M	57	143	113	117
1744	BC	2227	Y M	58	144	114	118
1743	BC	2228	Y M	59	145	115	119
1742	BC	2229	Y M	60	146	116	120
1741	BC	2230	Y M	61	147	117	121
1740	BC	2231	Y M	**Ishmael dies** in his 137th year (Gen 25:17; see 2095 YM)	62 -Jacob	148	118	122
1739	BC	2232	Y M	63	149	119	123
1738	BC	2233	Y M	64	150	120	124
1737	BC	2234	Y M	65	151	121	125
1736	BC	2235	Y M	66	152	122	126
1735	BC	2236	Y M	67	153	123	127

[Top | Flood | Abram | Exodus | David | Hezekiah | Jerusalem | JC | End Time | End Notes]

BC AD Years + or -		YM Years		**6000 Years of Mankind** Copyright © 2024 by Walter R. Dolen **Biblical Chronology Details** YM = Year of Mankind Begins in Sept/Oct 3 months before BC/AD dates	**Additional Details**	# of yrs	# of yrs	# of yrs
1734	BC	2237	Y M		68	154	124	128
1733	BC	2238	Y M		69	155	125	129
1732	BC	2239	Y M		70	156	126	130
1731	BC	2240	Y M		71	157	127	131
1730	BC	2241	Y M		72	158	128	132
1729	BC	2242	Y M		73	159	129	133
1728	BC	2243	Y M		74	160	130	134
1727	BC	2244	Y M		75	161	131	135
1726	BC	2245	Y M		76	162	132	136
1725	BC	2246	Y M		77	163	133	137
1724	BC	2247	Y M		78	164	134	138
1723	BC	2248	Y M		79	165	135	139
1722	BC	2249	Y M		80	166	136	140
1721	BC	2250	Y M		81	167	137	141
1720	BC	2251	Y M		82	168	138	142
1719	BC	2252	Y M		83	169	139	143
1718	BC	2253	Y M		84	170	140	144
1717	BC	2254	Y M		85	171	141	145
1716	BC	2255	Y M		86	172	142	146
1715	BC	2256	Y M		87	173	143	147

BC AD Years + or -		YM Years		**6000 Years of Mankind** Copyright © 2024 by Walter R. Dolen **Biblical Chronology Details** YM = Year of Mankind Begins in Sept/Oct 3 months before BC/AD dates	Additional Details	# of yrs	# of yrs	# of yrs
1714	BC	2257	Y M		88	174	144	148
1713	BC	2258	Y M		89	175	145	149
1712	BC	2259	Y M		90	176	146	150
1711	BC	2260	Y M	Joseph born **World population about: 144,000 to 2,500,000**	91	177	147	151
1710	BC	2261	Y M	1 - **Joseph first year**	92 - Jacob	178 of 430	148 of 400	152 I s a a c
1709	BC	2262	Y M	2	93	179	149	153
1708	BC	2263	Y M	3	94	180	150	154
1707	BC	2264	Y M	4	95	181	151	155
1706	BC	2265	Y M	5	96	182	152	156
1705	BC	2266	Y M	6	97	183	153	157
1704	BC	2267	Y M	7	98	184	154	158
1703	BC	2268	Y M	8	99	185	155	159
1702	BC	2269	Y M	9	100 - Jacob	186	156	160
1701	BC	2270	Y M	10 - Joseph	101	187	157	161
1700	BC	2271	Y M	11	102	188	158	162
1699	BC	2272	Y M	12	103	189	159	163
1698	BC	2273	Y M	13	104	190	160	164
1697	BC	2274	Y M	14	105	191	161	165
1696	BC	2275	Y M	15	106	192	162	166

BC AD Years + or -		YM Years		6000 Years of Mankind Copyright © 2024 by Walter R. Dolen **Biblical Chronology Details** YM = Year of Mankind Begins in Sept/Oct 3 months before BC/AD dates	Additional Details	# of yrs	# of yrs	# of yrs
1695	BC	2276	Y M	16	107	193	163	167
1694	BC	2277	Y M	17	108	194	164	168
1693	BC	2278	Y M	18	109	195	165	169
1692	BC	2279	Y M	19	110 - Jacob	196	166	170
1691	BC	2280	Y M	20 - Joseph	111	197	167	171
1690	BC	2281	Y M	21	112	198	168	172
1689	BC	2282	Y M	22	113	199	169	173
1688	BC	2283	Y M	23	114	200	170	174
1687	BC	2284	Y M	24	115	201	171	175
1686	BC	2285	Y M	25	116	202	172	176
1685	BC	2286	Y M	26	117	203	173	177
1684	BC	2287	Y M	27	118	204	174	178
1683	BC	2288	Y M	28	119	205	175	179
1682	BC	2289	Y M	**Isaac died in his 180th year** (Gen 35:28) 29 - Joseph	120	206	176	180
1681	BC	2290	Y M	**Joseph is 30** Beginning of the seven years of plenty (Gen 41:46-47) Joseph had two children (**Manasseh** and **Ephraim**) before the seven years of famine. (Gen 41:50-52)	121 - Jacob	207 of 430	177 of 400	
1680	BC	2291	Y M	31 - Joseph	122	208	178	
1679	BC	2292	Y M	32	123	209	179	
1678	BC	2293	Y M	33	124	210	180	
1677	BC	2294	Y M	34	125	211	181	

BC AD Years + or -		YM Years		**6000 Years of Mankind** Copyright © 2024 by Walter R. Dolen **Biblical Chronology Details** YM = Year of Mankind Begins in Sept/Oct 3 months before BC/AD dates	**Additional Details**	# of yrs	# of yrs	# of yrs
1676	BC	2295	Y M	35 - Joseph	126	212	182	
1675	BC	2296	Y M	36	127	213	183	
1674	BC	2297	Y M	37	128	214	184	
1673	BC	2298	Y M	38 - Joseph	129	215	185	
1672	BC	2299	Y M	**Jacob at 130 goes into Egypt** (Gen 47:9; 46:6) **Joseph is 39 when Jacob was 130** (Gen 41:46; 53:54; 45:6, 9-11; 47:8-9)	130- Jacob	216 of 430	186 of 400	
1671	BC	2300	Y M	40		217	187	
1670	BC	2301	Y M	41		218	188	
1669	BC	2302	Y M	42		219	189	
1668	BC	2303	Y M	43		220	190	
1667	BC	2304	Y M	44		221	191	
1666	BC	2305	Y M	45		222	192	
1665	BC	2306	Y M	46		223	193	
1664	BC	2307	Y M	47		224	194	
1663	BC	2308	Y M	48		225	195	
1662	BC	2309	Y M	49		226	196	
1661	BC	2310	Y M	50		227	197	
1660	BC	2311	Y M	51		228	198	
1659	BC	2312	Y M	52		229	199	
1658	BC	2313	Y M	53		230	200	
1657	BC	2314	Y M	54		231	201	

BC AD Years + or -		YM Years		6000 Years of Mankind Copyright © 2024 by Walter R. Dolen **Biblical Chronology Details** YM = Year of Mankind Begins in Sept/Oct 3 months before BC/AD dates	Additional Details	# of yrs	# of yrs	# of yrs
1656	BC	2315	Y M	55		232	202	
1655	BC	2316	Y M	56		233	203	
1654	BC	2317	Y M	57		234	204	
1653	BC	2318	Y M	58		235	205	
1652	BC	2319	Y M	59		236	206	
1651	BC	2320	Y M	60 - Joseph		237	207	
1650	BC	2321	Y M	61		238	208	
1649	BC	2322	Y M	62		239	209	
1648	BC	2323	Y M	63		240	210	
1647	BC	2324	Y M	64		241	211	
1646	BC	2325	Y M	65		242	212	
1645	BC	2326	Y M	66		243	213	
1644	BC	2327	Y M	67		244	214	
1643	BC	2328	Y M	68		245	215	
1642	BC	2329	Y M	69		246	216	
1641	BC	2330	Y M	70 - Joseph		247	217	
1640	BC	2331	Y M	71		248	218	
1639	BC	2332	Y M	72		249	219	
1638	BC	2333	Y M	73		250	220	
1637	BC	2334	Y M	74		251	221	

BC AD Years + or -		YM Years		6000 Years of Mankind Copyright © 2024 by Walter R. Dolen Biblical Chronology Details YM = Year of Mankind Begins in Sept/Oct 3 months before BC/AD dates	Additional Details	# of yrs	# of yrs	# of yrs
1636	BC	2335	Y M	75		252	222	
1635	BC	2336	Y M	76		253	223	
1634	BC	2337	Y M	77		254	224	
1633	BC	2338	Y M	78		255	225	
1632	BC	2339	Y M	79		256	226	
1631	BC	2340	Y M	80 - Joseph		257	227	
1630	BC	2341	Y M	81		258	228	
1629	BC	2342	Y M	82		259	229	
1628	BC	2343	Y M	83		260	230	
1627	BC	2344	Y M	84		261	231	
1626	BC	2345	Y M	85		262	232	
1625	BC	2346	Y M	86		263	233	
1624	BC	2347	Y M	87		264	234	
1623	BC	2348	Y M	88		265	235	
1622	BC	2349	Y M	89		266	236	
1621	BC	2350	Y M	90 - Joseph		267	237	
1620	BC	2351	Y M	91		268	238	
1619	BC	2352	Y M	92		269	239	
1618	BC	2353	Y M	93		270	240	
1617	BC	2354	Y M	94		271	241	

[Top | Flood | Abram | Exodus | David | Hezekiah | Jerusalem | JC | End Time | End Notes]

BC AD Years + or -		YM Years		6000 Years of Mankind Copyright © 2024 by Walter R. Dolen Biblical Chronology Details YM = Year of Mankind Begins in Sept/Oct 3 months before BC/AD dates	Additional Details	# of yrs	# of yrs	# of yrs
1616	BC	2355	YM	95		272	242	
1615	BC	2356	YM	96		273	243	
1614	BC	2357	YM	97		274	244	
1613	BC	2358	YM	98		275	245	
1612	BC	2359	YM	99		276	246	
1611	BC	2360	YM	100 - Joseph		277	247	
1610	BC	2361	YM	101		278	248	
1609	BC	2362	YM	102		279	249	
1608	BC	2363	YM	103		280	250	
1607	BC	2364	YM	104		281	251	
1606	BC	2365	YM	105		282	252	
1605	BC	2366	YM	106		283	253	
1604	BC	2367	YM	107		284	254	
1603	BC	2368	YM	108		285	255	
1602	BC	2369	YM	109		286	256	
1601	BC	2370	YM	**Joseph dies at 110 years old (Gen 50:22-26)**		287	257	
1600	BC	2371	YM	**Gap in chronological method... (Gap bridged by using the 430 year and the 400 year dates. See under 2083 YM)**		288 of 430	258 of 400	
1599	BC	2372	YM			289	259	
1598	BC	2373	YM			290	260	
1597	BC	2374	YM			291	261	

[Top | Flood | Abram | Exodus | David | Hezekiah | Jerusalem | JC | End Time | End Notes]

BC AD Years + or -		YM Years		6000 Years of Mankind Copyright © 2024 by Walter R. Dolen **Biblical Chronology Details** YM = Year of Mankind Begins in Sept/Oct 3 months before BC/AD dates	**Additional Details**	# of yrs	# of yrs	# of yrs
1596	BC	2375	Y M			292	262	
1595	BC	2376	Y M			293	263	
1594	BC	2377	Y M			294	264	
1593	BC	2378	Y M			295	265	
1592	BC	2379	Y M			296	266	
1591	BC	2380	Y M			297	267	
1590	BC	2381	Y M			298	268	
1589	BC	2382	Y M			299	269	
1588	BC	2383	Y M			300	270	
1587	BC	2384	Y M			301	271	
1586	BC	2385	Y M			302	272	
1585	BC	2386	Y M			303	273	
1584	BC	2387	Y M			304	274	
1583	BC	2388	Y M			305	275	
1582	BC	2389	Y M			306	276	
1581	BC	2390	Y M			307	277	
1580	BC	2391	Y M			308	278	
1579	BC	2392	Y M			309	279	
1578	BC	2393	Y M			310	280	
1577	BC	2394	Y M			311	281	

[Top | Flood | Abram | Exodus | David | Hezekiah | Jerusalem | JC | End Time | End Notes]

BC AD Years + or -		YM Years		**6000 Years of Mankind** Copyright © 2024 by Walter R. Dolen **Biblical Chronology Details** YM = Year of Mankind Begins in Sept/Oct 3 months before BC/AD dates	**Additional Details**	# of yrs	# of yrs	# of yrs
1576	BC	2395	Y M			312	282	
1575	BC	2396	Y M			313	283	
1574	BC	2397	Y M			314	284	
1573	BC	2398	Y M			315	285	
1572	BC	2399	Y M			316	286	
1571	BC	2400	Y M			317	287	
1570	BC	2401	Y M			318	288	
1569	BC	2402	Y M			319	289	
1568	BC	2403	Y M			320	290	
1567	BC	2404	Y M			321	291	
1566	BC	2405	Y M			322	292	
1565	BC	2406	Y M			323	293	
1564	BC	2407	Y M			324	294	
1563	BC	2408	Y M			325	295	
1562	BC	2409	Y M			326	296	
1561	BC	2410	Y M			327	297	
1560	BC	2411	Y M			328	298	
1559	BC	2412	Y M			329	299	
1558	BC	2413	Y M			330	300	
1557	BC	2414	Y M			331	301	

BC AD Years + or -		YM Years		6000 Years of Mankind Copyright © 2024 by Walter R. Dolen Biblical Chronology Details YM = Year of Mankind Begins in Sept/Oct 3 months before BC/AD dates	Additional Details	# of yrs	# of yrs	# of yrs
1556	BC	2415	Y M			332	302	
1555	BC	2416	Y M			333	303	
1554	BC	2417	Y M			334	304	
1553	BC	2418	Y M			335	305	
1552	BC	2419	Y M			336	306	
1551	BC	2420	Y M			337	307	
1550	BC	2421	Y M			338	308	
1549	BC	2422	Y M			339	309	
1548	BC	2423	Y M			340	310	
1547	BC	2424	Y M			341	311	
1546	BC	2425	Y M			342	312	
1545	BC	2426	Y M			343	313	
1544	BC	2427	Y M			344	314	
1543	BC	2428	Y M			345	315	
1542	BC	2429	Y M			346	316	
1541	BC	2430	Y M			347	317	
1540	BC	2431	Y M			348	318	
1539	BC	2432	Y M			349	319	
1538	BC	2433	Y M	Moses born		350	320	
1537	BC	2434	Y M	**Moses' first year** died in 2552 YM, son of 120 years (you count back from 2551 YM to find his first year)		351 of 430	321 of 400	

BC AD Years + or -		YM Years		6000 Years of Mankind Copyright © 2024 by Walter R. Dolen **Biblical Chronology Details** YM = Year of Mankind Begins in Sept/Oct 3 months before BC/AD dates	Additional Details	# of yrs	# of yrs	# of yrs
1536	BC	2435	Y M	2		352	322	
1535	BC	2436	Y M	3		353	323	
1534	BC	2437	Y M	4		354	324	
1533	BC	2438	Y M	5		355	325	
1532	BC	2439	Y M	6		356	326	
1531	BC	2440	Y M	7		357	327	
1530	BC	2441	Y M	8		358	328	
1529	BC	2442	Y M	9		359	329	
1528	BC	2443	Y M	10 - Moses		360	330	
1527	BC	2444	Y M	11		361	331	
1526	BC	2445	Y M	12		362	332	
1525	BC	2446	Y M	13		363	333	
1524	BC	2447	Y M	14		364	334	
1523	BC	2448	Y M	15		365	335	
1522	BC	2449	Y M	16		366	336	
1521	BC	2450	Y M	17		367	337	
1520	BC	2451	Y M	18		368	338	
1519	BC	2452	Y M	19		369	339	
1518	BC	2453	Y M	20 - Moses		370	340	
1517	BC	2454	Y M	21		371	341	

[Top | Flood | Abram | Exodus | David | Hezekiah | Jerusalem | JC | End Time | End Notes]

BC AD Years + or -		YM Years		6000 Years of Mankind Copyright © 2024 by Walter R. Dolen **Biblical Chronology Details** YM = Year of Mankind Begins in Sept/Oct 3 months before BC/AD dates	**Additional Details**	# of yrs	# of yrs	# of yrs
1516	BC	2455	Y M	22		372	342	
1515	BC	2456	Y M	23		373	343	
1514	BC	2457	Y M	24		374	344	
1513	BC	2458	Y M	25		375	345	
1512	BC	2459	Y M	26		376	346	
1511	BC	2460	Y M	27		377	347	
1510	BC	2461	Y M	28		378	348	
1509	BC	2462	Y M	29		379	349	
1508	BC	2463	Y M	30 - Moses		380	350	
1507	BC	2464	Y M	31		381	351	
1506	BC	2465	Y M	32		382	352	
1505	BC	2466	Y M	33		383	353	
1504	BC	2467	Y M	34		384	354	
1503	BC	2468	Y M	35		385	355	
1502	BC	2469	Y M	36		386	356	
1501	BC	2470	Y M	37		387	357	
1500	BC	2471	Y M	38		388	358	
1499	BC	2472	Y M	39		389	359	
1498	BC	2473	Y M	40 - Moses		390	360	
1497	BC	2474	Y M	41		391	361	

[Top | Flood | Abram | Exodus | David | Hezekiah | Jerusalem | JC | End Time | End Notes]

BC AD Years + or -		YM Years		6000 Years of Mankind Copyright © 2024 by Walter R. Dolen **Biblical Chronology Details** YM = Year of Mankind Begins in Sept/Oct 3 months before BC/AD dates	Additional Details	# of yrs	# of yrs	# of yrs
1496	BC	2475	Y M	42		392	362	
1495	BC	2476	Y M	43		393	363	
1494	BC	2477	Y M	44		394	364	
1493	BC	2478	Y M	45		395	365	
1492	BC	2479	Y M	46		396	366	
1491	BC	2480	Y M	47		397	367	
1490	BC	2481	Y M	48		398	368	
1489	BC	2482	Y M	49		399	369	
1488	BC	2483	Y M	50 - Moses		400	370	
1487	BC	2484	Y M	51		401	371	
1486	BC	2485	Y M	52		402	372	
1485	BC	2486	Y M	53		403	373	
1484	BC	2487	Y M	54		404	374	
1483	BC	2488	Y M	55		405	375	
1482	BC	2489	Y M	56		406	376	
1481	BC	2490	Y M	57		407	377	
1480	BC	2491	Y M	58		408	378	
1479	BC	2492	Y M	59		409	379	
1478	BC	2493	Y M	60 - Moses		410	380	
1477	BC	2494	Y M	61		411	381	

[Top | Flood | Abram | Exodus | David | Hezekiah | Jerusalem | JC | End Time | End Notes]

BC AD Years + or -		YM Years		6000 Years of Mankind Copyright © 2024 by Walter R. Dolen **Biblical Chronology Details** YM = Year of Mankind Begins in Sept/Oct 3 months before BC/AD dates	Additional Details	# of yrs	# of yrs	# of yrs
1476	BC	2495	Y M	62		412	382	
1475	BC	2496	Y M	63		413	383	
1474	BC	2497	Y M	64		414	384	
1473	BC	2498	Y M	65		415	385	
1472	BC	2499	Y M	66		416	386	
1471	BC	2500	Y M	67		417	387	
1470	BC	2501	Y M	68		418	388	
1469	BC	2502	Y M	69		419	389	
1468	BC	2503	Y M	70 - Moses		420	390	
1467	BC	2504	Y M	71		421	391	
1466	BC	2505	Y M	72		422	392	
1465	BC	2506	Y M	73		423	393	
1464	BC	2507	Y M	74		424	394	
1463	BC	2508	Y M	75		425	395	
1462	BC	2509	Y M	76		426	396	
1461	BC	2510	Y M	77		427	397	
1460	BC	2511	Y M	78		428	398	
1459	BC	2512	Y M	79		429	399	

[Top | Flood | Abram | Exodus | David | Hezekiah | Jerusalem | JC | End Time | End Notes]

BC AD Years + or -		YM Years		6000 Years of Mankind Copyright © 2024 by Walter R. Dolen **Biblical Chronology Details** YM = Year of Mankind Begins in Sept/Oct 3 months before BC/AD dates	Additional Details	# of yrs	# of yrs	# of yrs
1458	BC	2513	Y M	80 - Moses **Exodus** **This year began the 40 years of wandering for Israel; First of 480 years from the Exodus to Solomon's 4ᵗʰ year of his reign.** (1 Kings 6:1) Notice: Because it is impossible to figure the chronology during the following years from shortly after Israel came into their Promised Land until the forth year of Solomon we use the following scripture which breaches the gap: **1 Kings 6:1:** "And it came to pass in the four hundred and eightieth year after the children of Israel came out of the land of Egypt, in the forth year of Solomon's reign over Israel, in the month Zif, which is the second month, that he [Solomon] began to build the house of the Becoming-One." Click here to go to the 480th year. Note: Israel entered Egypt with about 70 souls and left about 214 years later with about 70,000 by doubling their numbers each 20 years, 3.5% each year, a *very* high rate. See https://beone.ws/exodusnumbers.html	**430 years of sojouring ends**, that began 2084 YM **400 years of affliction ends**, that began 2114 YM 1ˢᵗ year of 40 years of wondering begins 1st of year of the 480 yrs to Solomon' 4ᵗʰ Year (inclusive counting) **World's population: about 250,000 to 2,000,000 +or-** Note: from about 1500AD to 1800AD (300 yrs) world's population doubled from .5 billion to 1 billion; from 1800 to 1930 (130yrs) it doubled again with better hygiene, food, & healthcare	430 of 430 1 of 40	400 1 of 4 8 0	
1457	BC	2514	Y M		Second year of Israel's wondering	2	2	
1456	BC	2515	Y M			3	3	
1455	BC	2516	Y M			4	4	
1454	BC	2517	Y M	85 - Moses		5	5	
1453	BC	2518	Y M			6	6	
1452	BC	2519	Y M			7	7	
1451	BC	2520	Y M			8	8	
1450	BC	2521	Y M			9	9	
1449	BC	2522	Y M			10	10	
1448	BC	2523	Y M			11	11	
1447	BC	2524	Y M			12	12	
1446	BC	2525	Y M			13	13	

BC AD Years + or -		YM Years		6000 Years of Mankind Copyright © 2024 by Walter R. Dolen Biblical Chronology Details YM = Year of Mankind Begins in Sept/Oct 3 months before BC/AD dates	Additional Details	# of yrs	# of yrs	# of yrs
1445	BC	2526	Y M			14	14	
1444	BC	2527	Y M	95 - Moses		15	15	
1443	BC	2528	Y M			16	16	
1442	BC	2529	Y M			17	17	
1441	BC	2530	Y M			18	18	
1440	BC	2531	Y M			19	19	
1439	BC	2532	Y M			20	20	
1438	BC	2533	Y M			21	21	
1437	BC	2534	Y M			22	22	
1436	BC	2535	Y M			23	23	
1435	BC	2536	Y M			24	24	
1434	BC	2537	Y M	105 - Moses		25	25	
1433	BC	2538	Y M			26	26	
1432	BC	2539	Y M			27	27	
1431	BC	2540	Y M			28	28	
1430	BC	2541	Y M			29	29	
1429	BC	2542	Y M			30	30	
1428	BC	2543	Y M			31	31	
1427	BC	2544	Y M			32	32	
1426	BC	2545	Y M			33	33	

[Top | Flood | Abram | Exodus | David | Hezekiah | Jerusalem | JC | End Time | End Notes]

BC AD Years + or -		YM Years		**6000 Years of Mankind** Copyright © 2024 by Walter R. Dolen **Biblical Chronology Details** YM = Year of Mankind Begins in Sept/Oct 3 months before BC/AD dates	**Additional Details**	# of yrs	# of yrs	# of yrs
1425	BC	2546	Y M			34	34	
1424	BC	2547	Y M	115 - Moses		35	35	
1423	BC	2548	Y M			36	36	
1422	BC	2549	Y M			37	37	
1421	BC	2550	Y M	118 - Moses		38	38	
1420	BC	2551	Y M	119 - Moses		39	39	
1419	BC	2552	Y M	**Israel's wandering ends; Israel goes into the Promised land; law reiterated by Moses; Moses dies** **Notice:** Because it is impossible to figure the chronology during the following years from shortly after Israel came into their Promised Land we use the following scripture to fill the gap: **1 Kings 6:1:** "And it came to pass **in the four hundred and eightieth year after the children of Israel came out of the land of Egypt, in the forth year of Solomon's reign** over Israel, in the month Zif, which is the second month, that he [Solomon] began to build the house of the Becoming-One." **Click here to go to the 480th year.**	Moses dies at 120 years	40	40 of 480	
1418	BC	2553	Y M	**Israel's first year in the Promised Land** and plants new crops.	**Counting fifteen periods of 49 year periods = 735** years. A Jubilee occurred *after* seven 7 year periods.	1 of 735	41 of 480	
1417	BC	2554	Y M			2	42	
1416	BC	2555	Y M			3	43	
1415	BC	2556	Y M			4	44	
1414	BC	2557	Y M			5	45	
1413	BC	2558	Y M			6	46	
1412	BC	2559	Y M			7	47	
1411	BC	2560	Y M			0	48	

[Top | Flood | Abram | Exodus | David | Hezekiah | Jerusalem | JC | End Time | End Notes]

BC AD Years + or -		YM Years		**6000 Years of Mankind** Copyright © 2024 by Walter R. Dolen **Biblical Chronology Details** YM = Year of Mankind Begins in Sept/Oct 3 months before BC/AD dates	**Additional Details**	# of yrs	# of yrs	# of yrs
1410	BC	2561	Y M			9	49	
1409	BC	2562	Y M			10	50	
1408	BC	2563	Y M			11	51	
1407	BC	2564	Y M			12	52	
1406	BC	2565	Y M			13	53	
1405	BC	2566	Y M			14	54	
1404	BC	2567	Y M			15	55	
1403	BC	2568	Y M			16	56	
1402	BC	2569	Y M			17	57	
1401	BC	2570	Y M			18	58	
1400	BC	2571	Y M			19	59	
1399	BC	2572	Y M			20 of 735	60	
1398	BC	2573	Y M			21	61	
1397	BC	2574	Y M			22	62	
1396	BC	2575	Y M			23	63	
1395	BC	2576	Y M			24	64	
1394	BC	2577	Y M			25	65	
1393	BC	2578	Y M			26	66	
1392	BC	2579	Y M			27	67	
1391	BC	2580	Y M			28	68	

BC AD Years + or -		YM Years		6000 Years of Mankind Copyright © 2024 by Walter R. Dolen **Biblical Chronology Details** YM = Year of Mankind Begins in Sept/Oct 3 months before BC/AD dates	**Additional Details**	# of yrs	# of yrs	# of yrs
1390	BC	2581	YM			29	69	
1389	BC	2582	YM			30	70	
1388	BC	2583	YM			31	71	
1387	BC	2584	YM			32	72	
1386	BC	2585	YM			33	73	
1385	BC	2586	YM			34	74	
1384	BC	2587	YM			35	75	
1383	BC	2588	YM			36	76	
1382	BC	2589	YM			37	77	
1381	BC	2590	YM			38	78	
1380	BC	2591	YM			39	79	
1379	BC	2592	YM			40 of 735	80	
1378	BC	2593	YM			41	81	
1377	BC	2594	YM			42	82	
1376	BC	2595	YM			43	83	
1375	BC	2596	YM			44	84	
1374	BC	2597	YM			45	85	
1373	BC	2598	YM			46	86	
1372	BC	2599	YM			47	87	
1371	BC	2600	YM			48	88	

[Top | Flood | Abram | Exodus | David | Hezekiah | Jerusalem | JC | End Time | End Notes]

BC AD Years + or -		YM Years		**6000 Years of Mankind** Copyright © 2024 by Walter R. Dolen **Biblical Chronology Details** YM = Year of Mankind Begins in Sept/Oct 3 months before BC/AD dates	**Additional Details**	# of yrs	# of yrs	# of yrs
1370	BC	2601	Y M			49	89	
1369	BC	2602	Y M			50	90	
1368	BC	2603	Y M			51	91	
1367	BC	2604	Y M			52	92	
1366	BC	2605	Y M			53	93	
1365	BC	2606	Y M			54	94	
1364	BC	2607	Y M			55	95	
1363	BC	2608	Y M			56	96	
1362	BC	2609	Y M			57	97	
1361	BC	2610	Y M			58	98	
1360	BC	2611	Y M			59	99	
1359	BC	2612	Y M			60 of 735	100	
1358	BC	2613	Y M			61	101	
1357	BC	2614	Y M			62	102	
1356	BC	2615	Y M			63	103	
1355	BC	2616	Y M			64	104	
1354	BC	2617	Y M			65	105	
1353	BC	2618	Y M			66	106	
1352	BC	2619	Y M			67	107	
1351	BC	2620	Y M			68	108	

BC AD Years + or -		YM Years		6000 Years of Mankind Copyright © 2024 by Walter R. Dolen **Biblical Chronology Details** YM = Year of Mankind Begins in Sept/Oct 3 months before BC/AD dates	Additional Details	# of yrs	# of yrs	# of yrs
1350	BC	2621	Y M			69	109	
1349	BC	2622	Y M			70	110	
1348	BC	2623	Y M			71	111	
1347	BC	2624	Y M			72	112	
1346	BC	2625	Y M			73	113	
1345	BC	2626	Y M			74	114	
1344	BC	2627	Y M			75	115	
1343	BC	2628	Y M			76	116	
1342	BC	2629	Y M			77	117	
1341	BC	2630	Y M			78	118	
1340	BC	2631	Y M			79	119	
1339	BC	2632	Y M			80 of 735	120 of 480	
1338	BC	2633	Y M			81	121	
1337	BC	2634	Y M			82	122	
1336	BC	2635	Y M			83	123	
1335	BC	2636	Y M			84	124	
1334	BC	2637	Y M			85	125	
1333	BC	2638	Y M			86	126	
1332	BC	2639	Y M			87	127	
1331	BC	2640	Y M			88	128	

[Top | Flood | Abram | Exodus | David | Hezekiah | Jerusalem | JC | End Time | End Notes]

BC AD Years + or -		YM Years		6000 Years of Mankind Copyright © 2024 by Walter R. Dolen **Biblical Chronology Details** YM = Year of Mankind Begins in Sept/Oct 3 months before BC/AD dates	Additional Details	# of yrs	# of yrs	# of yrs
1330	BC	2641	Y M			89	129	
1329	BC	2642	Y M			90	130	
1328	BC	2643	Y M			91	131	
1327	BC	2644	Y M			92	132	
1326	BC	2645	Y M			93	133	
1325	BC	2646	Y M			94	134	
1324	BC	2647	Y M			95	135	
1323	BC	2648	Y M			96	136	
1322	BC	2649	Y M			97	137	
1321	BC	2650	Y M			98	138	
1320	BC	2651	Y M			99	139	
1319	BC	2652	Y M			100 of 735	140	
1318	BC	2653	Y M			101	141	
1317	BC	2654	Y M			102	142	
1316	BC	2655	Y M			103	143	
1315	BC	2656	Y M			104	144	
1314	BC	2657	Y M			105	145	
1313	BC	2658	Y M			106	146	
1312	BC	2659	Y M			107	147	
1311	BC	2660	Y M			108	148	

[Top | Flood | Abram | Exodus | David | Hezekiah | Jerusalem | JC | End Time | End Notes]

BC AD Years + or -		YM Years		6000 Years of Mankind Copyright © 2024 by Walter R. Dolen Biblical Chronology Details YM = Year of Mankind Begins in Sept/Oct 3 months before BC/AD dates	Additional Details	# of yrs	# of yrs	# of yrs
1310	BC	2661	YM			109	149	
1309	BC	2662	YM			110	150	
1308	BC	2663	YM			111	151	
1307	BC	2664	YM			112	152	
1306	BC	2665	YM			113	153	
1305	BC	2666	YM			114	154	
1304	BC	2667	YM			115	155	
1303	BC	2668	YM			116	156	
1302	BC	2669	YM			117	157	
1301	BC	2670	YM			118	158	
1300	BC	2671	YM			119	159	
1299	BC	2672	YM			120 of 735	160 of 480	
1298	BC	2673	YM			121	161	
1297	BC	2674	YM			122	162	
1296	BC	2675	YM			123	163	
1295	BC	2676	YM			124	164	
1294	BC	2677	YM			125	165	
1293	BC	2678	YM			126	166	
1292	BC	2679	YM			127	167	
1291	BC	2680	YM			128	168	

[Top | Flood | Abram | Exodus | David | Hezekiah | Jerusalem | JC | End Time | End Notes]

BC AD Years + or -		YM Years		6000 Years of Mankind Copyright © 2024 by Walter R. Dolen **Biblical Chronology Details** YM = Year of Mankind Begins in Sept/Oct 3 months before BC/AD dates	Additional Details	# of yrs	# of yrs	# of yrs
1290	BC	2681	Y M			129	169	
1289	BC	2682	Y M			130 of 735	170 of 480	
1288	BC	2683	Y M			131	171	
1287	BC	2684	Y M			132	172	
1286	BC	2685	Y M			133	173	
1285	BC	2686	Y M			134	174	
1284	BC	2687	Y M			135	175	
1283	BC	2688	Y M			136	176	
1282	BC	2689	Y M			137	177	
1281	BC	2690	Y M			138	178	
1280	BC	2691	Y M			139	179	
1279	BC	2692	Y M			140 of 735	180 of 480	
1278	BC	2693	Y M			141	181	
1277	BC	2694	Y M			142	182	
1276	BC	2695	Y M			143	183	
1275	BC	2696	Y M			144	184	
1274	BC	2697	Y M			145	185	
1273	BC	2698	Y M			146	186	
1272	BC	2699	Y M			147	187	

[Top | Flood | Abram | Exodus | David | Hezekiah | Jerusalem | JC | End Time | End Notes]

BC AD Years + or -		YM Years		6000 Years of Mankind Copyright © 2024 by Walter R. Dolen **Biblical Chronology Details** YM = Year of Mankind Begins in Sept/Oct 3 months before BC/AD dates	Additional Details	# of yrs	# of yrs	# of yrs
1271	BC	2700	Y M			148	188	
1270	BC	2701	Y M			149	189	
1269	BC	2702	Y M			150	190	
1268	BC	2703	Y M			151	191	
1267	BC	2704	Y M			152	192	
1266	BC	2705	Y M			153	193	
1265	BC	2706	Y M			154	194	
1264	BC	2707	Y M			155	195	
1263	BC	2708	Y M			156	196	
1262	BC	2709	Y M			157	197	
1261	BC	2710	Y M			158	198	
1260	BC	2711	Y M			159	199	
1259	BC	2712	Y M			160	200	
1258	BC	2713	Y M			161	201	
1257	BC	2714	Y M			162	202	
1256	BC	2715	Y M			163	203	
1255	BC	2716	Y M			164	204	
1254	BC	2717	Y M			165	205	
1253	BC	2718	Y M			166	206	
1252	BC	2719	Y M			167	207	

[Top | Flood | Abram | Exodus | David | Hezekiah | Jerusalem | JC | End Time | End Notes]

BC AD Years + or -		YM Years		**6000 Years of Mankind** Copyright © 2024 by Walter R. Dolen **Biblical Chronology Details** YM = Year of Mankind Begins in Sept/Oct 3 months before BC/AD dates	Additional Details	# of yrs	# of yrs	# of yrs
1251	BC	2720	Y M			168	208	
1250	BC	2721	Y M			169	209	
1249	BC	2722	Y M			170 of 735	210 of 480	
1248	BC	2723	Y M			171	211	
1247	BC	2724	Y M			172	212	
1246	BC	2725	Y M			173	213	
1245	BC	2726	Y M			174	214	
1244	BC	2727	Y M			175	215	
1243	BC	2728	Y M			176	216	
1242	BC	2729	Y M			177	217	
1241	BC	2730	Y M			178	218	
1240	BC	2731	Y M			179	219	
1239	BC	2732	Y M			180	220	
1238	BC	2733	Y M			181	221	
1237	BC	2734	Y M			182	222	
1236	BC	2735	Y M			183	223	
1235	BC	2736	Y M			184	224	
1234	BC	2737	Y M			185	225	
1233	BC	2738	Y M			186	226	
1232	BC	2739	Y M			187	227	

BC AD Years + or -		YM Years		6000 Years of Mankind Copyright © 2024 by Walter R. Dolen **Biblical Chronology Details** YM = Year of Mankind Begins in Sept/Oct 3 months before BC/AD dates	Additional Details	# of yrs	# of yrs	# of yrs
1231	BC	2740	Y M			188	228	
1230	BC	2741	Y M			189	229	
1229	BC	2742	Y M			190 of 735	230 of 480	
1228	BC	2743	Y M			191	231	
1227	BC	2744	Y M			192	232	
1226	BC	2745	Y M			193	233	
1225	BC	2746	Y M			194	234	
1224	BC	2747	Y M			195	235	
1223	BC	2748	Y M			196	236	
1222	BC	2749	Y M			197	237	
1221	BC	2750	Y M			198	238	
1220	BC	2751	Y M			199	239	
1219	BC	2752	Y M			200	240	
1218	BC	2753	Y M			201	241	
1217	BC	2754	Y M			202	242	
1216	BC	2755	Y M			203	243	
1215	BC	2756	Y M			204	244	
1214	BC	2757	Y M			205	245	
1213	BC	2758	Y M			206	246	
1212	BC	2759	Y M			207	247	

		[Top | Flood | Abram | Exodus | David | Hezekiah | Jerusalem | JC | End Time | End Notes]				

BC AD Years + or -		YM Years		**6000 Years of Mankind** Copyright © 2024 by Walter R. Dolen **Biblical Chronology Details** YM = Year of Mankind Begins in Sept/Oct 3 months before BC/AD dates	**Additional Details**	# of yrs	# of yrs	# of yrs
1211	BC	2760	Y M			208	248	
1210	BC	2761	Y M			209	249	
1209	BC	2762	Y M			210 of 735	250 of 480	
1208	BC	2763	Y M			211	251	
1207	BC	2764	Y M			212	252	
1206	BC	2765	Y M			213	253	
1205	BC	2766	Y M			214	254	
1204	BC	2767	Y M			215	255	
1203	BC	2768	Y M			216	256	
1202	BC	2769	Y M			217	257	
1201	BC	2770	Y M			218	258	
1200	BC	2771	Y M			219	259	
1199	BC	2772	Y M			220	260	
1198	BC	2773	Y M			221	261	
1197	BC	2774	Y M			222	262	
1196	BC	2775	Y M			223	263	
1195	BC	2776	Y M			224	264	
1194	BC	2777	Y M			225	265	
1193	BC	2778	Y M			226	266	
1192	BC	2779	Y M			227	267	

BC AD Years + or -		YM Years		**6000 Years of Mankind** Copyright © 2024 by Walter R. Dolen **Biblical Chronology Details** YM = Year of Mankind Begins in Sept/Oct 3 months before BC/AD dates	**Additional Details**	# of yrs	# of yrs	# of yrs
1191	BC	2780	Y M			228	268	
1190	BC	2781	Y M			229	269	
1189	BC	2782	Y M			230 of 735	270 of 480	
1188	BC	2783	Y M			231	271	
1187	BC	2784	Y M			232	272	
1186	BC	2785	Y M			233	273	
1185	BC	2786	Y M			234	274	
1184	BC	2787	Y M			235	275	
1183	BC	2788	Y M			236	276	
1182	BC	2789	Y M			237	277	
1181	BC	2790	Y M			238	278	
1180	BC	2791	Y M			239	279	
1179	BC	2792	Y M			240 of	280	
1178	BC	2793	Y M			241	281	
1177	BC	2794	Y M			242	282	
1176	BC	2795	Y M			243	283	
1175	BC	2796	Y M			244	284	
1174	BC	2797	Y M			245	285	
1173	BC	2798	Y M			246	286	
1172	BC	2799	Y M			247	287	

BC AD Years + or -		YM Years		6000 Years of Mankind Copyright © 2024 by Walter R. Dolen **Biblical Chronology Details** YM = Year of Mankind Begins in Sept/Oct 3 months before BC/AD dates	Additional Details	# of yrs	# of yrs	# of yrs
1171	BC	2800	YM			248	288	
1170	BC	2801	YM			249	289	
1169	BC	2802	YM			250 of 735	290 of 480	
1168	BC	2803	YM			251	291	
1167	BC	2804	YM			252	292	
1166	BC	2805	YM			253	293	
1165	BC	2806	YM			254	294	
1164	BC	2807	YM			255	295	
1163	BC	2808	YM			256	296	
1162	BC	2809	YM			257	297	
1161	BC	2810	YM			258	298	
1160	BC	2811	YM			259	299	
1159	BC	2812	YM			260	300	
1158	BC	2813	YM			261	301	
1157	BC	2814	YM			262	302	
1156	BC	2815	YM			263	303	
1155	BC	2816	YM			264	304	
1154	BC	2817	YM			265	305	
1153	BC	2818	YM			266	306	
1152	BC	2819	YM			267	307	

[Top | Flood | Abram | Exodus | David | Hezekiah | Jerusalem | JC | End Time | End Notes]

BC AD Years + or -		YM Years		**6000 Years of Mankind** Copyright © 2024 by Walter R. Dolen **Biblical Chronology Details** YM = Year of Mankind Begins in Sept/Oct 3 months before BC/AD dates	**Additional Details**	# of yrs	# of yrs	# of yrs
1151	BC	2820	YM			268	308	
1150	BC	2821	YM			269	309	
1149	BC	2822	YM			270 of 735	310 of 480	
1148	BC	2823	YM			271	311	
1147	BC	2824	YM			272	312	
1146	BC	2825	YM			273	313	
1145	BC	2826	YM			274	314	
1144	BC	2827	YM			275	315	
1143	BC	2828	YM			276	316	
1142	BC	2829	YM			277	317	
1141	BC	2830	YM			278	318	
1140	BC	2831	YM			279	319	
1139	BC	2832	YM			280	320	
1138	BC	2833	YM			281	321	
1137	BC	2834	YM			282	322	
1136	BC	2835	YM			283	323	
1135	BC	2836	YM			284	324	
1134	BC	2837	YM			285	325	
1133	BC	2838	YM			286	326	
1132	BC	2839	YM			287	327	

[Top | Flood | Abram | Exodus | David | Hezekiah | Jerusalem | JC | End Time | End Notes]

BC AD Years + or -		YM Years		**6000 Years of Mankind** Copyright © 2024 by Walter R. Dolen **Biblical Chronology Details** YM = Year of Mankind Begins in Sept/Oct 3 months before BC/AD dates	**Additional Details**	# of yrs	# of yrs	# of yrs
1131	BC	2840	YM			288	328	
1130	BC	2841	YM			289	329	
1129	BC	2842	YM			290	330	
1128	BC	2843	YM			291	331	
1127	BC	2844	YM			292	332	
1126	BC	2845	YM			293	333	
1125	BC	2846	YM			294	334	
1124	BC	2847	YM			295	335	
1123	BC	2848	YM			296	336	
1122	BC	2849	YM			297	337	
1121	BC	2850	YM			298	338	
1120	BC	2851	YM			299	339	
1119	BC	2852	YM			300 of 735	340 of 480	
1118	BC	2853	YM			301	341	
1117	BC	2854	YM			302	342	
1116	BC	2855	YM			303	343	
1115	BC	2856	YM			304	344	
1114	BC	2857	YM			305	345	
1113	BC	2858	YM			306	346	
1112	BC	2859	YM			307	347	

BC AD Years + or -		YM Years		6000 Years of Mankind Copyright © 2024 by Walter R. Dolen Biblical Chronology Details YM = Year of Mankind Begins in Sept/Oct 3 months before BC/AD dates	Additional Details	# of yrs	# of yrs	# of yrs
				[Top	Flood	Abram	Exodus	David	Hezekiah	Jerusalem	JC	End Time	End Notes]				
1111	BC	2860	Y M			308	348	
1110	BC	2861	Y M			309	349	
1109	BC	2862	Y M			310	350 of 480	
1108	BC	2863	Y M			311	351	
1107	BC	2864	Y M			312	352	
1106	BC	2865	Y M			313	353	
1105	BC	2866	Y M			314	354	
1104	BC	2867	Y M			315	355	
1103	BC	2868	Y M			316	356	
1102	BC	2869	Y M			317	357	
1101	BC	2870	Y M			318	358	
1100	BC	2871	Y M			319	359	
1099	BC	2872	Y M			320	360	
1098	BC	2873	Y M			321	361	
1097	BC	2874	Y M			322	362	
1096	BC	2875	Y M			323	363	
1095	BC	2876	Y M			324	364	
1094	BC	2877	Y M			325	365	
1093	BC	2878	Y M			326	366	
1092	BC	2879	Y M			327	367	

BC AD Years + or -		YM Years		6000 Years of Mankind Copyright © 2024 by Walter R. Dolen Biblical Chronology Details YM = Year of Mankind Begins in Sept/Oct 3 months before BC/AD dates	Additional Details	# of yrs	# of yrs	# of yrs
1091	BC	2880	Y M			328	368	
1090	BC	2881	Y M			329	369	
1089	BC	2882	Y M			330	370	
1088	BC	2883	Y M			331	371	
1087	BC	2884	Y M			332	372	
1086	BC	2885	Y M			333	373	
1085	BC	2886	Y M			334	374	
1084	BC	2887	Y M			335	375	
1083	BC	2888	Y M			336	376	
1082	BC	2889	Y M			337	377	
1081	BC	2890	Y M			338	378	
1080	BC	2891	Y M			339	379	
1079	BC	2892	Y M			340 of 735	380 of 480	
1078	BC	2893	Y M			341	381	
1077	BC	2894	Y M			342	382	
1076	BC	2895	Y M			343	383	
1075	BC	2896	Y M			344	384	
1074	BC	2897	Y M			345	385	
1073	BC	2898	Y M			346	386	
1072	BC	2899	Y M			347	387	

[Top | Flood | Abram | Exodus | David | Hezekiah | Jerusalem | JC | End Time | End Notes]

BC AD Years + or -		YM Years		6000 Years of Mankind Copyright © 2024 by Walter R. Dolen **Biblical Chronology Details** YM = Year of Mankind Begins in Sept/Oct 3 months before BC/AD dates	Additional Details	# of yrs	# of yrs	# of yrs
1071	BC	2900	Y M			348	388	
1070	BC	2901	Y M			349	389	
1069	BC	2902	Y M			350	390	
1068	BC	2903	Y M			351	391	
1067	BC	2904	Y M			352	392	
1066	BC	2905	Y M			353	393	
1065	BC	2906	Y M			354	394	
1064	BC	2907	Y M			355	395	
1063	BC	2908	Y M			356	396	
1062	BC	2909	Y M			357	397	
1061	BC	2910	Y M			358	398	
1060	BC	2911	Y M			359	399	
1059	BC	2912	Y M			360 of 735	400 of 480	
1058	BC	2913	Y M			361	401	
1057	BC	2914	Y M			362	402	
1056	BC	2915	Y M			363	403	
1055	BC	2916	Y M			364	404	
1054	BC	2917	Y M			365	405	
1053	BC	2918	Y M			366	406	
1052	BC	2919	Y M			367	407	

[Top | Flood | Abram | Exodus | David | Hezekiah | Jerusalem | JC | End Time | End Notes]

BC AD Years + or -		YM Years		*6000 Years of Mankind* Copyright © 2024 by Walter R. Dolen **Biblical Chronology Details** YM = Year of Mankind Begins in Sept/Oct 3 months before BC/AD dates	**Additional Details**	# of yrs	# of yrs	# of yrs
1051	BC	2920	Y M			368	408	
1050	BC	2921	Y M			369	409	
1049	BC	2922	Y M			370	410	
1048	BC	2923	Y M			371	411	
1047	BC	2924	Y M			372	412	
1046	BC	2925	Y M			373	413	
1045	BC	2926	Y M			374	414	
1044	BC	2927	Y M			375	415	
1043	BC	2928	Y M			376	416	
1042	BC	2929	Y M			377	417	
1041	BC	2930	Y M			378	418	
1040	BC	2931	Y M			379	419	
1039	BC	2932	Y M			380 of 735	420 of 480	
1038	BC	2933	Y M			381	421	
1037	BC	2934	Y M			382	422	
1036	BC	2935	Y M			383	423	
1035	BC	2936	Y M			384	424	
1034	BC	2937	Y M			385	425	
1033	BC	2938	Y M			386	426	
1032	BC	2939	Y M			387	427	

[Top | Flood | Abram | Exodus | David | Hezekiah | Jerusalem | JC | End Time | End Notes]

BC AD Years + or -		YM Years		6000 Years of Mankind Copyright © 2024 by Walter R. Dolen **Biblical Chronology Details** YM = Year of Mankind Begins in Sept/Oct 3 months before BC/AD dates	**Additional Details**	# of yrs	# of yrs	# of yrs
1031	BC	2940	Y M			388	428	
1030	BC	2941	Y M			389	429	
1029	BC	2942	Y M			390	430	
1028		2943				391	431	
1027		2944				392	432	
1026		2945				393	433	
1025		2946				394	434	
1024		2947				395	435	
1023	BC	2948	Y M			396	436	
1022	BC	2949	Y M	1 **David first year as King** of Judah and Israel, United Kingdom	This year is ascertained by counting back from Solomon's 4th year	397 of 735	437 of 480	
1021	BC	2950	Y M	2		398	438	
1020	BC	2951	Y M	3		399	439	
1019	BC	2952	Y M	4		400 of 735	440 of 480	
1018	BC	2953	Y M	5 David king of Judah and Israel (united kingdom)		401	441	
1017	BC	2954	Y M	6		402	442	
1016	BC	2955	Y M	7		403	443	
1015	BC	2956	Y M	8		404	444	
1014	BC	2957	Y M	9		405	445	
1013	BC	2958	Y M	10 David king of Judah and Israel (united kingdom)		406	446	
1012	BC	2959	Y M	11 -		407	447	

			6000 Years of Mankind Copyright © 2024 by Walter R. Dolen **Biblical Chronology Details** YM = Year of Mankind Begins in Sept/Oct 3 months before BC/AD dates	Additional Details	# of yrs	# of yrs	# of yrs
BC AD Years + or -		YM Years					
1011	BC	2960	YM	12 - **David sin with Bathsheba** and against Uriah is the beginning of the 390 years of iniquity for Israel (2 Sam 11:12-27; 12:1 ff; etc.) See 3344 YM for the end of the 390 years. This year is not certain.	390 of Israel's iniquity begins (Eze 4:3-6)	408 of 735	448	1 of 390 yrs
1010	BC	2961	YM	13		409	449	2
1009	BC	2962	YM	14		410	450	3
1008	BC	2963	YM	15- David king of Judah and Israel (united kingdom)		411	451	4
1007	BC	2964	YM	16		412 of 735	452 of 480	5
1006	BC	2965	YM	17		413	453	6
1005	BC	2966	YM	18		414	454	7
1004	BC	2967	YM	19		415	455	8
1003	BC	2968	YM	20 David king of Judah and Israel (united kingdom)		416	456	9
1002	BC	2969	YM	21		417	457	10
1001	BC	2970	YM	22		418	458	11
1000	BC	2971	YM	23		419	459	12
999	BC	2972	YM	24		420	460	13
998	BC	2973	YM	25 David king of Judah and Israel (united kingdom)		421	461	14
997	BC	2974	YM	26		422	462	15
996	BC	2975	YM	27		423	463	16
995	BC	2976	YM	28		424	464	17
994	BC	2977	YM	29		425	465	18
993	BC	2978	YM	30 David		426	466	19

Navigation header: [Top | Flood | Abram | Exodus | David | Hezekiah | Jerusalem | JC | End Time | End Notes]

[Top | Flood | Abram | Exodus | David | Hezekiah | Jerusalem | JC | End Time | End Notes]

BC AD Years + or -		YM Years		**6000 Years of Mankind** Copyright © 2024 by Walter R. Dolen **Biblical Chronology Details** YM = Year of Mankind Begins in Sept/Oct 3 months before BC/AD dates	**Additional Details**	# of yrs	# of yrs	# of yrs
992	BC	2979	Y M	31		427	467	20
991	BC	2980	Y M	32		428	468	21
990	BC	2981	Y M	33		429	469	22
989	BC	2982	Y M	34		430	470	23
988	BC	2983	Y M	35 David king of Judah and Israel (united kingdom)		431	471	24
987	BC	2984	Y M	36		432	472	25
986	BC	2985	Y M	37		433	473	26
985	BC	2986	Y M	38		434	474	27
984	BC	2987	Y M	39		435	475	28
983	BC	2988	Y M	40 David last year		436	476	29
982	BC	2989	Y M	**1 Solomon first year as King of Judah and Israel**[40] **(united kingdom)** about 30 years old		437	477	30
981	BC	2990	Y M	2		438	478	31
980	BC	2991	Y M	3		439	479	32
979	BC	2992	Y M	4 Solomon king of Judah and Israel (united kingdom)	480th year since the Exodus (1 Kings 6:1) & the 440th year since Israel went into the Promised Land.	440 of 735	480	33 of 390
978	BC	2993	Y M	5		441		34
977	BC	2994	Y M	6		442		35
976	BC	2995	Y M	7		443		36
975	BC	2996	Y M	8		444		37
974	BC	2997	Y M	9		445		38

BC AD Years + or -		YM Years		6000 Years of Mankind Copyright © 2024 by Walter R. Dolen **Biblical Chronology Details** YM = Year of Mankind Begins in Sept/Oct 3 months before BC/AD dates	Additional Details	# of yrs	# of yrs	# of yrs
973	BC	2998	Y M	10 Solomon king of Judah and Israel (united kingdom)		446		39
972	BC	2999	Y M	11		447		40
971	BC	3000	Y M	12		448		41
970	BC	3001	Y M	13		449		42
969	BC	3002	Y M	14		450		43
968	BC	3003	Y M	15 Solomon		451		44
967	BC	3004	Y M	16		452		45
966	BC	3005	Y M	17		453		46
965	BC	3006	Y M	18		454		47
964	BC	3007	Y M	19		455		48
963	BC	3008	Y M	20 Solomon king of Judah and Israel (united kingdom)		456		49
962	BC	3009	Y M	21		457		50
961	BC	3010	Y M	22		458		51
960	BC	3011	Y M	23		459		52
959	BC	3012	Y M	24		460		53
958	BC	3013	Y M	25		461		54
957	BC	3014	Y M	26		462		55
956	BC	3015	Y M	27		463		56
955	BC	3016	Y M	28		464		57
954	BC	3017	Y M	29		465		58

[Top | Flood | Abram | Exodus | David | Hezekiah | Jerusalem | JC | End Time | End Notes]

BC AD Years + or -		YM Years		6000 Years of Mankind Copyright © 2024 by Walter R. Dolen **Biblical Chronology Details** YM = Year of Mankind Begins in Sept/Oct 3 months before BC/AD dates	**Additional Details**	# of yrs	# of yrs	# of yrs
953	BC	3018	YM	30 Solomon king of Judah and Israel (united kingdom)		466		59
952	BC	3019	YM	31		467		60
951	BC	3020	YM	32		468		61
950	BC	3021	YM	33		469		62
949	BC	3022	YM	34		470		63
948	BC	3023	YM	35 Solomon king of Judah and Israel (united kingdom)		471		64
947	BC	3024	YM	36		472		65
946	BC	3025	YM	37		473		66
945	BC	3026	YM	38		474		67
944	BC	3027	YM	39		475		68
943	BC	3028	YM	40 **Solomon dies** and Rehoboam finishes his reign as **the united kingdom of Israel spilt into two: one the kingdom of Judah** and the other **the kingdom of Israel** (Samaria)	1- **Jeroboam's 1st year, King of Israel (Samaria)** [22] (1 Kings 12:20; 14:20). Jeroboam takes his reign after king Rehoboam ruled, after Israel rebelled because of the harshness, and after he came back from Egypt where he had fled from Solomon (1 Kings 11:40-12:20). He used the *non-accessional year method* of counting his regnal years, as did Israel afterward	476 of 735		69 of 390
942	BC	3029	YM	1 **Rehoboam first year, King of Judah** [17] start of his first official year	2 - Jeroboam War between Rehoboam and Jeroboam "all their days" (1 Kings 14:30; 15:6)	477		70
941	BC	3030	YM	2	3	478		71
940	BC	3031	YM	3	4	479		72
939	BC	3032	YM	4	5	480		73

BC AD Years + or -		YM Years		6000 Years of Mankind Copyright © 2024 by Walter R. Dolen **Biblical Chronology Details** YM = Year of Mankind Begins in Sept/Oct 3 months before BC/AD dates	Additional Details	# of yrs	# of yrs	# of yrs
938	BC	3033	Y M	5 **Shishak**, King of Egypt, came to war against Jerusalem and took treasures, shields of gold, etc in the 5th year of Rehoboam (1 Kings 14:25-27)	6	481		74
937	BC	3034	Y M	6	7	482		75
936	BC	3035	Y M	7	8	483		76
935	BC	3036	Y M	8	9	484		77
934	BC	3037	Y M	9	10	485		78
933	BC	3038	Y M	10 Rehoboam king of Judah	11	486		79
932	BC	3039	Y M	11	12	487		80
931	BC	3040	Y M	12	13	488		81
930	BC	3041	Y M	13	14	489		82
929	BC	3042	Y M	14	15	490		83
928	BC	3043	Y M	15 Rehoboam king of Judah	16	491		84
927	BC	3044	Y M	16	17	492		85
926	BC	3045	Y M	17 Rehoboam last year 1 **Abijam** [3] His first year is a co-reign with Rehoboam's last year. In the 18th year of Jeroboam of Israel (2 Chr 13:1)	18	493		86
925	BC	3046	Y M	2 Abijam	19	494		87
924	BC	3047	Y M	3 Abijam 1 **Asa king of Judah first year** [41] (1 Kinga 15:9-10) Asa first year was a co-reign with Abijam in Abijam's last year, for Abijam was at war against Jeroboam (see 2 Chron 13:2-3)	20	495 of 735		88 of 390
923	BC	3048	Y M	2 Asa	21 - Jeroboam 1- **Nadab** [2} begins to co-reign with Jeroboam in his last 2 years (1 Kings 15:25) because when Jeroboam had made war with Abijam he was injured (2 Chr 13:15) and didn't regain his strength (2 Chron 13:20)	496		89

[Top | Flood | Abram | Exodus | David | Hezekiah | Jerusalem | JC | End Time | End Notes]

BC AD Years + or -		YM Years		6000 Years of Mankind Copyright © 2024 by Walter R. Dolen Biblical Chronology Details YM = Year of Mankind Begins in Sept/Oct 3 months before BC/AD dates	Additional Details	# of yrs	# of yrs	# of yrs
922	BC	3049	Y M	3 Asa	22 Jeroboam last year 2 - Nadab co-reign 1 - **Baasha** [24] first year started after he killed Nadab (1 Kings 15:28, 33). He then killed the rest of Jeroboam's family (1 Kings 15:29)	497 of 735		90
921	BC	3050	Y M	4	2 - Baasha War between Asa of Judah and Baasha all their days except 10 years of peace (1 Kings 15:16, 32; 2 Chr 14:1)	498		91
920	BC	3051	Y M	5 Asa	3	499		92
919	BC	3052	Y M	6	4	500		93
918	BC	3053	Y M	7	5	501		94
917	BC	3054	Y M	8	6	502		95
916	BC	3055	Y M	9	7	503		96
915	BC	3056	Y M	10 Asa king of Judah	8 Baash king of Israel	504		97
914	BC	3057	Y M	11	9 Baash king of Israel	505		98
913	BC	3058	Y M	12	10	506		99
912	BC	3059	Y M	13	11	507		100
911	BC	3060	Y M	14	12	508		101
910	BC	3061	Y M	15 Asa	13	509		102
909	BC	3062	Y M	16	14	510		103
908	BC	3063	Y M	17 Asa, no war this year. Asa's 17th year was the house of Asa's 35th year, that is, the house beginning with Rehoboam (2 Chron 15:19; see next item)	15	511 of 735		104 of 390
907	BC	3064	Y M	18 - Asa, was the 36th year of Asa's house rule (house of Rehoboam) or the 36th inclusive year of the split kingdom (2 Chr 16:1)	16	512		105

[Top	Flood	Abram	Exodus	David	Hezekiah	Jerusalem	JC	End Time	End Notes]							

BC AD Years + or -		YM Years		6000 Years of Mankind Copyright © 2024 by Walter R. Dolen **Biblical Chronology Details** YM = Year of Mankind Begins in Sept/Oct 3 months before BC/AD dates	Additional Details	# of yrs	# of yrs	# of yrs
906	BC	3065	Y M	19	17	513		106
905	BC	3066	Y M	20 Asa king of Judah	18	514		107
904	BC	3067	Y M	21	19	515		108
903	BC	3068	Y M	22	20 Baash king of Israel	516		109
902	BC	3069	Y M	23	21	517		110
901	BC	3070	Y M	24	22	518		111
900	BC	3071	Y M	25 Asa	23	519		112
899	BC	3072	Y M	26 in this year Baasha {Israel} came against Judah (2 Ch 16:1, should be 26th year not 36, copy error?)	24 Baash king of Israel 1- **Elah** first year [2]	520		113
898	BC	3073	Y M	27 Asa	2 - Elah (1 Kings 16:6,8) **Zimri** kills Elah in his 2nd year and reigns 7 days (1 Kings 16:10, 15) **1 Omri made king of Israel[12]** by the people (1 Kings 16:16) **Note**: With Omri's reign Israel changed the start of their regnal year from fall to fall to spring to spring until the reign of Jehu. Zimi kills himself (1 Kings 16:18). During this time **Tibni** [5]was also made king over Israel. Thus half follower Tibni and half Omri (1 Kings 16:21) 2 - Omri / 2 - Tibni **Note**: Regnal year changed to Spring during either Omri's or Ahad's reign. **Note**: This regnal year begin 6 months before Judah's regnal year.	521 of 735	O m r i' s "h o u s e" of 42 yrs 1	114 of 390
897	BC	3074	Y M	28	3 - Omri / 3 - Tibni	522	2	115
896	BC	3075	Y M	29	4 - Omri / 3 - Tibni	523	3	116

BC AD Years + or -		YM Years		6000 Years of Mankind Copyright © 2024 by Walter R. Dolen **Biblical Chronology Details** YM = Year of Mankind Begins in Sept/Oct 3 months before BC/AD dates	Additional Details	# of yrs	# of yrs	# of yrs
895	BC	3076	YM	30 Asa king of Judah		524	4	117
894	BC	3077	YM	31	5 - Omri / 4 - Tibni	525	5	118
893	BC	3078	YM	32	6 - Omri / ? - Tibni Tibni died and Omri solely reigned over Israel in Asa's 31st year (1 Kings 16:22-23). Omri starts to build Samaria (1 Kings 16:23-24)	526	6	119
892	BC	3079	YM	33	7 - Omri After Omri ruled in Tirzah for 6 years and after he started building Samaria, he moved the capitol from Tirzah to Samaria (1 Kings 16:23-24).	527	7	120 121
891	BC	3080	YM	34	8 Omri 9	528	8	122
890	BC	3081	YM	35 Asa	10	529	9	123
889	BC	3082	YM	36	11	530	10	124
888	BC	3083	YM	37		531 of 735	11	125 of 390
887	BC	3084	YM	38	12 - Omri last year 1 - **Ahab** first year [22] (1 Kings 16:29) Because of the non-accession year method Ahab's first year officially included Omri's 12th.	532	12	126
886	BC	3085	YM	39 Asa disease in his feet (2 Chron 16:12)	2- Ahab 3	533	13	127
885	BC	3086	YM	40 Asa king of Judah	4	534	14	128
884	BC	3087	YM	41 Asa last year 1 **Jehoshaphat king of Judah** [25] (1 Ki 22:41-43)	5	535	15	129
883	BC	3088	YM	2	6	536	16	130
882	BC	3089	YM	3	7	537	17	131

BC AD Years + or -		YM Years		6000 Years of Mankind Copyright © 2024 by Walter R. Dolen **Biblical Chronology Details** YM = Year of Mankind Begins in Sept/Oct 3 months before BC/AD dates	Additional Details	# of yrs	# of yrs	# of yrs
881	BC	3090	Y M	4	8	538	18	132
880	BC	3091	Y M	5 Jehoshaphat	9	539	19	133
879	BC	3092	Y M	6	10	540	20	134
878	BC	3093	Y M	7	11	541	21	135
877	BC	3094	Y M	8	12	542	22	136
876	BC	3095	Y M	9	13	543	23	137
875	BC	3096	Y M	10 Jehoshaphat king of Judah	14	544	24	138
874	BC	3097	Y M	11	15	545	25	139
873	BC	3098	Y M	12	16 Ahab	546	26	140
872	BC	3099	Y M	13	17	547	27	141
871	BC	3100	Y M	14	18 - Ahab	548	28	142
870	BC	3101	Y M	15 Jehoshaphat	19	549	29	143
869	BC	3102	Y M	16	20 - Ahab	550	30	144
868	BC	3103	Y M	17 **Jehoshaphat** king of Judah **Jehoram** first co-reign Jehoram co-reign of 2 years (2 Kings 1:16-17) because during these two years king Jehoshaphat had joined himself with Ahab to war against Syria (see "Ahaziah"); and because Jehoshaphat after this war and Ahab's death had to defend Judah against Moah who was coming to invade Judah (2 Chr 20:1-25, 22); and because Jehoshaphat had joined with Ahaziah to build ships to go to Tharshish and to go to Ophir for gold, an adventure that did not work because the ships were "broken" (Chr 20:35-37; 1 Kings 22:48-49)	21 Ahab king of Israel 1 - **Ahaziah** first year [2] (1 Kings 22:51-52)	551 of 735	31	145 of 390
867	BC	3104	Y M	18 **Jehoshaphat** 2 - Jehoram's second year of co-reign		552	32	146

BC AD Years + or -		YM Years		**6000 Years of Mankind** Copyright © 2024 by Walter R. Dolen **Biblical Chronology Details** YM = Year of Mankind Begins in Sept/Oct 3 months before BC/AD dates	**Additional Details**	# of yrs	# of yrs	# of yrs
866	BC	3105	Y M	19	22- Ahab last year 2 - Ahaziah 1 - **Jehoram** first year [12] Ahab was killed in battle. Ahaziah dies after two years of injury. Jehoram (Joram) of Israel begins his 12 year reign after Ahaziah died (2 Kings 1:17-18; 3:1). This regnal year began in the first part of the 18th year of Jehoshaphat (2 Kings 3:1) **Elijah** warns Ahaziah (2 Kings 1L1ff)	553	33	147
865	BC	3106	Y M	20 Jehoshaphat	2 - Jehoram [Joram] king of Israel Wars with Mesha king of Moab during this reign (2 Kings 4-27)	554	34	148
864	BC	3107	Y M	21	3	555	35	149
863	BC	3108	Y M	22 **Jehoshaphat** King of Judah	4	556	36	150
862	BC	3109	Y M	23 **Jehoshaphat** King of Judah **3 - Jehoram of Judah co-reign resumes** (2 Kings 8:16-17; 2 Chr 21:3, 5; see above)	5 -Joram [Jehoram] (2 Kings 8:16-17)	557	37	151
861	BC	3110	Y M	24 **Jehoshaphat** 4 - Jehoram of Judah co-reign	6	558	38	152
860	BC	3111	Y M	25 **Jehoshaphat last year** 5 - Jehoram of Judah co-king	7 - Jehoram king of Israel	559	39	153
859	BC	3112	Y M	6 **Jehoram king of Judah solo King**	8	560	40	154
858	BC	3113	Y M	7 Jehoram got a disease of the bowels in his last two years of reign (2 Chr 21:18-19) as foretold by prophecy (2 Chr 21:15).	9 10 -	561	41	155
857	BC	3114	Y M	8 **Jehoram** dies and **Ahaziah** reigns in his place	11 - Jehoram king of Israel	562	42 Om ri's hou se yrs	156

BC AD Years + or -		YM Years		**6000 Years of Mankind** Copyright © 2024 by Walter R. Dolen **Biblical Chronology Details** YM = Year of Mankind Begins in Sept/Oct 3 months before BC/AD dates	**Additional Details**	# of yrs	# of yrs	# of yrs
856	BC	3115	Y M	1 **Ahaziah**[3] **king of Judah first year as solo king** [1] Jehoram's legal rule over Judah did not end until he died in his second year of illness (2 Chr 21:18-20), which was in his 8th year of rule. The inhabitants of Jerusalem made Ahaziah king in Jehoram of Israel's 11th year (2 Chr 22:1 with 2 Kings 9:29). But his official year of reign, according to Judah's method also included part of the 12th year of Jehoram of Israel (see 2 Kings 8:25-26). **Ahaziah became king after he was a 42 year "son" of Omri's ruling house** (see endnotes and 3rd column to the right for the count). His mother was a daughter of Omri, king of Israel.	12 - Jehoram king of Israel This regnal year began 6 months prior to the regnal year in Judah. -------------------------- 1- **Jehu** [28] killed Jehoram (Israel's king) and killed Ahaziah (Judah's king) (2 Chron 22:7-9; 2 Kings 9:21-28) because he was related to Omri and he killed all the house of Ahab, then he became king of Israel and tried to reform Israel. **He changes the regnal year back to fall to fall and begins to use the accessional year method.**	563 of 735		157 of 390
855	BC	3116	Y M	1 - **Athaliah Queen of Judah first illegal year** [6] Athaliah is the mother of Ahaziah kills all the royal seed, or so she thought (2 Kings 11:1). But Joash, a son of Ahaziah, was safely hidden from Athaliah for 6 years (2 Kings 11:2-3; 2 Chr 22:12). Queen Athaliah rules Judah for the six years when Joash was *hidden* (2 Chr 22:12; 2 Kings 11:3). Thus Athaliah took the kingdom and reigned as queen, "Athaliah did reign over the land" (2 Kings 11:3; 2 Chr 22:12). **(This year counted as Joash first year, since Athaliah illegally usurped the kingdom.)**		564		158
854	BC	3117	Y M	2 Athaliah illegal reign (counted as Joash's 2nd year)	2 Jehu king of Israel	565		159
853	BC	3118	Y M	3 Athaliah illegal reign (counted as Joash's 3rd year)	3	566		160
852	BC	3119	Y M	4 Athaliah illegal reign (counted as Joash's 4th year)	4	567		161
851	BC	3120	Y M	5 Athaliah illegal reign (counted as Joash's 5th year)	5	568		162
850	BC	3121	Y M	6 Athaliah illegal reign (counted as Joash's 6th year)	6	569		163
849	BC	3122	Y M	7 **Joash king of Judah reigns** [40] Athaliah was killed (2 Chr 23:1-15). Joash was a son of 7 years after the 6 years of hiding when he began to reign in the 7th year of Jehu of Israel (2 Chr 24:1; 2 Kings 11:21; 12:1). This means that Joash was but a very young child when queen Athaliah killed the rest of the royal seed (cf. "His nurse," in 2 Kings 11:2 & 2 Chr 22:11). Jehoiada the priest instructed Joash (Jehoash) in his early years of reign (2 Kings 12:2).	7	570 of 735		164 of 390
848	BC	3123	Y M	8 - Joash	8	571		165
847	BC	3124	Y M	9	9	572		166
846	BC	3125	Y M	10 Joash king of Judah	10 Jehu king of Israel	573		167

BC AD Years + or -		YM Years		6000 Years of Mankind Copyright © 2024 by Walter R. Dolen **Biblical Chronology Details** YM = Year of Mankind Begins in Sept/Oct 3 months before BC/AD dates	**Additional Details**	# of yrs	# of yrs	# of yrs
845	BC	3126	Y M	11	11	574		168
844	BC	3127	Y M	12	12	575		169
843	BC	3128	Y M	13	13	576		170
842	BC	3129	Y M	14	14	577		171
841	BC	3130	Y M	15 Joash king of Judah	15	578		172
840	BC	3131	Y M	16	16 Jehu king of Israel	579		173
839	BC	3132	Y M	17	17	580		174
838	BC	3133	Y M	18	18	581		175
837	BC	3134	Y M	19	19	582		176
836	BC	3135	Y M	20 Joash king of Judah	20 Jehu king of Israel	583		177
835	BC	3136	Y M	21	21	584		178
834	BC	3137	Y M	22	22	585		179
833	BC	3138	Y M	23	23 Jehu 1 - **Jehoahaz** [17] son Jehu reigns as co-king in Israel (2 Kings 13:1). **Hazael of Syria** oppressed Israel during all the days of Jehoahaz these days (2 Kings 13:22).	586 of 735		180 of 390
832	BC	3139	Y M	24	24 - Jehu king of Israel 2 - Jehoahaz King of Israel	587		181
831	BC	3140	Y M	25 Joash king of Judah	25 - Jehu king of Israel 3 - Jehoahaz King of Israel	588		182
830	BC	3141	Y M	26	26 - Jehu king of Israel 4 - Jehoahaz King of Israel	589		183
829	BC	3142	Y M	27	27 - Jehu king of Israel 5 - Jehoahaz King of Israel	590		184
828	BC	3143	Y M	28	28 - Jehu last year 6 - Jehoahaz King of Israel	591		185

[Top | Flood | Abram | Exodus | David | Hezekiah | Jerusalem | JC | End Time | End Notes]

BC AD Years + or -		YM Years		6000 Years of Mankind Copyright © 2024 by Walter R. Dolen Biblical Chronology Details YM = Year of Mankind Begins in Sept/Oct 3 months before BC/AD dates	Additional Details	# of yrs	# of yrs	# of yrs
827	BC	3144	Y M	29	7	592		186
826	BC	3145	Y M	30 Joash king of Judah	8	593		187
825	BC	3146	Y M	31	9	594		188
824	BC	3147	Y M	32	10	595		189
823	BC	3148	Y M	33	11	596		190
822	BC	3149	Y M	34	12	597		191
821	BC	3150	Y M	35 Joash king of Judah	13	598		192
820	BC	3151	Y M	36	14	599		193
819	BC	3152	Y M	37	15 - Jehoahaz 1 - **Jehoash first year** [16]	600		194
818	BC	3153	Y M	38 Joash 1 - **Amaziah king of Judah first year (co-reigns)** [29] (2 Kings 14:1-2) amaziah's first 3 years are as co-reign with his wounded father's 38th to 40th years (2 Chr 24:24-15).	16 - Jehoahaz 2 - Jehoash king of Israel	601 of 735		195 of 390
817	BC	3154	Y M	39 Joash 2 - Amaziah's second year (co-reigns)	17 - Jehoahaz last year 3 - Jehoash	602		196
816	BC	3155	Y M	40 Joash last year 3 - Amaziah's third year (co-reigns)	4 - Jehoash king of Israel	603		197
815	BC	3156	Y M	4 - **Amaziah solo reign begins**	5	604		198
814	BC	3157	Y M	5 Amaziah	6	605		199
813	BC	3158	Y M	6	7	606		200
812	BC	3159	Y M	7	8	607		201
811	BC	3160	Y M	8	9	608		202
810	BC	3161	Y M	9	10 - Jehoash king of Israel	609		203
809	BC	3162	Y M	10 Amaziah king of Judah	11	610		204

BC AD Years + or -		YM Years		6000 Years of Mankind Copyright © 2024 by Walter R. Dolen **Biblical Chronology Details** YM = Year of Mankind Begins in Sept/Oct 3 months before BC/AD dates	Additional Details	# of yrs	# of yrs	# of yrs
808	BC	3163	Y M	11	12	611		205
807	BC	3164	Y M	12	13	612		206
806	BC	3165	Y M	13	14	613		207
805	BC	3166	Y M	14	15 - Jehoash king of Israel	614		208
804	BC	3167	Y M	15 Amaziah Amaziah of Judah lived in 15 years after Jehoash of Israel's death (2 Kings 14:17; 2 Chr 25:25)	16 - Jehoash last year 1 - **Jeroboam II** first year [41] (2 Kings 14:16, 23)	615 of 735		209 of 390
803	BC	3168	Y M	16	2	616		210
802	BC	3169	Y M	17	3 - Jeroboam II king of Israel	617		211
801	BC	3170	Y M	18	4	618		212
800	BC	3171	Y M	19	5	619		213
799	BC	3172	Y M	20 Amaziah king of Judah	6	620		214
798	BC	3173	Y M	21	7	621		215
797	BC	3174	Y M	22	8	622		216
796	BC	3175	Y M	23	9	623		217
795	BC	3176	Y M	24	10 - Jeroboam II king of Israel	624		218
794	BC	3177	Y M	25 Amaziah	11	625		219
793	BC	3178	Y M	26	12	626		220
792	BC	3179	Y M	27	13	627		221
791	BC	3180	Y M	28	14	628		222
790	BC	3181	Y M	29 Amaziah king of Judah	15	629		223

BC AD Years + or -		YM Years		6000 Years of Mankind Copyright © 2024 by Walter R. Dolen **Biblical Chronology Details** YM = Year of Mankind Begins in Sept/Oct 3 months before BC/AD dates	Additional Details	# of yrs	# of yrs	# of yrs
789	BC	3182	Y M	**Interregnum Period?** Starting in Jeroboam king of Israel II's 16th year The Bible fails to tell us who ruled or judged Judah during this period (3181-3191 YM), or if there was an interregnum, or a catastrophe Nevertheless, the count of years is not lost since Jeroboam II of Israel had a continuous reign through this period, and the count of year of mankind for this period is found by comparing bother the reigns of Judah and Israel.	16 - Jeroboam II king of Israel	630 of 735		224 of 390
788	BC	3183	Y M	**Catastrophes**: Sometime in this period of Uzziah and Jeroboam's rule there was a great "earthquake" and other wide catastrophes (Amos 1:1; Zech 14:5; see in CP3, "Astronomical Chaos"). This may or may not account for the apparent interregnum periods.	17	631		225
787	BC	3184	Y M		18	632		226
786	BC	3185	Y M		19	633		227
785	BC	3186	Y M		20 - Jeroboam II king of Israel	634		228
784	BC	3187	Y M		21	635		229
783	BC	3188	Y M		22	636		230
782	BC	3189	Y M		23	637		231
781	BC	3190	Y M		24	638		232
780	BC	3191	Y M		25	639		233
779	BC	3192	Y M	**Catastrophes**: Sometime in this period of Uzziah and Jeroboam's rule there was a great "**earthquake**" and other wide catastrophes (Amos 1:1; Zech 14:5; see in CP3, "Astronomical Chaos"). This may or may not account for the apparent interregnum periods.	26 - Jeroboam II king of Israel	640		234
778	BC	3193	Y M	**1 - Uzziah (Azariah) first year as king of Judah** [52] He may have reigned in someway after Amaziah's death (2 Chr 26:3; 25:25-28; 26:1; 2 Kings 15:1-4). But his reign was not counted until Jeroboam's 27th year. He began his official reign when he was 16 years old (2 Chr 26:3) in 3188 YM. Butthe count of years of man is not lost because Jeroboam of Israel reigned continuously throughout this period. Because of 2 Chron 25:28 & 26:1, it is uncertain if there was an interregnum period between Amaziah of Judah and Uzziah (Azariah) of Judah.	27	641 of 735		235 of 390
777	BC	3194	Y M	2	28	642		236

[Top	Flood	Abram	Exodus	David	Hezekiah	Jerusalem	JC	End Time	End Notes]						

BC AD Years + or -		YM Years		**6000 Years of Mankind** Copyright © 2024 by Walter R. Dolen **Biblical Chronology Details** YM = Year of Mankind Begins in Sept/Oct 3 months before BC/AD dates	**Additional Details**	# of yrs	# of yrs	# of yrs
776	BC	3195	Y M	3	29	643		23?
775	BC	3196	Y M	4	30 - Jeroboam II king of Israel	644		238
774	BC	3197	Y M	5 Uzziah (Azariah)	31	645		23?
773	BC	3198	Y M	6	32	646		24(
772	BC	3199	Y M	7	33	647		24?
771	BC	3200	Y M	8	34	648		242
770	BC	3201	Y M	9	35	649		24?
769	BC	3202	Y M	10 Uzziah (Azariah) king of Judah	36 - Jeroboam II king of Israel	650		244
768	BC	3203	Y M	11	37	651		24?
767	BC	3204	Y M	12	38	652		24(
766	BC	3205	Y M	13	39	653		24?
765	BC	3206	Y M	14	40	654		24?
764	BC	3207	Y M	15 Uzziah (Azariah) king of Judah	41 - Jeroboam II king of Israel, last year	655		24?
763	BC	3208	Y M	16	**Interregnum Period** Zachariah in someway may have reigned or governed after the death of his father, Jeroboam II (2 Kings 14:29), or there may be an interregnum. Nevertheless the count of years of man is not lost because Uzziah's reign continues in Judah throughout this period.	656 of 735		25(of 39(
762	BC	3209	Y M	17		657		25?
761	BC	3210	Y M	18		658		252
760	BC	3211	Y M	19		659		25?

[Top | Flood | Abram | Exodus | David | Hezekiah | Jerusalem | JC | End Time | End Notes]

BC AD Years + or -		YM Years		6000 Years of Mankind Copyright © 2024 by Walter R. Dolen Biblical Chronology Details YM = Year of Mankind Begins in Sept/Oct 3 months before BC/AD dates	Additional Details	# of yrs	# of yrs	# of yrs
759	BC	3212	YM	20 Uzziah (Azariah) king of Judah	Interregnum Period for Israel	660		254
758	BC	3213	YM	21		661		255
757	BC	3214	YM	22		662		256
756	BC	3215	YM	23		663		257
755	BC	3216	YM	24		664		258
754	BC	3217	YM	25 Uzziah (Azariah)	Interregnum Period for Israel	665		259
753	BC	3218	YM	26		666		260
752	BC	3219	YM	27		667		261
751	BC	3220	YM	28		668		262
750	BC	3221	YM	29		669		263
749	BC	3222	YM	30 Uzziah (Azariah) king of Judah	Interregnum Period for Israel	670		264
748	BC	3223	YM	31		671		265
747	BC	3224	YM	32		672		266
746	BC	3225	YM	33		673		267
745	BC	3226	YM	34		674		268
744	BC	3227	YM	35 Uzziah (Azariah)		675		269
743	BC	3228	YM	36		676		270
742	BC	3229	YM	37		677		271

BC AD Years + or -		YM Years		6000 Years of Mankind Copyright © 2024 by Walter R. Dolen **Biblical Chronology Details** YM = Year of Mankind Begins in Sept/Oct 3 months before BC/AD dates	**Additional Details**	# of yrs	# of yrs	# of yrs
741	BC	3230	Y M	38	Zachariah first year [6 months] He reigned 6 months and then was killed in this period (2 Kings 15:8-10. These 6 months was the last 6 months of his would be 23th year.... Scripture is not clear if Zachariah also ruled before this year	678		272
740	BC	3231	Y M	39	1 - **Shallum** first year [1 month] Shallum reigns a month, probably the first month of Judah's regnal year (2 Kings 15:13) after he killed Zachariah (2 Kings 15:10). Shallum reign is to be counted as the whole year. **Menahem** begins to reign. He kills Shallum and reigns 10 years (2 Kings 15;14, 17); His first regnal year is the next year since Israel at this time was using the accessional year method as was Judah. See cp206.	679 of 735		273 of 390
739	BC	3232	Y M	40 Uzziah (Azariah) king of Judah	1 - **Menahem king of Israel** first year [10] See year above for details.	680		274
738	BC	3233	Y M	41	2 - - Menahem king of Israel **Pul king or co-king of Assyria** came against the land of Israel (Samaria), but Menahem gave Pul tribute so as "to confirm the kingdom in his hand" (2 Kings 15:19-20). But **Tiglath-pileser** of Assyria "he carried them [Israel] away" (1 Chr 5:26, 6:2; 2 Kings 15:29). **Pul = Tiglath-pileser, apparently in Babylon.**	681		275
737	BC	3234	Y M	42	3 - Menahem king of Israel	682		276
736	BC	3235	Y M	43	4	683		277
735	BC	3236	Y M	44	5	684		278
734	BC	3237	Y M	45 Uzziah (Azariah)	6	685		279

[Top | Flood | Abram | Exodus | David | Hezekiah | Jerusalem | JC | End Time | End Notes]

BC AD Years + or -		YM Years		**6000 Years of Mankind** Copyright © 2024 by Walter R. Dolen **Biblical Chronology Details** YM = Year of Mankind Begins in Sept/Oct 3 months before BC/AD dates	**Additional Details**	# of yrs	# of yrs	# of yrs
733	BC	3238	Y M	46 Azariah (Uzziah) became a leper sometime in his later years (2 Kings 15:5) because of his transgressions (2 Chr 26:16-20). He stayed a leper until he died (2 Chr 26:21). **Note:** Jotham,the son of Uzziah, judged the latter part of Azariah's official reign because of the king's leprosy (2 Chr 26:21; 2 Kings 15:5).	7	686		280
732	BC	3239	Y M	47	8	687		281
731	BC	3240	Y M	48	9	688		282
730	BC	3241	Y M	49	10 - Menahem king of Israel last year	689		283
729	BC	3242	Y M	50	1 - **Pekahiah** first year [2] king of Israel	690		284
728	BC	3243	Y M	51	2 - Pekahiah	691		285
727	BC	3244	Y M	52 Uzziah (Azariah) king of Judah, last year	1 - **Pekah** first year [20] king of Israel. He reigns 20 years after he killed Pekahiah (2 Kings 15:25-27)	692 of 735		286 of 390
726	BC	3245	Y M	1- **Jotham first year as king of Judah** [16] Jotham begins his 16 year reign in the 2nd year of Pekah (2 Kings 15:32-33). He began to reign after his father's death (2 Kings 15:7).	2	693		287
725	BC	3246	Y M	2	3	694		288
724	BC	3247	Y M	3	4	695		289
723	BC	3248	Y M	4	5 - Pekah king of Israel	696		290
722	BC	3249	Y M	5 Jotham king of Judah	6	697		291
721	BC	3250	Y M	6	7	698		292
720	BC	3251	Y M	7	8	699		293
719	BC	3252	Y M	8	9	700		294
718	BC	3253	Y M	9	10 - Pekah king of Israel	701		295
717	BC	3254	Y M	10 Jotham king of Judah	11	702		296

[Top | Flood | Abram | Exodus | David | Hezekiah | Jerusalem | JC | End Time | End Notes]

BC AD Years + or -		YM Years		6000 Years of Mankind Copyright © 2024 by Walter R. Dolen **Biblical Chronology Details** YM = Year of Mankind Begins in Sept/Oct 3 months before BC/AD dates	Additional Details	# of yrs	# of yrs	# of yrs
716	BC	3255	Y M	11	12 - Pekah king of Israel	703		297
715	BC	3256	Y M	12	13	704		298
714	BC	3257	Y M	13	14	705		299
713	BC	3258	Y M	14	15 - Pekah king of Israel	706		300
712	BC	3259	Y M	15	16 - Pekah	707		301
711	BC	3260	Y M	16 Jotham king of Judah last year 1 - **Ahaz first year** [16] Ahaz begins his 16 year reign in the 17th year of Pekah of Israel after Jotham died (2 Kings 16:1-2; 15:38)	17	708		302 of 390
710	BC	3261	Y M	2	18	709		303
709	BC	3262	Y M	3	19	710		304
708	BC	3263	Y M	4	20 - Pekah king of Israel	711		305
707	BC	3264	Y M	5 Ahaz king of Judah	Hoshea kills Pekah in his 20th year and reigns in his place (2 Kings 15:30).[4]	712		306
706	BC	3265	Y M	6	In this period Israel was overran by the **Assyrians' Tiglath-pileser** and Judah "kneeled" to him. "I am thy seervant and thy son," said Judah's king Ahaz to Tiglath-pileser. (2 Kings 15:29; 16:7-18) And **Hosea ("Asusi") was placed as governor** or "king" of Israel during this period: "Paqaha [Pekah] their king they deposed and I placed Ausi [Hoshea] over them as king" (see pages 258 and 256-257 in the *Archaeology and the Old Testament*, by Unger).	713 of 735		307
705	BC	3266	Y M	7		714		308
704	BC	3267	Y M	8	**Regnal years changed under Assyrian influence**	715		309
703	BC	3268	Y M	9	Israel's regnal years now spring to spring	716		310

[Top	Flood	Abram	Exodus	David	Hezekiah	Jerusalem	JC	End Time	End Notes]							

BC AD Years + or -		YM Years		**6000 Years of Mankind** Copyright © 2024 by Walter R. Dolen **Biblical Chronology Details** YM = Year of Mankind Begins in Sept/Oct 3 months before BC/AD dates	**Additional Details**	# of yrs	# of yrs	# of yrs
702	BC	3269	Y M	10 Ahaz king of Judah		717		311
701	BC	3270	Y M	11	1 yr of Sargon's co-reign? Both **Shalmaneser** and **Sargon** *were* co-king or princes under king **Tiglath-Pileser** who wore the Tiara. Tiglath-Pileser was making war over a great area (2 King19:11) and needed princes to take his place in case of his death. We did not know the exact death of Tiglath-Pileser or Shalmaneser.	718		312
700	BC	3271	Y M	12 Ahaz's		719 of 735		313 of 390
699	BC	3272	Y M	13	1 - **Hoshea** king of Israel began his official **reign over Israel** in the Spring 6 months after Ahaz began his 12 yr. The beginning of Israel's regnal years changed from the Fall to fall to Spring to Spring due to Assyrians influence.	720		314
698	BC	3273	Y M	14 Ahaz king of Judah	2 - Hoshea	721		315
697	BC	3274	Y M	15 Ahaz king of Judah 1 - **Hezekiah's first year as King of Judah** [29] Hezekiah begins his 29 year reign as co-ruler with Ahaz at 25 years old (2 Kings 18:1-2)	3 - Hoshea 3rd year included the first part of Hezekiah's first year (2 Kings 18:1-2) 4 - Hoshea	722		316
696	BC	3275	Y M	16 Ahaz King of Judah's last year 2 - Hezekiah co-reign	5 - Hoshea	723		317
695	BC	3276	Y M	3 - Hezekiah 1 - **Manasseh [55]** begins his co-reign at12 years old as a son of Hezekiah (2 Kings 21:1; 20:21). Since Hezekiah was 25 years old when he started his co-rule with king Ahaz, then Hezekiah must had been approximately 15 years old when Manasseh was born. **The difference between this chronology of the Bible and others** is that we have Manasseh co-ruling with his father at an early age because Hezekiah wanted his offspring to be the next king of Judah incase the kings of Assyria came and killed him in battle. Assyria was causing havoc in the region. The dynasty and heritage of Judah and the promises to David were at stake. Judah's co-king method	6 - Hoshea	724	1 M a n a s s e h	318

[Top | Flood | Abram | Exodus | David | Hezekiah | Jerusalem | JC | End Time | End Notes]

BC AD Years + or -		YM Years		**6000 Years of Mankind** Copyright © 2024 by Walter R. Dolen **Biblical Chronology Details** YM = Year of Mankind Begins in Sept/Oct 3 months before BC/AD dates	**Additional Details**	# of yrs	# of yrs	# of yrs
694	BC	3277	Y M	4 - Hezekiah king of Judah		725	2	319
693	BC	3278	Y M	5 - Hezekiah	7 - Hoshea **Shalmaneser** now king of Assyria begins the siege against Samaria (Israel's land) for 3 years starting in the 4th year of Hezekiah, which was the 7th of Hosea (2 Kings 18:9)	726	3	320
692	BC	3279	Y M	6 Hezekiah king of Judah	8 - Hoshea *Note:* **Sargon King of Assyria became King with the Tiara** after Shalmaneser died during the battle in Samaria, [Grayson, *Assyrian and Babylonian Chronicles*, p. 73].	727 of 735	4 M a n a s s e h	321 of 390
691	BC	3280	Y M	7 Hezekiah king of Judah 5 - Manasseh co-reign	9 **Hosea last year** included the first part of Hezekiah's 6th year. "At the end of three years Samaria (Israel's land) was taken" (2 Kings 18:10) The king of Assyria carry away people of Israel to Assyria (2 Kings 18:11)- **End of the Kingdom of Israel**	728	5	322
690	BC	3281	Y M	8 - Hezekiah king of Judah 6 - Manasseh co-reign	**12 Yr of Sargon King of Assyria** **Sennacherib,** his son was co-king (Prince) of Assyria, under Sargon his father, who wore the Tiara. Compare 12th year of Sargon with the first campaign of Sennacherib (Luckenbill, *Ancient Records of Assyria*, vol 2, pp. 14, w/ 116, 128, 133, 140, 153) Thus, the 12th year of Sargon is the first year of Sennacherib, if we believe these writings. 13 -	729	6	323
689	BC	3282	Y M	9 - Hezekiah 7 - Manasseh co-reign	14 -	730	7	324
688	BC	3283	Y M	10 Hezekiah king of Judah 8 - Manasseh (co-reign)	15 - Sargon	731	8	325

BC AD Years + or -		YM Years		6000 Years of Mankind Copyright © 2024 by Walter R. Dolen **Biblical Chronology Details** YM = Year of Mankind Begins in Sept/Oct 3 months before BC/AD dates	**Additional Details**	# of yrs	# of yrs	# of yrs
687	BC	3284	Y	11 Hezekiah king of Judah		732	9	326
			M	9 - Manasseh co-reign	16 -			
686	BC	3285	Y	12 -Hezekiah	**Sennacherib co-king of Assyria** (w/ Sargon) during this time came up against all the fortified cities of the kingdom and land of Judah (2 Kings 18:13; Isa 36:1-2). This a a part of Sennacherib's 3rd campaign (Luckenbill, vol 2, p. 120). The king of Assyria, sent a great army against Jerusalem (2 Kings 18:16-17)	733	10	327
			M					
685	BC	3286	Y	13 - Hezekiah		734	11	328 of 390
			M	11 - Manasseh (co-reign)	There were multiple kings of Assyria who came against Judah during this era of war. Apparently **Sennacherib** was a co-king, while **Sargon** was the head king. There were kingS of Assyria attacking the lands (2Kings 19:11; Isa 37:11)		M a n a s s e h	
					18 Yr of Sargon **Sennacherib (co-king) unable to conquer Jerusalem returns to Nineveh in Assyria.** After his father's death, he became solo king.			
684	BC	3287	Y	**14th yr Hezekiah**		735	12	329
			M	12 - Manasseh (co-reign) **Sennacherib**, king of Assyria, came against Judah (2 Kings 18:13). This was the year before the Jubilee as implied by 2 Kings 19:29 (see Lev 25:8-10, 20-22, 2-5). **Note**: the "this year" of 2 Kings 19:29 is the 7th year of the 7th cycle of 7 years. This year was Hezekiah's 14th year (cf. 2 Kings 19:29 with 2 Kings 18:13) The "second year" is the 8th year of Lev 25:22, which is the Jubilee year, and the "third year" is the 9th year of Lev 25:22). This 14th year occurred after a count of 15 seven sevens of years from the time Israel first went into the promised land. **See 2553 YM is 1 of 735 years.** **In this year Sennacherib's army is destroyed** (2 Ki 19:35) and the sign of the LONG DAY occurred (2 Ki 20:1-11; Isa 38:6-8). These two events may be interrelated. This is another sign of Astronomical Chaos (Velikovsky, *Worlds in Collision*, Part II Chapter 2; *Chronology Papers*, CP3).	Sometime later **Sennacherib** was then killed by his sons (Grayson, p. 81), Adrammelech and Sharezer (2 Kings 19:36-37); and Sennacherib's son **Esarhaddon** became king. At this time we cannot determine from the Bible	15th 49 yr c y c l e e n d s		

and secular evidence when Sennacherib was killed and when Esarhaddon became King in Assyria.

[Top | Flood | Abram | Exodus | David | Hezekiah | Jerusalem | JC | End Time | End Notes]

BC AD Years + or -		YM Years		**6000 Years of Mankind** Copyright © 2024 by Walter R. Dolen **Biblical Chronology Details** YM = Year of Mankind Begins in Sept/Oct 3 months before BC/AD dates	**Additional Details**	# of yrs	# of yrs	# of yrs
683	BC	3288	Y M	**15th Hezekiah** **This was a Jubilee year** 13 - Manasseh (co-reign) The *count* of the Jubilee years and the Sabbatical rest of the land began for Israel only *after* they came into the land in 2552 YM (Lev 25:2). This count began only *after* they planted their first crop in 2553 YM. (cf. Lev 25:2ff w/ Josh 5:12; 24:13). From this first planting in 2553 YM you count 15 cycles of 49 years to 3287 YM for a total of 735 years (inclusive counting). Thus, the next year in 3288 YM is the 50th year or the Jubilee of the **15th cycle of 49 years** after Israel came into the land. **First of 15 added years to Hezekiah's reign.** (2 Kings 20:6) **This was a Jubilee year** With the information under 3287 YM, the year 3288 was a Jubilee year (2 Ki 19:29 [cf. Lev 25:20-22, see "God's Appointed Times"]; 2 Kings 18:13 — indicates 2 Ki 19:29 was the 14th year of Hezekiah; 20:5-6 — indicates that Hezekiah would live for 15 more years; & 18:2 — indicates Hezekiah thus ruled for 29 years [14 + 15 = 29 years]).		13	330
682	BC	3289	Y M	16 Hezeliah 14 - Manasseh (co-reign)		14	331
681	BC	3290	Y M	17 - Hezekiah king of Judah 15 - Manasseh co-reign		15	332
680	BC	3291	Y M	18 Hezeliah 16 - Manasseh (co-reign)		16	333
679	BC	3292	Y M	19 - Hezekiah king of Judah 17 - Manasseh (co-reign)		17	334 of 390
678	BC	3293	Y M	20 - Hezekiah 18 - Manasseh (co-reign)		18	335
677	BC	3294	Y M	21 - Hezekiah king of Judah 19 - Manasseh co-reign		19	336
676	BC	3295	Y M	22 Hezeliah 20 - Manasseh (co-reign)		20	337
675	BC	3296	Y M	23 - Hezekiah king of Judah 21 - Manasseh co-reign		21	338
674	BC	3297	Y M	24 - Hezekiah 22 - Manasseh co-reign		22	339
673	BC	3298	Y M	25 - Hezekiah king of Judah 23 - Manasseh (co-reign)		23	340
672	BC	3299	Y M	26 - Hezekiah king of Judah 24 - Manasseh (co-reign)		24	341
671	BC	3300	Y M	27 - Hezekiah 25 - Manasseh (co-reign)		25	342

[Top | Flood | Abram | Exodus | David | Hezekiah | Jerusalem | JC | End Time | End Notes]

BC AD Years + or -		YM Years		6000 Years of Mankind Copyright © 2024 by Walter R. Dolen **Biblical Chronology Details** YM = Year of Mankind Begins in Sept/Oct 3 months before BC/AD dates	Additional Details	# of yrs	# of yrs	# of yrs
670	BC	3301	Y M	28 - Hezekiah 26 - Manasseh			26	343
669	BC	3302	Y M	**29th yr of Hezekiah, his last year as king of Judah** 27 - Manasseh co-king			27	344
668	BC	3303	Y M	28 - **Manasseh king of Judah, first as solo king** of Judah			28	345
667	BC	3304	Y M	29 - Manasseh king of Judah			29	346
666	BC	3305	Y M	30			30	347
665	BC	3306	Y M	31			31	348
664	BC	3307	Y M	32			32	349
663	BC	3308	Y M	33 - Manasseh king of Judah			33	350
662	BC	3309	Y M	34			34	351
661	BC	3310	Y M	35			35	352
660	BC	3311	Y M	36			36	353
659	BC	3312	Y M	37			37	354
658	BC	3313	Y M	38 - Manasseh king of Judah			38	355
657	BC	3314	Y M	39			39	356
656	BC	3315	Y M	40			40	357
655	BC	3316	Y M	41			41	358
654	BC	3317	Y M	42			42	359
653	BC	3318	Y M	43 - Manasseh king of Judah			43	360
652	BC	3319	Y M	44			44	361
651	BC	3320	Y M	45			45	362

BC AD Years + or -		YM Years		6000 Years of Mankind Copyright © 2024 by Walter R. Dolen **Biblical Chronology Details** YM = Year of Mankind Begins in Sept/Oct 3 months before BC/AD dates	**Additional Details**	# of yrs	# of yrs	# of yrs
650	BC	3321	Y M	46			46	363
649	BC	3322	Y M	47			47	364
648	BC	3323	Y M	48			48	365
647	BC	3324	Y M	49			49	366
646	BC	3325	Y M	50			50	367
645	BC	3326	Y M	51			51	368
644	BC	3327	Y M	52			52	369
643	BC	3328	Y M	53 - Manasseh king of Judah **Last Year**			53	370
642	BC	3329	Y M	54			54	371
641	BC	3330	Y M	**55 Manasseh's last year**			55	372
640	BC	3331	Y M	1 - **Amon** 1 [2]				376
639	BC	3332	Y M	2 - Amon				377
638	BC	3333	Y M	**Josiah 1ˢᵗ year, king of Judah** [31] Remember his regnal year starts 3 months before BC years. Thus it started in 639 BC. He was a son of eight years when he began to rule(2 Kings 22:1)				378
637	BC	3334	Y M	2				379
636	BC	3335	Y M	3				380
635	BC	3336	Y M	4				381
634	BC	3337	Y M	5 - Josiah king of Judah				382
633	BC	3338	Y M	6				383
632	BC	3339	Y M	7				384

[Top | Flood | Abram | Exodus | David | Hezekiah | Jerusalem | JC | End Time | End Notes]

BC AD Years + or -		YM Years		6000 Years of Mankind Copyright © 2024 by Walter R. Dolen **Biblical Chronology Details** YM = Year of Mankind Begins in Sept/Oct 3 months before BC/AD dates	Additional Details	# of yrs	# of yrs	# of yrs
631	BC	3340	Y M	8 - Josiah begins to seek after God (2 Chron 34:3)				385
630	BC	3341	Y M	9				386
629	BC	3342	Y M	10 - Josiah king of Judah				387
628	BC	3343	Y M	11				388
627	BC	3344	Y M	12 - Josiah begins to purge Judah and Jerusalem high places of worship and the idols (2 Chron 34:3-7)				389
626	BC	3345	Y M	13 - Josiah king of Judah **Jeremiah begins his 23 year of prophesying** that ends with the destruction of Jerusalem [3385 YM] **This ended of Ezekiel's 390 years (Ezek 4:5; 1:1)** **Beginning of the 390 years was 2960YM**	**End of Ezekiel's 390 years (Ezek 4:5)** Israel's iniquity since David's misadventure was 390 years at this point in time. David was king of the united empire of Israel with Judah as 1 of 12 "states."		1st of 23	390
625	BC	3346	Y M	14 **Count of Ezekiel's 40 years for Judah's sins** (Ezek 4:6)	Judah enters their 40 years **as the last remnant of the David's kingdom.**		2	1 of 40
624	BC	3347	Y M	15 - Josiah king of Judah			3	2
623	BC	3348	Y M	16			4	3
622	BC	3349	Y M	17			5	4
621	BC	3350	Y M	18 - **Josiah finds the book of the law** and purges Judah of idols (2 Kings 22:3-23:1-25; 2 Chron 34:8ff). He keep a great Passover feast (2 Chron 35:16-19)			6	5
620	BC	3351	Y M	19			7	6
619	BC	3352	Y M	20 - Josiah king of Judah			8	7
618	BC	3353	Y M	21			9	8
617	BC	3354	Y M	22			10	9
616	BC	3355	Y M	23			11	10
615	BC	3356	Y M	24			12	11

[Top | Flood | Abram | Exodus | David | Hezekiah | Jerusalem | JC | End Time | End Notes]

BC AD Years + or -		YM Years		6000 Years of Mankind Copyright © 2024 by Walter R. Dolen **Biblical Chronology Details** YM = Year of Mankind Begins in Sept/Oct 3 months before BC/AD dates	Additional Details	# of yrs	# of yrs	# of yrs
614	BC	3357	Y M	25 - Josiah king of Judah			13	12
613	BC	3358	Y M	26			14	13
612	BC	3359	Y M	27			15	14
611	BC	3360	Y M	28			16	15
610	BC	3361	Y M	29			17	16
609	BC	3362	Y M	30 - Josiah king of Judah	17th Nabopolassar		18	17
608	BC	3363	Y M	31 Josiah/**Jehoahaz. Josiah is killed** the archers of **Necho, king of Egypt** (2 Chron 35:20-24) **Jehoahaz**, Josiah's son, was made king by the people and he reigned for only three months. Jehoahaz was taken by Necho to Egypt and put **Eliakim**, Jehoahaz's brother, as king of Judah and changed his name to **Jehoiakim.** (2 Chron 36:1-4)			19	18
607	BC	3364	Y M	1 - **Jehoiakim** [11] king of Judah Regnal year began in Sept/Oct of 608 BC **Beginning of the 70 years,** counting Judah's Fall to Fall years (2 Chron 36:1-5).	18th Nabopolassar Nebuchadnezzar co-reign may have started herein **1 of 70** years of Jeremiah & Daniel (see "70 years of desolation" in Appendix of CP)	1 of 70	20	19
606	BC	3365	Y M	2	19 - **Nabopolassar Nebuchadnezzar** co-reigns 2 of 70	2	21	20 of 40
605	BC	3366	Y M	3 - Jehoiakim king of Judah "In the third year of the reign of Jehoiakim king of Judah came Nebuchadnezzar king of Babylon unto Jerusalem, and besieged it" (Daniel 1:1)	20 - **Nabopolassar Nebuchadnezzar** co-reigns 3 of 70	3	22	21
604	BC	3367	Y M	4 - Jerhoiakim **This year was the 23rd year of Jeremiah's prophesying.** (Jer 25:3) "The word that came to Jeremiah concerning all the people of Judah in the **fourth year of Jehoiakim** the son of Josiah king of Judah, that was the **first year of Nebuchadnezzar king of Babylon**" (Jer 25:1)	21 - Nabopolassar **Nebuchadnezzar co-kingship** "Against Egypt, against the army of **Pharaoh-necho** king of Egypt, which was by the river Euphrates in Carchemish, which Nebuchadnezzar [co-king] king of Babylon smote in the fourth year of Jehoiakim the son of Josiah king of Judah" (Jeremiah 46:2) Year 4 of 70	4	23	22

[Top | Flood | Abram | Exodus | David | Hezekiah | Jerusalem | JC | End Time | End Notes]

BC AD Years + or -		YM Years		6000 Years of Mankind Copyright © 2024 by Walter R. Dolen **Biblical Chronology Details** YM = Year of Mankind Begins in Sept/Oct 3 months before BC/AD dates	Additional Details	# of yrs	# of yrs	# of yrs
					1 - **Nebuchadnezzar king first year of solo reign** as per custom he didn't count his co-reign with his father	5		
603	BC	3368	Y M	5	Year 5 of 70, etc.			23
					2		6	
602	BC	3369	Y M	6				24
					3 - Nebuchadnezzar		7	
601	BC	3370	Y M	7				25
					4		8	
600	BC	3371	Y M	8				26
					5 - Nebuchadnezzar		9	
599	BC	3372	Y M	9				27
					6		10	
598	BC	3373	Y M	10				28
					7 - Nebuchadnezzar "**In the seventh year**, the month of Kislev, the king of Akkad [Babylon] mustered his troops, marched to the Hatti-land, and encamped against the city of Judah and on the second day of the month of Addaru [12th] he seized the city and captured the king [Jehoiachin]. He appointed there a king of his own choice [Zedekiah], received its heavy tribute and sent them to Babylon." (BM 21946 Reverse side line 11-13; D.J. Wiseman, *Chronicles of Chaldaean Kings*, p. 73; Grayson, p. 102)	11		

Nebuchadnezzar's attacked Jerusalem in the last part of his 7th year (Jer 52:28; BM 21946 reverse side lines 12 & 13), and at the beginning of his 8th regnal year Nebuchadnezzar took Jehoiachin, his mother, and his servants back to Babylon with him and put **Zedekiah** (Mattaniah) to be king of Judah (2 Kings 24:11-17).

Year 11 of the 70 years

[Top | Flood | Abram | Exodus | David | Hezekiah | Jerusalem | JC | End Time | End Notes]

BC AD Years + or -		YM Years		*6000 Years of Mankind* Copyright © 2024 by Walter R. Dolen **Biblical Chronology Details** YM = Year of Mankind Begins in Sept/Oct 3 months before BC/AD dates	**Additional Details**	# of yrs	# of yrs	# of yrs
597	BC	3374	YM	**11 Jehoiakim/ Jehoiachin** Jehoiakim dies At the very last part of the 7th year of Nebuchadnezzar (his 7th regnal year started 6 months prior to Jehoiakim's 11th year and continued into the first 6 months of Jehoiakim's 11th), in Jehoiakim's 11th year, Jehoiakim died and his body was cast outside the gates of Jerusalem, but afterward buried (Jer 22:18-19; 36:30; 2 Kings 23:36-24:6). After Jehoiakim died in his 11th year, then **Jehoiachin** reigned for 3 months and 10 days (2 Chr 36:9). **Note:** Concerning his age, Jehoiachin was 18 years old ("son of 18 years") when he began to reign (2 Kings 24:8); not 8 years old ("son of 8 years") (2 Chron 36:9). But he was a "son" of 8 years under the influence of Nebuchadnezzar because the last half of the 11th year of Jehoiakim, was also the 8th year since Nebuchadnezzar's first assault on Jerusalem (Dan 1:1-6; 2 Chr 6-7). "And Jehoiachin the king of Judah went out to the king of Babylon, he, and his mother, and his servants, and his princes, and his officers: and the king of Babylon took him in the **eighth year** of his reign" (Kings 24:12), which is the last half of Jehoiakim's 11th year.			29
					8 - Nebuchadnezzar **Year 12 of the 70 years** *First year of Jehoiachin Captivity.* The count of the years of the captivity began in 3374 YM. **These are the same years of captivity mentioned in the book of Ezekiel** (cf. Ez. 1:2 w/ Ez. 24:1-2 & 2Ki 24:20-25:1-2; note Ezek 1:2; 8:1; 20:1; 24:1; 26:1; 29:1; 29:17; 30:20; 31:1; 32:1; 33:21) Ezekiel used the Babylon years – their year began in the Spring.	12	
596	BC	3375	YM	**1 Zedekiah [11]** Last king of Judah (2 Kings 24:18; Chr 36:10-11)			30 of 40
					9 - Nebuchadnezzar	13	
595	BC	3376	YM	2			31
					10 - Nebuchadnezzar	14	
594	BC	3377	YM	3			32
					11 - Nebuchadnezzar	15	
593	BC	3378	YM	4			33
					12 - Nebuchadnezzar	16	
592	BC	3379	YM	5 - Zedekiah			34
					13 - Nebuchadnezzar	17	
591	BC	3380	YM	6			35
					14 - Nebuchadnezzar	18	
590	BC	3381	YM	7			36

[Top | Flood | Abram | Exodus | David | Hezekiah | Jerusalem | JC | End Time | End Notes]

BC AD Years + or -		YM Years		6000 Years of Mankind Copyright © 2024 by Walter R. Dolen **Biblical Chronology Details** YM = Year of Mankind Begins in Sept/Oct 3 months before BC/AD dates	**Additional Details**	# of yrs	# of yrs	# of yrs
					15 - Nebuchadnezzar	19		
589	BC	3382	Y M	8 - **Zedekiah**				37
					16 - Nebuchadnezzar	20		
588	BC	3383	Y M	9 - Zedekiah **Jerusalem was besieged** by Nebuchadnezzar in the 9th through and into the 11th year of Zedekiah's reign (2 Kings 25:1-2; Ezek 24:1; Jer 52:5-12, 29) "In the ninth year of Zedekiah king of Judah, in the tenth month, came **Nebuchadrezzar** king of Babylon and all his army against Jerusalem, and they besieged it" (Jeremiah 39:1).	17 - Nebuchadnezzar	21		38
587	BC	3384	Y M	10				39
					18 - Nebuchadnezzar "The word that came to Jeremiah from the LORD in the tenth year of Zedekiah king of Judah, which *was* the **eighteenth year of Nebuchadrezzar**. And at that time the king of Babylon's army was besieging Jerusalem:" (Jeremiah 32:1-2) ***11th year of Jehoiachin's captivity***	22		
586	BC	3385	Y M	11 - **Zedekiah** last year **Jerusalem was burned** in the *last* part of the 11th year of Zedekiah, which was in the beginning of the 19th of Nebuchadnezzar (2 Kings 25:8ff; Jer 52:12ff) and the 11th year of Jehoiachin's captivity on the fifth month of the Hebrew calendar near the end of Zedekiah's 11 year. 40th year of Jeremiah's prophesying ends (13h year of Josiah to 11th of Zedekiah. [Jer 1:2-3; 25:3]) End of 430 years (390 + 40 = 430) of Ezek 4:1-6 Beginning of 390 years in 2960 YM Beginning of 40 years in 3346 YM	**Year 22 of the 70 years**			40

End of Judah's Kingdom

BC AD Years + or -		YM Years		6000 Years of Mankind Copyright © 2024 by Walter R. Dolen **Biblical Chronology Details** YM = Year of Mankind Begins in Sept/Oct 3 months before BC/AD dates	**Additional Details**	# of yrs	# of yrs	# of yrs
					19- Nebuchadnezzar "And in the fifth month, on the seventh *day* of the month, which *is* the **nineteenth year of king Nebuchadnezzar** king of Babylon, came Nebuzaradan, captain of the guard, a servant of the king of Babylon, unto Jerusalem: , and the king's house, and all the houses of Jerusalem, and every great *man's* house burnt he with fire. And all the army of the Chaldees, that *were with* the captain of the guard, brake down the walls of Jerusalem round about. Now the rest of the people *that were* left in the city, and the fugitives that fell away to the king of Babylon, with the remnant of the multitude, did Nebuzaradan the captain of the guard carry away" (2 Kings 25:8-11). *12th year of Jehoiachin's captivity* **Year 23 of the 70 years**	23	
585	BC	3386	YM	**Judah Under Others** **Gedaliah** made governor of the land of Judah (Jeremiah, chap. 40); Gedaliah was later killed (Jer 41:2).			
					20 - Nebuchadnezzar	24	
584	BC	3387	YM				
					21 - Nebuchadnezzar	25	
583	BC	3388	YM				
					22 - Nebuchadnezzar	26	
582	BC	3389	YM				
					23- Nebuchadnezzar Nebuzaradan took away more captives to Babylon (Jer 52:30)	27	
581	BC	3390	YM		**Year 27 of the 70 years** *16th year of Jehoiachin's captivity*		
					24 - Nebuchadnezzar	28	
580	BC	3391	YM				
					25 - Nebuchadnezzar	29	
579	BC	3392	YM				

[Top | Flood | Abram | Exodus | David | Hezekiah | Jerusalem | JC | End Time | End Notes]

BC AD Years + or -		YM Years		6000 Years of Mankind Copyright © 2024 by Walter R. Dolen **Biblical Chronology Details** YM = Year of Mankind Begins in Sept/Oct 3 months before BC/AD dates	Additional Details	# of yrs	# of yrs	# of yrs
					26 - Nebuchadnezzar	30		
578	BC	3393	Y M					
					27 - Nebuchadnezzar	31		
577	BC	3394	Y M					
					28 - Nebuchadnezzar	32		
576	BC	3395	Y M					
					29 - Nebuchadnezzar	33		
575	BC	3396	Y M					
					30 - Nebuchadnezzar	34		
574	BC	3397	Y M					
					31 - Nebuchadnezzar	35		
573	BC	3398	Y M					
					32 - Nebuchadnezzar	36		
572	BC	3399	Y M	14th year after Jerusalem' destruction	**25th year of Jehoiachin's captivity (Ezek 40:1)**			
					33 - Nebuchadnezzar	37		
571	BC	3400	Y M					
					34 - Nebuchadnezzar	38		
570	BC	3401	Y M					
					35 - Nebuchadnezzar	39		
569	BC	3402	Y M		Year 39 of the 70 years			
					36 - Nebuchadnezzar	40		
568	BC	3403	Y M					
				Absolute BC/AD Date see text	37- Nebuchadnezzar **Absolute Date** **in the 37th year of** **Nebuchadnezzar** there is evidence from the **astronomical cuneiform tablet** VAT 4956 that the 37th year was from 568 to 567 BC (see CP3 for details). This is our connection between the Christian Era (BC-AD) system and the Year of Man (YM) system. **Year 41 of the 70 years**	41		
567	BC	3404	Y M	Dates in this shaded area are absolute because of the astronomical tablet (VAT 4956) indicates that this is *an* absolute BC date and because the ruling years of the Nebuchadnezzar and the years of the Hebrew Biblical Judean kings complement each other. **Absolute BC/AD Date** see text				

BC AD Years + or -		YM Years		**6000 Years of Mankind** Copyright © 2024 by Walter R. Dolen **Biblical Chronology Details** YM = Year of Mankind Begins in Sept/Oct 3 months before BC/AD dates	**Additional Details**	# of yrs	# of yrs	# of yrs
					38 - Nebuchadnezzar	42		
566	BC	3405	YM		39 - Nebuchadnezzar	43		
565	BC	3406	YM		40 - Nebuchadnezzar	44		
564	BC	3407	YM		41 - Nebuchadnezzar	45		
563	BC	3408	YM		42 - Nebuchadnezzar	46		
562	BC	3409	YM		**43 - Nebuchadnezzar Last year** Year 47 of 70	47		
561	BC	3410	YM					
560	BC	3411	YM		**1- Evil-Merodach 1st year** [2] takes Jehoiachin out of prison in the 37th year of Jehoiachin's captivity (Jer 52:31; 2 Kings 25:27). **Evil-Merodach** takes Jehoiachin out of prison in the 37th year of Jehoiachin's captivity, which was "in the year" that Evil-Merodach "began to reign," 3409 ½ - 3411 ½ YM (Jer 52:31; 2 Kings 25:27). The Parker & Dubberstein's *Babylonian Chronology 626- B.C. - A,D. 75*, p. 28, shows the year was 561-560 BC. **Year 48 of the 70 years** *37th year of Jehoiachin's captivity*	48		
					2 - Evil-Merodach last year	49		
559	BC	3412	YM		1 - **Nergal-shar-usur** [4]	50 of 70		

BC AD Years + or -		YM Years		6000 Years of Mankind Copyright © 2024 by Walter R. Dolen **Biblical Chronology Details** YM = Year of Mankind Begins in Sept/Oct 3 months before BC/AD dates	**Additional Details**	# of yrs	# of yrs	# of yrs
558	BC	3413	Y M					
					2 - Nergal-shar-usur	51		
557	BC	3414	Y M					
					3 - Nergal-shar-usur	52		
556	BC	3415	Y M					
					4 - Nergal-shar-usur	53		
555	BC	3416	Y M			1 **Nabonidus** [17] Year 54 of the 70 years	54		
554	BC	3417	Y M			The Parker & Dubberstein's *Babylonian Chronology 626-B.C. - A,D.* 75, p. 29, shows the year was 555-554 BC.			
					2 Nabonidus	55		
553	BC	3418	Y M			3 Nabonidus	56		
552	BC	3419	Y M			4 Nabonidus	57		
551	BC	3420	Y M			Year 57 of the 70 years			
					5 Nabonidus	58		
550	BC	3421	Y M			6 Nabonidus	59		
549	BC	3422	Y M	**Belshazzar co-reign** (See Nabonidus Chronicle [BM35382, col II])	7 Nabonidus **Belshazzar co-reign** (See Nabonidus Chronicle [BM35382, col II])	60 of 70		
548	BC	3423	Y M					
					8 Nabonidus (Belshazzar co-reign) Year 61 of the 70 years	61		
547	BC	3424	Y M			9 Nabonidus (Belshazzar co-reign)	62		
546	BC	3425	Y M			10 Nabonidus (Belshazzar co-reign)	63		
545	BC	3426	Y M			11 Nabonidus (Belshazzar co-reign)	64		
544	BC	3427	Y M			12 Nabonidus (Belshazzar co-reign)	65		
543	BC	3428	Y M			(Belshazzar co-reign) Year 65 of the 70 years			

BC AD Years + or -		YM Years		6000 Years of Mankind Copyright © 2024 by Walter R. Dolen **Biblical Chronology Details** YM = Year of Mankind Begins in Sept/Oct 3 months before BC/AD dates	Additional Details	# of yrs	# of yrs	# of yrs
					13 Nabonidus (Belshazzar co-reign)	66		
542	BC	3429	YM		14 Nabonidus (Belshazzar co-reign)	67		
541	BC	3430	YM		15 Nabonidus (Belshazzar co-reign)	68		
540	BC	3431	YM		16 Nabonidus (Belshazzar co-reign) Year 69 of the 70 years	69		
539	BC	3432	YM	"[1] The date 539 for the Fall of Babylon has been reckoned from the latest dates on the contracts of each king in this period, counting from the end of Nabopolassar's reign in 605 B.C., *viz.*, Nebuchadrezzar, 43: Amel-Marduk, 2: Nergal-shar-usur, 4: Labashi-Marduk (accession only): Nabonidus, 17 = 66 (Clay, *Pennsylv. Bab. Exp.*, Series A, VIII, 4. See also Pinches, *T.S.B.A.* VI, 486;" *Cambridge Ancient History*, Vol. III, 1929, p. 224, footnote 1).	17 - Nabonidus last year (Belshazzar co-reign) begins in the Spring of 539 BC (April) [see *Babylonian Chronology*; Parker & Dubberstein, p. 29]	70		
538	BC	3433	YM	**See paragraph cp202-206 in the *6000 Years of Mankind* to understand the accessional year method of counting regnal years**	**Year 70 of 70** Go to the Beginning of 70 **Fall of Babylon** Cyrus / Darius the Mede *accessional* year in Nabonidus' 17th year **1 Cyrus/Darius the Mede** Cyrus / Darius' first *official* year begins in spring of 538 (accessional year counting method) [see *Babylonian Chronology*, by Parker & Dubberstein, p. 29]			
537	BC	3434	YM		2 - Cyrus			
536	BC	3435	YM		3 - Cyrus			
535	BC	3436	YM		4 - Cyrus			
534	BC	3437	YM		5 - Cyrus			
533	BC	3438	YM		6 - Cyrus			
532	BC	3439	YM		7 - Cyrus			
531	BC	3440	YM		8 - Cyrus			

BC AD Years + or -		YM Years		*6000 Years of Mankind* Copyright © 2024 by Walter R. Dolen **Biblical Chronology Details** YM = Year of Mankind Begins in Sept/Oct 3 months before BC/AD dates	**Additional Details**	# of yrs	# of yrs	# of yrs
530	BC	3441	Y M					
					9 - Cyrus			
529	BC	3442	Y M					
					1 - Cambyses (1ˢᵗ King of Dan 11:2) The Parker & Dubberstein's *Babylonian Chronology 626-B.C. - A.D. 75*, p. 30, shows the year was 529-528 BC.			
528	BC	3443	Y M					
					2 - Cambyses			
527	BC	3444	Y M					
					3 - Cambyses			
526	BC	3445	Y M					
					4 - Cambyses			
525	BC	3446	Y M					
					5 - Cambyses			
524	BC	3447	Y M					
					6 - Cambyses			
523	BC	3448	Y M	Some information on this tablet is found in the 1976, *Ancient Planetary Observations and the Validity of Ephemeris Time,*, by Robert R. Newton. (pp. 110, 131, 135, 139, 144, 503, 513, 523, 711-715). Also see text in our book.				
					7 - Cambyses **Astronomical Tablet** The tablet that describes the 7th year (523-522 BC) of Kambyses (Cambyses) with various astronomical positions is found in Franz Xaver Kugler's *Sternkunde und Sterndienst in Babel*, published in 1907, pages 70-71.			
522	BC	3449	Y M					
					8 - Cambyses (1ˢᵗ King of Dan 11:2) began in the spring of 522 BC			
521	BC	3450	Y M					

BC AD Years + or -		YM Years		6000 Years of Mankind Copyright © 2024 by Walter R. Dolen **Biblical Chronology Details** YM = Year of Mankind Begins in Sept/Oct 3 months before BC/AD dates	**Additional Details**	# of yrs	# of yrs	# of yrs
520	BC	3451	Y M	**Darius l** first *official* year of reign began in 521 Begins in the spring of 521 BC (*Babylonian Chronology*, p. 30).	**Bardiya** (2ⁿᵈ King of Dan 11:2) claimed kingship **Darius l** begins his **first** *official* **regnal year** in the sping of 521 BC. (3ʳᵈ king of Dan 11:2) The Parker & Dubberstein's *Babylonian Chronology 626- B.C. - A.D. 75*, p. 30, shows the year was 521-520 BC. 2			
519	BC	3452	Y M		3			
518	BC	3453	Y M		4			
517	BC	3454	Y M		5			
516	BC	3455	Y M		6			
515	BC	3456	Y M		7			
514	BC	3457	Y M		8			
513	BC	3458	Y M		9			
512	BC	3459	Y M		10			
511	BC	3460	Y M		11			
510	BC	3461	Y M		12			
509	BC	3462	Y M		13			
508	BC	3463	Y M		14			
507	BC	3464	Y M		15			
506	BC	3465	Y M		16			
505	BC	3466	Y M		17			

BC AD Years + or -		YM Years		**6000 Years of Mankind** Copyright © 2024 by Walter R. Dolen **Biblical Chronology Details** YM = Year of Mankind Begins in Sept/Oct 3 months before BC/AD dates	**Additional Details**	# of yrs	# of yrs	# of yrs
504	BC	3467	Y M		18			
503	BC	3468	Y M		19			
502	BC	3469	Y M		20			
501	BC	3470	Y M		21			
500	BC	3471	Y M		22			
499	BC	3472	Y M		23			
498	BC	3473	Y M		24			
497	BC	3474	Y M		25			
496	BC	3475	Y M		26			
495	BC	3476	Y M		27			
494	BC	3477	Y M		28			
493	BC	3478	Y M		29			
492	BC	3479	Y M		30			
491	BC	3480	Y M		31			
490	BC	3481	Y M		32			
489	BC	3482	Y M		33			
488	BC	3483	Y M		34			
487	BC	3484	Y M		35			
486	BC	3485	Y M		36 - Darius l (last year)			
485	BC	3486	Y M	Spelling: Xerxes = Gk ; **Ahasuerus = Heb ;** Khsayarsan = Old Persian; Ahsiarsu = Akkadian				

[Top | Flood | Abram | Exodus | David | Hezekiah | Jerusalem | JC | End Time | End Notes]

BC AD Years + or -		YM Years		6000 Years of Mankind Copyright © 2024 by Walter R. Dolen Biblical Chronology Details YM = Year of Mankind Begins in Sept/Oct 3 months before BC/AD dates	Additional Details	# of yrs	# of yrs	# of yrs
					1 - **Xerses** (**Ahasuerus**) (4th King of Dan 11:2) The Parker & Dubberstein's *Babylonian Chronology 626-B.C. - A.D.* 75, p. 31, shows the year was 485-484 BC.			
484	BC	3487	Y M					
					2			
483	BC	3488	Y M					
					3			
482	BC	3489	Y M					
					4			
481	BC	3490	Y M					
					5			
480	BC	3491	Y M					
					6 -			
479	BC	3492	Y M	Invasion of Greece (4th King of Dan 11:2)				
					7 **Xerxes l** **Queen Esther** (Est. 2:16ff) The Parker & Dubberstein's *Babylonian Chronology 626-B.C. - A.D.* 75, p. 31, shows the year was 479-478 BC.			
478	BC	3493	Y M					
					8			
477	BC	3494	Y M					
					9			
476	BC	3495	Y M					
					10			
475	BC	3496	Y M					
					11			
474	BC	3497	Y M					
					12			
473	BC	3498	Y M					
					13			
472	BC	3499	Y M					
					14			
471	BC	3500	Y M					
					15			
470	BC	3501	Y M					
					16			
469	BC	3502	Y M					
					17			

BC AD Years + or -		YM Years		6000 Years of Mankind Copyright © 2024 by Walter R. Dolen **Biblical Chronology Details** YM = Year of Mankind Begins in Sept/Oct 3 months before BC/AD dates	Additional Details	# of yrs	# of yrs	# of yrs
468	BC	3503	Y M					
467	BC	3504	Y M		18			
466	BC	3505	Y M		19			
465	BC	3506	Y M		20			
464	BC	3507	Y M		21 Xerxes (last year)			
463	BC	3508	Y M		1 - Artaxerxes I			
462	BC	3509	Y M		2			
461	BC	3510	Y M		3			
460	BC	3511	Y M		4 - Artaxerxes I			
459	BC	3512	Y M		5 - Artaxerxes I			
458	BC	3513	Y M		6			
					7 Artaxerxes I **The announcement of the 70 weeks of years** declared in this year; the count of years start in the next year. (Ezra 7:7, 12-13ff; Daniel 9:24-25) The Parker & Dubberstein's *Babylonian Chronology 626-B.C. - A.D. 75*, p. 32, shows the year was 458-457 BC.		1 of 483 yrs	
457	BC	3514	Y M	**First year of Daniels count of 69 sevens of years. Beginning of the 69 weeks of years or 483 years from his 7th year** (Ezra 7:7, 12-13ff; Daniel 9:24-25) This count of years begins in the fall of 458.			2	
456	BC	3515	Y M				3	
455	BC	3516	Y M				4	
454	BC	3517	Y M				5	
453	BC	3518	Y M				6	

BC AD Years + or -		YM Years		6000 Years of Mankind Copyright © 2024 by Walter R. Dolen **Biblical Chronology Details** YM = Year of Mankind Begins in Sept/Oct 3 months before BC/AD dates	Additional Details	# of yrs	# of yrs	# of yrs
				[Top | Flood | Abram | Exodus | David | Hezekiah | Jerusalem | JC | End Time | End Notes]				
452	BC	3519	Y M				7	
451	BC	3520	Y M				8	
450	BC	3521	Y M				9	
449	BC	3522	Y M				10	
448	BC	3523	Y M				11	
447	BC	3524	Y M				12	
446	BC	3525	Y M				13	
445	BC	3526	Y M				14	
444	BC	3527	Y M				15	
443	BC	3528	Y M				16	
442	BC	3529	Y M				17	
441	BC	3530	Y M				18	
440	BC	3531	Y M				19	
439	BC	3532	Y M				20	
438	BC	3533	Y M				21	
437	BC	3534	Y M				22	
436	BC	3535	Y M				23	
435	BC	3536	Y M				24	
434	BC	3537	Y M				25	
433	BC	3538	Y M				26	

[Top | Flood | Abram | Exodus | David | Hezekiah | Jerusalem | JC | End Time | End Notes]

BC AD Years + or -		YM Years		**6000 Years of Mankind** Copyright © 2024 by Walter R. Dolen **Biblical Chronology Details** YM = Year of Mankind Begins in Sept/Oct 3 months before BC/AD dates	**Additional Details**	# of yrs	# of yrs	# of yrs
432	BC	3539	Y M				27	
431	BC	3540	Y M				28	
430	BC	3541	Y M				29	
429	BC	3542	Y M				30	
428	BC	3543	Y M				31	
427	BC	3544	Y M				32	
426	BC	3545	Y M				33	
425	BC	3546	Y M				34	
424	BC	3547	Y M				35	
423	BC	3548	Y M				36	
422	BC	3549	Y M				37	
421	BC	3550	Y M				38	
420	BC	3551	Y M				39	
419	BC	3552	Y M				40	
418	BC	3553	Y M				41	
417	BC	3554	Y M				42	
416	BC	3555	Y M				43	
415	BC	3556	Y M				44	
414	BC	3557	Y M				45	
413	BC	3558	Y M				46	

BC AD Years + or -		YM Years		6000 Years of Mankind Copyright © 2024 by Walter R. Dolen **Biblical Chronology Details** YM = Year of Mankind Begins in Sept/Oct 3 months before BC/AD dates	Additional Details	# of yrs	# of yrs	# of yrs
412	BC	3559	Y M				47	
411	BC	3560	Y M				48	
410	BC	3561	Y M				49	
409	BC	3562	Y M				50	
408	BC	3563	Y M				51	
407	BC	3564	Y M				52	
406	BC	3565	Y M				53	
405	BC	3566	Y M				54	
404	BC	3567	Y M				55	
403	BC	3568	Y M				56	
402	BC	3569	Y M				57	
401	BC	3570	Y M				58	
400	BC	3571	Y M				59	
399	BC	3572	Y M				60	
398	BC	3573	Y M				61	
397	BC	3574	Y M				62	
396	BC	3575	Y M				63	
395	BC	3576	Y M				64	
394	BC	3577	Y M				65	
393	BC	3578	Y M				66	

BC AD Years + or -		YM Years		6000 Years of Mankind Copyright © 2024 by Walter R. Dolen **Biblical Chronology Details** YM = Year of Mankind Begins in Sept/Oct 3 months before BC/AD dates	Additional Details	# of yrs	# of yrs	# of yrs
392	BC	3579	Y M				67	
391	BC	3580	Y M				68	
390	BC	3581	Y M				69	
389	BC	3582	Y M				70	
388	BC	3583	Y M				71	
387	BC	3584	Y M				72	
386	BC	3585	Y M				73	
385	BC	3586	Y M				74	
384	BC	3587	Y M				75	
383	BC	3588	Y M				76	
382	BC	3589	Y M				77	
381	BC	3590	Y M				78	
380	BC	3591	Y M				79	
379	BC	3592	Y M				80	
378	BC	3593	Y M				81	
377	BC	3594	Y M				82	
376	BC	3595	Y M				83	
375	BC	3596	Y M				84	
374	BC	3597	Y M				85	
373	BC	3598	Y M				86	

[Top | Flood | Abram | Exodus | David | Hezekiah | Jerusalem | JC | End Time | End Notes]

BC AD Years + or -		YM Years		6000 Years of Mankind Copyright © 2024 by Walter R. Dolen **Biblical Chronology Details** YM = Year of Mankind Begins in Sept/Oct 3 months before BC/AD dates	Additional Details	# of yrs	# of yrs	# of yrs
372	BC	3599	Y M				87	
371	BC	3600	Y M				88	
370	BC	3601	Y M				89	
369	BC	3602	Y M				90	
368	BC	3603	Y M				91	
367	BC	3604	Y M				92	
366	BC	3605	Y M				93	
365	BC	3606	Y M				94	
364	BC	3607	Y M				95	
363	BC	3608	Y M				96	
362	BC	3609	Y M				97	
361	BC	3610	Y M				98	
360	BC	3611	Y M				99	
359	BC	3612	Y M				100	
358	BC	3613	Y M				101	
357	BC	3614	Y M				102	
356	BC	3615	Y M				103	
355	BC	3616	Y M				104	
354	BC	3617	Y M				105	
353	BC	3618	Y M				106	

[Top | Flood | Abram | Exodus | David | Hezekiah | Jerusalem | JC | End Time | End Notes]

BC AD Years + or -		YM Years		**6000 Years of Mankind** Copyright © 2024 by Walter R. Dolen **Biblical Chronology Details** YM = Year of Mankind Begins in Sept/Oct 3 months before BC/AD dates	**Additional Details**	# of yrs	# of yrs	# of yrs
352	BC	3619	Y M				107	
351	BC	3620	Y M				108	
350	BC	3621	Y M				109	
349	BC	3622	Y M				110	
348	BC	3623	Y M				111	
347	BC	3624	Y M				112	
346	BC	3625	Y M				113	
345	BC	3626	Y M				114	
344	BC	3627	Y M				115	
343	BC	3628	Y M				116	
342	BC	3629	Y M				117	
341	BC	3630	Y M				118	
340	BC	3631	Y M				119	
339	BC	3632	Y M				120	
338	BC	3633	Y M				121	
337	BC	3634	Y M				122	
336	BC	3635	Y M				123	
335	BC	3636	Y M				124	
334	BC	3637	Y M				125	
333	BC	3638	Y M				126	

BC AD Years + or -		YM Years		6000 Years of Mankind Copyright © 2024 by Walter R. Dolen **Biblical Chronology Details** YM = Year of Mankind Begins in Sept/Oct 3 months before BC/AD dates	Additional Details	# of yrs	# of yrs	# of yrs
332	BC	3639	YM				127	
331	BC	3640	YM				128	
330	BC	3641	YM				129	
329	BC	3642	YM				130	
328	BC	3643	YM				131	
327	BC	3644	YM				132	
326	BC	3645	YM				133	
325	BC	3646	YM				134	
324	BC	3647	YM				135	
323	BC	3648	YM				136	
322	BC	3649	YM				137	
321	BC	3650	YM				138	
320	BC	3651	YM				139	
319	BC	3652	YM				140	
318	BC	3653	YM				141	
317	BC	3654	YM				142	
316	BC	3655	YM				143	
315	BC	3656	YM				144	
314	BC	3657	YM				145	
313	BC	3658	YM				146	

BC AD Years + or -		YM Years		**6000 Years of Mankind** Copyright © 2024 by Walter R. Dolen **Biblical Chronology Details** YM = Year of Mankind Begins in Sept/Oct 3 months before BC/AD dates	**Additional Details**	# of yrs	# of yrs	# of yrs
312	BC	3659	Y M				147	
311	BC	3660	Y M				148	
310	BC	3661	Y M				149	
309	BC	3662	Y M				150	
308	BC	3663	Y M				151	
307	BC	3664	Y M				152	
306	BC	3665	Y M				153	
305	BC	3666	Y M				154	
304	BC	3667	Y M				155	
303	BC	3668	Y M				156	
302	BC	3669	Y M				157	
301	BC	3670	Y M				158	
300	BC	3671	Y M				159	
299	BC	3672	Y M				160	
298	BC	3673	Y M				161	
297	BC	3674	Y M				162	
296	BC	3675	Y M				163	
295	BC	3676	Y M				164	
294	BC	3677	Y M				165	
293	BC	3678	Y M				166	

[Top | Flood | Abram | Exodus | David | Hezekiah | Jerusalem | JC | End Time | End Notes]

BC AD Years + or -		YM Years		6000 Years of Mankind Copyright © 2024 by Walter R. Dolen **Biblical Chronology Details** YM = Year of Mankind Begins in Sept/Oct 3 months before BC/AD dates	Additional Details	# of yrs	# of yrs	# of yrs
292	BC	3679	YM				167	
291	BC	3680	YM				168	
290	BC	3681	YM				169	
289	BC	3682	YM				170	
288	BC	3683	YM				171	
287	BC	3684	YM				172	
286	BC	3685	YM				173	
285	BC	3686	YM				174	
284	BC	3687	YM				175	
283	BC	3688	YM				176	
282	BC	3689	YM				177	
281	BC	3690	YM				178	
280	BC	3691	YM				179	
279	BC	3692	YM				180	
278	BC	3693	YM				181	
277	BC	3694	YM				182	
276	BC	3695	YM				183	
275	BC	3696	YM				184	
274	BC	3697	YM				185	
273	BC	3698	YM				186	

BC AD Years + or -		YM Years		6000 Years of Mankind Copyright © 2024 by Walter R. Dolen **Biblical Chronology Details** YM = Year of Mankind Begins in Sept/Oct 3 months before BC/AD dates	Additional Details	# of yrs	# of yrs	# of yrs
272	BC	3699	Y M				187	
271	BC	3700	Y M				188	
270	BC	3701	Y M				189	
269	BC	3702	Y M				190	
268	BC	3703	Y M				191	
267	BC	3704	Y M				192	
266	BC	3705	Y M				193	
265	BC	3706	Y M				194	
264	BC	3707	Y M				195	
263	BC	3708	Y M				196	
262	BC	3709	Y M				197	
261	BC	3710	Y M				198	
260	BC	3711	Y M				199	
259	BC	3712	Y M				200	
258	BC	3713	Y M				201	
257	BC	3714	Y M				202	
256	BC	3715	Y M				203	
255	BC	3716	Y M				204	
254	BC	3717	Y M				205	
253	BC	3718	Y M				206	

[Top | Flood | Abram | Exodus | David | Hezekiah | Jerusalem | JC | End Time | End Notes]

BC AD Years + or -		YM Years		6000 Years of Mankind Copyright © 2024 by Walter R. Dolen **Biblical Chronology Details** YM = Year of Mankind Begins in Sept/Oct 3 months before BC/AD dates	Additional Details	# of yrs	# of yrs	# of yrs
252	BC	3719	Y M				207	
251	BC	3720	Y M				208	
250	BC	3721	Y M				209	
249	BC	3722	Y M				210	
248	BC	3723	Y M				211	
247	BC	3724	Y M				212	
246	BC	3725	Y M				213	
245	BC	3726	Y M				214	
244	BC	3727	Y M				215	
243	BC	3728	Y M				216	
242	BC	3729	Y M				217	
241	BC	3730	Y M				218	
240	BC	3731	Y M				219	
239	BC	3732	Y M				220	
238	BC	3733	Y M				221	
237	BC	3734	Y M				222	
236	BC	3735	Y M				223	
235	BC	3736	Y M				224	
234	BC	3737	Y M				225	
233	BC	3738	Y M				226	

[Top | Flood | Abram | Exodus | David | Hezekiah | Jerusalem | JC | End Time | End Notes]

BC AD Years + or -		YM Years		**6000 Years of Mankind** Copyright © 2024 by Walter R. Dolen **Biblical Chronology Details** YM = Year of Mankind Begins in Sept/Oct 3 months before BC/AD dates	Additional Details	# of yrs	# of yrs	# of yrs
232	BC	3739	Y M				227	
231	BC	3740	Y M				228	
230	BC	3741	Y M				229	
229	BC	3742	Y M				230	
228	BC	3743	Y M				231	
227	BC	3744	Y M				232	
226	BC	3745	Y M				233	
225	BC	3746	Y M				234	
224	BC	3747	Y M				235	
223	BC	3748	Y M				236	
222	BC	3749	Y M				237	
221	BC	3750	Y M				238	
220	BC	3751	Y M				239	
219	BC	3752	Y M				240	
218	BC	3753	Y M				241	
217	BC	3754	Y M				242	
216	BC	3755	Y M				243	
215	BC	3756	Y M				244	
214	BC	3757	Y M				245	
213	BC	3758	Y M				246	

[Top | Flood | Abram | Exodus | David | Hezekiah | Jerusalem | JC | End Time | End Notes]

BC AD Years + or -		YM Years		6000 Years of Mankind Copyright © 2024 by Walter R. Dolen **Biblical Chronology Details** YM = Year of Mankind Begins in Sept/Oct 3 months before BC/AD dates	Additional Details	# of yrs	# of yrs	# of yrs
212	BC	3759	YM				247	
211	BC	3760	YM				248	
210	BC	3761	YM				249	
209	BC	3762	YM				250	
208	BC	3763	YM				251	
207	BC	3764	YM				252	
206	BC	3765	YM				253	
205	BC	3766	YM				254	
204	BC	3767	YM				255	
203	BC	3768	YM				256	
202	BC	3769	YM				257	
201	BC	3770	YM				258	
200	BC	3771	YM				259	
199	BC	3772	YM				260	
198	BC	3773	YM				261	
197	BC	3774	YM				262	
196	BC	3775	YM				263	
195	BC	3776	YM				264	
194	BC	3777	YM				265	
193	BC	3778	YM				266	

BC AD Years + or -		YM Years		6000 Years of Mankind Copyright © 2024 by Walter R. Dolen **Biblical Chronology Details** YM = Year of Mankind Begins in Sept/Oct 3 months before BC/AD dates	Additional Details	# of yrs	# of yrs	# of yrs
192	BC	3779	Y M				267	
191	BC	3780	Y M				268	
190	BC	3781	Y M				269	
189	BC	3782	Y M				270	
188	BC	3783	Y M				271	
187	BC	3784	Y M				272	
186	BC	3785	Y M				273	
185	BC	3786	Y M				274	
184	BC	3787	Y M				275	
183	BC	3788	Y M				276	
182	BC	3789	Y M				277	
181	BC	3790	Y M				278	
180	BC	3791	Y M				279	
179	BC	3792	Y M				280	
178	BC	3793	Y M				281	
177	BC	3794	Y M				282	
176	BC	3795	Y M				283	
175	BC	3796	Y M				284	
174	BC	3797	Y M				285	
173	BC	3798	Y M				286	

BC AD Years + or -		YM Years		6000 Years of Mankind Copyright © 2024 by Walter R. Dolen **Biblical Chronology Details** YM = Year of Mankind Begins in Sept/Oct 3 months before BC/AD dates	Additional Details	# of yrs	# of yrs	# of yrs
172	BC	3799	Y M				287	
171	BC	3800	Y M				288	
170	BC	3801	Y M				289	
169	BC	3802	Y M				290	
168	BC	3803	Y M				291	
167	BC	3804	Y M				292	
166	BC	3805	Y M				293	
165	BC	3806	Y M				294	
164	BC	3807	Y M				295	
163	BC	3808	Y M				296	
162	BC	3809	Y M				297	
161	BC	3810	Y M				298	
160	BC	3811	Y M				299	
159	BC	3812	Y M				300	
158	BC	3813	Y M				301	
157	BC	3814	Y M				302	
156	BC	3815	Y M				303	
155	BC	3816	Y M				304	
154	BC	3817	Y M				305	
153	BC	3818	Y M				306	

BC AD Years + or -		YM Years		6000 Years of Mankind Copyright © 2024 by Walter R. Dolen Biblical Chronology Details YM = Year of Mankind Begins in Sept/Oct 3 months before BC/AD dates	Additional Details	# of yrs	# of yrs	# of yrs
				[Top | Flood | Abram | Exodus | David | Hezekiah | Jerusalem | JC | End Time | End Notes]				
152	BC	3819	Y M				307	
151	BC	3820	Y M				308	
150	BC	3821	Y M				309	
149	BC	3822	Y M				310	
148	BC	3823	Y M				311	
147	BC	3824	Y M				312	
146	BC	3825	Y M				313	
145	BC	3826	Y M				314	
144	BC	3827	Y M				315	
143	BC	3828	Y M				316	
142	BC	3829	Y M				317	
141	BC	3830	Y M				318	
140	BC	3831	Y M				319	
139	BC	3832	Y M				320	
138	BC	3833	Y M				321	
137	BC	3834	Y M				322	
136	BC	3835	Y M				323	
135	BC	3836	Y M				324	
134	BC	3837	Y M				325	
133	BC	3838	Y M				326	

[Top | Flood | Abram | Exodus | David | Hezekiah | Jerusalem | JC | End Time | End Notes]

BC AD Years + or -		YM Years		6000 Years of Mankind Copyright © 2024 by Walter R. Dolen **Biblical Chronology Details** YM = Year of Mankind Begins in Sept/Oct 3 months before BC/AD dates	Additional Details	# of yrs	# of yrs	# of yrs
132	BC	3839	YM				327	
131	BC	3840	YM				328	
130	BC	3841	YM				329	
129	BC	3842	YM				330	
128	BC	3843	YM				331	
127	BC	3844	YM				332	
126	BC	3845	YM				333	
125	BC	3846	YM				334	
124	BC	3847	YM				335	
123	BC	3848	YM				336	
122	BC	3849	YM				337	
121	BC	3850	YM				338	
120	BC	3851	YM				339	
119	BC	3852	YM				340	
118	BC	3853	YM				341	
117	BC	3854	YM				342	
116	BC	3855	YM				343	
115	BC	3856	YM				344	
114	BC	3857	YM				345	
113	BC	3858	YM				346	

BC AD Years + or -		YM Years		**6000 Years of Mankind** Copyright © 2024 by Walter R. Dolen **Biblical Chronology Details** YM = Year of Mankind Begins in Sept/Oct 3 months before BC/AD dates	**Additional Details**	# of yrs	# of yrs	# of yrs
112	BC	3859	Y M				347	
111	BC	3860	Y M				348	
110	BC	3861	Y M				349	
109	BC	3862	Y M				350	
108	BC	3863	Y M				351	
107	BC	3864	Y M				352	
106	BC	3865	Y M				353	
105	BC	3866	Y M				354	
104	BC	3867	Y M				355	
103	BC	3868	Y M				356	
102	BC	3869	Y M				357	
101	BC	3870	Y M				358	
100	BC	3871	Y M				359	
99	BC	3872	Y M				360	
98	BC	3873	Y M				361	
97	BC	3874	Y M				362	
96	BC	3875	Y M				363	
95	BC	3876	Y M				364	
94	BC	3877	Y M				365	
93	BC	3878	Y M				366	

[Top | Flood | Abram | Exodus | David | Hezekiah | Jerusalem | JC | End Time | End Notes]

BC AD Years + or -		YM Years		**6000 Years of Mankind** Copyright © 2024 by Walter R. Dolen **Biblical Chronology Details** YM = Year of Mankind Begins in Sept/Oct 3 months before BC/AD dates	**Additional Details**	# of yrs	# of yrs	# of yrs
92	BC	3879	Y M				367	
91	BC	3880	Y M				368	
90	BC	3881	Y M				369	
89	BC	3882	Y M				370	
88	BC	3883	Y M				371	
87	BC	3884	Y M				372	
86	BC	3885	Y M				373	
85	BC	3886	Y M				374	
84	BC	3887	Y M				375	
83	BC	3888	Y M				376	
82	BC	3889	Y M				377	
81	BC	3890	Y M				378	
80	BC	3891	Y M				379	
79	BC	3892	Y M				380	
78	BC	3893	Y M				381	
77	BC	3894	Y M				382	
76	BC	3895	Y M				383	
75	BC	3896	Y M				384	
74	BC	3897	Y M				385	
73	BC	3898	Y M				386	

			6000 Years of Mankind Copyright © 2024 by Walter R. Dolen **Biblical Chronology Details** YM = Year of Mankind Begins in Sept/Oct 3 months before BC/AD dates	Additional Details	# of yrs	# of yrs	# of yrs
BC AD Years + or -		YM Years					
72	BC	3899	Y M				387	
71	BC	3900	Y M				388	
70	BC	3901	Y M				389	
69	BC	3902	Y M				390	
68	BC	3903	Y M				391	
67	BC	3904	Y M				392	
66	BC	3905	Y M				393	
65	BC	3906	Y M				394	
64	BC	3907	Y M				395	
63	BC	3908	Y M				396	
62	BC	3909	Y M				397	
61	BC	3910	Y M				398	
60	BC	3911	Y M				399	
59	BC	3912	Y M				400	
58	BC	3913	Y M				401	
57	BC	3914	Y M				402	
56	BC	3915	Y M				403	
55	BC	3916	Y M				404	
54	BC	3917	Y M				405	
53	BC	3918	Y M				406	

[Top | Flood | Abram | Exodus | David | Hezekiah | Jerusalem | JC | End Time | End Notes]

BC AD Years + or -		YM Years		6000 Years of Mankind Copyright © 2024 by Walter R. Dolen Biblical Chronology Details YM = Year of Mankind Begins in Sept/Oct 3 months before BC/AD dates	Additional Details	# of yrs	# of yrs	# of yrs
52	BC	3919	Y M				407	
51	BC	3920	Y M				408	
50	BC	3921	Y M				409	
49	BC	3922	Y M				410	
48	BC	3923	Y M				411	
47	BC	3924	Y M				412	
46	BC	3925	Y M				413	
45	BC	3926	Y M				414	
44	BC	3927	Y M				415	
43	BC	3928	Y M				416	
42	BC	3929	Y M				417	
41	BC	3930	Y M				418	
40	BC	3931	Y M				419	
39	BC	3932	Y M				420	
38	BC	3933	Y M				421	
37	BC	3934	Y M				422	
36	BC	3935	Y M				423	
35	BC	3936	Y M				424	
34	BC	3937	Y M				425	
33	BC	3938	Y M				426	

[Top	Flood	Abram	Exodus	David	Hezekiah	Jerusalem	JC	End Time	End Notes]									

BC AD Years + or -		YM Years		**6000 Years of Mankind** Copyright © 2024 by Walter R. Dolen **Biblical Chronology Details** YM = Year of Mankind Begins in Sept/Oct 3 months before BC/AD dates	**Additional Details**	# of yrs	# of yrs	# of yrs
32	BC	3939	Y M				427	
31	BC	3940	Y M				428	
30	BC	3941	Y M				429	
29	BC	3942	Y M				430	
28	BC	3943	Y M				431	
27	BC	3944	Y M				432	
26	BC	3945	Y M				433	
25	BC	3946	Y M				434	
24	BC	3947	Y M				435	
23	BC	3948	Y M				436	
22	BC	3949	Y M				437	
21	BC	3950	Y M				438	
20	BC	3951	Y M				439	
19	BC	3952	Y M				440	
18	BC	3953	Y M				441	
17	BC	3954	Y M				442	
16	BC	3955	Y M				443	
15	BC	3956	Y M				444	
14	BC	3957	Y M				445	
13	BC	3958	Y M				446	

[Top | Flood | Abram | Exodus | David | Hezekiah | Jerusalem | JC | End Time | End Notes]

BC AD Years + or -		YM Years		6000 Years of Mankind Copyright © 2024 by Walter R. Dolen **Biblical Chronology Details** YM = Year of Mankind Begins in Sept/Oct 3 months before BC/AD dates	Additional Details	# of yrs	# of yrs	# of yrs
12	BC	3959	Y M				447	
11	BC	3960	Y M				448	
10	BC	3961	Y M				449	
9	BC	3962	Y M				450	
8		3963					451	
7		3964					452	
6	BC	3965	Y M				453	
5		3966					454	
4	BC	3967	Y M	1- Jesus Christ first year (started in the fall of 5 BC) **Yehoshua (Jesus) born** Herod was king when Jesus was born (Matt 2:1). Herod died between an eclipse of the moon and a Passover in 4 BC. (See Jack Finegan, *Handbook of Biblical Chronology*, pp 294-295[paragraph 504]Revised Ed. 1998)			455	
3	BC	3968	Y M	2			456	
2	BC	3969	Y M	3-			457	
1	BC	3970	Y M	4-			458	
1	A D	3971	Y M	5			459	
2	A D	3972	Y M	6 - Yehoshua (Jesus Christ)			460	
3	A D	3973	Y M	7			461	
4	A D	3974	Y M	8 -			462	
5	A D	3975	Y M	9 -			463	
6	A D	3976	Y M	10 -			464	
7	A D	3977	Y M	11- Yehoshua (Jesus Christ)			465	

[Top | Flood | Abram | Exodus | David | Hezekiah | Jerusalem | JC | End Time | End Notes]

BC AD Years + or -		YM Years		6000 Years of Mankind Copyright © 2024 by Walter R. Dolen **Biblical Chronology Details** YM = Year of Mankind Begins in Sept/Oct 3 months before BC/AD dates	Additional Details	# of yrs	# of yrs	# of yrs
8	A D	3978	Y M	12			466	
9	A D	3979	Y M	13			467	
10	A D	3980	Y M	14			468	
11	A D	3981	Y M	15			469	
12	A D	3982	Y M	16 - Yehoshua			470	
13	A D	3983	Y M	17			471	
14	A D	3984	Y M	18			472	
15	A D	3985	Y M	19			473	
16	A D	3986	Y M	20			474	
17	A D	3987	Y M	21 - Yehoshua (Jesus Christ)			475	
18	A D	3988	Y M	22			476	
19	A D	3989	Y M	23			477	
20	A D	3990	Y M	24			478	
21	A D	3991	Y M	25			479	
22	A D	3992	Y M	26 - Yehoshua			480	
23	A D	3993	Y M	27			481	
24	A D	3994	Y M	28			482	
25	A D	3995	Y M	29	**At the end of this year ends the 69 weeks of years.** Go to the beginning of the 483 years		483	

BC AD Years + or -		YM Years		**6000 Years of Mankind** Copyright © 2024 by Walter R. Dolen **Biblical Chronology Details** YM = Year of Mankind Begins in Sept/Oct 3 months before BC/AD dates	**Additional Details**	# of yrs	# of yrs	# of yrs
26	A D	3996	Y M	**30- Jehoshua (Jesus) was water baptized when he was about 30. This year began in Sep/Oct. 26 AD.** This year began after 69 weeks of years (Dan 9:24-25). There is the last week of years of the "seventy weeks" prophecy. During the last week "shall Messiah be cut off" (v. 26), and "in the middle of the week, he shall cause the sacrifice and the offering will cease" (v. 27). This prophecy was cut off after the first half of the 70th week. The last half of the last week will occur in the 1260 days (42 months) mentioned in the book of Daniel and Revelation, which is the last 3 ½ years of the old age. Read our *Prophecy Papers* for more info.	Jesus' 30 year began in the Sept/Oct of 26 AD Beginning of the first half of the 70th week of years of Daniel's prophecy. Go below for the last half of the 70th week of years.	JC 30		
27	A D	3997	Y M	31 Christ's 31th year began in the Fall of 27 AD				
28	A D	3998	Y M	32- began in the Fall of 28 AD		3.5 Yrs		
29	A D	3999	Y M	33- began in the Fall of 29AD	3rd year of the 3 ½ years			
30	A D	4000	Y M	33 ½ - **Jehoshua (Jesus) Crucified** at 33 ½ yrs (in his 33th year) on a Passover, on 14th of Nisan/Abib, on April , 5, 30 AD, Julian date. **4th millennium ends** The week of 7 days previewed and predicted the week of seven millenniums. To God a day is like a 1000 years (Psa 90:4; 2 Pet 3:8; Rev 20:2, 3, 4, 5, 6, 7) The 1000 years in the book of Revelation is in the seventh millennium. The 7 days of the week is a type of the antitype week of millenniums. Christ died at the end of the 4th day of the week (Wednesday); Christ died at the end of the 4th millennium. This is type and antitype.	**Last ½ year of the 3 ½ years** This prophecy was cut off in the middle of a week of days (Wednesday) and also in the middle of the last week of years (Type and antitype). The last half of the last week of years will occur in the 1260 days (42 months) mentioned in the book of Revelation.			
31	A D	4001	Y M	First full year after his resurrection, as King of Kings, yet to take his Kingdom. **5th millennium starts.**	**First year of the 2000 years** before the real holy of holies (JC) appears and begins his 1000 year Kingdom of God. See endnotes 4 for more info. Read NM16: nm662-665 to understand the 2000 years.			1 of 200
32	A D	4002	Y M					2

[Top | Flood | Abram | Exodus | David | Hezekiah | Jerusalem | JC | End Time | End Notes]

BC AD Years + or -		YM Years		6000 Years of Mankind Copyright © 2024 by Walter R. Dolen Biblical Chronology Details YM = Year of Mankind Begins in Sept/Oct 3 months before BC/AD dates	Additional Details	# of yrs	# of yrs	# of yrs
33	A D	4003	Y M					3
34	A D	4004	Y M					4
35	A D	4005	Y M					5
36	A D	4006	Y M					6
37	A D	4007	Y M					7
38	A D	4008	Y M					8
39	A D	4009	Y M					9
40	A D	4010	Y M					10 of 2000
41	A D	4011	Y M					11
42	A D	4012	Y M					12
43	A D	4013	Y M					13
44	A D	4014	Y M					14
45	A D	4015	Y M					15
46	A D	4016	Y M					16
47	A D	4017	Y M					17
48	A D	4018	Y M					18
49	A D	4019	Y M					19
50	A D	4020	Y M					20
51	A D	4021	Y M					21
52	A D	4022	Y M					22

[Top | Flood | Abram | Exodus | David | Hezekiah | Jerusalem | JC | End Time | End Notes]

BC AD Years + or -		YM Years		6000 Years of Mankind Copyright © 2024 by Walter R. Dolen **Biblical Chronology Details** YM = Year of Mankind Begins in Sept/Oct 3 months before BC/AD dates	**Additional Details**	# of yrs	# of yrs	# of yrs
53	AD	4023	YM					23
54	AD	4024	YM					24
55	AD	4025	YM					25
56	AD	4026	YM					26
57	AD	4027	YM					27
58	AD	4028	YM					28
59	AD	4029	YM		.			29
60	AD	4030	YM					30
61	AD	4031	YM					31
62	AD	4032	YM					32
63	AD	4033	YM					33
64	AD	4034	YM					34
65	AD	4035	YM					35
66	AD	4036	YM					36
67	AD	4037	YM					37
68	AD	4038	YM					38
69	AD	4039	YM					39
70	AD	4040	YM	Temple destroyed by the Romans after 3 years				40 200
71	AD	4041	YM					41
72	AD	4042	YM	**Table Years Cut Off Here Resumes Below at 2012 AD**				42

[Top | Flood | Abram | Exodus | David | Hezekiah | Jerusalem | JC | End Time | End Notes]

BC AD Years + or -		YM Years		6000 Years of Mankind Copyright © 2024 by Walter R. Dolen **Biblical Chronology Details** YM = Year of Mankind Begins in Sept/Oct 3 months before BC/AD dates	Additional Details	# of yrs	# of yrs	# of yrs
2012	AD	5982	YM	**Table Years Resumes**				1982
2013	AD	5983	YM					1983
2014	AD	5984	YM					1984
2015	AD	5985	YM					1985
2016	AD	5986	YM					1986
2017	AD	5987	YM					1987
2018	AD	5988	YM					1988
2019	AD	5989	YM					1989
2020	AD	5990	YM					1990 of 2000
2021	AD	5991	YM					1991
2022	AD	5992	YM					1992
2023	AD	5993	YM					1993
2024	AD	5994	YM					1994
2025	AD	5995	YM					1995
2026	AD	5996	YM					1996

[Top | Flood | Abram | Exodus | David | Hezekiah | Jerusalem | JC | End Time | End Notes]								

BC AD Years + or -		YM Years		**6000 Years of Mankind** Copyright © 2024 by Walter R. Dolen **Biblical Chronology Details** YM = Year of Mankind Begins in Sept/Oct 3 months before BC/AD dates	**Additional Details**	# of yrs	# of yrs	# of yrs
2027	A D	5997	Y M	**Last 3 ½ years of the 70 weeks of years of Daniel and the book of Revelation.** [Date depends on when the 10 nations turn into 7 nations.]	**1ˢᵗ year of the 1290/1260 days of Daniel and Revelation.** **Begins in November/December of 2026**	3.5 Yrs		1997 of 2000
2028	A D	5998	Y M		2			1998
2029	A D	5999	Y M		3			1999
2030	A D	6000	Y M	**The Great antitypical Pentecost** (May/June) depending on when the barley crop is ready March/April. See NM16 and *Prophecy Papers*. This was the 2000 year since Christ's death and resurrection (nm664). **This date depends on the premises we described in the first chapter of the book the, *6000 Years of Mankind* and 10 to 7** **This ends the kingdom of Satan** (The adversary of the True God)	**Last ½ year of the 1290/1260 days** **Last part of the 3 ½ years of the 70 weeks of years of Daniel** It ends after the two witnesses of the book of Revelation lay dead on the street (Rev 11:6-11) for last half of a week of days (mid Wed. to the end of the 7ᵗʰ day, Sabbath/ Saturday.			2000
2031	A D	6001	Y M	This YM year begins about 3 months before the AD date in Sept/Oct. of 2030 **This year will start the seventh millennium,** the 1000 years mentioned in the book of Revelation. **Kingdom of God**	Go to the first half of the last week of 70 weeks of years of Daniel			2001

10 Nations to 7

Taken from the Prophecy Papers paragraphs pr183-184

1290 Days

pr183> The "abomination" is the *individual* Beast or the *system* of the Beast. And according to Daniel 12:11 it is set up 1290 days from (away from) when the daily sacrifice is taken away [pr173ff]. The real daily sacrifice is taken away at Christ's return. Since the abomination can't be "set up" *after* Christ returns, then it is set up *before* Christ returns. It is set up *before* Christ's physical return. It is set up (or given or bestowed on the world) 1290 days *from* when the daily sacrifice is taken away, or from before the time of Christ's return. (It is the abomination or detestable thing that destroys that is set up on the 1290th day before Christ's return.)

Pr 184> But we have seen that for 1260 days the Beast of Revelation will rule before Christ returns, and that this Beast will be of seven nations. Therefore it is the ten nations, or a first end-of-the-age Beast that will be set up 1290 days before Christ physically returns. And it will exist for 30 days as ten nations with one mind (Rev 17:13). This is the "one hour" (a short period of time) that the ten nations will be together. But these nations' power goes to "the horn that looked more imposing than the others and that had eyes and a mouth that spoke boastfully" and the seven-member league (Dan 7:20, NIV). This leader takes control through his deceit and craftiness (Dan 7:23-25) 1260 days before Christ returns, as explained in PR2 & 3 (Beast Papers). Thus, the ten-nation league will rule for 30 days, *from* the 1290th day before Christ physically returns *to* the 1260th day before Christ returns. This **"backward count"** of the 1290 days is not an unusual method of counting. For example, the Greeks and Romans counted days in their month backward at times:

- "In this [Grecian] system, the count in the last decade [of the month] was backwards, i.e., counting from high to low towards the end of the month ... " (*Greek and Roman Chronology*, P. 60).
- "The designation of the days within the month was made by a peculiarly Roman system. The first day of the month was called *Kalendae*, the 5th (or 7th in a 31 day month), was called the *Nonae*, and the 13th (or 15th in a 31 day month) was called the *Idus*. These are the named days, and other days in the month were designated by counting back from these named days, counting inclusively" (*Greek and Roman Chronology*, p. 154).

Appendix

70 years of desolation begins

Note: *The beginning of the overpowering of Jerusalem & Judah, and the land and nations around Judah began in the beginning of Jehoiakim's reign. This began the 70 years of desolation for land and nations of the area* (Jer 27:1-11; Dan 9:2; Jer 25:9, 11; 29:10).

cp422» There is confusion over the 70 year prophecy by Jeremiah. Some see several 70 year periods; they think that Zechariah 1:12 and 7:5 are different 70 year periods than Jeremiah's. Some think that the 70 years were not up until a few years after Cyrus took the Babylonian kingdom. But a close look at the pertinent scriptures tell us that the 70 years was not only concerning the desolation of Jerusalem (Dan 9:2), but also "this land and against its inhabitants, *and against all these nationS round about*" (Jer 25:9). "This whole land shall be a desolation, and an astonishment; and *these nationS shall serve the king of Babylon seventy years*" (Jer 25:11). Furthermore, "when the seventy years are accomplished, I will punish the king of Babylon, and that nation" (Jer 25:12). This is very important, "when seventy years are accomplished," what was to happen? — "I will punish the king of Babylon and that nation." Thus, clearly when the seventy years are over is when the king of Babylon and the nation of Babylon is punished. *And* "after the seventy years be accomplished for Babylon I will visit you, and perform my good word toward you, in causing you to return to this place" (Jer 29:10). Thus, when the seventy years are accomplished, then Babylon and their king will be punished *and* God will bring back Judah to their land. Therefore we find the end of the 70 years at the time when Babylon is defeated, its kingship is ended, and Judah is first returned to its land.

cp423» Prophecy said that Cyrus was to perform God's will including "saying to Jerusalem, Thou shalt be built; and to the temple, Thy foundation shall be laid" (Isa 44:28 ff). And in the first year of Cyrus "that the word of the LORD spoken by the mouth of Jeremiah might be accomplished, the LORD stirred up the spirit of Cyrus..." (2 Chron 36:22, see v. 21). Jeremiah spoke of the accomplishment of the seventy years and the punishment of Babylon and the return of Judah to their land. Jeremiah's word as well as the word of Isaiah was accomplished by Cyrus (compare 2 Chron 36:22-23 and Ezra 1:1-3 with Isa 44:28-45:2). It was king Cyrus who "brought forth the vessels of the house of the LORD, which Nebuchadnezzar had brought forth out of Jerusalem, and had put them in the house of his gods" (Ezra 1:7). It was through Cyrus's actions that Babylon and their king were destroyed (*Nabonidus Chronicle*; Dan 5; *Darius the Mede*, p. 73; Finegan [1964], ¶ 334; etc.). It was through Cyrus's actions that Judah was returned to their land starting in Cyrus's first year (2 Chr 36:22ff; Ezra 1:1-4; 5:13ff; etc.).

cp424» Daniel 1:1-2 tells us *when* Nebuchadnezzar first took vessels out of the temple and first besieged Jerusalem. Daniel 1:1 said this happened in the "third year of the reign of Jehoiakim king of Judah." But this does not mean that the third year of Jehoiakim was when the 70 years began because the 70 years not only included the "desolation of Jerusalem" but also included "all the nations round about" and "*these nations* shall serve the king of Babylon seventy years." Jeremiah was not only a prophet of Judah but "a prophet unto the nations" (Jer 1:5; see 1:10).

cp425» It was not when the nations of this area were completely or *totally defeated* that the 70 years began, but at the *very beginning* of these things. Parallel time periods, for example, are the flood (see under 1559 YM), the 400 years (see 2114 YM), and the 430 years (see 2084 YM). The flood was counted from the very first rain drop, the 400 years was counted from the first affliction of Abraham's "seed," and the 430 years was counted from the very first year that Abraham (Abram) was called in Mesopotamia and then began his sojourning out of his family's land of nativity. The *count* of the 70 years began with Babylon's New Year's day in 3363 ½ YM (Spring of 608 BC) because this was the count of years of Nebuchadnezzar's dynasty not Judah's: "these nations shall serve the king [Nebuchadnezzar's dynasty] of Babylon seventy years" (Jer 25:11; 27:6-7; Isa 23:15-17, see below). It was in the *beginning* of the reign of Jehoiakim that Nebuchadnezzar was given "all these lands into the hand of Nebuchadnezzar the king of Babylon":

> In the *beginning of the reign of Jehoiakim* the son of Josiah king of Judah came this word unto Jeremiah from the Lord, saying, {2} Thus saith the Lord to me; Make thee bonds and yokes, and put them upon thy neck, {3} And send them to the king of Edom, and to the king of Moab, and to the king of the Ammonites, and to the king of Tyrus, and to the king of Zidon ... {6} And now have I given all these lands into the hand of Nebuchadnezzar the king of Babylon, my servant; and the beasts of the field have I given him also to serve him. {7} And all nations shall serve him, and his son, and his son's son, until the very time of his land come: and then many nations and great kings shall serve themselves of him. {8} And it shall come to pass, that the nation and kingdom which will not serve the same Nebuchadnezzar the king of Babylon, and that will not put their neck under the yoke of the king of Babylon, that nation will I punish, saith the LORD, with the sword, and with the famine, and with the pestilence, until I have consumed them by his hand (Jer 27:1-8, KJV).

From cuneiform evidence we also see that Nebuchadnezzar as crown prince marched for his father and conquered lands across the Euphrates in the land of Hatti beginning in the 19th year of his father, which is the first year of Jehoiakim thus in the beginning of Jehoiakim's reign (see CP5: Notes and Figure; BM 22047, lines 5ff).

cp426» Apparently, these 70 years are the same 70 years that the city of "Tyre shall be forgotten seventy years, according to the days of one king" (Isa 23:15-17). The city of Tyre was also destroyed by Nebuchadnezzar (Jer 27:1-3, 8; Ezek 26:7ff) and suffered in the 70 year dynasty of Nebuchadnezzar until Cyrus destroyed Babylon and its kingship (See Notes).

British Museum Tablet # 21946

cp427» This clay tablet is part of the clay tablets called the Assyrian and Babylonian Chronicles (Grayson, *Assyrian and Babylonian Chronicles*, 1972 [Grayson, Eisenbrauns verison 2000, as Chron. 5, p. 99]). The information on these clay tablets were compiled in the Persian period and written in the Akkadian language in cuneiform script from earlier material; some tablets may have been written in the Seleucid period (Sidney Smith, *Babylonian Historical Texts*, pp. 1, 27, 98; D.J. Wiseman, *Chronicles of Chaldaean Kings*, pp. 1-5). Normally in these tablets the most important events were written for each year of a king's reign. The "most important events" for the 21st year of Nabopolassar was the defeat of the Egyptian army near Carchemish, the conquering of all of Hatti-land, the death of king Nabopolassar and the accession of the king's son and crown prince, Nebuchadnezzar. The only *specific* date for any of these events is the death of king Nabopolassar and the accession of Nebuchadnezzar. Normally specific dates are not given in these chronicles. The only date as to when Nebuchadnezzar destroyed the army of Egypt was given as "at that time Nebuchadnezzar conquered the whole area of Hatti-country" (BM 21946, obverse side, line 8). Because of the little detail we do have, it is unclear as to the exact date when the last part of the Egyptian army was destroyed. Were they all destroyed before Nebuchadnezzar's coronation or after when Nebuchadnezzar went back to Hatti-land? Jeremiah 46:2 says that Nebuchadnezzar destroyed the Egyptian army in the 4th year of Jehoiakim. But BM 21946 may seem to some to say the army was destroyed *before* the 4th year of Jehoiakim.

From British Museum Tablet # 21946:

cp428» "[In the twenty-first year - see BM 22047] the king [Nabopolassar] of Akkad [Babylon] stayed in his own land, Nebuchadrezzar his eldest son, the crown-prince, mustered [the Babylonian army] and took command of his troops; he marched to Carchemish [Gal-ga-mes] which is on the bank of the Euphrates, and crossed the river [to go] against the Egyptian army which lay in Carchemish [Gal-ga-mes]... fought with each other and the Egyptian army withdrew before him. He accomplished their defeat and to non-existence [beat?] them. As for the rest of the Egyptian army which had escaped from the defeat [so quickly that] no weapon had reached them, in the district of Hamath the Babylonian troops overtook and defeated them so that not a single man [escaped] to his own country. At that time Nebuchadnezzar conquered the whole area of the Hatti-country."

cp429» Notice that at the time that the Egyptian troops, who had escaped the attack at Carchemish, were defeated was "at that time Nebuchadrezzar conquered the whole area of the Hatti-country." The clay tablet begins with a general description of what happened in the 21st year of Nabopolassar and says that at the time the Egyptians from Carchemish were defeated was also the time the whole Hatti-country was defeated. The question becomes, when precisely was this?

BM 21946 Continues:

cp430» "For twenty-one years Nabopolassar had been king of Babylon. On the 8th of the month of Ab [5th month] he died [lit. "the fates"]: in the month of Elul [6th month] Nebuchadrezzar returned [*ana*] to Babylon and on the first day of the month of Elul [6th month] he sat on the royal throne in Babylon. In the 'accession year' Nebuchadrezzar went back again [*ana* - "marched"] to Hatti-land and until the month of Sebat [11th month] marched unopposed through the Hatti-land; in the month of Sebat he took the heavy tribute of the hatti-territory to Babylon" (D.J. Wiseman, *Chronicles of Chaldaean Kings*, pp. 67-69; and see Grayson, *Assyrian and Babylonian Chronicles*, pp. 99-102).

As we see next, Hatti-land included Judah or Jerusalem.

Hatti-land Is The Land That Included Judah:

cp431» "In the seventh year, the month of Kislev [9th month], the king of Akkad [Babylon] mustered his troops, marched to the Hatti-land, and encamped against the city of Judah and on the second day of the month of Addaru [12th] he seized the city and captured the king. He appointed there a king of his own choice, received its heavy tribute and sent them to Babylon." (BM 21946 Reverse side line 11-13; D.J. Wiseman, *Chronicles of Chaldaean Kings*, p. 73; Grayson, *Assyrian and Babylonian Chronicles*, p. 102)

Third or Fourth Year

cp432» We see from BM 21946 that king Nebuchadnezzar took the whole Hatti-land in his accession year which was the 21st year of Nabopolassar which was the last half of the third year of king Jehoiakim through the first half of the fourth year of Jehoiakim (see chart). He returned to Babylon in the 6th month because his father died in the 5th month.

cp433» Now notice Jeremiah 46:2: "Against Egypt, against the army of Pharaoh-necho king of Egypt, which was by the river Euphrates in Carchemish, which Nebuchadrezzar king of Babylon smote in the fourth year of Jehoiakim the son of Josiah king of Judah." This verse says that Nebuchadnezzar destroyed the Egyptian army in the 4th year of Jehoiakim. Because of Jeremiah 46:2 we suspect that the Egyptian army was not *completely* defeated until after the time Nebuchadnezzar returned to Babylon for his coronation:

> "As for the rest of the Egyptian army which had escaped from the defeat [so quickly that] no weapon had reached them, in the district of Hamath the Babylonian troops overtook and defeated them so that not a single man [escaped] to his own country" (BM 21946, see in context above).

Vessels and Captives Taken in 3rd Year

cp434» In Daniel, it said that King Nebuchadnezzar took Jerusalem in Jehoiakim's third year, and took away "vessels of the house of God, which he carried into the land of Shinar [Babylon] to the house of his god, and he brought the vessels into the treasure house of his god" and *King* Nebuchadnezzar took captives "among these were of the children of Judah, Daniel, Hananiah, Mishael, and Azariah" (Dan 1:1-7; 2 Chr 36:7). The 3rd year of Jehoiakim started in the last half of the 20th year of

Nabopolassar and ended at about the time Nebuchadnezzar was crowned in the 21st year of Nabopolassar (see chart).

King v. Crown Prince

cp435» Daniel called Nebuchadnezzar *king* in Jehoiakim's 3rd year (Dan 1:1). Daniel called Belshazzar a *king* also (Dan 7:1 & 8:1). But in the so-called Babylonian Chronicles Nebuchadnezzar is called the crown prince (*mar sarri*), but not king, in Nabopolassar's 19th, 20th, and 21st years, which corresponds to Jehoiakim's 1st, 2nd, and 3rd years (BM 22047, see charts). Also Belshazzar is called the crown prince (*mar sarri*), but not king, as early as the seventh year of Nabonidus (BM 35382, Nabonidus Chronicle). In the 3rd year of Jehoiakim, according to the Babylonian Chronicle Nebuchadnezzar was the crown prince, but to Daniel he was KING. Beginning in the 7th year of Nabonidus, according to the Nabonidus Chronicle, Belshazzar was crown prince, but to Daniel he was KING. In fact both Nebuchadnezzar and Belshazzar were co-kings with their fathers. In the Bible other "crown princes" ruling with their fathers were also called KINGS (for example, Jehoshaphat & Jehoram, 3103 YM). When Daniel calls a crown prince of Babylon, "king," he is in agreement with a previous Biblical custom.

cp436» In Jehoiakim's first through third year (Nabopolassar's 19-21st yrs.), Nebuchadnezzar was "crown-prince" (BM 21946). Still later, in the last part of Jehoiakim's 3rd year (Nabopolassar's 21st), Nebuchadnezzar "sat on the royal throne" as sole king in the 6th month after his father died in the 5th month (BM 21946). Nebuchadnezzar was crown prince before the 6th month, but in the 6th month he became the sole king. According to the Babylonian Chronicle his first *official* year began the next year (BM 21946; see CP5: Notes).

Belshazzar

cp437» In the book of Daniel king Belshazzar is mentioned as the last king of Babylon. But until this century (20th) the name of king Belshazzar was not found in secular or non Jewish writings. He was found in Josephus' *Antiquities of the Jews*, as "Baltasar," but he thought it was another name for "Naboandelus" [Nabonidus] (book 9, chap 11, ¶ 2). Although the crown prince in the Nabonidus Chronicle is not called by any other name except the crown prince (*mar sarri*), this crown prince is identified by name in other documents beside the Bible:

> "In the fifth year of Nabonidus, for example, a business document records a loan of money from a certain Nabu-mukinahi, 'the scribe of Belshazzar, the son of the king.' In the seventh year, an astrological report of a certain Shumukin reads, 'I have observed the Great Star [Venus] and I shall study this with regard to a favorable interpretation for my lord Nabonidus, king of Babylon, as well as to my lord Belshazzar, the son of the king.'[33]"
>
> "[33] Bern. Alfrink in *Biblica* 9 (1928):187-205; Raymond P. Dougherty in JAOS 48 (1928):1113, 117, 124; idem, *Nabonidus and Belshazzar*, pp. 82f., 97f."
>
> (Jack Finegan, *Archaeological History of the Ancient Middle East*, pp. 132-133 & 190)

In another cuneiform document, "Verse Account of Nabonidus," Nabonidus is actually said to have entrusted the kingship to Belshazzar, his son (Ancient Near East Tests, James B. Pritchard, 1969, p. 313).

Egyptian Army was Defeated in What Year?

cp438» Nebuchadnezzar as crown prince (co-king or "king" according to Daniel) first attacked the army of Egypt near Carchemish. Some of the Egyptian army withdrew before him to the district of Hamath. This is where the Pharaoh took king Jehoahaz of Judah several years earlier. "And Pharaoh-nechoh put him in bands at Riblah in the land of Hamath, that he might not reign in Jerusalem; and put the land to a tribute of a hundred talents of silver, and a talent of gold." (2 Ki 23:33) It was to this garrison in the territory of Hamath that the remains of the Egyptian army fled after the rout from Nebuchadnezzar's army near Carchemish (BM 21946, Obv. line 1-6; Jer 46:2a). Nebuchadnezzar and/or his army pursued the rest of the Egyptian troops and by the fourth year of Jehoiakim "all the kings of the Hatti-land came before him and he received their heavy tribute" (BM 21946, Obverse side, lines 12-13, 15-17).

Two Possibilities Concerning The First Attack By Nebuchadnezzar On Jerusalem And Daniel's 3 Years of Training:

cp439» (1) *3rd Year/21st Year.* In the 21st year of Nabopolassar, either before this clash in Carchemish or after it when Nebuchadnezzar and/or his troops were pursuing the Egyptian army, somehow and in someway (there are no details in the Bible or the Babylonian Chronicles) Nebuchadnezzar made king Jehoiakim his prisoner and "bound him in fetters to carry him to Babylon." (2 Chr 36:6) He also took vessels from the temple as well as "children of Israel, and of the king's seed, and of the princes" back to Babylon (2 Chr 35:7; Dan 1:3, 2-7). But Jehoiakim was not brought to Babylon in his third year for he ruled for 11 years and died in Israel. He may have paid a heavy tribute (as he gave to Egypt – 2Ki 23:35)to escape being brought to Babylon at that time while promising to be a subject to Babylon. (2Kings 24:1)

(2) *3rd Year/20th Year.* Another possibility was that Jehoiakim was taken in the first half of his 3rd year, which would have been Nabopolassar's 20th year, a year in which Nebuchadnezzar was also "king" according to Daniel's thinking or "crown prince" (*mar sarri*) according to the Babylonian Chronicles.

Daniel's Three Years of Training

cp440» Notice that among those brought to Babylon was Daniel who among others were given study to "teach the learning and the tongue of the Chaldeans ... so nourishing them *three* years, that at the end thereof they might stand before the king" (Dan 1:4-5, 6). Now by comparing the scriptures we see that the *three* years of training was up in the beginning of the *second* year of Nebuchadnezzar's reign (Dan 1:4-5, 17-19; 2:1-2, 5, 12-13). In order for the 2nd year of Nebuchadnezzar to be after the 3rd year of training, Daniel's training must have begun in the 20th year of Nabopolassar. Scripture does say Daniel was taken in the 3rd year of Jehoiakim. The 3rd year of Jehoiakim was the last half of Nabopolassar's 20th year through the first half of his 21st year. It so happens that,

> "In the twentieth year ... in the month of Tisri [7th month; 3rd year of Jehoiakim] the king of Addad [Babylon] mustered his army, marched along the bank of the Euphrates and pitched his camp at Quramati which is on the bank of the

Euphrates. He sent his troops [with Nebuchadnezzar leading?, see below] across the Euphrates and they seized the towns of Sunadiri, Elammu and Dahammu which are in the country across the river [Hatti-land, where Judah was also located]. Spoil from them they took. In the month of Sebat, the king of Akkad [Babylon] returned to his own country. The Egyptian army which had crossed the Euphrates at Carchemish came against the Babylonian army which was stationed in Quramati, but the Babylonian army withdrew quickly and retreated. In the twenty-first year the king of Addad (stayed) in his own land. Nebuchadrezzar his eldest son, the crown prince, mustered the Babylonian army and ..." (BM 22047, lines 16-28, Wiseman, trans.).

cp441» This text did not say where the crown prince was in the 20th year, but if the 19th year is any indication the crown prince, Nebuchadnezzar, was helping his father also in the 20th year even if the text did not say so,

"The nineteenth year: In the month Sivan the king of Akkad [Babylon] mustered his army and Nebuchadnezzar, his eldest son, the crown prince, mustered his army. They marched .." (BM 22047, lines 5-7, Grayson's trans., p. 97).

Nebuchadnezzar Co-King 3 Years with Nabopolassar

cp442» If the kings of Israel and Judah are any indication, kings made their sons co-kings (crown princes), either in time of war and/or when they were sick or getting old and sickly. Thus, it is possible in the last half of the 20th year of Nabopolassar, which was in the 3rd year of Jehoiakim, that Nebuchadnezzar was helping his father as he did in the 19th year, and besieging Jerusalem (Dan 1:1) as his father was besieging other cities in Hatti-land, or as he was camped at Quramati by the river Euphrates. In fact, from the 19th into the 21st year, Nebuchadnezzar was co-king with his father, Nabopolassar.

I believe possibility (2) above is most likely.

Intercalary Months

cp443» Nebuchadnezzar was coronated in the first day of the sixth month after he returned in the sixth month. We have an apparent contradiction. How can he return in the sixth month and be also coronated in the first day of the sixth month? It must surely take more than one day to plan and have a coronation. But if there were two months of Elul or two sixth months, as there was when intercalary months were needed this would explain it:

"In the period covered by this study the Babylonian calendar year was composed of lunar months, which began when the thin crescent of the new moon was first visible in the sky at sunset. Since the lunar year was about eleven days shorter than the solar year, it was necessary at intervals to intercalate a thirteenth month, either a second Ululu (the sixth month) or a second Addaru (the twelfth month) in order that New Year's Day, Nisanu 1, should not fall much before the spring of the year (late March and early April).

... This meant that seven lunar months must be intercalated over each nineteen-year period.

The specific years in which the intercalations were to be made, however, and whether they should be second Addarus or second Ululus remained to be determined empirically — a process which lasted some centuries" (Parker and Dubberstein, *Babylonian Chronology 626 B.C. - A.D. 75*, p. 1).

cp444» Through the reading of some letters of this period their contents imply that "the order for the intercalary month was not sent out until presumably in the 6th or 12th month itself, the statement implying that the present Ululu or Addaru was to be followed by an intercalated Ululu or Addaru" (Parker and Dubberstein, p. 2). "These letters also make it clear that no established system which fixed the seven intercalations at definite points within the nineteen-year period existed at the beginning of the Persian period. Letter No. 15 implies that intercalary orders were even issued within a few weeks of the beginning of an intercalary month" (p. 2). No standardized system for the placement of these months in the 19 year cycle has been found before about 367 BC (p. 2).

cp445» At the time of Nebuchadnezzar Judah also had a lunar-solar calendar similar to Babylon's calendar. So depending when the Babylonian and Judah's calendars placed their intercalary months, either calendar could be off synchronism by a month. This means that the 6th month on the Babylonian calendar that year could have been the 7th month of Judah's calendar. This would answer the question of how Nebuchadnezzar could return in the 6th month, but was also coronated on the first of the 6th month. This may show that there were two months of Elul (6th month) that year, and not that he returned in the 6th month, the very first day, and was coronated that same day. Although not impossible, I would think it would take more than one day to prepare the coronation ceremony. Yet it may have been a simple ceremony. The fact is that we do not know the answer to this. Because Nebuchadnezzar's defeat of the Egyptian forces came towards the end of Jehoiakim's 3rd year, and into the beginning of the 4th year, and because of the possibility of the non-synchronism of the calendars of each country, we can understand Jeremiah's statement that the Egyptians were smote in the 4th year of Jehoiakim (see chart).

JEHOIAKIM	Judah's Months	NABOPOLASSAR/ NEBUCHADNEZZAR	DANIEL'S three years of training (Dan 1.5)
3rd Year	7	Babylon's months	
Some time in Jehoiakim's 3rd year Nebuchadnezzar besieged Jerusalem and takes vessels from the temple as well as sons of Israel, the king's seed, and princes. Among these captives was Daniel. (Dan 1.1-?)	8 9 10 11 12	8 20th of Nabopolassar (2nd year co-reign for Nebuchadnezzar) 9 10 11 12	(1)
	1 2 3 4 5	1 21st of Nabopolassar (3rd co-reign for Neb.) 2 3 In Nebuchadnezzar's 3rd year as "Crown Prince" he attacks the Egyptians at Carchemish 4 5 Nebuchadnezzar's father dies	(2)
Nebuchadnezzar destroying the rest of the Egyptian army	6	6 Neb. returns home	
Nebuchadnezzar and/or troops destroys the Egyptian army	7 8	6 (Intercalary month Neb. coronation on 1st) 7	
4th Year of Jehoiakim	9 10 11 12	8 This year is also Nebuchadnezzar's accessional year (MU.SAG) 9 10 11 12	
		1 NEBUCHADNEZZAR'S 1st Sole Yr	(3)
5th Year of Jehoiakim 3rd yr Dan. Training	7	1 2nd Year	
6th Year	7		

Ur of the Chaldeans

(This is taken from the notes of the Seed Paper. This paper is from the Prophecy Papers. It is inserted here because of possible interest to chronologists)

cp446» Abraham (Abram) came from the "Ur of the Chaldeans" (Gen 11:31). The "Ur of the Chaldeans" mentioned in the Bible is not the city identified as "Ur" by many today. The contemporary "Ur" is hundreds of miles southeast of Haran and Ebla on *this* side of the Euphrates river. That is, on the side (this side) of the Euphrates river nearest Jerusalem. But the Biblical "Ur of the Chaldeans" was *across* the river Euphrates in northwestern Mesopotamia somewhere near Haran. Archeological finds and Biblical proof indicate this.

cp447» This "Ur of the Chaldeans" is most likely the same Ur that is mentioned to be "in the territory of Haran" in the Ebla Clay tablets discovered in 1975, not the Ur on *this side* of the river Euphrates southeast of the Mesopotamian region. The contemporary "Ur" is located in the southeastern territory of the Sumero-Akkadian Empire and had a different culture and language than Abraham's.

Ur of Abraham was located near Haran in Mesopotamia

cp448» There is Biblical proof that the city of "Ur" that Abraham came from was near Haran:

> Abram, Lot, and Terah "went forth with them from *Ur of the Chaldees*, to go into the land of Canaan; and they came unto *Haran*, and dwelt there" (Gen 11:31).
> "Thus says the LORD God of Israel, your fathers dwelt *on the other side of the river* [Euphrates] in old time ... and I took your father Abraham from the other side of the river [Euphrates]" (Joshua 24:2, 3).

cp449» Thus, Abraham came from the *other* side of the river (from Jerusalem's viewpoint). That river being the Euphrates. But the contemporary identification of the so-called "Ur of Chaldeans" is on *this* side of the river (from Jerusalem's viewpoint).

> "The God of Glory appeared unto Abraham, when he was in Mesopotamia, *before* he dwelt in Haran" (Acts 7:2).

cp450» Abraham came from Mesopotamia. The word Mesopotamia means *"the country between the rivers"* (*Unger's Bible Dict.*, "Mesopotamia"). These rivers being the Euphrates and Tigris. But the contemporary "Ur" is not located *between* the rivers. Originally the word "mesopotamia" stood only for the northwestern region between the rivers Euphrates and Tigris (*Unger's Bible Dict.*, 3rd Ed., "Mesopotamia"). Albert Clay mistakenly wrote in 1907:

> "In former years Urfa, not far from Harran, was identified as the ancestral city of the patriarch [Abraham], but it is now [1907] fifty years since Rawlinson identified the mounds known as Mugayyar, in the southern part of the valley, as the home of Abraham. Ur is a very ancient city" (*Light on the Old Testament from Babel*, by Albert T. Clay, pub. 1907).

The former identification of Urfa as the area where the old Ur was located is much closer than the new and wrong identification of Ur.

Ur of the Chadeans by the River Chebar

cp451» Abraham came "out of the land of the Chaldeans" (Acts 7:4). This is what Genesis 11:31 and other verses say:

- "And they went forth with them *from Ur of the Chaldees*" (Gen 11:31).
- "You the LORD God, who did choose Abram, and brought him forth *out of Ur of the Chaldees*, and gave him the name of Abraham" (Neh 9:7).
- "I am the LORD that brought you *out of Ur of the Chaldees*" (Gen 15:7).
- "The *land of the Chaldeans by the river Chebar* .." (Ezek 1:3).

cp452» In Abraham's time the Biblical land of the Chaldeans where Ur was located was northwestern Mesopotamia. It was close to the Armenians (*Ramses II and His Time*, by I. Velikovsky, pp. 170, 168ff; note Gurney, *Hittites*, Chap VI; see endnote). The Biblical Chaldean language was the Aramean or Syriac language (Dan 2:4). The Biblical river Chebar was "in the land of the Chaldeans" (Ezek 1:3). This river *Chebar may* be the present day river *Khabor* in northeast Syria near Haran and *Ur*fa and south of Armenia in Turkey. Later the Chaldeans moved southward to Babylon and were known in Ezekiel's time as the "Babylonians of Chaldea, the land of their nativity" (Ezek 23:15). But in contemporary literature the "Ur of Chaldeans" is located hundreds of miles in a southeastern direction from the Chaldeans' northwestern Mesopotamian homeland.

Land of Abraham's Nativity is the real Ur of the Chadeans

cp453» The real Ur of the Chaldeans was the land of Abraham's nativity or birth:

- God told Abraham in Mesopotamia to "get you out of *your country, and from your kindred*" (Acts 7:3).
- Haran was a brother of Abram [Gen 11:27], and Haran died "in the land of his nativity [Hebrew, "his (place of) birth"], in *Ur of the Chaldees*" (Gen 11:28).
- When Abram went out of Ur he was told by God, "get out of your country, and from your kindred [Hebrew: "your (place of) birth"]" (Gen 12:1). And "get you out of your country, and from your kindred [Greek, "relations"]" (Acts 7:3).
- "The LORD ... took me from my father's house [family], and from the land of my kindred [Hebrew, '(place of) birth']" (Gen 24:7).

Abraham Was An Aramean

Abraham's birthplace, his nativity, was in *northwestern* Mesopotamia in the land of Syria or Aram or Padan-Aram (rivers of Aram):

> "And Abraham said unto his eldest servant of his house ... you shall go unto *my* country, and to *my* kindred, and take a wife unto my son Isaac ... and the servant took ten camels ... and went to *Mesopotamia* unto the city of Nahor [the name of Abraham's brother] ... and Isaac was forty years old when he took Rebekah to wife, the daughter of Bethuel the *Syrian of Padan-Aram*, the sister to Laban the Syrian [Hebrew - "Aramite"]" (Gen 24:2, 4, 10; 25:20).

cp454» Syrians are Aramites or Arameans who lived between the rivers (Euphrates & Tigris), in the land of Aram, northwestern Mesopotamia. This area was Abraham's birthplace. Abraham was called a Hebrew (Gen 14:13). "Hebrew" comes from a Hebrew word (*eber*) which means: "across (the river)." Abraham the Hebrew came from across the Euphrates river.

cp455» One of the fathers of Moses was Jacob (Israel) who was perishing from famine in Palestine before he went down to Egypt (Gen chap 42ff). Thus, Moses said, "My father was a perishing *Aramean*, and he went down to Egypt" (Deut 26:5, see Hebrew text).

Review

cp456» Abraham went forth out of Ur of the Chaldeans "to go unto the land of Canaan, and they came unto Haran and dwelt there" (Gen 11:31). This "Ur" was his homeland, his birthplace. He was born there with his brother Haran (Gen 11:27-28). When God spoke to Abraham in Ur of the Chaldeans, in Mesopotamia, he told Abraham to move away from his birthplace, his relatives, his kindred, and from his fathers house (family) (Gen 12:1; Acts 7:2-4, see above). Because Abraham spoke in a Semitic tongue, because his own country was the Ur of Chaldeans, because one of the Chaldeans' languages was a Semitic tongue (Dan 2:4 - "Syriac" or "Aramaic"), this is one reason why we can say that the real "Ur of Chaldeans" was located in northwestern Mesopotamia near Ebla and Haran (the name of Abraham's brother). It was not the southeastern "Ur" with its different language and culture. This southeastern "Ur" is actually spelled, "Urim" not *Ur* (*The Sumerians*, S. N. Kramer, pp. 28 & 298). But the "Ur of the Chaldeans" was probably the "Ur" mentioned in the Ebla tablets that was located "in the territory of Haran" (*Ebla Tablets*, p. 42; *Ebla*, by Bermant and Weitzman, 1979, p. 190; *Riv. Bibl.* [1977], p.236).

Ebla Tablets' Proof

cp457» A Professor Paolo Matthiae of the Rome University has been excavating the Tell Mardikh (Ebla) since 1964. In 1968 he discovered a statue bearing the name Ibbit-Lim, a king of Ebla. The kingdom of Ebla was known to a few because Ebla is mentioned in Sumerian, Akkadian, and Egyptian texts (*Ebla Tablets*, pp. 11-12). Professor Giovanni Pettinato, University of Rome, is the epigrapher working on the tablets. He has written the book, *The Archives of Ebla* (1981) and wrote in such journals as *Biblical Archaeologist* (May, 1976).

cp458» The reports on the Ebla tablets reveal that the culture of Ebla had a Semitic language, "a forerunner of all the Canaanite dialects, which include Ugaritic, Phoenician, and Hebrew" (*National Geographic*, Dec, 1978, p. 749; *The Archives of Ebla*, by Giovanni Pettinato, 1981, pp. 56, 65). Many of the personal names in the Ebla tablets closely resemble Hebrew names: *Abramu* (Abraham), *Esaum* (Esau), and *Saulum* (Saul) (*Nat. Geo.* Dec, 1978, p. 736). The old city state of Ebla with its Semitic language was only about 100 miles from Haran, while the other and more southern "Ur" (Urim) with its different language was about 600 miles away — a large distance in those days. Along with the Biblical proof, we conclude that Abram, who spoke in a Semitic tongue, came from the "Ur of Chaldeans" which was much closer to Haran and Ebla than the southeastern "Ur." It was in this northwestern area where a Semitic culture existed. It was from this area that Abraham came from.

Ur was in the Territory of Haran

cp459» Clifford Wilson in his paperback book called *Ebla Tablets* writes of his disappointment on finding "a city of Ur is referred to in the trade tablets. It is described as being 'in the territory of Haran.' " (p. 42) Not only does the Ebla tablets mention Ur, but they say it is in the territory or locality of Haran. This is further proof that Abraham's city of Ur was near Haran in northwestern Mesopotamia, not the contemporary "Ur" hundreds of miles southeast of Haran and Ebla.

cp460» But Mr. Wilson was "somewhat disappointed." Why was he disappointed? "I am the producer of a number of audio-visuals on Bible backgrounds, and one of them is based on Sir Leonard Wooley's findings at the city of Ur" (Wilson, p. 42; and see C.L. Woolley, *Ur of the Chaldees*, 1929, 1982). It was the southeastern "Ur," first identified by Henry Rawlinson in the middle 1800's, that Wooley helped to popularize as being the "Ur of Chaldeans." Instead of Mr Wilson seeing that he made a mistake, instead of reviewing the Biblical data as we have, Wilson comes up with a weak excuse to retain the contemporary "Ur" as the Ur of Abraham (p. 44).

Chaldeans Language Confusion

cp461» At one time the so-called "Syriac" language (Dan 2:4) or the "Aramaic" language was called Chaldee. Notice "Chaldee" in such books as *The New Englishman's Hebrew and Chaldee Concordance*, or the *Hebrew and Chaldee Lexicon* by Gesenius. Before the mistaken identification of the southeastern "Ur" for the Biblical "Ur of Chaldeans," the Aramaic tongue was identified with the Chaldeans. "It [Aramaic] was formerly inaccurately called Chaldee (Chaldaic) because spoken by the Chaldeans of the book of Daniel (2:4-7:28). But since the Chaldeans are known to have generally spoken Akkadian, the term Chaldee has been abandoned" (*Unger's Bible Dict.*, "Aramaic").

cp462» Yet the Chaldeans did speak Aramaic (Syriac) and other local languages. In Daniel's time they used the Akkadian-Babylonian language, and the Syriac or Aramean language (*Ramses II*, p. 171ff & Dan 2:4ff). The city state of Ebla also used two or more languages in their writings: the Semitic Paleo-Canaanite language, and the "Sumerian script, with Sumerian logograms adapted to represent Akkadian words and syllables" (*Ebla Tablets*, p. 24). "The schematic presentation of the verbal, nominal, and pronominal systems warrants classifying Eblaite in the West Semitic group.... For this reason I prefer to classify Eblaite as a Canaanite Language, thanks to its close relationship with Ugaritic, Phoenician, and Biblical Hebrew.... Eblaite becomes a chronological companion of Old Akkadian of the East Semitic group" (Pettinato, *...Ebla*, p.65). But "the bilingualism of the tablets is only apparent. Though 80 percent of the words are Sumerian and only 20 percent are Eblaite, all of them were read as Eblaite. The Sumerian terms are in reality logograms which the scribes translated without difficulty into their own language when they read them" (*...Ebla*, by Pettinato, p. 57).

cp463» It should be noted that there is no recorded evidence that the southeastern "Ur" had a Semitic culture or wrote with a Semitic script. Although one must be careful. The famous H.C. Rawlinson in about the 1850's mistakenly designated the Sumerian language as the "Akkadian" or "Scythian or Turanian" language (*The Sumerians*, p. 20). "In short, Rawlinson had definitely discovered the Sumerians and their language, except that he designated them quite erroneously first as Babylonian Scyths and then as Akkadians, the very term now used for the Semites of the land...the term 'Akkadian' continued to be used [incorrectly] for several decades" (p. 20, 21). So you must be careful when studying old writings concerning the Sumerian language.

Babylonians and the Hittites

cp464» Velikovsky tries to connect the Babylonians with the Hittites (*Ramses II*, chapters IV ff). Gurney in his book, *The Hittites*, may in someway also connect them:

> "Akkadian. This is the name now universally given to the well-known Semitic language of Babylonia and Assyria; to the Hittites, however, it was known as 'Babylonian'. It was widely used in the Near East for diplomatic

correspondence and documents of an international character, and the Hittite kings followed this custom when dealing with their southern and eastern neighbours. Many Hittite treaties and letters are therefore wholly in Akkadian and were available in translation long before the great bulk of the archive of Boghazkoy had been deciphered. In addition, as mentioned above, Akkadian words are common in texts written in Hittite, but it is generally held that this is a form of allography.... Two languages only — Hittite and Akkadian — were used by the Hittite kings for their official documents" (Chap VI, pp. 125, 117).

To Summarize

cp465» The above Biblical evidence clearly indicates that the real "Ur of Chaldeans" was the Semitic speaking one, located in northwestern Mesopotamia. Outside of the Ebla evidence, the internal evidence of the Bible should have made it plain to Sir Leonard Woolley and the others that the "Ur of Chaldeans" was not some foreign culture to the Semitic Abraham, but Abraham's own culture and homeland. This "Ur" is mentioned in the Ebla tablets as being near Haran. The Ebla culture used a Semitic language and had similar names as the ones used by the Hebrews. The culture of Ebla was located near the city of Haran and near northwestern Mesopotamia at approximately the same time as Abraham lived. It was Abraham, a Semitic speaking Hebrew, who left his own homeland, where his relatives lived so as to go into the land of Canaan. Abraham's homeland was the "Ur of Chaldees" which is also close to or the same as Padan-Aram, located in northern Mesopotamia. From his homeland, Abraham went to Canaan, by first going through and living in Haran for a few years. Haran was also located in Mesopotamia, or between the two rivers. But the contemporary "Ur" is located far from northwestern Mesopotamia; it had a different culture than Abraham's. Thus, this southern Ur (*Urim*) is not Abraham's own country.

Flood Chart

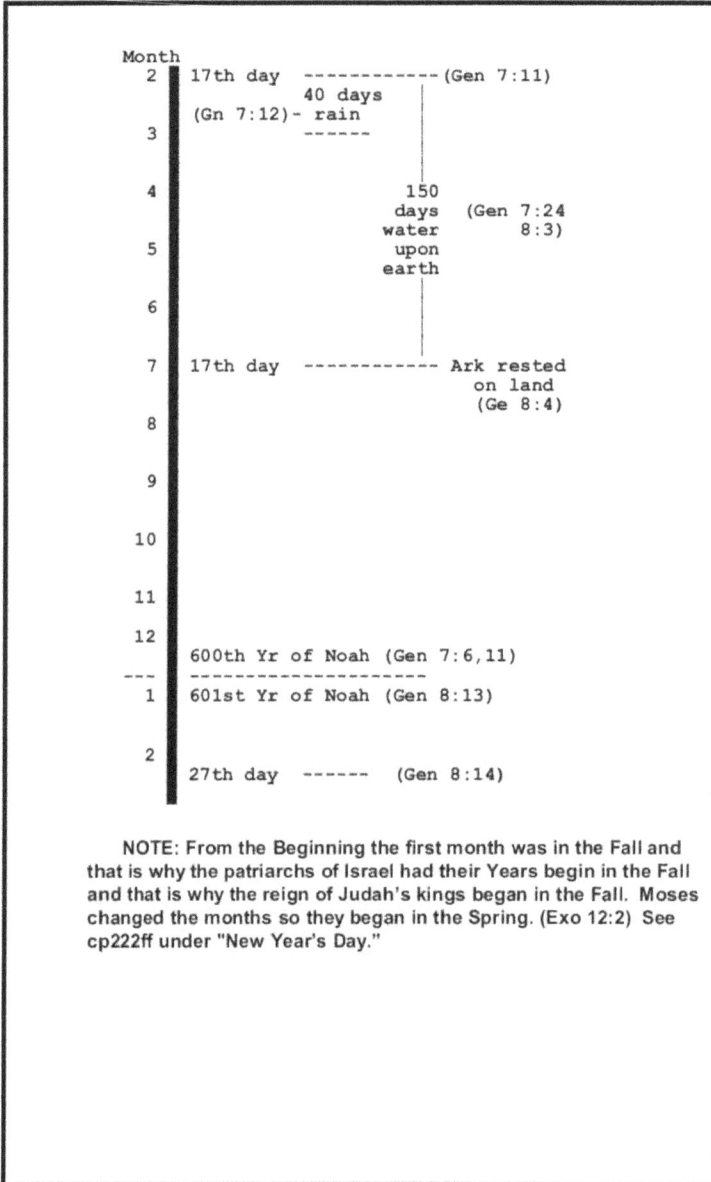

```
Month
  2    17th day  ------------ (Gen 7:11)
              40 days
       (Gn 7:12)- rain
  3            ------

  4                    150
                       days   (Gen 7:24
                      water        8:3)
  5                    upon
                      earth

  6

  7    17th day  ------------ Ark rested
                               on land
                               (Ge 8:4)
  8

  9

 10

 11

 12
       600th Yr of Noah (Gen 7:6,11)
 ---   --------------------
  1    601st Yr of Noah (Gen 8:13)

  2
       27th day  ------   (Gen 8:14)
```

NOTE: From the Beginning the first month was in the Fall and that is why the patriarchs of Israel had their Years begin in the Fall and that is why the reign of Judah's kings began in the Fall. Moses changed the months so they began in the Spring. (Exo 12:2) See cp222ff under "New Year's Day."

Index

Page 380

Your Notes

End Notes

1. The years for the Patriarchs always began on the first new moon in the Fall (Sept/Oct) in memory of the creation of man.

2.

Population Growth *Estimates* After the Flood		
3.5 % Population Growth Each Year		
Fast increase in population population still took about 140 years to reach 1000		
Double Population Growth	**Doubles Each 20 Years**	Years of Man (YM)
8 Noah's Family	1-20 years	1656 YM [ab. 2318 BC]
16	20	1676
32	40	1696
64	60	1715
128	80	1736
256	100	1756 In the time of Peleg, the earth was divided (people divided by language & race*) [Gen 10:25] 1757-1997 YM
512	120	1776
1024	140	1796
2048	160	1816 **Cush begot Nimrod – the Rebellion***
4096	180	1836
8192	200	1856
16384	220	1876 [Nimrod? Babylon*]
The Earth divided by language, race, culture and wars in Peleg's time*		

Double Population Growth	**Doubles Each 40-70 Years** depending on wars, famines, plagues, etc.	
32000	290	1946
64000	360	2016 YM [1955 BC]
See our *6000 Years of Mankind* for other estimates of population		

* In the Bible the time of the Babylonian division of mankind is only approximate since the scriptures are vague to the exact chronological time frame. We only give our time frame as an example.

3. In 2 Kings 8:26-27 it says Ahaziah of Judah was a "son of 22 years" (see Hebrew text) when he began to reign, thus, he was 22 years old when he began to reign. But in 2 Chron 22:2 it says Ahaziah is a "son of 42 years" (see Hebrew text). Now Ahaziah's mother Athaliah was the daughter of Omri, King of Israel (2 Kings 8:26; 2 Chr 22:2-3). This means that Ahaziah was a son of Omri's house, which at that time (the beginning of 3115 YM) was 42 years old. Omri's rule began in 3073 YM. You add 42 years and you come to 3115 YM. This year was when Ahaziah's began to reign after Jehoram's death. The Hebrew word *ben* (Strong's #1121), has a broad meaning in Hebrew: meaning sometimes a literal "son" or sometimes also a grandson, a subject, a quality or condition, etc.'

4. Note that although 2 Kings 15:30 speaks of Jotham's 20th year, we know that Pekah died in his 20th year since he ruled only 20 years (2 Kings 15:27). Therefore Pekah was killed in his 20th year and Hoshea began his reign in *what would have been* Jotham's 20th year, if he was still king, or that is, Hoshea began to reign in the *20th* year of the house of Jotham. Hoshea did not co-reign with Pekah, because he killed Pekah so he could rule, thus Hoshea's first year of reign began after Pekah's last year (accessional year method).

www.ingramcontent.com/pod-product-compliance
Lightning Source LLC
Chambersburg PA
CBHW062011090426
42811CB00005B/818